M000204754

Inventing the Third World

Histories of Internationalism

Series Editors:

Jessica Reinisch, Birkbeck, University of London, UK
David Brydan, King's College London, UK

Editorial Board:

Tomoko Akami, Australian National University, Australia
Martin Conway, University of Oxford, UK
Adom Getachew, University of Chicago, USA
Sandrine Kott, University of Geneva, Switzerland
Stephen Legg, University of Nottingham, UK
Su Lin Lewis, University of Bristol, UK
Erez Manela, Harvard University, USA
Samuel Moyn, Yale University, USA
Alanna O'Malley, Leiden University, Netherlands
Kiran Klaus Patel, Ludwig Maximilian University of Munich, Germany
Tehila Sasson, Emory University, USA
Frank Trentmann, Birkbeck University of London, UK
Heidi Tworek, University of British Columbia, Canada

This book series features cutting-edge research on the history of international cooperation and internationalising ambitions in the modern world. Providing an intellectual home for research into the many guises of internationalism, its titles draw on methods and insights from political, social, cultural, economic and intellectual history. It showcases a rapidly expanding scholarship which has begun to transform our understanding of internationalism and the modern world.

Cutting across established academic fields such as European, World, International and Global History, the series critically examines historical perceptions of geography, regions, centres, peripheries, borderlands and connections across space in the history of internationalism. It includes both monographs and edited volumes that shed new light on local and global contexts for international projects; the impact of class, race and gender on international aspirations; the roles played by a variety of international organisations and institutions; and the hopes, fears, tensions and conflicts underlying them.

The series is published in association with Birkbeck's Centre for the Study of Internationalism, and edited by Jessica Reinisch (Birkbeck) and David Brydan (King's College London).

Published:

Organizing the 20th-Century World: International Organizations and the Emergence of International Public Administration, 1920-1960s, edited by Karen Gram-Skjoldager, Haakon Andreas Ikonomou & Torsten Kahlert

Internationalists in European History: Rethinking the Twentieth Century, edited by Jessica Reinsich and David Brydan

International Cooperation in Cold War Europe: The United Nations Economic Commission for Europe, 1947-64, by Daniel Stinsky

Placing Internationalism: International Conferences and the Making of the Modern World, edited by Stephen Legg, Mike Heffernan, Jake Hodder & Benjamin Thorpe

Forthcoming:

Relief and Rehabilitation for a Postwar World?, edited by Samantha K. Knapton and Katherine Rossy

Inventing the Third World

In Search of Freedom for the Postwar Global South

Edited by
Gyan Prakash and Jeremy Adelman

BLOOMSBURY ACADEMIC
LONDON • NEW YORK • OXFORD • NEW DELHI • SYDNEY

BLOOMSBURY ACADEMIC
Bloomsbury Publishing Plc
50 Bedford Square, London, WC1B 3DP, UK
1385 Broadway, New York, NY 10018, USA
29 Earlsfort Terrace, Dublin 2, Ireland

BLOOMSBURY, BLOOMSBURY ACADEMIC and the Diana logo are trademarks of
Bloomsbury Publishing Plc

First published in Great Britain 2023

Cover design: Terry Woodley
Cover image © A group of women, some of whom are veiled, applauds at a military
parade celebration of Algerian independence, November 1, 1962. Photo by FERNAND
PARIZOT/AFP via Getty Images

A catalogue record for this book is available from the British Library.

A catalog record for this book is available from the Library of Congress.

ISBN: HB: 978-1-3502-6815-9
ePDF: 978-1-3502-6816-6
eBook: 978-1-3502-6817-3

Series: Histories of Internationalism

Typeset by Deanta Global Publishing Services, Chennai, India

To find out more about our authors and books visit www.bloomsbury.com and
sign up for our newsletters.

Contents

Figures

Preface

The end of the Second World War and the eclipse of empires brought a wave of efforts to reimagine the world in the future tense. Nation-states emerging from the shadows of colonial rule gathered at Bandung to chart alternative destinies and to challenge global inequalities. The result was nothing less than an effort to reimagine the world order in a way that stood in direct contrast to the liberal regime designed in Bretton Woods and in San Francisco as the Second World War drew to a close. Anticolonialism and development dreaming envisioned a less hierarchical, more pluralistic, and more distributive arrangement. As the current world order gets caught ever more tightly into an impasse, this volume looks back at the proliferating alternative visions under the mantle of the Third World. Avoiding the tendency to treat alternatives as doomed, utopian projects, the volume seeks to recover the world-changing aspirations of the Third World project as well as its cultural and intellectual breakthroughs.

By inventing the Third World, writers, artists, musicians, and photographers sought to create new institutions of solidarity, new expressions, and alternative narratives than the liberal and/or imperial ones they had inherited. In so doing, they also created substitute channels, networks, and associations to circulate and exchange their insights, ideas, and cultural production from universities to book prizes, foundations and literary festivals, magazines and movies, many of which moved across borders but outside the dominant circuitry of what we now call the Global North. They built a nonaligned movement to strike a different path from Cold War geopolitics. Equally important, writers, artists, photographers, and musicians experimented with cultures of hope and possibility. Viewed from different points in what we now call the Global South, or what was then called—in a triumphal chorus—the Third World, there was a search for new meanings of freedom, self-determination, and the promise of development. Out of this moment came efforts in the South to create new histories of global relations (Walter Rodney, *How Europe Underdeveloped Africa*, and dependency theory), new heroes and icons (Che Guevara, Napalm Girl), new repertoires (Little Red Books, photos of atrocity in Sharpeville, or Saigon), and new genres (Mumbai jazz, the tropical novel). Such aspirations for collective freedom and justice coexisted and competed with the ideals of individual rights and artistic and cultural freedom globally disseminated by *LIFE*, George Orwell's *Animal Farm* and *1984*. At once nationally rooted and internationally oriented, these projects placed the promises of decolonization and struggles for social and racial justice at the center of global history. These efforts to remake the world constituted a new epoch that intersected with and thus altered the trajectories of the global Cold War. In this sense, this volume flips the traditional narrative that locates the struggle over decolonization within a framework of East-West conflict and instead embeds the Cold War within a longer epic over empire.

The chapters in this anthology were presented and discussed at a workshop in the Princeton Institute for Regional and International Studies, featuring colleagues from the United States, Latin America, Asia, Europe, and Africa. During that gathering, we explored the global history of the Cold War era from perspectives outside its usual framing and focus on actors outside geopolitical war rooms. Our theme was the yearnings for freedom in Asia, Africa, and Latin America from around the time of the post–Second World War decolonization to the late 1970s. At a time when globalization is met with retreats to national borders, we asked participants to revisit the moment when national freedom projects were unabashedly international because they envisioned alternative world orders and to explore the historical conditions of their possibility. The chapters ranged from studies of visual culture, literature, and journalism to the circulation of academic writings and art exhibitions. The sum of all these parts affirmed the existence of cultural understandings of freedom in the Third World and a shared search for alternative world orders, and thus enables readers to gain insight into a radically different "global cultural cold war" than the one we commonly associate with the East-West divide. It will show that the period that is customarily defined as the Cold War era was also marked by attempts to inaugurate a different epoch—one to achieve global racial and social justice and imagined a different kind of peace. The editors would especially like to express their appreciation to the staff of the Princeton Institute for International and Regional Studies, its Director and our colleague and collaborator, Stephen Kotkin, to Poorvi Bellur for her assistance on the final stages, and to the wonderful editors at Bloomsbury.

On the Threshold of the Third World[1]

Homi K. Bhabha

Where Was the Third World? Where Is It *Now*?

The opening sentences of Gyan Prakash and Jeremy Adelman's introduction to this expansive and invigorating volume invite us to revisit the innovative ideals of the Third World that now appear to a host of historians to be a closed chapter. "The Third World," they write "appears as an obsolete term, the coinage of another age, a closed chapter in world history." This dark foreboding is surpassed by a dazzling array of twelve chapters that prove, to the contrary, that the political coinage and moral economy of the "Third World" might well be the most trenchant critique we have of the soiled currency of neoliberal ethno-nationalism.

Globalization, driven by the priorities of financial markets and political majoritarianism, deploys new technologies to encompass those parts of the world that gravitate toward power and privilege—be it in the North or the South. Outside these enclaves lie those who resist the mimetic lure of global accumulation and appropriation: in most cases, their local histories and political circumstances do not permit them to compete for globalization's glittering prizes. These peoples and countries remain, three-quarters of a century later, the wretched of the earth. Where once the Third World was a challenging call to fight global inequality and injustice—a call to solidarity in the cause of planetary transformation and the redistribution of the balance of power—today, there is callous contempt for "shithole countries" and a peremptory dismissal of "failed states." In his 2004 landmark text *Globalization and Its Discontents,* Joseph Stiglitz warned us of the ravaging effects of "free-market fundamentalism" which, a decade later, has brought in its wake a rash of related fundamentalisms that fester on the global body politic: religious fundamentalism, populist fundamentalism, and xenophobic fundamentalism. Stiglitz reminds us that the IMF's imposition of "conditionalities" on loan-making to poor countries results in a kind of neocolonial world-making. It is invariably justified as establishing free markets, individual freedoms, and economic development in the interests of the "world community."

The binary opposition between First World and Third World, despite its polarities and pitfalls, generates a dialectical discourse with stakes in an international debate about the definition and distribution of "public goods." Do universal goods, with their normative implications, disavow "foreign" cultural values and disregard historical differences in favor of First World priorities? Or, in Amartya Sen's language, should global public goods be construed as "capabilities" tailored to the complex and diverse needs of specific lives? In the context of the Cold War, this dialectical discourse faced postcolonial countries with difficult "international" choices—which side are you on?—as Fanon argues in *The Wretched of the Earth*. Nonetheless, the dialectical struggle inherent in the project of the Third World represented a conflict of goals and values signified in "contradictions" of contested beliefs and antagonistic economic models.

Today, the dialectical tension associated with the concept of the Third World has given way to a global bipolar dynamic consisting of sectoral profitability, selective connectivity, and accelerated networks of algorithmic advances. Profound asymmetries in opportunity and equality are portrayed as anachronistic problems of parts of the world that resist "coming up to speed" with the global agenda. I am reminded of the truth of Fanon's riposte to the Eurocentric demand that the Third World should adopt Western paradigms of development: "No, we do not want to catch up with anyone."[2] As the global juggernaut speeds past, the severity of the discontents of globalization are diminished in scale and rapidly disappear in the rear-view mirror.

In such a world, the *speed* of neoliberal capitalist exploitation and expansion generates a narrative of progress invested in networked oases of accumulation and "disruptive innovation" (to use the business school jargon) that treat the rest of the world as a global wasteland. The endemic and recurrent problems of global justice, global health, global climate change, and global migration somehow slip through these networked chains of neoliberal command. They are looked upon with disdain as anachronistic "works in progress" left over from another time. If the accelerated speed of command and control is the shibboleth of the global world, the solidarity of the synchronic development of ideas, cultures, and opportunities (an optimistic utopian project, it must be admitted) was the keyword of Third-Worldism.

Let's look through the rear-view mirror for a moment and ask, *Where was the Third World?*

In their introduction, the editors tell of Jawaharlal Nehru taking the podium at the opening of the Asians Relations Conference in 1947, pointing to a map of Asia and declaring, "We stand at the end of an era and the *threshold* of a new period of history." The flow of Nehru's soaring rhetoric moves too swiftly from the "end" of an era to the inauguration of a "new" history. He flies over the fact that to stand on a historical *threshold* is to place oneself at a point of *transition* in the duration of the present—somewhere in-between the lessons of the past and the labors of the future—experiencing the "ends" of colonialism while concurrently, devising and deciphering the "means" of postcolonial life-worlds to come.

In his conversation with Nehru at the Bandung conference, Richard Wright immediately saw Nehru as a visionary leader who stood courageously on the threshold of a historic transition of power in India, while addressing a similar series of transitions across Asia, Africa, and the Third World. Indeed, there is hardly a finer articulation of the political integrity and ethical aspiration of the idea of the Third World than Nehru's speech, *Tryst with Destiny,* delivered at midnight on August 14, 1947, to the Constituent Assembly of India. *Yeah*, Nehru spoke "in the midnight hour"[3] to dedicate all Indian's "to the service of India, and her people, and to the still larger cause of humanity," and at the stroke of the midnight hour, as he put it, he dedicated India to the service of the world—the Third World in particular: "Those dreams are for India, but they are also for the world, for all the nations and peoples are too closely knit together today for any one of them to imagine that it can live apart." The greatness of the Nehruvian vision, as Wright encountered it at Bandung, lay in its ability keep a tryst with the complexities of historical transition. Nehru sought an "interstitial" internationalism founded on thresholds that linked newly independent states to each other, rather than throwing up geopolitical frontiers and economic barriers to keep them apart. Solidarity, not sovereignty, is the goal of threshold-thinking. Nehru, as Wright quickly saw, attempted to maintain a prescient, if precarious, balance on both sides of the postcolonial threshold: Wright asks,

> Of what does [Nehru's] greatness consist? It consists of his being what his country is: part East, part West. If one day Nehru says that the perplexities facing Asia are moral, then he is acting in a Western manner; if the next day he says that the world is gripped by a power struggle, he is looking upon life as an Asian. From his point of view, he is not merely playing with ideas; *he is a reflection of what his India* is, a halfway house between East and West.[4]

Nehru's productive and ambivalence gives him access to a translational, global cosmopolitanism that is part East and part West, but the Asian perspective that articulates the threshold between East and West—the formative fulcrum—is capable of building a *Lebenswelt* that is new and different, and this is what Wright heard in Nehru's speech. As I read both Nehru and Wright, I see an emphasis on the *nation*—as a threshold of subaltern hospitality accessible to the half-way house—rather than on the sovereignty of the *state* that frequently bars its windows and locks its doors against the lives and times of others, foreigners, strangers.

Wright's polarised presentation of the world divided between East and West is as problematic today as it was at Bandung. It has a queasy Kiplingesque echo that I would not entertain. However, "half-way house," as a metaphor of political and cultural mediation across national borders, is an interesting figure of speech. It invokes the aspirational ambition of the idea of Third World as a political forum of networked regional solidarities that are de-centred in the very process of struggling for, and achieving, postcolonial freedoms. Here, in my view, there is an implicit appeal to political freedom as an-ongoing process of threshold-thinking that arises out of the experiments and exigencies of transitionality in the attempt to negotiate an intersectional society and an inter-cultural polity. Perhaps this is why W. E. B. DuBois frequently hyphenates the word *inter*-national.

The appeal to threshold-thinking, when it enters the annals of historical writing, or contemporary witnessing, activates an agency of mediation that *writes* transition in the language of intermediacy. The intermediate, I suggest, is not "in the middle," but "in-the-midst-of": an interstitial space of reflection and representation; a gap in time—the time of the threshold—that reaches out for a spatial trope with which to figure *transition* as history and concept. The mediation between parties, countries or cultures, is often a process of transference across a gap of interests, intentions and inheritances—not unlike the metaphoric transfer of meaning—in order to negotiate a translation of terms and conditions. The "gap" is seminal to thought and action caught between past and future, as Hannah Arendt argues:

> [I]t would be of some relevance to notice that the appeal to thought arose in the
> oddin-between period which sometimes inserts itself into historical time when
> not only the later historians but the actors and witnesses, the living themselves,
> become aware of *an interval in time which is altogether determined by things that
> are no longer and by things that are not yet.* In history, these intervals have shown
> more than once that they may contain the moment of truth. [my emphasis][5]

The half-way house, configured in this way, is a metonym of mediation: its portals
enable the free movement of peoples and ideas across the threshold. The half-way
house, in the way of all metonyms, signifies a "whole" house whose spaces are diverse
yet interconnected, and whose windows share a landscape, but catch the light at
different times of the day. The call to assemble a Third World is a call to alterity, not
unity; and Bandung provided post-colonial states with a platform of aspiration and
action aimed at the convergence of interests, not a consensus of ideological positions.

Third World nationhood is a process of developing dynamic, evolving
neighborhoods, unhindered by the sovereign possessions of the Cold War State. At
their best, these visions of freedom resist the manacles of capitalist and militaristic
"progress" legitimised by a moral economy of racial inequality. The political rhetoric
of imperial dominance and Cold War dependency are remarkably similar, despite
their distance in time and place. They share a racist intent in their enunciations of
the prophecy and profitability of Western Progress, and those recruited to labour in
its interests are the very ones excluded from its promise: the colonised are classified
as being historically "backward," while Third World nations are condemned to being
inherently "immature."

To herd hordes of enslaved subjects and colonised peoples—" the wretched of
the earth"—in the service of driving the very machines of capitalist profitability that
mangle them, body and soul, in the cause of Progress, is at the heart of Fanon's ethical
critique of an Enlightenment modernity gone rogue.

> But what matters now is not a question of profitability, not a question of increased
> productivity, not a question of production rates. No, it is not a question of back to
> nature. It is the very basic question of not dragging man in directions which mutilate
> him, of not imposing on his brain tempos that rapidly obliterate and unhinge it. The
> notion of catching up must not be used as a pretext to brutalize man, to tear him
> from himself and his inner consciousness, to break him, to kill him.

To achieve a new world order—the Third World—is more than a historical and political
mission; it requires nothing less than an alternative ontology and psychology—a new
humanism, in Fanon's phrase—that refuses the tragic Sisyphean task of struggling to roll
the rock up the pinnacle of Progress to see it come crashing down . . . again and again:

> No, we do not want to catch up with anyone. But what we want is to walk in the
> company of man, every man, night and day, for all times. It is not a question of
> stringing the caravan out where groups are spaced so far apart they cannot see the
> one in front, and men who no longer recognize each other, meet less and less and

talk to each other less and less. The Third World must start over a new history of man . . .[6]

Temperamentally, no two postcolonial thinkers could be more at odds than Nehru and Fanon, and yet they share a vision of hospitality that opens doors on both sides of the threshold. Fanon's conclusion to *The Wretched of the Earth* is an unforgiving attack on the very idea of Europe as an icon of civility or civilization. "The Third World must start over a new history of man," Fanon declares, "which takes account of not only the occasional prodigious theses maintained by Europe but also its crimes, the most heinous of which have been committed at the very heart of man." But then, as he utters his last words on the matter, Fanon stands with Nehru on threshold of a revisionary hospitality—not without anxiety and hostility—and defines a "new humanism" that transcends the sum of the parts. In that act Fanon attempts to suture (not suppress) the wounds of the colonial past: "For Europe, for ourselves and for humanity, comrades, we must make a new start, develop a new way of thinking, and endeavor to create a new man."[7]

At its best, such threshold-thinking in the construction of the Third World— what I have here called interstitial internationalism and elsewhere, translational cosmopolitanism—is a lasting challenge to the narrow borders of disciplinary thought. Third World intellectuals are more likely to be engaged with public-facing interventions problems rather than professional protocols. Nehru is a historian, an essayist and a politician; Fanon, a psychiatrist, phenomenologist, and an activist. Their trysts with destiny are also trysts with the tasks of cultural translation. There are several instances, in this volume, where the displacement of disciplines reveals new thresholds of representation-as-translation across art, culture, and intellectual discourse. The Third World inaugurated new parameters of citizenship— national, not nationalistic— which initiated imaginative forces of transitional and translational cultural agency in the broadest sense.

This volume is alive with such translational trysts. Agustín reveals, as he puts it, "the central role of intellectuals and books in the dissemination of the ideas, values and images on which rising non-aligned solidarities were built. . . . [The]efficiency of the Third-Worldism and non-aligned politics was often based on the intersected elective affinities of diverse state and non-state actors involved in its construction, however unequal or asymmetric these actors may have been." In a remarkable act of translation, Penny M. Von Easchen argues that "We Shall Overcome" resonated with audiences in India. Renowned Indian poet Girija Kumar Mathur contributed a literal translation in Hindi, "Hum Honge Kaamyab." Regularly sung by school children in India during the 1980s, the multilinguistic song has been described as an "unofficial national anthem." And in her chapter on the color black in the work of F. Newton Souza, Atreyee Gupta draws our attention to black as a weapon of the weak: "when wielded by the disenfranchised in the second half of the twentieth century, the color black—the Négritude poetics of the color black, the black of the Black Panthers, the black flag of dispersed anarchist groups across the world—functioned as (a)chromatic contractions of resistance." In opening our minds to these life-enhancing Third World border-crossing projects in politics and the arts, the closed minds and policed borders of the prevalent ethno-nationalist regimes of our times seem both retrograde and repressive. The view from the rear-view mirror looks considerably better.

The ethno-populist systems of power of our global moment impose carceral histories and geographies on much of the world-order today. Minorities barred from citizenship; refugees barred from borders; speech barred from opinion; dissidents barred from public discourse; protesters barred from the park or the *maidan;* Black lives barred from protection. The prison-house of the present, which exists in more places than we care to name, is an attempt to build walls of exclusion and interdiction where there should be a free and equal passage across the thresholds of public life and its divergent, even disjunctive, social values. This is surely what Frantz Fanon proposed as being both the trial and the testimony of an imminent Third World Order.

Counterintuitively, Fanon proposes that a sense of "nationhood" must develop from an awareness of the thresholds and transitions that exist between countries, regions, and cultures. It is from this "space in-between" that the Third World emerges, recognizing differential histories and representing diverse interests that constitute a country, peoples, or a region. The Third World moves beyond the claims of sovereign nationalism and the confines of tribal patriotism. "A national consciousness," Fanon argues, "*which is not nationalism* [and] is alone capable of giving us an international dimension"[8] is one in which the national culture is built on the politics of difference—"the outcomes of tensions internal and external to a society as a whole, and its multiple layers."[9]

To negotiate these tensions internal and external to a society—to cross and recross these diverse worldly thresholds—opens the door to a politics of radical hospitality in which the idea of the Third World finds its moral compass and its historical moorings.

Notes

1   For my dear friend Gyan, whose raucous belly laugh echoes through the years.
2   Fanon, *WE*, 238.
3   Any resemblance to Wilson Pickett's Motown Records Classic *In the Midnight Hour* is entirely coincidental.
4   Richard Wright, 141–2.
5   Hannah Arendt, Between Past and Future, 29.
6   Fanon, *WE*, 238.
7   Fanon, *WE*, 235–9.
8   Fanon, *WE*, 179.
9   Fanon, *WE*, 177.

Introduction

Imagining the Third World: Genealogies of Alternative Global Histories

Gyan Prakash and Jeremy Adelman

Today, the "Third World" appears as an obsolete term, the coinage of another age, a closed chapter in world history. If mentioned, it is with embarrassment, sometimes with scare quotes. The new order dominated by neoliberalism discards it as anachronistic, a relic of the Cold War era when the world was partitioned into three regions; the triumph of market fundamentalism and flat-world euphoria brought down communism and rebaptized the Third World as "emerging markets." To recall the Third World is to dredge up failed dreams and forgettable nightmares.

This volume returns to the ruins of the pre-1989 era to explore in its history an understanding of the present that does not presuppose that, from the moment of its creation a third world was a doomed one. It argues that the Third World was never only a geopolitical entity, a mere cartographic descriptor produced by a bipolar Cold War, a residual from a clash between a capitalist "West" and communist "East." It was also an idea, an emancipatory imagination of an alternative future, and one that was more committed than either the "First" or "Second" Worlds to demolishing empires and unburdening colonial peoples as a necessary condition for world order and peace.[1] As the halo of globalization has slipped in recent years and the fantasy of ever-emerging markets has faded, the memories of those visions of an alternative world order need to be exhumed.

World-defining summits at Bandung in 1955, the 1966 Tricontinental Conference in Havana, and the 1972 gathering of the UN Conference on Trade and Development in Santiago were its expressions at the geopolitical level. But the idea of the Third World drew force from decolonization in Africa and Asia, and from Latin American dreams of a more equitable development in the face of imperialism. Together, they aspired for far-reaching social changes and global relations free of domination. It was an attempt to reenvision the world globally and locally, free from the legacies of slavery, colonialism, and imperialism. We return to it not as nostalgia for the world we have lost but to locate in its history an account of the present that has installed the market as the global Zeitgeist of our future, a destiny for which there is neither escape nor choice. This came about, we argue, by discarding the Third World imaginary's faith in human interventions, in the power of politics, in the transformative potential of art and literature to remake the world in a different image.

The imagination of the Third World coincided with and changed the course of the Cold War. But the Third World also preceded and exceeded it. Its origins and ambitions lay in the energies released by decolonization and the struggles for a non-dominated world, which constitute the central epochal upheavals of the twentieth century. To return to the Third World, then, is to rethink the global history of the modern world from its margins, to challenge the definition of the period after the Second World War as the epoch of Cold War, and assert that efforts to reimagine an order free from imperial domination constituted a powerful historical arc of the epoch.

This rethinking must begin with returning to anticolonialism as central to the aspirations that drove the emergence of the idea of the Third World. Empire came to be seen as the source of competition and conflict; it was also the machinery that held back the majority of the world's population. Of course, anticolonialism is as old as colonialism itself. We can go back to the Haitian Revolution of 1791 whose historical salience has been "silenced," as Michel-Rolph Trouillot put it, by the historiography on the "age of revolutions."[2] Then there was the 1857 Rebellion in India, the 1865 Morant Bay Rebellion in Jamaica, the effort among Cuban, Puerto Rican, and Filipino insurgents to fight Spanish and then American occupiers after 1898. That year, a man called Surontiko Samin began to preach a withdrawal from the world in north-central Java, a rejection of bank credit, school fees, and despised tax collectors. His followers, when asked for their place of birth, could reply: "I was born on earth." All the Dutch imperial authorities could hear were rumors of peasant revolt. Then came the 1899–1901 Boxer Revolt in China, the uprisings in southwestern Africa—and by 1907 there was, for all intents and purposes, an Afro-Asian underground of sedition.[3]

But what was distinctive about the Third World project was not the resistance to imperialism but its internationalist character. Imperialism and colonialism constituted a system of worldwide domination, requiring its dismantling on a global scale. The origin of this internationalist idea can be found in the famous last sentence of Marx's *Communist Manifesto*: "The proletarians have nothing to lose but their chains. They have a world to win." Marx's words were directed against capitalism that, in his view, respected no national boundaries, and he saw colonialism as part of primitive accumulation. By the early twentieth century, Hobson and Lenin had developed Marx's formulation on capitalism's global nature into full-fledged theories of imperialism. The period leading up to the First World War and its aftermath witnessed outbreaks of anti-imperialist opposition that, if not immediately inspired by this legacy of critiques of imperialism, nevertheless began to confront it globally.

Although the standard view attributes the Third World's internationalist imagination to the establishment of postcolonial nation-states after the Second World War, Manu Goswami convincingly argues that visions of a post-imperial internationalism go back to the early twentieth century.[4] She writes of the Indian sociologist-philosopher Benoy Kumar Sarkar, who advanced a remarkably internationalist vision of an anti-imperial future. Central to his anti-imperialism was a demand for equality in all spheres—from politics to culture, to intellectual thought, to education. He did not, however, fetishize the nation as the only form to achieve this equality, regarding it not as an organic expression of some culture or spirit but as a historically contingent and local expression of political freedom secured by military and territorial power. Sarkar advanced these ideas in his voluminous writings and speeches in Europe, the United States, and India. He was not alone in stating universalist anti-imperialism. Goswami refers to the writings of the Peruvian writer José Carlos Mariátegui, who wrote that the so-called Indian problem in Latin America could only be solved by an internationalist anticolonial solidarity. A Marxist who resisted the Comintern straightjacket, Mariátegui did not believe that all societies had to march their way through the same stages of history on their way to a universal utopia mapped out by Europeans. Indeed, European empires ensured that they could not follow a prescribed universal path; any effort to modernize in the peripheries of the world economy was condemned to run into deep-seated legacies of colonial structures. Peru, a case in point, seceded formally from Spain a century earlier—but it still carried the heritage of a racially stratified order on its shoulders, with immiserated indigenous people in the highlands and "whitened" urbanites on the coast. When Mariátegui dreamed of a Latin American brand of socialism across borders, it had to start with the fact of world colonialism and create alternative and inclusive alliances and coalitions with all kinds of subject peoples— and not just the lionized proletariat of Marxist eschatology. The "Indian problem"— for liberal internationalists—was presented as a moral one. Indeed, all appeals to "the conscience of civilization" in the name of a humanitarian and enlightened order, which included antislavery campaigns, defenses of aboriginal peoples, denounced colonizing nations while still invoking the precept of an advanced white, European, morality. No wonder, Mariátegui mused, these humanitarian campaigns were futile and Indians and the descendants of slaves still lay in wait. In words that anticipated recent criticisms of humanitarian imperialism, Mariátegui warned that "humanitarian teachings have not halted or hampered European imperialism, nor have they reformed its methods." They could only begin to change the world if they recognized and examined the imperial roots of their own faiths in order to transcend them in pursuit of a more truly alternative world order.[5]

The internationalism of such anticolonial imaginations has to be set in the context of the global nature of imperialism itself. Those who lived in the imperial world thought and imagined the future in the context of the global political modernity that imperialism had fashioned. The nation-form did not appear as the only embodiment of political freedom. Intellectuals envisioned transnational solidarities to achieve freedom and equality denied by imperialism.[6] The Bolshevik Revolution's repudiation of unequal treaties imposed by the tsarist regime and the establishment of the Comintern in 1919 signaled an international struggle against capitalism and imperialism. And although the League of Nations can be viewed as a counterrevolutionary project to manage colonial territories on behalf of the European empires and spoke the language of Anglo-Saxon privilege in endorsing national self-determination,[7] its establishment in 1919 was a recognition of imperialism as an international system.

The opposition to such a global system and the attempts to manage it were immediate; just as imperial forces lived in a perpetual state of alert about peasant unrest or seditious plots being hatched in the canteens alongside the dockyards of Shanghai, Bombay, and Buenos Aires, the spectacle of something wider, connected, and concerted began to haunt world elites at the end of the First World War. There is lively debate among historians of China about the nature of the "New Culture" espoused by students and intellectuals during the May Fourth movement of 1919.[8] But whatever the range and reach of modernity advanced by May Fourth, it is clear the movement was directed against predatory foreign interests while inhabiting the political and cultural space forged by imperialism. Gandhi's sharp break from the British Empire after the Amritsar massacre of 1919, and his subsequent conjoining of the non-cooperation movement of 1920–2 with the Islamic opposition to the dismemberment of the Ottoman Empire, also resisted imperialism as a world system. This internationalist character of the resistance to colonialism was also evident in the League Against Imperialism conference in Brussels in 1927, bringing together anti-imperialist activists from around the world, including Jawaharlal Nehru from India and Mohammed Hatta from Indonesia. The 1930s witnessed concerted efforts by Black intellectuals and activists to mount a global anticolonial struggle based on the recognition that imperialism was underpinned by racial oppression going back to slavery. Together, W. E. B. Du Bois, C. L. R. James, and George Padmore forged a powerful pan-Africanism that envisioned a global revolution against the intertwined racial and colonial domination.[9]

It was not by coincidence that just as Gandhi severed whatever remained of his faith in the British in 1919 that DuBois also rounded on Woodrow Wilson. DuBois had gone to Paris that year as an envoy for the National Association for the Advancement of Colored People and made an overture to Wilson to treat Black soldiers equally, to consider the "future of Africa" in talks about self-determination. DuBois was also a lifelong champion of what he saw as Japanese-inspired internationalism after the Japanese navy routed Russia's fleet in 1905, and he was dismayed when Wilson spurned Japan's proposal for a clause in the new peace treaty that declared all races to be equal and for its signatories to abolish racial discrimination. For two decades, DuBois had insisted that "the color line" was not just an American "problem." So long as Africa was colonized, so long as empires carved the world into racially coded dominions, the color line was a global one. After his disenchantment with Wilson in Paris, DuBois returned home to the horror of Red Summer, when white supremacists spread terror, especially directed again Black veterans returning from the European front. In despair, DuBois published his ominous *Darkwater: Voices from Within the Veil*. Its pages reveal a mind in anguish after the hope for an anti-racial and postcolonial world got drowned in the bloodletting.[10]

If 1919 parted the waters for rival internationalisms, socialist and capitalist, imperial and postcolonial, that year set in motion some basic thinking about alternatives from within what we now call the Global South. Underlying the struggles against imperialism was a desire to build a different world. This is often overlooked by the standard view that sees the postwar decolonization and the establishment of postcolonial nation-states as the successful diffusion of the European model of national sovereignty. In fact, anticolonial nationalism had larger and different ambitions.[11] Black intellectuals and activists, for example, redefined national self-determination away from the Westphalian model of sovereignty. Viewing empire as enslavement, they envisioned an egalitarian world order premised on the end of racial and economic inequality.[12] Such a vision of a different world order also called for a radical restructuring of colonized societies shaped by enslavement. For, if empire was enslavement, then its end demanded freedom and equality not only at the global level but also at the local level. Gandhi did not have the well-developed understanding of empire as enslavement advanced by Black intellectuals, but even he did not think of *swaraj* (self-rule) as a mere replacement of alien government with self-government. This is evident, for example, in his 1909 text, *Hind Swaraj*. At the time, Gandhi had not broken from the political framework of imperialism. He did so only after his return to India from South Africa and following the Amritsar massacre in 1919. But even in this early text, Gandhi stated that his concept of *swaraj* did not mean only native rule in place of foreign rule. He famously wrote that he did not want "English rule without the Englishman." Underlying his ideal of *swaraj* was a critique for what he called the "modern civilization," a rejection of imperial politics, culture, and economy, which he saw rooted in the violence of domination. In its place, he advanced the idea of a nonmodern civilization, based on nonviolence and nondomination. As Indians dressed in homespun cloth marched on the streets, boycotted foreign cloth, withdrew from schools and colleges, and refused to cooperate with the colonial administration during the 1920–2 non-cooperation movement, the psychological hold of British rule crumbled and a new world became imaginable.

If, through the 1930s and 1940s, anticolonial intellectuals and political activists explored and advanced ideas about a world without empire, the Second World War revolutionized anticolonialism because it intensified and industrialized the conflict and brought the underground to the surface—and gave it guns. From Japan's invasion of Manchuria in 1931, gathering force with German predatory policies in the east and the Italian invasion of Abyssinia in 1935, as empires reached down deep into colonized societies to recruit soldiers and mobilize resources, the opposition to colonialism also deepened to include and ally growing numbers of students, workers, and peasants. As Japan rolled into China and seized the outposts of European empires in Asia, the whole continent was thrown into turmoil. Old patterns of social and political authority were shattered. "This was Asia's revolutionary moment," write Bayly and Harper, "when many previously disempowered groups in society—women, the young, workers and peasants—took the political initiative to rebuild their communities, salvage their livelihoods and regain their dignity."[13] Outside of Europe, this was a longer and bloodier struggle than the European one of which it was a part. In Japanese-occupied Asia, 24 million people would die, another 3 million Japanese, and 3.5 million would starve to death in India alone to sustain Britain's war effort.[14] A sense of epochal change was in the air as the world appeared on the brink of turning upside down.

It was against this background of the Second World War and its aftermath that Jawaharlal Nehru opened the Asian Relations Conference in New Delhi on March 23, 1947. He stood in front of an enormous illuminated map of the continent and declared: "We stand at the end of an era and the threshold of a new period of history." Although Nehru planned no revolutionary overthrow of the old order, there is no doubt that the soaring rhetoric of the "new period of history" was responding to yearnings for radically new beginnings that had been building up since the early twentieth century across the imperially dominated world. From this moment on, the postcolonial states took the lead in the struggle to build a new world order after empire. Bandung was the institutional expression of the efforts by decolonized nations to chart a path in a world now in the throes of the Cold War. Nation-states were in the lead to build a Third World, but decades of struggle against colonialism and the threat of its recurrence in the form of the Cold War were very much part of Bandung. Richard Wright, the African American writer, who was at Bandung, wrote:

> It was the kind of meeting that no anthropologist, no sociologist, no political scientist would ever have dreamed of staging; it was too simple, too elementary, cutting through outer layers of disparate social and political and cultural facts down to the bare brute residues of human existence: races and religions and continents. Only brown, black, and yellow men who had long been made agonizingly self-conscious, under the rigors of colonial rule, of their race and their religion could have felt the need for such a meeting. There was something extra-political, extra-social, almost extra-human about it.[15]

Wright's observations about this effort to make the experience of colonial domination the basis for a postcolonial transformation with something "extra human" was in tune with Fanon's idea that the exertion of sheer will would produce a radical national culture of decolonization. His conviction that Marxism would have to be stretched to fit colonial realities and to imagine postcolonial futures can be viewed as a call for creativity in thought and action.[16] The creative energy to remake the international order with anticolonial political solidarity was amply present in Bandung, as Richard Wright noted.

Recently, Bandung has come back into scholarly focus.[17] Back also is the renewed attention to the "spirit" of Bandung. This is to be welcomed, for, as Su Lin Lewis and Carolien Stolte argue, the conflation of Afro-Asian solidarity with nonalignment and the precedence accorded to "realpolitik" over the "romance" of Bandung have obscured traditions of non-state anticolonial thought and transnational solidarity that preceded and followed the extraordinary 1955 conference.[18] Anticolonial thought brimmed with creative energy. Consider, for example, the title of Gandhi's journal—*Young India*—and the name of his publishing house—Navjivan Press (New Life Press). This appeal to youth and newness spoke of the desire to reach beyond the present and the inherited to fashion something fresh and different. Gary Wilder argues that the post-1945 period was an era of "world-historical opening," showing how Aimé Césaire and Leopold Sénghor viewed decolonization as an opportunity to remake the world with transnational alliances and polities.[19] Intellectuals and activists organized conferences and built networks—"Other Bandungs"—to forge Afro-Asian solidarity against imperialism in the period leading up to Bandung. Later[20] radical left-wing women activists, not content with the achievement of national independence in their respective countries, organized conferences, and formed transnational non-state alliances to combine their anti-imperialism with demands for women's rights as laborers and peasants.[21] And, although nation-states organized the conference, "whatever paucity the Bandung moment may have had as a political philosophy, it nevertheless laid the groundwork for the global emergence of a critical, postcolonial, antiimperial intellectual ethic."[22] This was expressed, for example, in the works of such artists as Maqbool Fida Hussain of India and Gazbia Sirry of Egypt.

Anticolonialism, then, was a fecund body of thought that animated imaginations of a world after empire—in which a Third World would enjoy the same freedoms and unprogrammed futures as the other worlds. Some scholars have pitted nation-state sovereignty against federations as more expansive and a deeper form of anticolonial thinking. But, as Getachew shows, that anticolonial nationalism was never the European, Westphalian model but a form that envisaged the dismantling of the unequal order fashioned by colonialism and imperialism. Leaders like Kwame Nkrumah and Michael Manley placed the postcolonial nation in an international frame, and even experimented with federalism to undo the political and economic inequities of the international order.[23] Outside the initiatives by postcolonial leaders and states, there was a robust body of thoughts and actions by non-state activists, intellectuals, writers, and artists that strove to envision and realize a world after colonialism. The involvement of communists and the World Peace Council in several of these initiatives has often been treated through the Cold War lens. But whatever the manipulation of such activities, the activists involved in these projects were not Soviet dupes. The anticolonial ideas and energies animating their projects preceded and exceeded the Cold War.

Yet another source was communism. In China, India, and elsewhere, writers and observers on the Left had always had to reckon with the legacies of empire and the centrality of the peasantry. So, communists had to place the effects of the world economy at the center of their diagnosis for revolution—and the party often served as the latticework for radical solidarities.

But what was communism? Beyond Europe, it came to mean many things. Indeed, it was in the Third World that European experiments in alternative forms of communist social organization—such as Tito's Yugoslavia—got reinvented as a more organic and compatible system of progress. Latin America, which had long thrown off formal colonialism, witnessed communist intellectuals from transnational networks under the WPC umbrella. These networks would eventually feed the efforts to imagine the Third World. Communism and national liberation struggles against imperialism joined together in preparing the building blocks of Tricontinentalism. What pushed Latin American communists to the forefront of progressive internationalism was the heightened centrality of the power of the United States and its multinationals like the United Fruit Company, suspected of being the hidden force behind the 1954 overthrow of the democratically elected government of Jacobo Arbenz in Guatemala. Indeed, the Communist Party had actively supported Arbenz even though he made clear his differences with them. One young Argentine doctor had gone to Guatemala in solidarity with the reform esprit. His name was Ernesto "Che" Guevara. In the rubble from the bombing by the air force of the capital, he would swear to wage a globalized war against American imperialism. After fleeing north to Mexico, which had itself been a haven for communist and anarchists seeking refuge after the Spanish Civil War, he would meet with Cuban exiles led by Fidel Castro. But it is worth noting that not all "communist" networks functioned like a seamless alliance of anti-imperial malcontents. Behind the scenes, there was great feuding over what communism would mean. For the heirs of Mariátegui's heterodoxy, the Third World, because of the legacies of colonialism, needed to chart its own brand of struggle, one that made anti-imperialism at least as important, if not more important, than proletarian alliance-building. By the late 1950s, on the eve of the Cuban Revolution and informed by the Sino-Soviet split, there was a ferocious debate among Third World communists about the spirit and strategy of revolutionary solidarity. For the Argentine Marxist José Aricó, reckoning with Marx's own blind spots and condescensions about European colonialism was, if anything, an opening, an opportunity, to rethink radical internationalism in a new key—even if it meant challenging orthodoxies from Moscow.[24]

A third was a yearning to master time, to catch up or even to surpass the other "worlds." The Third World was, for many, co-terminus with the idea of development, so much so that the Third World idea got reimported into the First World as a liberatory turn, emancipating all societies from the unevenness and unfairness of modernization. There was, of course, a drive to "develop" the Third World using First World technologies, expertise, and markets. As the Nationalist regime in China crumbled and Mao seized power, and as many decolonizing efforts from Malaya to South Africa took inspiration, Washington branded "technical assistance," rolled out in the form of President Harry Truman's Point Four Program in 1949, to use development as a means to thwart the radical turn. This was in large measure *because* development was such a compelling way to envision a future free of oppression and scarcity. By mastering time, planning it, accelerating it, Third Worlders could reverse the legacies of colonialism—which had always been much more than formal political subjugation. In India, Ghana, Brazil, to "develop" meant to become free of domination and it would eventually cascade into international organizations and alliances as diverse as the United Nations Commission for Latin America and Caribbean (where a turn toward "dependency analysis" would incubate) to the UN Conference on Trade and Development (where schemes for helping primary exporters coursed through the swelling ranks of international development "advisers"). Development became a kind of platform for dreaming of alternative histories of the future.

Needless to say, utopian visions in the name of capturing and redirecting time could also go awry. Where the virus of compressing years into quintiles spread most was in the communist world; what the master-planners of capitalism dreamed up was nothing compared to the development utopias of party chiefs. In 1957, Comrade Khrushchev announced at a gathering of world party leaders to celebrate the fortieth anniversary of the October Revolution that the Soviet Union was committed to eclipsing American industrial output in fifteen years. Not to be outdone and frustrated that China was still inching after one Five Year Plan, Mao's proclamation of a Great Leap Forward to outdo British industrial output in fifteen years, plunged much of China back into the stone age. In the euphoria, the missile scientist Qian Xuesen waxed "How High Will Grain Yields Be?" in *China Youth Daily* to convince doubters of the promise of "Sputnik" expectations. Mao began to rethink his own fevered projections: surpassing the UK may take only two or three years, "especially in steel production." As it became clear that any advance on the industrial front required better carts— without railroads or trucking, "cartification" was the aim—making ball bearings gained urgency for home factories. "Every household a factory, every home ringing with a ding-dong sound" was the slogan. Though the output was useless, *People's Daily* celebrated national "bearingification" as a monumental breakthrough. Meanwhile, "right deviationists" and "degenerate peasants" blamed for tripping progress were rounded up; reports of local food shortages were dismissed as "temporary crises." Thirty million people starved to death in three years in humanity's worst manufactured famine.[25]

By the 1960s, declared the "development decade" by the UN General Assembly, more and more critics grew disenchanted with the gap between the dreams and the realities. The Martiniquian psychiatrist Frantz Fanon had gone to Algeria and helped the insurgents there. When it came to the development experts and social scientific certainty, his bitterness shone through. After serving in North African hospitals, he invoked the acidic words of an unnamed "Senegalese patriot" disenchanted with the promises of the poet-president Senghor: "We asked for the Africanization of the top jobs and all Senghor does is Africanize the Europeans." Fanon did not think much of the "narcissistic monologues" of the colonial bourgeois and their academics, or the efforts to jump-start nations with "theoretical knowledge" invoked to "regiment the masses according to a predetermined schema." His prose drips with disdain, especially for the intellectuals who rid colonies of their European masters while having assimilated the colonizer's culture, and so authoring a kind of "self-hatred that characterizes racial conflict in segregated societies." He became convinced that true liberation required a violent cleansing; moving from Lyon to Algiers put him on the road to write one of the twentieth-century's most wrenching works, *Les Damnés de la terre*. Written in Fanon's dying months, from April to July 1961, the book's wrath aimed to slice through the mist of development's false hopes. "The Third World," he concluded,

> must start over a new history of man which takes account of not only the occasional prodigious theses maintained by Europe but also its crimes, the most heinous have been committed at the very heart of man, the pathological dismembering of his functions and the erosion of his unity, and in the context of the community, the fracture, the stratification and the bloody tensions fed by class, and finally, on the immense scale of humanity the racial hatred, slavery, exploitation and, above all, the bloodless genocide whereby one and a half billion have been written off.[26]

The result was the globalization of Third World aspirations that provoked a counter-movement to contain it—and to radicalize it, and with it waves of enchantments and disenchantments, hopes and despairs, utopias and dystopias. These three core aspirations changed the discourse, diplomacy, and landscape of actors involved in the imagining and creation of the world order after 1945—and opened a field that was at once political, cultural, social, and economic, upon which great battles over the meaning of global order would be waged. This contest cannot be reduced to sideshows of a global Cold War, not least because it preceded it, and one might say endured long after the Cold War ended.

The Third World was an attempt to reimagine the world and its history. New cultural and intellectual expressions spoke of this soaring world-changing ambition. Politics produced bursts of creativity as artists and intellectuals searched for alternative cultural and aesthetic vocabularies to understand and undo the experiences of colonialism, racial and imperialist oppression. The extraordinary ferment in postcolonial literature came out of these efforts. The Kenyan writer Ngugi wa Thiong wrote about the alienating effects of colonialism. Africans were expected to view their world according to European cultural representations and values, creating a vast gap between Jane Austen's images of manners from the lived African experience. Ngugi's *The River Between* (1965) turned against such expectation. He wrote about a division in an African community brought about by Christianization, prompting the younger generation to make something of their own, inspired by their own imagination.[27] Ngugi's novel is redemptive, like Chinua Achebe's *Things Fall Apart* (1958), recovering community and belonging denied to African societies by colonialism. Ngugi even published his later novels first in Gikuyu rather than English to resist the dominance of Europhone languages and insist on the importance of language to identity. The Caribbean writings of George Lamming and Edward Braithwaite seized on texts by such European canonical figures as Homer and Shakespeare and repurposed their narratives of travel, discovery, and dispossession into tales of reconnections to the past after historical experiences of loss and dispossession. But perhaps no aesthetic turn more defined the search for new ways of imagining time than the rise of magical realism in Latin America, with the novels of Jorge Amado and Gabriel García Márquez as its best sellers. The image of butterflies floating out of peoples' mouths and time wandering in circles coexisted with an affection for Ché-style praxis (and not a few of the boom writers were open about their support for armed insurrection); what they shared was a faith in the power of voluntarism, for making history anew.[28]

But with rising disappointments with the limits of national independence in the 1960s and the 1970s, mere re-appropriation of the colonial cultural inheritances appeared inadequate. To lose faith in the guerrilla fighter-turned-warlord did not mean throwing in the towel and accepting European or North American norms. If anything, disenchantment could sharpen the edge of the Third World critique of the global order of things. In *Petals of Blood* (1977), Ngugi wrote about an African community turned into an industrial wasteland by an alliance of native and international capital, dashing the promises of national independence. Fanon, Amílcar Cabral, Cuba, and Mao stood for the new radical spirit. The Argentinian filmmakers Fernando Solanas and Octavio Getino captured this new spirit in their 1969 manifesto for Third Cinema.[29] Calling for "a culture *of* and *for* the revolution, a subversive culture capable of contributing to the downfall of capitalist society," the manifesto aligned itself to "a worldwide liberation movement whose moving force is to be found in Third World countries." This manifesto was part of movements across the world for a new kind of cinema to represent the realities of inequalities and oppression and as artistic vehicles of change.[30] Among others, the Italian Giles Pontecorvo, Ousman Sembene of Senegal, Tomás Gutiérrez Alea of Cuba, and Glauber Rocha, the most prominent exponent of Cinema Novo in Brazil, expressed this drive for films that broke from the Hollywood's commercialism and aesthetic conventions, and experimented with cinematic styles to represent the conditions of imperialist oppression and inequality. Ritwik Ghatak and the Alternative Cinema movement in the early 1970s India were similarly politically motivated explorations. These films were set in different cultural locations and addressed their specific conditions, but their black-and-white, documentary-style cinematography, artisanal production, and a focus on cognition and critique rather than seamless narratives were aimed to forge a "third aesthetic" outside the Euro-American film practice and theory, and meant as political interventions to transform the conditions of capitalist and imperialist oppression.

The global Cold War was fought to shape and control the Third World; the history of the Third World is what made the Cold War a global struggle. It even fueled worldwide anxieties to contain the spread of communism under the aegis of the Congress for Cultural Freedom. Backed by the Central Intelligence Agency and incubated in Western Europe, the CCF became a globe-spanning effort to support artists and intellectuals in Mexico, India, Burma, Chile, and elsewhere to roll back the influence of radicals. While the CCF intellectuals could eventually ruminate on the end of ideology in Europe and North America, they could not ignore the challenge to its ideology posed by the question of development and alternatives in the Third World. Indeed, they understood the world outside the Euro-American bloc in terms of the question of development and modernization, but could not come up with an answer. They proceeded with efforts to win "hearts and minds." If the CCF and the US State Department promoted jazz tours, these, rather than serving geopolitical objectives, ended up being enlisted for local cultural purposes. Thus, while Jazz became part of Bombay Cinema music, Soviet book publishing fostered a progressive visual culture of framing pictures. Rival literary conferences revealed perspectives at odds with the goals of the Cold War sponsors.

The authors in this volume retrace the lineages of this cultural project, one that crossed boundaries and cultivated a hope that local struggles for justice were connected to a wider worldmaking process and in that sense to overcome the solitudes of colonialism. One of the deepest legacies of empire, which fueled Fanon's recognition that the most dramatic struggle of all over the minds and hearts of Third Worlders, was in Third World minds. As much as we tend to think of the Third World as counter to the First or Second Worlds, as an idea, the Third World was above all a construct to create a different historiography and narrative consciousness for the Third World, one free from the scripts of empire. To be backward, underdeveloped, colored, peasant, to live in another time because one lived beyond a European space was, for Fanon, cognitive agony. It was in the service to heal those pains and recognize those agonies that Third World writers, artists, musicians, architects created their own prizes, magazines, conferences, universities, diplomatic practices—an internationalism in an entirely new key—looked to each other. In so doing, they projected views of world order that put words like "freedom," "peace," and "development" into motion to rival the bristling belligerence of rival military-industrial alliances of NATO and the Warsaw Pact.

The authors also probe the important shifts and contested meanings of the Third World imaginary. The year 1960, for instance, marked a turn. With much of Africa decolonized by 1960, Algeria becoming the "Mecca of Revolution,"[31] and the Cuban Revolution serving as an inspiring example, the newly emergent states strove to institutionalize Third-Worldism and provide it with uniformity. Bandung, the Non-Aligned Movement, and diplomacy at the UN were expressions of this process, much of it identified with the language of peace and development. With the cycle of decolonization having passed its peak, and with the more radical insurgencies in Cuba, Algeria, and Vietnam, appeals to peace gave way to calls for revolution. These raised the geopolitical stakes. The Bay of Pigs and the Cuban missile crisis, the CIA-directed assassination of Patrice Lumumba, and the escalating Sino-Soviet split highlighted the pressures exerted by geopolitics on desires and imaginations for a new, post-imperial, and more equitable world once they were commandeered by states. The geopolitical struggle, however, should not make us lose sight of the fact that underpinning the conflict were decades of creative anti-imperial and emancipatory creative thinking and practices of writers, artists, intellectuals, and activists. Indeed, as many of the chapters in this book illustrate, the search for freedom and nondomination at a global scale could contain within it many possible meanings under the portmanteau of Third World.

Together, the chapters in this volume illuminate the worldmaking power of the Third World imaginary. This volume views post–Second World War global history from the South. Its aim is to explore the many ways in which artists, writers, intellectuals, and activists created alternative visions of world order. Challenging the customary definition of this history as the era of the Cold War, the volume insists that it was the epoch of Third World imaginings, attempts to reenvision and remake the world after colonialism and imperialism. Seen from the South, the Cold War was embedded within a longer, more epic, struggle over empire and freedom as a defining and lasting feature of world-making.[32] The Third World was never only a geopolitical space, an entity left over after the East and West partitioned their spheres. It was also an idea, an emancipatory imagination of an alternative future. Imagining such a future intersected with superpower rivalry but also exceeded it, changed it, and did so by design. A tableau of ideas and forces made up the Third World imaginary. The papers of this anthology describe them in rich, world-spanning, detail. They bring into view the cultural histories of decolonization and place them in conversation with geopolitics, thus bringing together fields and inquiries that do not speak to each other. In this fashion, thinking about the Cold War in world history is a strategy for generating new debates about peace, freedom, and equality that are not reducible to the familiar geopolitics of missile launchers and the foggy streets of John Le Carré novels.

Four transversal themes challenge us to rethink the Cold War, world imaginings, and the role of artists and intellectuals in laying out alternative visions of global order that defied the East-West divides and preceded the flat-earth nostrums of neoliberalism. These four themes inform a different history of globalization, one that challenged hierarchies and dependencies while still insisting on cross-border sharing and integration as a premise for an equitable and peaceable globalism. While the authors avoid the traps of nostalgia, they are united in their commitment to explore and excavate visions of global interdependence before it became the hostage of market fundamentalism and pared-down individualism.

First, the Third World served as a coinage for thinking about a different world order, one that was to be moral, equitable, inclusive, possibly a different globalism before globalization. All of the authors illuminate the ways in which actors looked across borders for ideas, inspirations, performances, and fears because the point of departure was a quest for peace, for antiracism, and even a more robust idea of citizenship and democracy that imagined an integrated world, but one forged in a very different rhetoric and with different solidarities than the superpower alignments struggled to impose. It culminated in the 1970s, with proposals for a New International Economic

Order, one that seized upon the moment of détente to push forward on a new global architecture. The Cold War, therefore, looks less like a standoff between superpowers than a war of imaginings, one that turned lethal in India, Congo, and Chile. But it began as a war of world imaginings.

A different world order meant confronting a tension running through liberal and socialist globalisms and seeking strategies to reconcile universalism and cultural differences beyond the familiar civilizational hierarchies of the old imperial defaults. To imagine a Third World as a premise of a different, inclusive world order meant confronting empire head on as a condition of existence. As Cindy Ewing shows in her chapter, beginning with Indonesia's dispute with the Netherlands to its international condemnation of France in North Africa, the Arab-Asian group worked collectively to confront colonial powers in enshrining national sovereignty in the human rights covenant. This precursive activity to the Bandung conference pinpoints the urgency of decolonization within what would be called the Non-Aligned Movement; freeing the world from domination was central to its charge, even if it posed challenges to coalition building under a banner of peace. Fast forwarding to the 1960s, Patrick Iber explains how some of these rifts could widen as Third World ideas of redistribution and freedom became more radical and parted ways with the moderate, reformist, esprit of the 1950s. Tricontinentalism pushed coalition members within and across the Third World to make agonizing choices and exclusions that lurked below the surface of the earlier Third World internationalism depicted by Ewing. Few aspects fueled the militant turn more than the circulation of idealized images and stories of how peasant armies in Vietnam fought off Sikorski helicopters while getting razed by Napalm. University students in El Salvador followed the news of the Tet Offensive of 1968 like partisans and would come to believe that they would be heirs to the Viet Cong. Mélida Anaya Montes (aka Ana María) studied the Vietnamese resistance to French and American forces closely and became one of the commanders of the Farabundo Martí Liberation Front in El Salvador and imagined a victory in Central America following a script from Indochina.[33] The radical turn pushed nonalignment to a new level and announced a new fusion of struggles in Latin America and Africa. It was also a provocation and revealed internal splits.

Peace and solidarity contained under them a second principle. Anticolonialism and anti-imperialism did more than call for a new model of an inclusive world order, it also appealed to a more just and equitable one. The idea of the Third World buoyed dreams of development free from unequal relations globally and locally and drove the imaginings of this new order. The ideas and actors were diverse—ranging from anticolonial nationalists to communists, political activists to artists and intellectuals. But what they shared was a view that the old rules and institutions of the world order were rigged to favor the haves over have-nots. They sought redistribution and development. Agustín Cosovschi's chapter is an excellent example of how the equity-seeking language of socialism became a bridge between Yugoslavian and Chilean writers; it was also a socialism that sought to side-step the more rigid formulae prescribed by Beijing or Moscow. The idea of development and redistribution was frightening enough, as Daniel Steinmetz-Jenkins shows in his study of American modernization theory, that prominent social scientists from the Global North were forced to wrestle with their own conceits about the end of ideology—just as the Third World was giving ideology new, potent, meanings.

Third, the practices of making the Third World as an idea depended on networks, meetings points, conferences, nodes and cities from Bombay to Dakar, from Moscow to MIT. The activist undergrounds of pre-1939 surfaced, spread, and linked up in ways that pooled grievances and shared intellectual and cultural repertoires. Because it posed itself as a contest over the global imagination, cultural actors, and the praxis of what political scientists call "soft power," were instrumental to the diplomatic cause of alliance-making. Some of these networks sprung from communist circuitry, as Marcelo Ridenti shows of Latin American writers, especially the celebrated Brazilian Jorge Amado, in Europe. Universities also became nodes for a different kind of social science and historiography. Andreas Eckert's profile of Walter Rodney, his lecture circuiting and his presence in Dar es Salam as he wrote *How Europe Underdeveloped Africa*, is an important example of how advocates of the Third World idea created alternative channels, agencies, and symbols of respectability and recognition. London and Dakar became global hubs for a cultural exchange and performance, so that musicians like Paul Robeson and Bhupen Hazarika could look beyond the standard centers of New York and give entirely new significance to the meaning of "We Shall Overcome" against a backdrop of the First World Festival of Negro Arts in Senegal in 1966.

Fourth, there was an active business of performing and sharing that circulated Third World appeals across borders—and into remote corners. The place of media, books, painting, recorded music, radio, circulation of photography proliferated the instruments of exchange in this new economy and expanded the kinds of actors who participated in it. Atreyee Gupta delves into the London-based Indian artist Francis Newton Souza's explorations of the aesthetics of the color black and its meanings in relation to colonialism and slavery. Naresh Fernandes relates the story of the State Department-sponsored tours by Jazz Ambassadors in Mumbai, hoping to repair the image of race discrimination in the United States. But jazz had an earlier history in the city, and these tours only helped to consolidate jazz's place in Bombay film music. Jazz also burst beyond the boundaries of internationalism set by the Cold War and evolved into a series of performances and festivals called Jazz Yatra, a journey of jazz. The music was defined as "Indo-Afro-American," and musicians saw the Third World as a source of catalyzing jazz. Jessica Bachman tracks how Soviet propaganda material was assimilated into a visual portrait of culture featuring communists and Third World revolutionaries. Her article reminds us of the circulation of iconic images of Che, Lumumba, Angela Davis that were to become part of the visual Third World imaginary. Monica Popescu writes about the rival conferences of African writers organized by the battling superpowers. The assembled writers, however, did not play to the assigned scripts, showing that the Third World writers and intellectuals had minds of their own. Together, Gupta, Fernandes, Bachman, and Popescu reiterate that the Third World imaginary cannot be neatly folded into a Cold War narrative. Nor did artists and musicians, writers and performers hew obediently to political masters. The touring circuit, translations, galleries, pushed aesthetic commitments beyond the realpolitik of state formation.

The 1970s appear as a capstone decade to the story because it was then that internal fissures, lurking in Ewing's exploration of the early Non-Aligned Movement all the way to the impasses and divisions among Latin American writers in Ridenti's chapter, came into the open. It was a decade that yielded the highest forms of Third World internationalism. By this time, the Tricontinentalism had radicalized the "spirit" of Bandung. For if the 1955 meeting of the newly independent postcolonial nations in Indonesia built on the experiences under European colonialism, the 1966 Havana conference advanced, as Anne Garland Mahler suggests, a more fluid notion of power and resistance. Tricontinentalism saw imperial power as deterritorialized, and interlinked with capitalism and racial domination, requiring a global struggle of all exploited peoples.[34] This notion of radical, global solidarity of the oppressed was present in Third Cinema, the internationalism of the Black Panther movement in the United States, and political and cultural mobilizations against the Vietnam War. The Havana conference did not produce these movements, but they expressed the Tricontinental ideology of the transnational solidarity of the oppressed.

It was against this background of rising demand for a change in the global order that the idea of a New International Economic Order (NIEO) emerged as one project of economic restructuring. Indeed, the NIEO was not only a reflection of increasing frustration about the limits of political sovereignty in a world of nations and the glacial change from development, it was also an effort on the part of Third World leaders to thwart younger, more radical activists—many of whom were abandoning factories and universities to form or join insurgent groups. When the president of Mexico, Luis Echeverría Álvarez, traveled to Santiago, Chile, in April 1972, it was ostensibly to attend a conference of the United Nations Conference on Trade and Development. But he used the occasion to steal the thunder of radicals in Mexico to denounce developed countries for not living up to their promises, to announce the creation of a Charter of Economic Rights and Duties of States, and the right of Third World nations to seize control of their resources from shady multinational corporations and the protection rackets of industrial societies. "The solidarity we demand," he exclaimed, "is a condition of survival." *El Día*'s headline the next day was euphoric: "THE THIRD WORLD WILL PARTICIPATE IN WORLD ECONOMIC DECISIONS."[35] The promise of a new order, however, remained a promise.

Another was the workings of the Independent Commission chaired by the former West German chancellor, Willy Brandt, but a circle dominated by voices from the Third World. Its report, *North-South: A Program for Survival*, carried the spirit of the NIEO forward and spotlighted the divide—etched in a map that came to exemplify an alternative to old Cold War fissures between East and West, now definitively between North and South, not between capitalism and communism but between haves and have-nots, between poor and rich. This was *the* global rift. The program also fused the hope for global redistribution with a dream of global peace and disarmament. Indeed, as the report argued, it was the arms race and weaponized rivalry between superpower belligerents that aggravated the drain of resources from the South to the North. The call for disarmament as a precondition for redistribution—in the name of what the report coined as "globalization"—fused the important strains of Third-Worldism into one.[36]

The "Brandt Line"

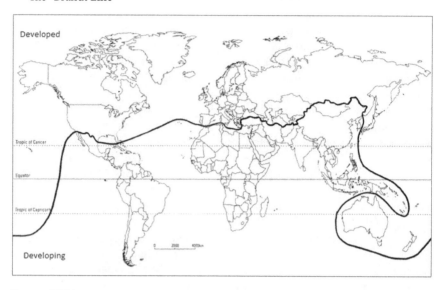

Source: Wiki

The 1970s also witnessed the ways in which hopes for freedom and equality on a global scale could push in directions that the Third World champions had not anticipated—to challenge forms of colonialism not just between countries but within them, and even within other forms of "domestic" hierarchy. Global rights-talk within the United Nations created a space for challenging gender hierarchies. It is not as if the question of gender equity was new to Third World imagination. Women organized a number of conferences before and after Bandung—All India Women's Conference (Lahore, 1932), Conference of Women of Asia (Beijing, 1949), Asia Conference for the Relaxation of International Tensions (New Delhi, 1955), the Asian-African Women's Conference (Colombo, 1958), and the First Afro Asian Women's Conference (Cairo, 1961). These conferences, as recent research shows, not only advanced anticolonial and transnational women's solidarity but also spoke about gender inequities.[37] Although this Third World feminism may have been overshadowed by the masculine language of militant, armed struggle and the male-dominated leadership of postcolonial states, it was always a live part of anticolonial solidarity.

Thus, the Commission on the Status of Women, created in 1946, got pushed along with many other institutions to respond to more radical demands. New entities, like feminist nongovernmental organizations, pushed for a world assembly devoted only to women's grievances (male-dominated states were better known for their foot dragging). It culminated in a two-week long conference in Mexico City. The first UN world conference of and about women was a landmark in a different model of solidarity. It was not, however, without its conflicts. There were famous struggles over the microphone, between Northerners and Southerners, Left and Right. As the charismatic wife of a Bolivian tin miner, Domitila Barrios de

Chungara reminded attendees, women may get short-shrift on a massive scale. But they are no less united than the rest of the world. While a crowd chanted "Domitila! Domitila! Domitila!," the stocky and nearly toothless (she'd been beaten a few days earlier) activist had the mic: "How can we speak of equality among women? We can't speak of equality between games of canasta. Women cannot be equals any more than poor and rich countries." Domitila became the voice of a dissident, Third-Worldist, counterpoint to the European and North American feminist NGO's who'd led the organization of the event while Ukrainian delegates went on a hunger strike in support of Soviet dissidents back home. The three-world rifts ran through the global feminist calls for unity. But as Jocelyn Olcott has reminded us, it would be easy to let these public—and mediatized—rifts dominate the narrative, obscuring a more fundamental way in which there was a common cry coming from women on a global stage demanding respect and equality. The gathering led to profound shifts in policy and development finance, and was, after all, a stage upon which women from all parts of a divided planet could challenge each other and demystify essentialized and universal ideas of womanhood. It was a powerful moment of exchange in part because Third World women were heavily represented and because it took place in a Third World capital.[38]

The critique of hierarchies also turned inward and thereby raised questions about the line separating Third from other worlds or even the Brandt line between North and South. In 1969, in an effort to right historic wrongs against native peoples, the government of Canada proposed sweeping reforms in a "White Paper," which promised "positive recognition" of "Indian culture to Canadian life." The Indian Association of Alberta shot back. "These are nice sounding words which are intended to mislead everybody. The only way to maintain our culture is for us to remain as Indians." Integration, the protestors argued, meant colonial assimilation.[39] Here too, by 1974, patriarchal traditions among native people were coming in for scrutiny. And yet, indigenous criticisms of the world order crossed world borders. Marie Smallface Marule, a Blood Indian from southern Alberta, had worked in Zambia as a volunteer and married a South African antiapartheid activist. When the couple returned to live in Ottawa, their home became a hub of global rethinking. One British Columbian chief, George Manuel, overheard a Tanzanian diplomat, Mbuto Milando, use the term "the Fourth World" in one of the meetings at Smallface's house. Manuel, who had been active across the Americas, consulted Maori leaders in New Zealand, visited Saami people in Scandinavia, and celebrated the tenth anniversary of independence in Tanzania. It was there, especially in the effort to create village-based shared economies called Ujamaa, that Manuel saw hope for an alternative that sliced through the false hopes of national developmentalism. He would author the landmark book in 1975, *The Fourth World: An Indian Reality*, which outlined a counter-colonial narrative that united native peoples worldwide in a struggle against settlement in the First, Second, and Third Worlds.[40]

At the same time, the 1970s also saw retreat, defeat, setbacks, and disenchantment. As Srirupa Roy explores in her chapter, Indira Gandhi's last-ditch failed attempt to salvage the older model of postcolonial nation-building and developmentalism with the announcement of Emergency (1975–7) was followed by the discourse of "curative democracy" in India that spoke in the language of morality of the people. Its new rhetoric of conditional democracy turned the focus inward, away from politically forged internationalism while also opening itself to the language of the market. This was a sign of change. Even as the 1970s witnessed the high point of the Third World project, it would also see the spread of authoritarianism, civil strife, and warlordism across the Third World in response to political turmoil from below.

There is a tendency to look back upon the Third World as a doomed utopian ensemble, a moment in which former colonial peoples dared to imagine alternatives to empires and market rules designed elsewhere. Its rise and fall, in this narrative, was indexed to a project for an alliance of sovereign nation-states to replace empires. Distorted and disfigured by the pressures of Cold War militarization and the proliferation of proxy wars, the hope of decolonization and peace, redistribution and development, got mangled up by external forces. By the early 1980s, the pressures of the debt crisis, Mexico's announcement in the summer of 1982 that it could not honor its payments to banks, all but sealed the hopes for a nonaligned world and a different world order.

But there was more: the traps and agonies of Third-Worldism did not lie in wait, planted by Cold Warriors before the aspirations of self-determination finally took flight in Asia, Africa, and Latin America. As so many chapters in this volume attest, there was a deeper tension, possibly an irresolvable flaw, in the Third World imaginary sewn in the very project itself. It was this: to be free in a world of empires and superpowers required the creation and construction of state powers capable of negotiating redistribution, planning development, and sowing alliances. The narrative of freedom and nondomination could be tracked into projects of national sovereignty and state-building. While the imaginary was greater than geopolitics and is what made it so utterly global because it transcended states and statists, Third-Worldism was vulnerable to capture by states and their leaders. For Nehru and Tito, Lázaro Cárdenas and Séjou Touré, may have yearned for a different world order, but they also seized upon the rhetoric of Bandung to double down on the powers of nation-states. The more radical turn of the Tricontinental may have changed the complexion and alliances, and swung its weight behind armed insurgency, but it did not dislodge the role of the nation-state at the center of visions for the future. The artists and journalists, historians and musicians, found themselves at odds as much with state leaders at home as they did with the peddlers of superpower narratives and their symbolic capital, their literary prizes and their Ivy League sirens.

The idea of the Third World signaled a hope for an alternative world. As an idea, it sparked imaginations and mobilized a wide array of cultural actors and brokers. Because it was an idea, it also had a pulse independent from and capable of outliving the economic and political dynamics of state formation. The pressures of structural adjustment, new commercial supply chains, and the retreat of welfare and development during the 1980s pushed societies into a logic of markets to eclipse the logic of states. But these pressures, and the inequities they sired, also gave new meaning to alternative imaginaries and purpose to their afterlives. The idea of the Third World may have dissolved with the summitry and statism that loomed so large from the 1940s to the 1970s. But the idea of alternatives did not.

Notes

1 According to Vijay Prashad, "Third World Was Not a Place. It Was a Project." See Vijay Prashad, *The Darker Nations: A People's History of the Third World* (New York: New Press, 2008), xv.

2 Michel-Rolph Trouillot, *Silencing the Past: Power and the Production of History* (Boston: Beacon Press, 1995).

3 Tim Harper, *Underground Asia: Global Revolutionaries and the Assault on Empire* (Cambridge, MA: Harvard University Press, 2021), 233.

4 Manu Goswami, "Imaginary Futures and Colonial Internationalisms," *American Historical Review*, 117: 5 (2012), 1461–85.

5 José Carlos Mariátegui, *Siete ensayos de interpretación de la realidad peruana* (Lima: Biblioteca Amauta, 1995), 32–3; Goswami, "Imaginary Futures and Colonial Internationalisms," 1474–5.

6 Recent scholarship has argued that nation-state sovereignty was not the only anticolonial alternative; intellectuals and activists also advanced the idea of federations. See Frederick Cooper, *Citizenship between Empire and Nation: Remaking France and French Africa, 1945-1960* (Princeton: Princeton University Press, 2014) and Gary Wilder, *Freedom Time: Negritude, Decolonization, and the Future of the World* (Durham: Duke University Press, 2015).

7 Adom Getachew, *Worldmaking after Empire* (Princeton: Princeton University Press, 2019), 37–52.

8 Kai-Wing Chow, Tze-ki Hon, Hunh-yok Ip, and Don C. Price, "Introduction," *Beyond the May Fourth Paradigm*, ed. Kai-Wing Chow, Tze-ki Hon, and Don C. Price (Lanham: Lexington Books, 2008), 1–23.

9 Penny M. Von Eschen, *Race Against Empire: Black Americans and Anticolonialism, 1937–1957* (Ithaca: Cornell University Press, 1997), 7–21; Getachew, *Worldmaking after Empire*, 67–70. Priyamvada Gopal's *Insurgent Empire: Anticolonial Resistance and British Dissent* (New York: Verso, 2019) places dissent and resistance by anticolonial Black intellectuals at the heart of the British Empire.

10 David Levering Lewis, *W. E. B. Du Bois: The Fight for Equality and the American Century, 1919–1963* (New York: Henry Holt, 2000), 11–15.

11 Karuna Mantena, "Popular Sovereignty and Anti-colonialism," in *Popular Sovereignty in Historical Perspective*, ed. Richard Bourke and Quentin Skinner (Cambridge: Cambridge University Press, 2016), 297–316.

12 Getachew, *Worldmaking after Empire*, 71–106.

13 Christopher Bayly and Tim Harper, *Forgotten Wars: Freedom and Revolution in Southeast Asia* (Cambridge: Belknap, 2007), 517.

14 Harper, *Underground Asia*, 641.

15 Richard Wright, *The Color Curtain* (Cleveland and New York: The World Publishing Company, 1956), 13–14.

16 Frantz Fanon, *The Wretched of the Earth* (New York: Grove Press, 1991), 40.

17 See, for examples, *Making a World after Empire: The Bandung Moment and Its Political Afterlives*, ed. Christopher Lee (Athens: Ohio University Press, 2010); Luis Eslava, Michael Fakhri, and Vasuki Nesiah, eds., *Bandung, Global History, and International Law: Critical Pasts and Pending Futures* (Cambridge: Cambridge University Press, 2017).

18 Sun Lin Lewis and Carolien Stolte, "Other Bandungs: Afro-Asian Internationalisms in the Early Cold War," *Journal of World History*, 30, no. 1–2 (2019): 1–19.

19   Wilder, *Freedom Time*, 1.

20   See Sun Lin Lewis and Carolien Stolte, "Other Bandungs," and Carolien Stolte, "'The People's Bandung': Local Anti-Imperialists on an Afro-Asian Stage," *Journal of World History*, 30, no. 1–2 (2019): 125–56; and Reem Abou-El-Fadl, "Building Egypt's Afro-Asian Hub: Infrastructures of Solidarity and the 1957 Cairo Conference," *Journal of World History*, 30, no. 1–2 (2019): 157–92.

21   Elizabeth Armstrong, "Before Bandung: The Anti-Imperialist Women's Movement in Asia and the Women's International Democratic Federation," *Signs* 41, no. 2 (2016): 305–31.

22   Atreyee Gupta, "After Bandung: Transacting the Nation in a Postcolonial World," in *Postwar: Art Between the Pacific and the Atlantic 1945-1965*, ed. Okwui Enwezor, Katy Siegel, and Ulrich Wilmes (Munich: Prestel, 2017), 636.

23   Getachew, *Worldmaking after Empire*, 107–41.

24   José Aricó, "Razones políticas de un desencuentro," in his *Marx y América Latina* (México: FCE, 2010), 149–55.

25   Yang Jisheng, *Tombstone: The Great Chinese Famine, 1958-1962* (New York: Farrar, Strauss and Giroux, 2008), xviii–xxi, 77.

26   Frantz Fanon, *The Wretched of the Earth* (New York: Grove, 2004), 10, 68, 232, 238.

27   Elleke Boehmer, *Colonial and Postcolonial Literature: Migrant Metaphors* (New York: Oxford University Press, 1995), 189–90.

28   Ibid., 199–206.

29   Fernando Solanas and Octavio Getino, "Toward a Third Cinema," *Tricontinental*, no. 14 (October 1969), 107–32, https://ufsinfronteradotcom.files.wordpress.com/2011/05/tercer-cine-getino-solanas-19691.pdf.

30   See the essays on Jim Pines and Paul Willemen, eds., *Questions of Third Cinema* (London: BFI publications, 1989).

31   Jeffrey James Byrne, *Mecca of Revolution: Algeria, Decolonization, and the Third World Order* (New York: Oxford University Press, 2016).

32   In fact, Bhakti Shringarpure views the Cold War as an afterlife of colonialism, impacting the postcolonial world by reconstituting the binaries of civilized/uncivilized and into capitalism/socialism and democracy/communism. See her *Cold War Assemblages: Decolonization to Digital* (New York: Routledge, 2019).

33   Joaquín M. Chávez, *Poets & Prophets of the Resistance: Intellectuals & the Origins of El Salvador's Civil War* (New York: Oxford University Press, 2017), 65 and 237–8.

34   Anne Garland Mahler, *From the Tricontinental to the Global South: Race, Radicalism, and Transnational Solidarity* (Durham: Duke University Press, 2018).

35   Christy Thornton, *Revolution in Development: Mexico and the Governance of the Global Economy* (Berkeley and Los Angeles: University of California Press, 2021), 172.

36   Report of the Independent Commission on International Development Issues, *North-South: A Program for Survival* (Cambridge, MA: MIT Press, 1980), 13.

37   See Armstrong, "Before Bandung"; Armstrong, Elizabeth and Vijay Prashad, "Bandung Women: Vietnam, Afghanistan, Iraq, and the Necessary Risks of Solidarity,". in *In Interrogating Imperialism: Conversations on Gender, Race, and War*, ed. Robin Riley and Naeem Inayatullah (London: Palgrave-Macmillan, 2006). Shobna Nijhawan, "International Feminism from an Asian Center: The All-Asian Women's Conference (Lahore, 1931) as a Transnational Feminist Moment," *Journal of Women's History* 29, no. 3 (2017): 12–36.

38   Jocelyn Olcott, *International Women's Year: The Greatest Consciousness-Raising Event in History* (New York: Oxford University Press, 2017), 1–3.

39 Indian Association of Alberta, Citizen Plus (Red Paper), 1970, in Keith D. Smith, ed., *Strange Visitors: Documents in Indigenous-Settler Relations in Canada from 1876* (Toronto: University of Toronto Press, 2014), 299.

40 Anthony Hall, *The American Empire and the Fourth World: The Bowl with One Spoon* (Montreal and Kingston: McGill-Queens University Press, 2003), 238.

1

The Third World before Afro-Asia

Cindy Ewing

Introduction

In the immediate years after 1945, a project of Asian unity anchored the Third World's reworking of global order. Led by some of the most prominent nationalists in South and Southeast Asia, the effort to build solidarity among Asian nations in the wake of the Second World War entailed reimagining the vast spatial realm between the Atlantic and Pacific Oceans as unified by postcolonial statehood. At the center of this reimagining was a politics of anti-imperialism that strove to end foreign occupation and forge new worlds after empire. In between Leninist and Wilsonian theories of self-determination, the anti-imperialism of Asian nationalists formed one pillar of what became an internationalist Third World project in the mid-twentieth century. In the 1940s and 1950s, Asian nationalists, not only political leaders but also writers, artists, intellectuals, jurists, and other activists, used the pregnant moment of the postwar to articulate an ambitious sociopolitical vision for the Third World around ideas of unity and brotherhood among formerly colonial peoples in Asia. Into the 1950s and 1960s, they deepened their links with African nationalists, reviving transnational solidarities formed in the early twentieth century while reimagining the global order anew, this time around the junction of Afro-Asia. Charting the history of the Third World, therefore, requires untangling its many and diverse projects, beginning with a recognition that its world-making was not a process of singular transformation but an evolving and changing crucible in which the relations of the South were remade according to different visions.

Recent scholarship on the Third World widely adopts Vijay Prashad's framing that "the Third World was not a place. It was a project."[1] This conceptualization of the Third World as a project rather than a static or fixed place echoes Frantz Fanon's language in *Les Damnés de la Terre*, which ascribed a shared revolutionary project to the "masse colossale."[2] Prashad's restoration of agency has been a landmark contribution to inquiry into the histories of the postcolonial; it imbues the Third World with a sense of motion and movement that recovers the concept from a framing steeped in developmentalism and mid-century modernization theory. Rather than attribute to the Third World a linear path of progress and accumulation, this revised understanding of the history of the Third World untethers its meaning from narratives of whiggish political economy, racialized stages of development, and civilizational discourse. This reframing is also intertwined with scholarly efforts to historicize and recover the Global South more broadly, not as a bounded space or group of peoples defined in relation to the Global North but toward a wide range of usages that are pliable and capacious in their conception of the Majority World.

This molding of the space and time dimensions of the Third World, however, does not make historicity any less important. To trace the history of the Third World from within its own self-understanding requires locating its projects in their contexts while specifying exactly who the colonial masses were and by whose definition they were known as such. By the same token, tracing a genealogy of the Third World might also pay attention to its exclusions and absences, thereby acknowledging that even in its breath, the Third World involved sharp definitions and divisions. In this respect, the Third World was not always coterminous with contemporary notions of the Global South, especially in the moments of its most visible self-articulation or in major periods of radicalization and transformation. The postwar project of fostering Asian unity, for example, sought to create South-South solidarities while advancing global decolonization in highly public and concrete ways. But it was also a project with specific aims that did not assume universal and immediate decolonization for all colonial peoples. This Third World, constructed before Afro-Asianism reoriented and expanded the imaginary of the Global South, was foremost interested in recovering sovereignty from empire through internationalist networks formed around pan-Asian ideas of brotherhood, or the "New Asia." In the immediate post-1945 era, the Third World was emerging around certain geographic orientations reflective of specific political aims by nationalist elites in Asia rather than a unified and universal convulsion by all masses toward the same vision for liberation.

A resurgence of scholarly interest in the Third World and its histories has drawn attention to the important role that diverse actors from Asia and Africa played in shaping global contexts through solidarity movements. This dynamic scholarship has shifted some emphasis away from a trained focus on the hegemony of great power nations like the United States in favor of more nuanced historical constructions of power and thick descriptions of the ways the Third World pursued the dismantling of empire. Other historians have focused on the inner life of the Third World and mapped networks of postcolonial solidarity and South-South connection, decentering the West and the tendency to paint the Global South as a place to compete over or win.[3] The history of the Third World is instead made up of plural pasts; many visions and projects constituted the alternative modernities of the Global South in the twentieth century.

Despite this sustained project of recovery, the historiography on the Third World has tended to remain muted on explaining what the Third World actually was.[4] The term, aside from its own elusive genealogy, continues to be problematic in its most basic usage, denoting neither a bounded geographic space or a specific group of people. As such, the term has generated a wide range of analogues, problematically serving as a stand-in for developmentalist tropes, racialized categories, or oversimplified political geographies. At the same time, as historians have engaged with the concept of the Third World beyond a Cold War lens, the term has also expanded discussion of the meanings of liberation, postcoloniality, anti-imperialism, and complex visions of modernity. There are grounds for similar concerns about the Global South as a prescriptive term, potentially reproducing power hierarchies and encasing complex societies within rigid orders. While this has been a productive area of scholarship in general, there remains a need for greater historical specificity and sourcing the key concepts and acts that constituted the making of the Third World.

Anglophone studies on the Third World share the common myth that the term was first coined by Alfred Sauvy in his renowned 1952 article, which drew the revolutionary politics of Asia and Africa into an analogy with the Third Estate in France.[5] This conception of the Third World, again drawing on the language of the masses, attributed a political program of leftist radicalism to the Third World based on an imagined equivalence with France in the late eighteenth century. Another French writer, Claude Bourdet, had also used the term at least since 1949 in the same register of revolutionary politics and mass mobilization of Asia and Africa, while a monograph published in 1956 by the French sociologist Georges Balandier first used "le tiers monde" as a title.[6] This understanding, therefore, located an origin story for the Third World in the abstract from outside the Third World itself. In later decades, throughout the 1960s and 1970s, the identification of the term with the radical left in Europe expanded transnational solidarity movements and intellectual networks that focused on, and interacted with, the Third World as part of the more explicitly socialist and radical ideology of Third-Worldism. Historians have begun to map different origins of this Third World from its incubation in eras outside of the mid-century and in extra-Third World sites like Paris and London, which had long been centers of intellectual life and radical politics.[7] Such studies help to recover more capacious Third World imaginations, depicting a more expansive universe from which to identify and trace anti-imperial projects.

French social theories about the Third World did not sit well with the leading lights of the Third World itself, however. Vijay Prashad notes that when Jawaharlal Nehru heard the term for the first time, he dismissed it out of hand. In this account, Nehru misheard the term as "third force" and criticized its implications of otherness and its framing of the world into divisions, which were defined by "armed strength, nuclear strength, ballistic strength, [and] monetary strength."[8] Instead, an earlier appearance of the term comes from within the Third World itself, when the Indian Council of World Affairs hosted the Asian Relations Conference in New Delhi in March and April of 1947. The British High Commissioner in New Delhi, Terence Shone, reported extensively on the conference as an official observer. He wrote, "It was sometimes suggested that Asia, or at least South East Asia, constituted a 'third world' which had its part to play in restoring to equilibrium a balance of power at present too exclusively dependent on the opposed worlds of America and Russia."[9] According to Vineet Thakur, Shone's phrasing suggests that he could have been using the conference's language despite a possibly disapproving inflection in his report. The conference materials also referred to the New Asia as Southeast Asia, referring to a region geographically broader than the contemporary meaning of the term and further supportive of Thakur's claim that Shone was likely invoking conference language. The emphasis on the political potential of this Third World to act in the world, not in revolution but in resistance to emerging Cold War dynamics shows a conception of the Third World that differs from the Sauvy definition but more closely adheres to Nehruvian internationalism and its emphasis on engaged yet neutral diplomacy for postcolonial states. Nehru's aspirations for the New Asia as promoted at the conference portray a Third World that would be engaged in international affairs and participate in the global order through the cooperation of the newly independent Asian nations.

Shone's report on the Asian Relations Conference offered a glimpse into one of the Third Worlds being imagined in 1947 before the Bourdet or Sauvy usages. This archival trace hints at the historical importance of the Asian Relations Conference in the making of the Third World. The staging of the first postcolonial conference in Asia, to the chagrin of British officials, showcased the centrality of common colonial experience to an emergent Third World imagination.

Origins of the New Asia

While the Asian Relations Conference brought together delegations from twenty-eight countries, its internationalism was rooted in Nehru's endeavor to unite the peoples and nations of Asia. The theme of "New Asia" that repeatedly appeared in the conference literature lay at the heart of the Third World project in 1947. At the same time that the idea of Asian unity looked outward, this project also concerned itself with fundamental questions of nation-building and internal order in postcolonial society, even as the conference expressly claimed not to be governmental or political in nature. Given the massive challenges faced by postcolonial governments in the late 1940s, no less the interim government in New Delhi, discussions at the conference turned towards the common problems of establishing peace after the withdrawal of empire shared by many of the delegations present. Not only was the colonial experience a source of identification among attendees of the Asian Relations Conference, but so were the realities created by the ending of empire as well.

To build enthusiasm for the Asian Relations Conference, Nehru undertook a diplomatic tour of Southeast Asia in March 1946, first flying to Singapore to meet with Lord Louis Mountbatten and then to Rangoon on a stopover. In Rangoon, Nehru met with Aung San to discuss future cooperation among Asian leaders now that the war had ended. Aung San enthusiastically supported the idea of a summit of Asian nations and echoed Nehru's unity rhetoric, itself a theme that had appeared frequently in Aung San's public statements throughout the war. Later that summer, Aung San hosted Ho Chi Minh and raised Nehru's initiative for holding a future Asian Relations Conference in their meeting. Nehru then announced that an "All Asia Conference" would take place in New Delhi in early 1947. He boasted in press interviews that prominent leaders such as Ho Chi Minh, Aung San, and Sukarno supported his initiative. Plans for the conference appeared in newspapers throughout India, Burma, Indonesia, and Vietnam, celebrating Asian unity and brotherhood. Rather than "splendid isolation," Nehru spoke publicly about how the futures of Asian peoples were interlinked, with

India's independence struggle at the heart of the pursuit of liberation in other parts of Asia.[10]

The Indian Council of World Affairs played a key role in developing Third World consciousness by framing the Asian Relations Conference as inclusive of all Asian peoples and specifically nongovernmental, striving to avoid political conflicts. The ICWA sent invitations to "all Asian countries and to Egypt," a phrasing developed in discussions during conference planning sessions on the geographic boundaries of the New Asia. The planners strove to be inclusive yet historically informed in their invitations, even as they envisioned the conference as merely the first in a series of such meetings.[11] This spatial conception of Asia in broad terms did not originate with the ICWA, however. Nehru and other Indian nationalists long talked about the importance of the Middle East and Egypt to the realization of India's nationalist aspirations during its independence struggle. At the 1927 conference in Brussels that established the League Against Imperialism, Nehru spoke of how much "our interests are the same . . . whether you come from China, Egypt or other distant countries."[12] Documents from throughout the post-independence period show that Egypt and China represented the poles of a key zone of Asian solidarity in Nehru's imagination. In a 1946 editorial, Nehru wrote, "A free India will link together the Middle East with China."[13]

In addition to enthusiastic responses from political, scholarly, and literary leaders in Burma and Ceylon, the Chinese delegation accepted its invitation through K. P. S. Menon, India's ambassador in Nanking. Menon added his wholehearted approval of China's attendance even though it was viewed by the conference planners as a "big" and, therefore, powerful country.[14] Also attending were the Soviet republics of Asia, which gave the conference a noticeable Central Asian presence, further expanding the geographic reach of the "New Asia."[15] Avoiding political division, the ICWA invited the Democratic Republic of Vietnam as well as French-controlled South Vietnam, Laos, and Cambodia while the largest foreign delegation came from Indonesia. Nehru personally ensured the presence of the Indonesian delegation at the Asian Relations Conference by sending a private plane to retrieve the Indonesian prime minister. Together, the invitations and responses charted the broad geographic outlines of New Asia.

The Asian Relations Conference opened on March 23, 1947, at the Purana Qila in central New Delhi.[16] Thousands watched the delegations proceed to the dais, which was decorated with an enormous map of Asia as a cartographic expression of the conference's vision.[17] The delegations represented Afghanistan, Armenia, Azerbaijan, Bhutan, Burma, Cambodia, Cochin-China (South Vietnam), Laos, Ceylon, China, Egypt, Georgia, India, Indonesia, Kazakhstan, Kirghizia, (South) Korea, Malaya, Mongolia, Nepal, Palestine, Persia, Philippines, Tajikistan, Thailand, Tibet, Turkey, Turkmenistan, Uzbekistan, and (North) Vietnam. Observers came from Australia, the Arab League, the United Kingdom, the Soviet Union, the United States, and the United Nations.

The opening speeches of the conference contained soaring rhetoric on the unity and brotherhood of Asian peoples, with an emphasis on their ancient ties prior to colonial rule. Although colonialism severed these bonds and forced Asian peoples into isolation, independence restored their natural links and the conference was an opportunity to establish a geographic zone free of external interference and foreign intervention. The Reception Committee chairman Shri Ram painted a picture of precolonial "free intercourse between India and her neighbouring countries" that was unencumbered by their supposedly technological or commercial weakness.[18] Ram attributed their isolation to colonialism, a theme that regularly appeared in the statements of delegates throughout the conference. Ram also used a long historical perspective to show the endurance of connections among Asians to proclaim that their present condition was not only temporary but also surmountable. Nehru echoed these sentiments in his plenary speech, "The idea of such a conference arose simultaneously in minds in many countries of Asia because there was a widespread awareness that the time has come for us, peoples of Asia to meet, to hold consultations and to advance together."[19]

The celebratory tenor of the conference stood in contrast to the recent communal riots in India over the previous year. Demonstrations were also taking place at the same time in opposition to another war in Asia: the French war in Indochina. In New Delhi, All India Students Federation hosted a conference of Indian youth and urged the interim government to recognize the Democratic Republic of Vietnam. The endorsement of Chandra Bose, a member of the interim cabinet and a prominent personality, amplified their efforts. Bose also called on the Indian people to view the war in Indochina as part of a broader Asian struggle for independence, linking the regionalist rhetoric espoused by Congress leaders such as Nehru with Ho Chi Minh's own calls for Asian brotherhood. Outside of the Purana Qila, efforts to unite Asian struggles for independence not only called for direct political action but also echoed the common resolution to fight imperialism through Asian unity. The Asian Relations Conferences were not the only venue through which transnational solidarities were made but rooted a burgeoning vision of an anti-imperialist Third World centered in, but not limited to, New Delhi.

Third World Support for Indonesian Independence

Despite the bold proclamations of the 1947 conference, the prospects for closer relations in the Third World still required the dedicated construction of a common identity. While some participants talked about holding another Asian Relations Conference the following year, no such plans emerged. The delegations did agree to the creation of the Asian Relations Organization to increase contact among the participant nations but it was not given resources or direction. Instead, a second Asian Relations Conference, also commonly referred to as the Inter-Asian Conference, materialized in January 1949 in response to the attack on Indonesia by the Dutch government. This second Asian Relations Conference called upon the "New Asia" to shift its attention toward political action and became a venue for Third World leaders to assert collective condemnation of imperialism. Rather than discussing social and cultural issues as in the first Asian Relations Conference, the 1949 gathering emphasized the necessity of Asian unity to oppose colonial rule through active and engaged diplomacy at the international level. This in turn had a transformative impact on the development of the United Nations and the way Third World nations saw themselves as actors within it.

The second Asian Relations Conference met from January 20 to 23, 1949, at Hyderabad House in New Delhi. In a collective statement, the fifteen national delegations insisted they gathered to "reinforce the United Nations and not to replace it."[20] As chairman, Nehru told the plenary that the attack was not only directed at Indonesia but posed a "challenge to a newly awakened Asia."[21] Unanimously, the conference declared the Dutch police action "a flagrant breach of the Charter of the United Nations."[22] The conference's first priority was to "to frame and submit to the Security Council a proposal which, if accepted by both parties concerned, would restore peace immediately to Indonesia."[23] Seated in the visitor's section were A. T. Lamping, the Dutch ambassador to India; Loy Henderson, the American ambassador to India; and the American journalist Harold Isaacs. Isaacs observed that "Nehru and his advisers . . . showed signs of being afraid of the communist coloration of the Viet Nam nationalist leadership."[24] Instead, as chairman, Nehru focused the deliberations on Indonesia to avoid any discussions of Vietnam. Though Nehru did not want to discuss the Indochina conflict, he was willing to involve himself in Indonesia. He even attempted to intervene covertly to send an RAF plane to retrieve Sutan Sjahrir despite the air blockade imposed by the Netherlands, though the mission failed.[25] Burma took a similar position. U Ba Maw proposed that an expeditionary force retrieve the republican leadership.[26] On January 22, the conference adopted three resolutions recommending that the delegations "should keep in touch with one another through normal diplomatic channels" and "instruct their representatives at the headquarters of the UN or their diplomatic representatives to consult among themselves."[27]

The conference marked the clear transformation of Nehru's project of Asian unity from the recovery of ancient ties to the active pursuit of global political change. In typically grand style, Nehru asserted, "We symbolize in particular the spirit of freedom and democracy which is so significant a feature of the new Asia."[28] However, in 1949, Nehru's geographic imagination began to reach further, viewing the "representatives of the free nations of Asia" as including "Australia, New Zealand and the Philippines on the one side to Egypt and Ethiopia on the other," representing "the vast area embracing half of the circumference of the globe and by far the greater part of its population."[29] This wider global vision for the Third World still relied on the foundation of the New Asia but extended to other nations outside of the 1947 participants.

Reflecting the state-led objectives of the conference, Nehru emphasized principles of statehood and identified nonintervention as the central principle of diplomacy in the region. "Asia," he said, "too long submissive and dependent and a plaything of other countries, will no longer brook any interference with her freedom."[30] Specifically, Nehru stated in his presidential address that the conference should prioritize "devis[ing] machinery."[31] He called upon the "free countries of Asia" to work together to establish a "permanent arrangement" for their ambassadors to meet and consult one another on international issues.[32] The delegations from the Philippines, Syria, Yemen, and Burma all supported the suggestion of a permanent secretariat, possibly based in

New Delhi. S. W. R. D. Bandaranaike then proposed a formal defense arrangement among Asian nations, but the Egyptian and Iraqi delegations rejected the idea of military commitments. The Egyptian delegate conceded that it might support a general regional organization but nothing further.[33] Nazim al-Qudsi called "a regional and permanent understanding within the framework of the United Nations" necessary for the "strengthening of political and economic ties with the countries of Asia here present."[34] However, not all Asian states were as enthused as suggested by Indian rhetoric. Meanwhile, D. S. Senanayake's comment that there was "an undercurrent of apprehension regarding the long-term possibility of Indian expansion involving Ceylon" illustrated how political tensions between nations remained under the surface of the conference discussions.[35]

As the Inter-Asian Conference discussed their recommendations, the UN Security Council met at Lake Success to decide how to respond to the ongoing crisis in Indonesia. The Indian delegation leader Benegal Rau called for reconstituting the Good Offices Committee as a full commission to enable the council's decisions to be implemented and announced that a conference was about to convene in New Delhi "to explore the possibilities of a peaceful solution, and to strengthen the hand of the Security Council."[36] The fifteen Asian states sent their recommendations in a letter to the president of the Security Council.[37] The Indian and Australian ambassadors also called upon the council to incorporate these recommendations, which were passionately criticized by the Dutch ambassador.[38] Meanwhile, the Indonesian delegation present at the UN expressed their public appreciation. The United States had now shifted its position to supporting Indonesian independence and withdrew aid to the Netherlands under the Brewster amendment.[39]

The Security Council also called for a cessation of hostilities and the restoration of the republican government in Jogyakarta.[40] Sponsored by the United States, the January 28 resolution omitted a Soviet amendment based on the New Delhi recommendations to order the Netherlands to withdraw all troops immediately. Only the Soviet Union, the Ukraine, Egypt, and Cuba supported the amendment, lacking the numbers to change the resolution.[41] The Security Council also called for a transfer of sovereignty by July 1, 1950, under the supervision of the newly renamed UN Commission for Indonesia from its former G.O.C. title. The Netherlands then submitted a request to the Security Council to hold round-table discussions, prompting Carlos Romulo to convene a "little New Delhi conference" in New York among the ambassadors of postcolonial nations. Romulo invited the same nineteen countries that met at the conference on Indonesia two months earlier, drawing directly on their recommendations.[42]

This seventeen-nation meeting reiterated the special interest of Third World nations in Indonesia's future. In May, fifteen nations in this group cosponsored a resolution at the Ad Hoc Committee "expressing the hope that a lasting settlement would be reached," which kept attention at the UN on Indonesia. With the constant monitoring of the Security Council, the Round Table Conference met at the Hague over the summer and succeeded in recognizing Indonesia's sovereignty. Marking a resolute victory for the Third World, Indonesia regained its independence on December 27, 1949, to be finalized by a popular constituent assembly.

The Arab-Asian Group's Third World Project

In the late 1940s, Third World leaders continued to agitate for independence and self-government at the United Nations, where they began to express solidarity with colonial peoples and act in unison at different committees within the UN. At the General Assembly, twelve Arab and Asian member-states began to coordinate their diplomatic activities as part of an informal Arab-Asian group, the predecessor to the later Afro-Asian bloc and later still, the G-77. The emergence of an Arab-Asian group in the late 1940s showed the importance of the UN as a meeting point for the Third World and how central decolonization was to the agenda of Third World collective action. The postcolonial elites appointed as permanent representatives and UN secretariat officials brought different visions of how the postwar global order should work and what their role within it should be, in particular emphasizing cases of decolonization and advocating for greater self-government. Their sometimes divergent perspectives created friction within the group even as it worked in concert to move debate forward, such as on the "questions" of the status of Indonesia, the former Italian colonies in Africa, and in the UN response to the outbreak of the Korean War.

Just as the group strove to bring greater attention to the specific needs of the Third World, it also struggled to define a political program and identify its long-term priorities. This led to individual members in the group pursuing separate agendas that polarized other members, such as Carlos Romulo's campaign for a Pacific Pact among noncommunist Asian states. Conflicts between members, such as India and Pakistan, also hindered cooperation and a sense of unity among Third World states or entering into conflict with other Third World states. Therefore, while the UN was a formative setting for the emergence of Third World solidarities such as the Arab-Asian group, the common goals pursued by these states did not translate into a uniform consensus on what decolonization meant or what postcolonial states should prioritize.

Third World solidarity at the UN was also deeply shaped by the conditions of an emerging Cold War. As the twelve Arab and Asian states drafted resolutions and coordinated their votes at the General Assembly, they also rejected accusations by other member-states that they were forming a formal bloc that might challenge apparent Anglo-American or Soviet dominance. Though the language of bloc politics appeared in some of the rhetoric seen at regional summits, diplomats from postcolonial nations instead emphasized transnational solidarity outside of rigid categories or alignments. One of the leaders of India's delegation, Benegal Rau, spoke often about the solidarity of independent nations without any reference to blocs. He called the recent election of Philippine delegate Carlos Romulo "a matter of special gratification to all Asian delegations" to remind the General Assembly of the Arab-Asian group's recent victories.[43]

Rau also tied Romulo's election to the Arab-Asian group's campaign for Indonesia's independence earlier that year. The Arab-Asian group emerged most clearly in their united campaign to support Indonesia and its pursuit of recognition at the United Nations. This campaign developed through direct consultations both at the UN and outside of the international organization, including a conference hosted in New

Delhi in January 1949 to foster Asian Relations around the cause of supporting the Indonesian republican cabinet. Through collective action, Rau explained that the Inter-Asian Conference "was momentous and the resolutions passed at the Conference had materially influenced the subsequent course of events."[44] Its importance, however, lay not only "the fact that such a conference was held" but that "it was the first time Asian Governments had come together for a political purpose."[45]

The other diplomats at the plenary would have been familiar with the actions of the Asian-Arab group and the New Delhi conference just earlier that year. In a speech, Rau provided the General Assembly with a short history of their collective efforts, recounting the 1947 and 1949 conferences. Illustrating postwar Third World consciousness, Rau asserted, "If the cultural Asian Conference of March 1947 had been a symbol of Asia's awakening to a new life, the political Conference of January 1949 might be said to mark the coming of age of Asia and the beginning of a process of active co-operation [*sic*] among the countries in that region of the world."[46] Through the combined efforts of the New Delhi conference and the Arab-Asian campaign, postcolonial elites played a direct role in Indonesia's independence struggle, transforming the UN into a necessary mediatory space for advancing decolonization. Their collective support for the Indonesian representative, Nico Palar, amplified his protest against the Dutch government while convincing the US delegation that it should support the Indonesian cause.

At the UN Security Council, Rau gave moral and political support to Indonesia not only as India's representative but also as the spokesperson for the Arab-Asian group. Upon becoming the official representative of the Indonesian Republic, Nico Palar stood before the General Assembly and thanked the Asian and Arab nations for "defending Indonesia's sovereign rights."[47] The addition of the Indonesian Republic to the Arab-Asian group strengthened and reinforced this new Third World presence at the UN, itself a forum for Third World cooperation but also a point of linkage across postcolonial state capitals and a regular meeting place for Third World leaders and anticolonial activists.

The postcolonial internationalism of the Arab-Asian group contributed to the growth of anticolonial and anti-imperial sentiment at the UN. Increasingly, through the efforts of postcolonial diplomats within the UN, different agencies and commissions engaged more frequently on colonial issues and held discussions about greater international oversight over colonial and dependent territories. Uniting these different activities was the regular refrain by members of the Arab-Asian group on the UN's eventual goal of statehood for all colonial peoples. Even though the group's members shared this commitment to decolonization, there was not always agreement on how exactly the group should support and advance independence. The representatives from Arab League states tended to call for immediate independence, while the representatives of the more recently decolonized states in Asia tended to state that the UN needed a more gradual approach.

While the Arab-Asian group expressed its objective as statehood for all colonial peoples, its members did not always agree on the best method to achieve it, with some delegations, namely from the Arab world, agitating for immediate independence and others, from South Asia, advising a more gradual approach to achieving self-government.

At the third General Assembly session, for example, the Indian delegation attempted to chart a middle path between disagreeing factions by suggesting the creation of new measures of accountability that would attend to the welfare of the inhabitants of trust territories. While the Indian delegation called attention to the problem of racial discrimination, it also sought to mollify discord by suggesting that the issue be discussed separately as its own agenda item.[48] This revised motion effectively severed the anti-discrimination campaign from the colonial question. Presented as a conciliatory and pragmatic gesture, this posture set the tone for the other Arab-Asian member-states as a tentative step forward.

Other members of the Arab-Asian group adopted this conciliatory approach. At the Third Committee of the General Assembly, the Burmese representative U Ba Maung campaigned for the Indian plan that Libya and Somaliland should be transferred to a UN-administered trusteeship so that "after a period of not less than 10 and not more than 20 years, these territories shall be independent or join with adjacent territories according to the wishes of the inhabitants as expressed by the plebiscites."[49] Pakistani foreign minister Zafarullah Khan also stressed the importance of UN administration if trusteeships were created. U Ba Maung reported, "The last item had to be left unresolved due to a rejection by the combined forces of Arab, Asiatic, Soviet, and Latin American blocs . . . needless to say, Burma voted against."[50] The Somali delegate leader sent a letter of thanks to Burmese prime minister U Nu for "the keen interest voiced by the new State of Burma and other Asiatic Powers in defence and protection of the rights of the subject, weak, and poor people like ourselves."[51] In the final vote, the Arab and Asian nations registered their collective dissent and managed to defeat the British-Italian proposal in the vote on May 11, 1949. The Libyan delegation leader, Mansour Kadadoran, sent letters to the Asian member-states thanking them for their "inspired and courageous opposition" to Italy's effort to regain control.[52] Unwilling to allow the decision to move forward, the General Assembly ultimately postponed further action on the item until the fourth full session.[53]

With their trusteeship proposal defeated, the United States and Great Britain yielded to the growing demand for Libya's independence and offered a new plan, newly containing a limited preparatory period for self-government that more closely resembled the gradual approach proposed by the Arab-Asian group. The Soviet Union, attempting to appeal to the Arab and Asian member-states, repeated calls for immediate independence while other non-Western states such as Haiti insisted on the need to solicit the opinions of the inhabitants. When opinion in the assembly swayed toward recognizing Libya's independence, Benegal Rau memorably praised the General Assembly for "acting for the first time like a world parliament."[54] Ever the lawyer, Rau added that "the best way of safeguarding that independence would be to allow the populations concerned to draw up their own constitution." Representing the Arab-Asian group, Rau provided new language in their joint draft resolution on a ten-year trusteeship, a commission of inquiry for Eritrea, and the establishment of judicial and legislative authorities through local councils. These terms were widely supported by the Asian and Arab states for empowering local leaders to govern. By heavily lobbying other member-states, these terms became incorporated into the final resolution. As a member of both the Italian Colonies subcommittee and the

International Law Commission, Rau gave his recommendation that a constitution be drawn up for Somaliland as well.[55] The Trusteeship Council accepted the suggestion, and on November 21, the General Assembly adopted a resolution calling for Libya's wholesale independence as a sovereign state by January 1, 1952.[56]

The focus on specific details and procedure by the Arab and Asian states produced a victory in their view for the cause of decolonization in North and East Africa. Rather than merely forcing the issue by calling for new votes, the group worked together to undermine other proposals and prepared alternate proposals with concrete suggestions that they believed would satisfy both the Trusteeship Council and the wider UN membership at the General Assembly. With Benegal Rau as the intellectual heart of the group, the postcolonial nations represented by the Arab-Asian group developed an increasingly unified collective voice at the United Nations aimed not only at responding to crisis but also creating internal rules and procedures that would formalize and accelerate decolonization. In addition to enlarging the role of the UN, these postcolonial elites also insisted on transparent and explicit steps toward devolution, helping to make the UN publicly supportive of national elections, individual petition rights, and constitution-making by indigenous populations.

At the conclusion of the fourth General Assembly session in December 1949, Romulo adopted Rau's language to encapsulate the assembly's accomplishments. From the chair he declared, "The General Assembly, acting for the first time as a world parliament with legislative powers, has reached a decision on the disposal of the former Italian colonies."[57] Romulo also cited the resolution on the Balkans, the commission in Korea, and the negotiations on Indonesia as "proof of the growing moral power of the General Assembly."[58] These resolutions showed that "no single power or group of powers can be said to dominate" while affirming "the great charter principles of self-determination and independence for all peoples."[59] Behind the scenes, Romulo also sought to mediate disputes between the Anglo-American and Soviet blocs, such as over disarmament and atomic control. Illustrative of the Arab-Asian group's working method, Rau also assisted Romulo in this effort to mediate the international dispute and drafted a plan for an international declaration on atomic control.[60] With this proposal, the Arab and Asian states collectively voiced their support for disarmament, which became a signature issue throughout the 1950s. The expansion of the Third World agenda, enabled by its growing ranks of new postcolonial member-states, upheld its central ideas of nonintervention and respect for sovereignty while pursuing greater political equality and decolonization.

Conclusion

One thread in the complex and multivalent history of the Third World was the set of connections forged by postcolonial elites after 1945. The Asian Relations Conferences of 1947 and 1949 marked two milestones in the genealogy of the Third World, staging a project for Asian unity that preceded more expansive initiatives for South-South solidarity. These gatherings enabled new exchanges, not all of which were state-based but rather part of an internationalist milieu that recognized the multiple roles and offices that postcolonial leaders often found themselves serving in, as activists, organizers, writers, academics, and also as legislators and diplomats. The conferences also worked alongside international diplomacy and efforts to transform the UN into a site to make anti-imperial claims. Post-independence India led the way in this engaged mode of postcolonial internationalism, based on an imagined Third World geography centred on the subcontinent and reaching outward toward North Africa and the Pacific. Reflecting on both conferences, Nehru laid out this Third World vision in a letter to Prime Minister Mohan Shumsher, "We have championed in the United Nations and elsewhere the cause of freedom in Asia, in Africa and even in other continents. . . . We cannot isolate ourselves in this world and in this Asia, which has progressively become more coordinated."[61] Although the means of politics were not always clearly defined, one manifestation of postcolonial internationalism was a focus by postcolonial elites on the UN and the cultivation of Third World cooperation in the form of the Arab-Asian group, whose focus on "colonial questions" showed that at least one important dimension of the Third World project involved diplomatic acts of anti-imperial resistance in formal institutions like the UN.

This story of unity, from its expansive imagination of postcolonial cooperation to its constrained geographic scope, helps to begin mapping a history of the invention of the Third World. Even though decolonization was the central issue of the Arab-Asian group's advocacy, its call for independence for colonial peoples was conditioned by the realities of international diplomacy surrounding trusteeship and postwar attempts to reassert colonial rule in Asia and Africa. As revealed by the early campaigns of Arab and Asian UN member-states in the late 1940s, anticolonial solidarity moved from symbolic gestures to concrete yet compromised negotiations for the granting of self-government, dependent on the circumstances and opportunities available at the UN. In the age of decolonization, the leaders of postcolonial states defined the nature of their engagement with the world in specific terms, thus laying the groundwork for Third World projects in different ideological registers and at different geographic scales. Over the next few decades, postcolonial elites continued to maintain an active presence at the UN where they pursued the right to national self-determination and other mechanisms in support of decolonization, even as they built and participated in other political networks. Instead of pursuing radical politics or revolution, the Arab-Asian group sought to use its collective voice to rethink global order itself, reshaping international institutions and laws toward a universal commitment to decolonization.

Notes

1 Vijay Prashad, *The Darker Nations: A People's History of the Third World* (New York: New Press, 2008), xv.
2 Frantz Fanon, *Les Damnés de la Terre* (Paris: Francois Maspero, 1961), 241.
3 Recent examples of the emerging literature on South-South connections include Christopher E. Goscha and Christian Ostermann, eds., *Connecting Histories: Decolonization and the Cold War in South East Asia, 1945-1962* (Stanford: Stanford University Press, 2009); Jeffrey James Byrne, *Mecca of Revolution: Algeria,*

Decolonization, and the Third World Order (Oxford: Oxford University Press, 2016); Anne Garland Mahler, *From the Tricontinental to the Global South: Race, Radicalism, and Transnational Solidarity* (Durham: Duke University Press, 2018); Michele L. Louro, Carolien Stolte, Heather Streets-Salter, and Sana Tannoury-Karam, eds., *The League against Imperialism: Lives and Afterlives* (Dordrecht: Leiden University Press, 2020).

4 This literature tends to situate the Third World in the Cold War. See Odd Arne Westad, *The Global Cold War: Third World Interventions and the Making of Our Times* (Cambridge: Cambridge University Press, 2005); Robert McMahon, ed., *Cold War in the Third World* (New York: Oxford University Press, 2013); Jason C. Parker, *Hearts, Minds, Voices: U.S. Cold War Public Diplomacy and the Formation of the Third World* (New York: Oxford University Press, 2016); Gregg Brazinsky, *Winning the Third World* (Chapel Hill: University of North Carolina Press, 2017).

5 Alfred Sauvy, "Trois Mondes, Une Planète," *L'Observateur*, August 14, 1952.

6 Leslie Wolf-Phillips, "Why 'Third World'?: Origin, Definition and Usage," *Third World Quarterly* ix (1987): 1311–27.

7 See Jennifer Anne Boittin, *Colonial Metropolis: the Urban Grounds of Anti-Imperialism and Feminism in Interwar Paris* (Lincoln: University of Nebraska Press, 2010); Marc Matera, *Black London: The Imperial Metropolis and Decolonization in the Twentieth Century* (Oakland: University of California Press, 2015); Michael Goebel, *Anti-Imperial Metropolis: Interwar Paris and the Seeds of Third World Nationalism* (Cambridge: Cambridge University Press, 2015); Christoph Kalter, *The Discovery of the Third World: Decolonization and the Rise of the New Left in France, c. 1956–1970* (Cambridge: Cambridge University Press, 2016).

8 Prashad, *The Darker Nations*, 11.

9 Shone quoted in Vineet Thakur, "An Asian Drama: The Asian Relations Conference, 1947," *The International History Review* 41, no. 3 (2019): 673–95.

10 Kalidas Nag, *New Asia* (Calcutta: P. Bharati, 1947), 16.

11 Asian Relations Organization, *Asian Relations: Being Report of the Proceedings of the First Asian Relations Conference, New Delhi, March-April, 1947* (New Delhi: Asian Relations Organization, 1948), 5.

12 "Speech at the Brussels Congress," February 10, 1927, A.I.C.C. File No. G.29(82-A)/1927, National Archives of India (NAI).

13 Jawaharlal Nehru, *The New York Times Magazine*, March 3, 1946, *SWJN* 1, Vol. 15, 512.

14 K. P. S. Menon to Ministry of External Affairs, F.542(3).C.A., NAI.

15 These nations included Georgia, Kazakhstan, Kirghizia, Tajikistan, Turkmenistan and Uzbekistan.

16 Indian Council of World Affairs, *Asia: A Souvenir Book issued by the Indian Council of World Affairs on the Occasion of the Asian Relations Conference, New Delhi, March 23-2 April 1947* (New Delhi: Indian Council of World Affairs, 1947).

17 *Asian Relations: Being Report of the Proceedings and Documentation of the First Asian Relations Conference, New Delhi, March-April 1947* (New Delhi: Asian Relations Organization, 1948), 13; 15–16.

18 Ibid., 17.

19 Renu Srivastava, *India and the Nonaligned Summits: Belgrade to Jakarta* (New Delhi: Northern Book Centre, 1995), 3.

20 "Asian Conference on Indonesia," *The Times of India*, January 13, 1949.

21 Jawaharlal Nehru, "Presidential Speech Delivered in New Delhi Inaugurating the Eighteen-Nation Conference on Indonesia, January 20, 1949," in *Jawaharlal Nehru's*

Speeches, September 1946-May 1949, Vol. 1 (New Delhi: Publications Division, Ministry of Information and Broadcasting, Govt. of India, 1954-58), 325–30.

22 "New Delhi Resolution on Indonesia," *The New York Times*, January 24, 1949.

23 Ibid.

24 See Harold R. Isaacs, "Problems of Nationalism," in *South Asia in the World Today*, ed. Phillips Talbot (New York: AMS Press, 1973), 159.

25 Rudolf Mrázek, *Sjahrir: Politics and Exile in Indonesia* (Ithaca: Southeast Asia Program, Cornell University, 1994), 335–6.

26 "Asia for the Asiatics," *The Chicago Tribune*, January 19, 1949.

27 "Asia's Moral Mandate on Indonesia to U.N. Body," *The Times of India*, January 22, 1949; "Delhi Conference Suggestions to Security Council," *The Times of India*, January 24, 1949.

28 Jawaharlal Nehru, *Independence and After* (New York: John Day, 1950), 297.

29 Ibid.

30 Ibid.

31 Nehru, "Presidential speech delivered in New Delhi inaugurating the eighteen-nation Conference on Indonesia, January 20, 1949."

32 Sunanda K. Datta-Ray, "Rediscovering Suvarnabhumi: India and South-east Asia," in *Indian Foreign Policy: Challenges and Opportunities*, ed. Atish Sinha and Madhup Mohta (New Delhi: Academic Foundation, 2007), 413.

33 *The Conference on Indonesia, January 20-23, 1949* (Delhi: Publications Division, Ministry of Information and Broadcasting, Govt. of India, 1949).

34 Quoted in Rami Ginat, *Syria and the Doctrine of Arab Neutralism: From Independence to Dependence* (Brighton: Sussex Academic Press, 2005), 87–8; David Kimche, *The Afro-Asian Movement: Ideology and Foreign Policy of the Third World* (Jerusalem: Israel Universities Press, 1973), 34.

35 T. A. Keenleyside, "Nationalist Indian Attitudes Towards Asia: A Troublesome Legacy for Post-Independence Indian Foreign Policy," *Pacific Affairs* 55, no. 2 (Summer 1982): 228–9.

36 United Nations, Security Council Official Records (SCOR), 401st meeting, January 17, 1949, Lake Success, New York, U.N. Doc. S/PV.401, http://repository.un.org/handle/11176/87208.

37 These recommendations stated: (1) Immediate withdrawal of Dutch forces from the Residency of Jogjakarta and their progressive withdrawal—positions held on December 18, 1948–March 15, 1949, when the interim government should come into existence; (2) Immediate removal of all restrictions on the Republic's trade; (3) Complete transfer of power to the U.S.I. not later than January 1, 1950.

38 SCOR, 403rd meeting, January 25, 1949, Lake Success, New York, S/PV.403; SCOR, 404–406th meetings, January 27, 1949, Lake Success, New York, U.N. Doc. S/PV.404-S/PV.406.

39 The United States shifted toward supporting Indonesian independence only in January 1949 when the US ambassador Philip Jessup condemned Dutch actions at the UN Security Council. See Amy Sayward, *The United Nations in International History* (London: Bloomsbury Academic, 2017), 34.

40 "New Delhi Resolution on Indonesia," *The New York Times*, January 24, 1949.

41 "U.N. Approves Plan for Free Indonesia: Seeks End to Fight," *The New York Times*, January 28, 1949.

42 Only Nepal and Ceylon did not attend, as they were not yet UN member-states.

43 United Nations, General Assembly Official Records, 4th Session, 222nd Plenary Meeting, September 21, 1949 (Lake Success, 1949), 10.

44 Ibid.
45 Ibid.
46 Ibid.
47 Nico Palar, Statement at UN General Assembly, September 28, 1950, Indonesian Mission to the United Nations File, Inventaris Arsip Lambertus Nicodemus Palar, No. 123, National Archives of the Republic of Indonesia.
48 General Assembly Official Records, 3rd Session, 1st Part, 4th Committee, 61st meeting, October 19, 1949 (Lake Success, 1949), 100.
49 U Ba Maung, Report, April 18, 1949, Acc. No. 38, 15/3(30), National Archives of Myanmar (NAM).
50 U Ba Maung, Report, May 1, 1949, Acc. No. 39, 15/3(30), NAM.
51 Adullahi Issa to U Nu, March 8, 1949, Acc. No. 321, NAM.
52 Mansour Kadadoran to U So Nyun, May 25, 1949, Acc. No. 39, NAM.
53 General Assembly Resolution 287(III), May 18, 1949, A/RES/287.
54 General Assembly Official Records, 280th Plenary Meeting, October 3, 1949 (Lake Success, 1949), 29.
55 "Propose Trusteeship for Italy's African Territory," *New Journal and Guide*, October 22, 1949.
56 United Nations, General Assembly Resolution 289(IV), November 21, 1949, A/RES/289.
57 "Steady UN Gains Cited by Romulo," *Los Angeles Times*, December 11, 1949.
58 Ibid.
59 Ibid.
60 "2 Nations Ask End of Atomic Selfishness," *The New York Times*, November 8, 1949; "India Will Bid UN Shift Atomic Work," *The New York Times*, September 26, 1949; Report on First Session of the International Law Commission, October 14, 1949, Acc. No. 14 15_3(17), NAM.
61 Jawaharlal Nehru to Mohan Shumsher Jung Bahadur Rana, June 9, 1949, *SWJN* 2, Vol. 11, 379.

2

From Peace to National Liberation

Mexico and the Tricontinental[1]

Patrick Iber

Introduction

In January 1966, coinciding with the seventh anniversary of the Cuban Revolution, delegates from around the world gathered in Havana. For months prior, in preparation for what was intended to be a historic event, trees had been planted and trash cleared away in an effort to beautify the city. For thirteen days, more than five hundred delegates and nearly three hundred observers met in the Hotel Habana Libre, the hotel that in the era of Fulgencio Batista had been a Hilton, hammering out a list of principles and commitments. The Tricontinental sought to unify the people of Asia, Africa, and Latin America, adding Latin America to the parts of the world then experiencing decolonization and forming an anti-imperialist alliance based on ideas of racial solidarity and a shared experience of economic exploitation. Though Latin America's countries had gained their independence much earlier, Latin America still suffered, argued Afro-Cuban scholar Walterio Carbonell, one of the intellectual authors of the conference, under the "disguised colonialism" of the United States.[2] The absent Che Guevara sent a message to the gathering, hoping for "two, three, many Vietnams."[3] The conference resolutions pledged that "the peoples of the three continents must reply to imperialist violence with revolutionary violence to safeguard hard-won independence, as well as to achieve the liberation of the peoples who are fighting to shake off the colonialist noose."[4]

Many of those gathered for the occasion came from the movements describing themselves as for the "national liberation" of their respective countries; many, also, were members of the World Peace Council, a Soviet-aligned body established in 1950. The conference represented the confluence of many interests, some in tension with each other. The Soviet policy of peaceful coexistence with capitalism and the Chinese policy of support for national liberation movements that was a source of the Sino-Soviet split were the most obvious. Cuba, reliant on Soviet support but committed to armed insurgency, hovered between the two. Castro publicly sided with the Soviets while using the conference as an opportunity to recruit new guerrilla fighters. The

Tricontinental Conference led to the creation of a permanent Organization of Solidarity with the People of Asia, Africa, and Latin America, known as OSPAAAL for its abbreviation in Spanish (the Organización de Solidaridad con los Pueblos de Asia, África y América Latina). OSPAAAL absorbed the Afro-Asian Peoples' Solidarity Organization (AAPSO), which had been formed in 1957. The Tricontinental also reflected a transition in Cuban foreign policy from sponsoring revolutionary efforts in Latin America toward greater engagement with Africa.[5]

Though the Tricontinental was often linked to the Bandung conference of 1955, the Bandung and Tricontinental came to emphasize different elements of the broader project of independence and anticolonialism. Bandung was committed to nonalignment in the Cold War and was attended by governments; the Tricontinental to armed struggle against imperialism and was made up of movements of national liberation. A report prepared for the Judiciary Committee of the U.S. Senate described the gathering as being held "to coordinate subversion and guerrilla activity on a worldwide basis, to exchange experiences, and to build further on what has already been constructed—meaning especially Cuba and Vietnam."[6] Few participants would have objected to the characterization. Amílcar Cabral, the agronomist and revolutionary socialist from Guinea-Bissau, began his address with the declaration that "We are not going to eliminate imperialism by shouting insults against it. For us, the best and worst shout against imperialism, whatever its form, is to take up arms and fight."[7] When Che Guevara was killed in Bolivia the next year in 1967, the OSPAAAL declaration praised his commitment to armed struggle and declared that "victory and a glorious future will develop from this direct confrontation with imperialism."[8]

Seen in this way, the Tricontinental looks like a product of Cuban diplomacy, and, of course, it was. Nevertheless, it can also be seen as a sequel to a conference held in Mexico five years earlier. That conference, with the unwieldy title of the Latin American Conference for National Sovereignty, Economic Emancipation, and Peace, sparked both a domestic political movement within Mexico and an international effort to extend the work done there to an alliance with Asia and Africa. This chapter will explore the overlooked role of Mexico's Lázaro Cárdenas in the organization of the Tricontinental. Cárdenas, who had been president of Mexico from 1934 to 1940 and oversaw substantial agrarian reform, aid to the Spanish Republic, and the nationalization of Mexico's oil industry, was considered by friends and enemies alike as Mexico's most left-wing statesman. This chapter shows how the Cold War placed his style of politics of national liberation into institutional alignment with Soviet propaganda, justifying either its repression (as occurred domestically) or its radicalization (as occurred internationally).

Lázaro Cárdenas and the Partisans of Peace

Lázaro Cárdenas had had a mostly quiet post-presidency. He had largely retreated from public life, even as the ruling party in Mexico that he had helped to shape veered in a more conservative direction. In 1954, when the CIA had helped overthrow the leftist government of Jacobo Arbenz in Guatemala, Cárdenas had issued a statement lamenting the damage done to the sovereignty of Guatemala. Then, in December 1955, word came that Cárdenas had been awarded the International Stalin Prize for Strengthening Peace among Peoples, better known as the Stalin Peace Prize. He chose to accept it.

The Stalin Peace Prize was part of the Soviet Union's Cold War diplomacy, one part of efforts to represent itself as the champion of peace against the interests of the warmongering West. It had also helped spur meetings of "Partisans of Peace" in Poland in 1948 and in New York and Mexico City in 1949. In 1950, this organizational work led to the creation of the World Peace Council, a body with Soviet support that coordinated peace efforts around the globe. In the early 1950s, the idea of peace was taken up by many left-wing artists outside of the Soviet Union (which was experiencing an exceptionally repressive phase under late Stalinism). Pablo Picasso, then probably the world's most famous artist, had joined the French Communist Party in 1944. He attended Peace events, and painted works devoted to the cause. In 1951, for example, he painted "Massacre in Korea," showing the murder of civilians by inhuman, robotic anticommunist forces.[9] The CIA described cultural aspects of the Cold War as the "battle for Picasso's mind," covertly helping establish parallel organizations devoted to the cause of "freedom" rather than that of "peace."[10]

The 1949 meeting in Mexico City, known as the Continental Congress for Peace, brought together sympathetic forces from around the Americas. It featured performances by the Chilean poet Pablo Neruda and the dancer Waldeen as well as appearances by the Mexican muralists Diego Rivera and David Álfaro Siqueiros. Lázaro Cárdenas gave his blessing, though without violating his custom of declining to appear in public in support of political causes.[11] Following the event, a Mexican Pro-Peace Committee was established to continue its work. The first important task was signature-gathering on behalf of the Stockholm Appeal, a worldwide campaign that called for international control of atomic weapons and declared their first use a war crime. The Mexican Committee set its sights on one million signatures. Most of the effort for collecting them came from the Mexican Communist Party, which directed its followers to apply limitless energy to the organization of local Peace Committees. Members of the national committee of the Pro-Peace group took to the streets to round up signatures from passersby; Diego Rivera himself spent a morning in front of the post office in Mexico City, making speeches in favor of peace next to signs reading "Damn the warmongers" and "Down with the atomic bomb." When the final tallies were presented, the Mexican Committee furnished 300,000 signatures.[12]

Rivera was among the prominent artists who devoted considerable time to the cause of Peace in the early 1950s. The culmination of his efforts—at least in artistic terms—was a quickly executed mural, *Pesadilla de guerra, sueño de paz* (Nightmare of war, dream of peace). The work, completed in 1952, shows the benevolent figures of Stalin and Mao standing with a Peace petition, offering a pen to figures representing the United Kingdom, France, and a gun-and-Bible-toting Uncle Sam. In the foreground, Frida Kahlo sits in a wheelchair, soliciting signatures from people on the street. The mural, which was intended for an exhibition in Paris, was rejected by the Mexican government as a provocation to its allies, but celebrated in a showing by the Communist Party and the Mexican Peace Committee.[13] Officially lost, the mural is sometimes rumored to have been taken to China or the Soviet Union, where it may or may not have survived.[14]

Rivera hoped that his painting might earn him readmission into the Mexican Communist Party. But, more broadly, it shows how, as with other "fellow-traveling" organizations, the Communist Party wanted both to control the actions of the campaign and to represent a broad front. It instructed its supporters not to be "sectarian" in their actions within Peace campaigns and as they formed local chapters. They struggled to achieve this goal. The party soon reported that "detrimental sectarianism" had caused communist groups to simply convert their own cells into Peace chapters, which was leading to inactivity and narrow support for their initiatives.[15] In broad terms, the Peace committee was managed by Mexico's Communist Party, and there is evidence that operational subsidies for publications came from the World Peace Council.[16]

In Mexico, many of the prominent organizers on behalf of the cause of peace were personally close to Lázaro Cárdenas. Heriberto Jara, the nominal head of the organization, was a close family friend. Elena Vázquez Gómez worked as Cárdenas's secretary: she and her partner Teresa Proenza, who edited the magazine *Paz*, were also close associates of Frida Kahlo and Diego Rivera during the early 1950s, when the painters devoted considerable emotional and physical energy to the "Peace" cause. Elena Vázquez Gómez had been an asset of Soviet intelligence during World War II. Proenza and Vázquez Gómez also organized a 1953 Continental Congress for Culture in Santiago, Chile, alongside Pablo Neruda.[17]

Cárdenas himself was not directly involved with the Mexican Pro-Peace Committee in the early years of the 1950s. The man who had once granted asylum to Stalin's enemy Trotsky would seem an unlikely choice for affiliation with a Soviet-aligned group. But Cárdenas, in spite of his sympathy and personal respect for Trotsky, and his deep frustration at the time of the Hitler-Stalin Pact, had never been anti-Soviet. In the 1940s, he had still never traveled outside of Mexico, which remained his sole point of reference. He associated anticommunism with the politics of the privileged. World events and personal contacts moved him toward opinions that aligned with those of the World Peace Council. Shocked by the use of nuclear weapons over Japan at the end of the Second World War, Cárdenas concluded that President Truman was a war criminal. In the Cold War context, he became an "anti-anticommunist" in opposition to dominant anticommunist political cultures. "Communism is the bogeyman of the rich and the hope of the poor," Cárdenas wrote in his diary in late 1946.[18]

After Stalin's death in 1953, the new Soviet leadership that came to power sought to de-Stalinize several aspects of Soviet life, including both culture and foreign affairs, and the idea of Peace faded somewhat as a cultural force. To improve domestic conditions, the USSR needed to decrease military spending and consequently sought reasonably good relations with the United States. World Peace Council rhetoric shifted from forceful anti-imperialism to antinuclear talk of peaceful coexistence. Though it remained unquestionably pro-Soviet, Nikita Khrushchev went as far as to suggest to the WPC leadership that it should act on principle, even if that meant going against the USSR. At the same time, however, Khrushchev believed that the Soviet Union was the only major power genuinely interested in peace, and that decolonizing Asia and

Africa would join a great "zone of peace" that would bring the "Third World" closer to the USSR over time.[19]

When Cárdenas was awarded the Stalin Peace Prize in 1955, his decision to accept it was made in that framework. The historian Frank Tannenbaum had been his friend and counselor in the 1930s, but the anarchism of his younger days had hardened into liberal anticommunism by the 1950s. When he heard of the award, he wrote Cárdenas to warn of the "diabolically clever" actions of the communists to "lay claim on you before the world." He continued:

> But you do not belong to them. Your life and work on behalf of the Mexican people lies within the Mexican tradition and is inspired by the democratic philosophy of the Western World. You believe in freedom, in justice, in a free press, free assembly, free speech, in human dignity and in that no man has a right to impose his ideas by force upon another. You do not believe in concentration camps or in liquidating people whose political opinions are different from yours, (as illustrated by the case of Trotsky) and you believe in the freedom and equality of little nations.[20]

Cárdenas did not see the matter in those terms. For him, accepting the Stalin Prize expressed approval of the steps that major powers had made toward peace with each other—talks held in Geneva in mid-1955 had reduced nuclear tensions—and the hope that a thaw in the Cold War would mean the end of interventions. To Tannenbaum, he replied:

> If the world is asking for peace; if the old allies of the past war have returned to meeting to try to find solutions to their differences . . . how can it hurt Mexico or a Mexican to accept the Peace Prize? You refer to the tradition of Mexico and Western democratic philosophy, and go on, "you believe in freedom, in justice, in a free press, freedom of assembly, human dignity, equality of small nations, etc." We really do believe in those things and we desire them for all to whom those liberties have been forbidden. If it is as you express, and there are peoples on other continents that live under oppression, we ought not to turn around and do the same thing by damaging "small nations" and suppressing freedom of expression.

In February 1956, the Soviet film director Grigori Alexandrov conferred the award in a lavish ceremony in Mexico City, referring to Cárdenas as a "paladin of democracy and independence," a defender of justice and of the interests of the Mexican people. Thousands packed the room to witness the event; thousands more waited outside to catch a glimpse of Cárdenas as he left. The multitude that turned out to see him was a sign of how many missed his leadership in a rapidly developing but capitalist Mexico. Famously impassive in public and unwilling to criticize his successors in office directly, the short speech that he made at the ceremony was oblique. He heralded improvements in relations between the great powers and, without mentioning Guatemala by name, of the importance of ending the Cold War because of the damage it had done to the sovereignty of smaller nations. Cárdenas described propaganda against Mexican Partisans of Peace as tendentious, saying that the aspiration for peace was shared by millions of men and women working for universal peace: it was the supreme ideal of the "people." Cárdenas's distrust of anticommunism led him to doubt that Tannenbaum's concentration-camps-and-secret-police description of the Soviet Union was accurate. But what he objected to most strongly was the Cold War logic that transformed criticism of the Soviet Union into a justification for oppressive intervention in the Western Hemisphere and beyond.[21]

His friend Heriberto Jara wrote to Lázaro Cárdenas in May 1957, after his prize had been awarded, trying to keep him involved in World Peace Council activity. But Cárdenas, while expressing sympathy, kept to his usual pattern of public silence. International overtures were more successful. The World Peace Council's president, Frédéric Joliot-Curie, died in late 1958, and was replaced by his close friend and associate J. D. Bernal, an Irish biologist and communist. Bernal, in keeping with the times, looked to reach out to noncommunist leaders who shared the values of the WPC and struck on the idea of inviting Lázaro Cárdenas to join the organization.[22] This offer didn't raise the problem of being perceived as interfering in Mexican politics. Cárdenas agreed to serve as a member of the World Peace Council, on the condition that he be allowed to send proxies in his stead to international meetings.[23]

Cárdenas, accompanied for much of the time by his son Cuauhtémoc, made his first lengthy trip outside of Mexico in the early months of 1959. He traveled to Paris, Moscow, Beijing, Tokyo, and finally the United States. In Moscow, he and Cuauhtémoc were greeted by the Soviet Peace Committee and taken to the Bolshoi Theater. In Beijing, they were met by Kuo Mo-jo, the most important personality on the Chinese Peace Committee. At the end of his trip, Cárdenas traveled from San Francisco to Chicago to Knoxville, Tennessee—where he examined approvingly the work of the Tennessee Valley Authority. In a diary entry, he noted:

> All the peoples of the world desire peace. The people of Europe, Latin America and the United States itself have serious internal problems, such as a lack of sources of work for their entire populations. . . . China with its 600 million inhabitants is solving that problem with an enormous impulse in agriculture while it also develops industry to absorb the excess rural population of each province. Other countries could do this too if the State, and not financiers and industrialists, directed their economies.[24]

When he returned to Mexico, the statements that Cárdenas made to the press set off another convulsion of speculation that he had been won over to communism, and indeed the trip did convince him of the superiority of socialist wealth redistribution. He also accepted the claims of the Soviet government and of China to be fully representative of their people—and he hadn't noticed the millions of deaths by starvation that resulted from China's Great Leap Forward, under way during his visit. But he was particularly enthusiastic about state-led development, regardless of the context in which it unfolded. In the early 1960s, Cárdenas defined the ideological program of the Mexican Revolution as "national sovereignty, economic emancipation, comprehensive agrarian reform, political democracy, union democracy, [and] freedom of worship and of the press" and he read this interpretation of the Mexican Revolution onto other revolutionary states. It was an imprecise analogy: "agrarian reforms" in the Soviet Union and China (but not Mexico) produced enormous humanitarian catastrophes. But Cárdenas's agenda was not really to defend the Soviet Union or China, and their situations were not as analogous to Mexico's as was the country that he noted in his diary really inspired hope: Cuba.[25]

Fidel Castro and Cárdenas had met before. In Mexico, training for invasion of Cuba in the mid-1950s, Castro had not been able to count on the automatic sympathy of the Mexican left. Both Cuban and Mexican communists thought of him as an "adventurer," and Cárdenas had been on good terms with then-president Fulgencio Batista, who was now the dictator Castro sought to overthrow. But Castro's allies reached out to Cárdenas when Fidel was threatened with deportation, and Cárdenas wrote on his behalf to President Adolfo Ruiz Cortines, asking him to honor Mexico's traditional right to asylum. Castro subsequently met with Cárdenas, who described him as a "young intellectual with a vehement temperament and the blood of a fighter." Cárdenas reasoned that if Castro were to be successful in overthrowing Batista, it would be because it was the will of the Cuban people.[26]

After his victory in 1959, when Cuba decreed its agrarian reform, Cárdenas compared the steps to Mexico's own actions and noted that he hoped that Cuba would take a socially integrated approach that would avoid the internal convulsions that Mexico had suffered. Invited to Cuba to celebrate July 26—the anniversary of the attacks on the Moncada barracks—Cárdenas appeared triumphantly alongside Fidel Castro. Cuba became the symbol of the democratic aspirations that Cárdenas had for Mexico, for a return to the values that he associated with the Mexican Revolution. He had some reservations about the course of the revolution that he kept private: he shocked visiting Cuban president Osvaldo Dorticós and the others in the room by telling him that he found the "climate of the Revolution . . . troubling" in 1960, but would never have said so publicly.[27]

The Cuban example was inspiring to many on the Mexican left, and its defense was largely posed in the language of democratic reform. In the new newsmagazine *Política*, where many of those associated with the Peace Movement wrote, democracy was presented as the goal of the Cuban Revolution. Cuba was described as the most democratic country in the region: in the words of Víctor Flores Olea, "a direct, plebiscitary, *concrete* [democracy] . . . in which people and Government are perfectly identified [with one another]." Fidel Castro himself told the assembled crowds in Cuba on May 1, 1960, that "[Cuba's previous rulers] invented a strange democracy in which you, who are the majority, counted for nothing. Democracy is that in which the majority governs; democracy is that in which the interests of the majority are defended . . . democracy is the right to bread, to work, to culture, and the right to count within society." That he made that argument in the context of announcing that there was no need to hold elections did not seem such a problem to those who believed in the unity of Cuba's government and its people.[28]

To its critics on the left, Mexico's government did not satisfy that sort of definition of democracy, because the interests of the people had been abandoned. That argument became even more compelling in August 1960, when the government used the social dissolution law to arrest and sentence the muralist David Álfaro Siqueiros to eight years in prison. Siqueiros, a member of Mexico's Communist Party, had made comments critical of the government of Mexico on trips to Cuba and Venezuela. The government argued that in advocating for the dictatorship of the proletariat, Siqueiros sought not only the dissolution of the Mexican government, but of Mexican society itself. But Siqueiros continued to paint while in prison, turning his work into a symbol of the power of freedom of expression over state repression. Pablo Neruda visited in January 1961 and composed a quick verse: "I have seen your painting jailed / which is like jailing a blaze // [. . .] Mexico is a prisoner alongside you." For political prisoners like himself, Siqueiros declared gallantly from behind bars, "jail is the same thing a battlefield [is to a soldier]."[29]

The Latin American Conference of 1961

In December 1959, Cuba's new foreign minister had approached the Mexican government about holding an "International Conference of Underdeveloped Nations" to be held in Havana: a distant precursor to the Tricontinental and an attempt to include Asia, Africa, and Latin America in a single project. But Brazil and Mexico were concerned that Cuba was seeking too much control over inter-American politics and demurred.[30] Instead of a project between governments, it would be representatives of "national liberation" movements that would push that project forward. In 1960 discussions began in Austria, at the International Institute of Peace that had been established in that city after the World Peace Council was expelled in 1956, and in Stockholm, then the headquarters of the World Peace Council, about holding a large Peace Congress somewhere in Latin America. In May, Olga Poblete, a Chilean feminist activist who was active in the international Peace Movement, sounded out Lázaro Cárdenas on the possibility of an "Afro-Asian-Latin American" congress, an idea that had been repeatedly raised by the Brazilian public health expert Valério Konder.[31] The Steering Committee eventually decided to hold an event in Mexico, and in December Latin American delegates—Domingos Vellasco of Brazil, Olga Poblete of Chile, and Tomás Alberto Casella of Argentina, all members of their local peace committees—arrived in Mexico to meet with Lázaro Cárdenas to plan the event. In mid-January, Cárdenas and the others issued a call to a Conferencia Latinoamericana por la Soberanía Nacional, la Emancipación Económica y la Paz: the Latin American Conference for National Sovereignty, Economic Emancipation, and Peace. The convocation argued that the people of Latin America, like those around the rest of the world, wanted to enjoy freedom and democratic rights, sovereignty, education and culture, independence, and economic development. The declaration asserted that all of these positive qualities were found most clearly in revolutionary Cuba.[32]

In spite of its foreign connections, Cárdenas worked to make sure that the conference could not be accused of foreign dependence. Socialist politician and union leader Vicente Lombardo Toledano remarked in December 1960 that individual contributions were needed to pay for the upcoming conference, as offers of financial support that had come from the Soviet bloc countries had been rejected so as to not invite criticism in Mexico. Clementina Batalla, a leader in the Soviet-aligned Women's

International Democratic Federation, was made treasurer of the 1961 conference.[33] She recorded each contribution and expenditure on behalf of the Mexican sponsoring committee and made the results available to the public. The conference sought to be seen, as both a point of pride and of political necessity, as being a fully national undertaking, and not the result of Soviet or Cuban manipulation. For a total bill of nearly $300,000 pesos, no single source dominated. Heriberto Jara made one of the largest personal contributions, of $6,000 pesos. Vicente Lombardo Toledano's labor federation did receive money from the Soviet Union to keep it operational and might have been a conduit for support of the conference, but his contribution was only $1,000 pesos. The donations of various communal farms dwarfed that amount many times over. If any foreign government managed to contribute to the conference, it was by circumventing rules in place to prevent it. Cárdenas sold a piece of property belonging to his family to help finance the event.[34] The International Institute for Peace made several airline tickets available to engineer Jorge L. Tamayo, but Cárdenas insisted on paying for them and the money for the tickets was returned. The need for the work to remain "Mexican" was well known throughout the movement. At an organizational meeting in March 1961, after Cárdenas had taken his leave, an Argentine journalist and Communist Party member proposed obtaining $100,000 pesos from Cuba for the printing of pamphlets, and offered to do so, but Tamayo told her that Cárdenas would not approve.[35]

When the event began, it did so against a background of US-Cuban tension. The United States had severed diplomatic relations with the island in January and had been covertly preparing an invasion force for some time. Those gathering in Mexico thought that their gathering might play some role in stopping an attack on Cuba: decades later, Lázaro's son Cuauhtémoc Cárdenas speculated that the conference had delayed the landing at the Bay of Pigs, which took place the next month.[36] Speaking at the inaugural event of the conference on March 5, 1961, to a room full of 4,000 people, Lázaro Cárdenas made explicit an argument that had existed embryonically from the beginning of Peace Movement campaigning: that there was a distinction between "revolution" and "war." The difference lay in ends, not means. War, argued Cárdenas, threatens to extinguish humanity, and those who bring it about do so intending to profit from it financially. Revolution, by contrast, seeks political and economic changes that favor the collectivity of the people who carry it out. Cárdenas was quick to add that respect for the will of the citizenry was the desired mechanism for change and that did not necessarily imply that violence was the only means for expressing it. What gave the Cuban example such an impact in Latin America, he argued, was that its government understood this distinction: the government and people of Cuba are pacifist, but they defend their revolution. Later in the event, the Brazilian delegate Domingos Vellasco called the Cuban government democratic, "of and for the people."[37]

During the conference, commissions were established to write resolutions around four areas of concern: national sovereignty, economic emancipation, peace, and common action. The national sovereignty commission produced recommendations asking for juridical equality between Latin American states, self-determination, nonintervention, anti-imperialism, anticolonialism, defense of the Cuban Revolution, condemnation of US military missions, and instruments of imperialism like the Organization of

American States. The economic emancipation group called for economic development, the right to strike, fiscal democracy, agrarian reform, nationalization, and the rights of workers to freedom, autonomy, and union democracy. Other resolutions expressed solidarity with Cuba and with Africa and Asia, in favor of economic cooperation and disarmament and in favor of individual liberty and the defense of political prisoners. "The defeat of imperialism is the fundamental condition of any development plan for our countries," read the final resolution: "The works of the Cuban Revolution show the way to put an end to foreign domination."[38]

Lázaro Cárdenas undertook to raise awareness for the causes of the Conferencia Latinoamericana in the manner he had used effectively during his presidency: by traveling out to villages in person. Accompanied by many of the Latin American and Chinese delegates to the conference—as well as novelist Carlos Fuentes, in his capacity as sympathetic journalist—Cárdenas traveled to Querétaro, Guanajuato, Jalisco, and Michoacán. In Guanajuato, Fuentes overheard citizens remark about Cárdenas: "Look at him, he is a true democrat." "He knows how to mix among the people." The path forward for Mexico's democratic reconstruction, reflected Fuentes, would be dependent not on one man, but on the active expression of popular will. "Comprehensive agrarian reform, union democracy, and political liberty," he wrote, "will not be gifts given to the people, nor will it be a single *caudillo* who obtains them for the people. It will be the people, organized . . . that achieves them."[39]

Organization continued. In May, a Provisional Committee for National Sovereignty, Economic Emancipation and Peace was formed, dedicated to disseminating the messages of the conference, especially freedom for political prisoners and defense of the Cuban Revolution. On August 4 and 5, a national assembly was held that established a Movement for National Liberation (MLN: Movimiento de Liberación Nacional), dedicated to the same causes as the March conference: national sovereignty, economic emancipation, and peace. It sought to unite all of the "democratic and progressive," "popular" interests without regard to party. The MLN espoused the subversive notions that the results of elections should reflect the outcomes desired by voters, and that demonstrations and speech should not be curtailed by the use of police violence. The document released to the public emphasized that the movement situated itself as a nationalist, rather than class-based organization, and called for the simultaneous pursuit of many objectives: full enforcement of the Constitution, freedom for political prisoners, a democratic, honest, and independent justice system, free expression of ideas, comprehensive agrarian reform, union and *ejido* democracy and autonomy, Mexican control over Mexico's natural resources, industrialization without recourse to foreign loans, just distribution of national wealth, independence, dignity, and international cooperation, solidarity with Cuba, trade with all countries, democracy, honor, and well-being, bread and freedom, sovereignty and peace.[40]

Though the movement mobilized, at a minimum, tens of thousands, its impact would be limited. What pressure the MLN could exert on the Mexican government came about mostly because of Lázaro Cárdenas. In the wake of the Conferencia Latinoamericana in 1961, President Adolfo López Mateos called a meeting with Cárdenas, pressuring him not to travel to Cuba. López Mateos tried generosity. He offered Cárdenas the opportunity to take charge of the PRI; the former president replied that he was not up to the job. Soon thereafter, Cárdenas declared that he belonged to "no party," simultaneously denying that he was a communist while also suggesting he did not see himself as part of the ruling party in Mexico. Although it was obvious that he had not been active within the machinery of the PRI for some time, such a declaration still came as a surprise and raised the possibility that Cárdenas, especially if he were expelled from the PRI, would take large numbers of supporters with him and create a genuine electoral threat to the stability of the regime. He was seen as the only person who had the power to really split the PRI, even though his private behavior suggested that he had no desire to do so. At the end of 1961, he accepted an executive position overseeing the Balsas River Commission, a regional development project based in his home state of Michoacán, hoping that in taking the post he might be able to influence López Mateos to grant clemency to the jailed political prisoners. Repeated meetings with López Mateos yielded no results, however, and opened him to charges of co-optation. Still, he continued to act as a bridge to the government.

Cárdenas had helped build the MLN to respond to problems in Mexico, aided by the transformed infrastructure of the World Peace Council. Even as it tried to emphasize its Mexican roots, it would soon come to pay a price for its international connections.[41] The Mexican government's relationship with the MLN was complex, as President Adolfo López Mateos wanted to claim ground as an advocate of international peace and coexistence.[42] Nevertheless, the United States, through the CIA, and the Mexican government, worked deliberately to undermine it: creating opposing front groups, monitoring and harassing its participants, and denying newsprint to affiliated publications.[43]

Even with these obstacles, the MLN brought a kind of energy to the Mexican left that it had not seen in years. Volunteers numbering at least in the tens of thousands fanned out across the country to try and mobilize support for progressive causes. Yet, most of the MLN's specific campaigns proved unsuccessful, undermined by government intervention. Organizing in Baja California Norte around the issue of salinity in the Colorado River, which harmed Mexican farmers, frightened the United States. Cuauhtémoc Cárdenas (seen by US officials as a communist sympathizer) seemed poised to be named to head the Mexicali Valley Irrigation District, so López Mateos pressured Lázaro Cárdenas to have his son withdraw from contention. López Mateos then send federal troops to the Mexicali Valley and forced a dissident, MLN-aligned leader to quiet down by threatening him with murder. A new peasant organization created in 1963 by MLN leaders, the Central Campesina Independiente, was supposed to be independent of the ruling party but was captured by it in little more than a year.[44]

The MLN, bringing together as it did several left-wing groups, inevitably suffered from internal tensions. Heriberto Jara, for example, thought that its young leaders had been seized by extremism and gave no credit for the good things that the PRI did. But its real threats to internal cohesion came from party leaders. Union leader and socialist politician Vicente Lombardo Toledano was apparently disappointed to learn that the Cuban Embassy had given its delegates instructions to deal with Alonso Aguilar Monteverde on the recommendation of Lázaro Cárdenas, ignoring members of his own Partido Popular Socialista, and began to complain publicly about the MLN.[45] Stating that he thought that the Peace Movement and the MLN should be separate undertakings, Lombardo Toledano took the PPS out of the MLN at mid-year. The remaining leadership of the MLN described the departure of the PPS as an act directed against the "representative sectors of the Mexican left"—placing Vicente Lombardo Toledano's organization outside of that category.[46]

In 1963, further conflicts arose regarding the 1964 presidential elections. Some, especially in the Communist Party, wanted to use the MLN to launch a presidential candidate, but the internal line had always been that the organization was multiparty and that members would work within their own parties to have them adopt the principles for which the MLN advocated. Nonetheless, the Communist Party created a People's Electoral Front and offered as a presidential candidate Ramón Danzós Palomino, a member of both the PCM and the MLN. While insisting that it did not want to damage the unity of the MLN, the PCM tried to recruit other members of the Movement to support the Electoral Front, creating distrust and resentment. Some disillusioned members, such as Cuauhtémoc Cárdenas, distanced themselves from the MLN, and the elections of 1964 proved to be the beginning of a long decline, as the organization ceased to be able to motivate the kind of unity and organizational drive that it had had for the eighteen months or so following its creation in late 1961. It had one concrete victory in 1964 when Siqueiros was released early from prison, freed by presidential decree on July 13—but even that had to wait until nearly the end of López Mateos's term in office, when it became clear that the action would be taken by his successor if he didn't do it himself.[47]

The Path to the Tricontinental

Many who worked for the MLN would later be involved in Mexico's student movement, and even the eventual split from the ruling party that led to the formation of the Partido de la Revolución Democrática after the contested election of 1988. But its immediate achievements were modest. Nevertheless, the conference was seen by many internationally as a first step toward a more ambitious international event. In May 1961, two months after the conference in Mexico, Brazilian doctor Valério Konder wrote to Cárdenas describing meetings held in New Delhi at which he had pushed for a common "tri-continental" meeting of representatives of the countries of Asia, Africa, and Latin America.[48] Conversations and outreach continued under the auspices of the World Peace Council. In September 1962, Cárdenas wrote twice to Fidel Castro, expressing sympathy with Castro's plight and the heroic struggle of the Cuban people. "Cuban sugar is today what Mexican oil once was," Lázaro Cárdenas had reasoned the previous year, and now, in his letter to Castro he extended the comparison: "The interests that are today rising up against Cuba also wanted to frustrate the nationalization of our oil by means of isolation and blockade." Cárdenas passed on a memorandum of the discussions at the World Peace Council, mentioning Castro's interest in the development of a Tricontinental Conference.[49] In October, a commission on convening the Tricontinental met in Stockholm, announcing the intention to continue to organize the forces working for "national independence, sovereignty, and peace"—the same framework as that of Mexico's conference of 1961.[50]

Ongoing organizing was complicated by tensions that had emerged within the World Peace Council, where the Soviet delegation had become the moderate one, far outstripped in its belief in the possibility of rapid social change by the Chinese. Khrushchev's efforts to sign agreements that decreased tensions with the United States were seen by the Chinese as "collaboration with U.S. imperialism," and a violation of the principles of national liberation. In 1962, the Chinese Peace Committee issued a decree that the Soviet delegation's 1956 decision to replace the Stalin Peace Prize with the Lenin Prize had been taken unilaterally and without consultation within the international Peace Movement, thus besmirching the great name of Stalin.[51] The Chinese Committee retaliated by issuing its own International Stalin Peace Prizes. For his part, Lázaro Cárdenas saw Sino-Soviet differences as debilitating to the unity of peoples in the fight against imperialism and tried to gather information to understand the tensions between the two countries.[52]

Still, the organizing continued. In December 1962, J. D. Bernal wrote to confirm the WPC secretariat's enthusiasm for a meeting of the nature proposed by Cárdenas. Bernal asked Cárdenas for help securing Latin American participation at the Conference of the Afro-Asian Solidarity Council in Dar es Salaam, which could be used to set up preparatory commissions for what he referred to as the "Three Continents Conference."[53] There were setbacks: in February 1963, the Latin American observers to the third Afro-Asian Peoples' Solidarity Conference in Tanganyika complained that they had not been allowed to express their views on the planning of a Tricontinental.[54] The next month, in Brazil, a Continental Congress of Solidarity with Cuba encountered trouble when visas were denied to foreign delegations (including Bernal himself) and the justice minister raided the building where planning was taking place. But in September and October, Cárdenas exchanged a special representative with Ghanaian President Kwame Nkrumah for planning purposes in what Nkrumah described as their common interests in the fight "against imperialism and neo-colonialism" and what Cárdenas described as the preparation of a "Second Latin American Conference for National Sovereignty, Economic Independence, and World Peace."[55] Finally, in Cairo, in September 1965, a preparatory committee of the Afro-Asian Peoples' Solidarity Organization decided to accept the invitation of the Cuban government to hold the Tricontinental Conference the following January. "Solidarity among the peoples of Africa, Asia and Latin America is a reality firmly established a long time ago," they wrote, papering over any differences. "[The Three Continents] all face the same problems . . . and the people of the Three Continents feel the profound need for solidarity that must exist between them and in coordinating their fight against the common enemy, North American imperialism."[56] The Tricontinental was born.

Mexico would not be a major participant in the project of the Tricontinental, but the diplomacy of Lázaro Cárdenas had been important to its creation. The sequel to the 1961 conference finally arrived, but with a new director in the chair. That earlier meeting represented the consolidation of an international agenda that Lázaro Cárdenas saw as the defense of his interpretation of the Mexican Revolution and his presidential administration: economic independence, national sovereignty, international solidarity, and peace. His evolving thought and reaction to the events of the Cold War make it clear how the cause of peace was linked to the defense of national sovereignty. Cárdenas saw in Cuba an analogous struggle, and its defense was already a major theme in 1961. Working through the World Peace Council, in the years after, political organizers from Mexico, Brazil, Argentina, and Chile pushed for unity with their African and Asian counterparts, in a context in which the defense of Cuba was the preeminent priority. Cuba seized the initiative and used the Tricontinental as part of its strategy for national defense.

The Tricontinental brought together the work being done in forums like AAPSO and the World Peace Council in defense of a program of anti-imperialism and state-led socialist economics. It did not end up representing Cárdenas's idea of a united front. "The organization for the Tricontinental Conference," he noted drily, "did not conform to that which was agreed upon in the Latin American Conference celebrated in Mexico in 1961."[57] The MLN, which was the domestic outgrowth of the conference of 1961, was a more direct reflection of his hopes. In the context of the broader Cold War, the history of the MLN sits awkwardly. Its origins were tied up in the work of Soviet front groups, yet it brought together a broader group of supporters and articulated a critique of Mexican democracy and defended civil liberties. It made a Stalinist like Siquerios a symbol of free expression, showing how contingent the idea of "democracy" was. It was a demonstration that—contrary to anticommunist Cold War propaganda—the defense of civil liberties could emerge from involvement with a Soviet "front" group, and that it was difficult yet possible to construct a financially and programmatically independent national political movement even amid such connections. Nevertheless, the foreign connections—the internationalism—were used as justifications for repression which were an important factor in dismantling the organization. The "spirit" of the Tricontinental and of the MLN diverged, though they declared similar goals. Those divergent paths—a vulnerable broad front of leftist political activity in the MLN and an insurrectionary internationalism in the Tricontinental—together show how the structure of the Cold War limited the strategies available to advocates of projects that they hoped would bring independence and emancipation.

Notes

1 This chapter reframes, reintroduces, and condenses the fifth chapter of my 2015 book *Neither Peace Nor Freedom* for a new context. Though I have taken the opportunity to rewrite many parts and have included research not referenced in that chapter, there is some overlap with the material in the book. I want to thank Harvard University Press for allowing us to reproduce a version of the chapter here.

2 Anne Garland Mahler, *From the Tricontinental to the Global South: Race, Radicalism, and Transnational Solidarity* (Durham: Duke University Press, 2018), 66.

3 Julio García Luis, ed., *Cuban Revolution Reader: A Documentary History of Fidel Castro's Revolution*, 2nd ed (Melbourne and New York: Ocean Press, 2008), 176.

4 United States Senate. Subcommittee to Investigate the Administration of the Internal Security Act and other Internal Security Laws of the Committee on the Judiciary, "The

Tricontinental Conference of African, Asian, and Latin American Peoples" (USGPO, 1966), 15.

5 On tensions at the Tricontinental, see Jorge I. Domínguez, *To Make a World Safe for Revolution: Cuba's Foreign Policy* (Cambridge, MA: Harvard University Press, 1989), 69–70. On Cuban engagement with Africa, see Piero Gleijeses, *Conflicting Missions: Havana, Washington, and Africa, 1959-1976* (Chapel Hill: University of North Carolina Press, 2002).

6 United States Senate. Subcommittee to Investigate the Administration of the Internal Security Act and other Internal Security Laws of the Committee on the Judiciary, "The Tricontinental Conference of African, Asian, and Latin American Peoples," 3.

7 Quoted in Vijay Prashad, *The Darker Nations: A People's History of the Third World* (New York: New Press, 2008), 107. As of 2020, Prashad is the director of Tricontinental: Institute for Social Research.

8 "The OSPAAAL Declaration," *Tricontinental*, (September–October 1967), 120.

9 Pierre Daix, *Picasso: Life and Art* (New York: Icon Editions, 1993), 305. For more on the general role of the World Peace Council and its relationship to the Soviet Union, see Lawrence S. Wittner, *One World or None: A History of the World Nuclear Disarmament Movement Through 1953* (Stanford, CA: Stanford University Press, 1993); Annie Kriegel, "'Lutte Pour La Paix' et 'Mouvement Pour La Paix' Dans La Stratégie et La Structure Du Mouvement Communiste International," in *L'Union Soviétique Dans Les Relations Internationales*, ed. Francis Conte and Jean-Louis Martres (Paris: Economica, 1982), 223–41.

10 Greg Barnhisel, *Cold War Modernists: Art, Literature, and American Cultural Diplomacy* (New York: Columbia University Press, 2015), 27. On the US side of the Cultural Cold War, see, among others, Hugh Wilford, *The Mighty Wurlitzer: How the CIA Played America* (Cambridge, MA: Harvard University Press, 2008); Frances Stonor Saunders, *The Cultural Cold War: The CIA and the World of Arts and Letters* (New York: New Press, 2000). I have written a larger guide to the literature: Patrick Iber, "The Cultural Cold War," in *Oxford Research Encyclopedia of American History* (Oxford University Press, 2019), https://doi.org/10.1093/acrefore/9780199329175.013 .760.

11 Lázaro Cárdenas, *Apuntes, 1941-1956* (México: Universidad Nacional Autónoma de México, 1973), 182, 220, 223, 235. For more on early Peace activities in Latin America, see chapter 2 of Iber, *Neither Peace Nor Freedom*, and the work of Marcelo Ridenti in this volume.

12 "Por un Millón de firmas," *Paz* 1, no. 9 (Diciembre 1951): 57; Heriberto Saucedo (Secretario de Finanzas del PCM), "Apliquemos nuestra política justa de finanzas," May 27–30, 1950, Partido Comunista Mexicano archive [PCM], box 22, folder 3, Centro de Estudios del Movimiento Obrero y Socialista [CEMOS]; "Se informa el resultado de las investigaciones practicidades por este Dependencia en relación con el Comité Mexicano por la Paz," September 8, 1950, Dirección Federal de Seguridad [DFS], Diego Rivera Barrientos file—versión pública, document 11-71-50, Archivo General de la Nación, Mexico [AGN].

13 Raquel Tibol, *Diego Rivera, Luces y Sombras* (Barcelona: Lumen, 2007), 291–300; Bertram David Wolfe, *The Fabulous Life of Diego Rivera* (New York: Stein and Day, 1963), 385–8; Salvador Novo, *La Vida En México En El Periodo Presidencial de Miguel Alemán* (México: Empresas Editoriales, 1967), 766–7; Mary K. Coffey, *How a Revolutionary Art Became Official Culture: Murals, Museums, and the Mexican State* (Durham: Duke University Press, 2012), 56–60. The Mexican government's decision

not to display the mural came after pressure from the US ambassador. Stephen R. Niblo, *War, Diplomacy, and Development: The United States and Mexico, 1938–1954* (Wilmington, DE: Scholarly Resources, 1995), 286.

14 Hugh Dellios, "Missing mural ignites Mexico's imagination," *Chicago Tribune*, June 1, 2004, https://www.chicagotribune.com/news/ct-xpm-2004-06-01-0406010149-story .html.

15 Letter from Juan Pablo Sainz Aguilar, 1951 or 1952, PCM archive, box 24, folder 1, CEMOS.

16 More details can be found in Iber, *Neither Peace Nor Freedom*, 150–4.

17 Raquel Tibol, *Frida Kahlo: An Open Life* (Albuquerque: University of New Mexico Press, 1993), 79; Frida Kahlo, Carlos Fuentes, and Sarah M. Lowe, *The Diary of Frida Kahlo : An Intimate Self-Portrait* (New York: H.N. Abrams, 1995), 257; Isolda Pinedo Kahlo, *Intimate Frida* (Bogotá, Colombia: Cangrejo, 2006), 192. Elena Vázquez Gómez has been identified as codenames "Elena" and "Seda" in the Venona decrypts. Mexico City to Moscow, January 15 and 21, 1944, accessed May 4, 2021, https:// www.nsa.gov/Portals/70/documents/news-features/declassified-documents/venona /dated/1944/15jan_kgb_personality_elena.pdf and https://www.nsa.gov/Portals/70 /documents/news-features/declassified-documents/venona/dated/1944/21jan_info _about_kgb.pdf.

18 Cárdenas, *Apuntes, 1941-1956*, 223.

19 The World Peace Council experienced structural changes that reflected its new posture. Its headquarters were moved from Prague to Vienna and increased efforts to combine forces with Christian peace groups. Austria, worried about WPC activities on its soil, requested that it leave in 1957; it dissolved and reformed at the same address as the International Institute for Peace. Clive Rose, *The Soviet Propaganda Network: A Directory of Organisations Serving Soviet Foreign Policy* (London and New York: Pinter Publishers; St. Martin's Press, 1988), 108–10. On Khrushchev, see Andrew Brown, *J. D. Bernal: The Sage of Science* (Oxford and New York: Oxford University Press, 2005), 415. On the Soviet Union and the Third World, see Michael E. Latham, "The Cold War in the Third World, 1963-1975," in *The Cambridge History of the Cold War*, ed. Melvyn Leffler and Odd Arne Westad, vol. 2 (Cambridge and New York: Cambridge University Press, 2010), 264; Roy Allison, *The Soviet Union and the Strategy of Non-Alignment in the Third World* (Cambridge and New York: Cambridge University Press, 1988).

20 Selden Rodman, *Mexican Journal* (New York: Devin-Adair Co., 1958), 259. Tannenbaum to Lázaro Cárdenas, February 24, 1956, Frank Tannenbaum papers, folder "Cárdenas," box 1, Columbia University Rare Books and Manuscripts Library, New York.

21 Lázaro Cárdenas to Tannenbaum, March 11, 1956, Frank Tannenbaum papers, folder "Cárdenas," box 1, Columbia; "Discurso de entrega por el Prof. Grigori Alexandrov, a nombre del 'Comité Adjudicador de los Premios Internacionales Stalin,'" Heribero Jara papers, box 36, folder 1428, Archivo Histórico de la Universidad Nacional Autónoma de México [AHUNAM]; Eric Zolov, "Between Bohemianism and a Revolutionary Rebirth: Che Guevara in Mexico," in *Che's Travels: The Making of a Revolutionary in 1950s Latin America*, ed. Paulo Drinot (Durham and London: Duke University Press, 2010), 270–1. "Discurso del General Lázaro Cárdenas," Heriberto Jara papers, folder 1428, box 36, AHUNAM.

22 On Bernal, see Brenda Swann and Francis Aprahamian, *J.D. Bernal: A Life in Science and Politics* (London and New York: Verso, 1999), ix–xx, 212–34.

23 Heriberto Jara to Lázaro Cárdenas, May 1957, Lázaro Cárdenas del Río papers [LCR], microfilm roll 23, AGN; Bernal to Cárdenas, July 31, 1959, Cárdenas to Bernal, October 7, 1959, LCR papers, section "Consejo Mundial de la Paz–I, 1949-1960," roll 23, AGN.

24 Cárdenas, *Apuntes, 1941-1956,* 88. For more on this trip, see Eric Zolov, *The Last Good Neighbor: Mexico in the Global Sixties* (Durham: Duke University Press, 2020), 24–9.

25 Cuauhtémoc Cárdenas Solórzano, *Sobre Mis Pasos* (México: Aguilar, 2010), 63. The one defining the Mexican Revolution is from 1961 and is in Cárdenas, *Apuntes, 1957-1966,* 210. The comparative mildness of Mexico's revolutionary experience is put in stark relief by Friedrich Katz, "Violence and Terror in the Mexican and Russian Revolutions," in *A Century of Revolution: Insurgent and Counterinsurgent Violence during Latin America's Long Cold War,* ed. Greg Grandin and Gilbert M. Joseph (Durham: Duke University Press, 2010), 45–61. On the hopes of Cárdenas for Cuba, see Cárdenas, *Apuntes, 1941-1956,* 91.

26 The meeting took place on August 2, 1956. Cárdenas, *Obras,* vol. II, 646–7.

27 "Se informa en relación con las actividades del Ing. Jorge L. Tamayo," June 11, 1960, DFS, Lázaro Cárdenas del Río—versión pública, binder 2, AGN.

28 Víctor Flores Olea, "Cuba, una democracia concreta," *Política* 1, no. 2 (May 15, 1960): 10--11; Castro is quoted in Carlos Fuentes, "Primero de mayo en la Habana," *Política* 1, no. 2 (Mayo 15, 1960): 46–7.

29 "El preso 46788/60," *Política* 1, no. 9 (September 1, 1960): 5–20; "La sentencia de David Álfaro Siqueiros y Filomeno Mata, se finca en informes policiacos, en opiniones y noticias periodistas, relacionado esto con las finalidades y principales del Partido Comunista Mexicano," Heriberto Jara papers, box 47, folder 1530, AHUNAM; Julio Scherer García, *La Piel y La Entraña (Siqueiros)* (México: Era, 1965), 12.

30 Zolov, *Last Good Neighbor,* 113.

31 Olga Poblete to LCR, May 20, 1960, LCR papers, section "Conferencia Latinoamericana y Tricontinental," roll 24, AGN.

32 Convocatoria, por Lázaro Cárdenas, Domingos Vellasco and Alberto T. Casella, January 17, 1961, PCM archive, box 40, folder 20, CEMOS.

33 The Women's International Democratic Federation is often described as a Soviet front group, but scholars have cautioned that this is an oversimplification. Jadwiga Pieper Mooney, "Fighting Fascism and Forging New Political Activism: The Women's International Democratic Federation (WIDF) in the Cold War," in *De-Centering Cold War History: Local and Global Change,* ed. Jadwiga Pieper Mooney and Fabio Lanza (London: Routledge, 2013), 52–72.

34 Zolov, *Last Good Neighbor,* 119.

35 "Se informa en relación con el Partido Popular Socialista," December 20, 1960, DFS, VLT-versión pública, volume 5, AGN; "Lista de personas, agrupaciones, comités de auspicio, municipios, etc. que cooperaron para los trabajos de la Conferencia Latinoamericana por la Soberanía Nacional, la Emancipación Económica, y la Paz," April 1961, Clementina Batalla de Bassols papers, gallery 7, box 3, folder 10, AGN; Jorge L. Tamayo to Victor Chkhikvadze, January 20, 1961, LCR papers, section "Consejo Mundial de la Paz–II: Enero a Diciembre de 1961," roll 23, AGN; Memorandum, March 14, 1961, DFS, document 11-6-61, Cuauhtémoc Cárdenas Solórzano file—versión pública, AGN; The Argentine journalist was Sara Goldenberg, editor of the Argentine Peace Council's magazine, *Queremos Vivir.* "Informe sobre Sara Goldenberg," February 27, 1961, DFS, file 11-6-61, AGN.

36 Cuauhtémoc Cárdenas, interview with author, Berkeley, California, May 2010.

37 Memo, March 5, 1961, DFS archive, file 11-6-1961, gallery 1, AGN.

38 *Conferencia Latinoamericana Por La Soberanía Nacional, La Emancipación Económica y La Paz: Documentos* (México, 1961). For more on the Peace Conference, and the broader context of relations between Mexico and Cuba, see Renata Keller, *Mexico's Cold War: Cuba, the United States, and the Legacy of the Mexican Revolution* (New York: Cambridge University Press, 2015).

39 Carlos Fuentes, "Siete días con Lázaro Cárdenas," *Política* I, no. 23 (April 1, 1961): 16, 22.

40 The executive and coordinating committee consisted of Alonso Aguilar Monteverde, Narciso Bassols Batalla, Enrique Cabrera, Cuauhtémoc Cárdenas, Enrique González Pedrero, Braulio Maldonado and Manuel Terrazas. "Movimiento de Liberación Nacional, bases generales de organización aprobadas por unanimidad en la asamblea nacional celebrada en la ciudad de México, D.F., los días 4 y 5 de agosto de 1961," Heriberto Jara papers, box 47, folder 1523, AHUNAM; Memo, October 30, 1961, DFS, file 11-6-61, AGN; "Llamamiento al pueblo mexicano del Movimiento de Liberación Nacional," *Siempre!*, no. 429 (September 13, 1961): 132–3.

41 Cárdenas, *Apuntes, 1957-1966*, 213–16; Kate Doyle, "After the Revolution: Lázaro Cárdenas and the Movimiento de Liberación Nacional," *National Security Archive Electronic Briefing Book*, May 31, 2004, http://www.gwu.edu/~nsarchiv/NSAEBB /NSAEBB124/index.htm; Olga Pellicer de Brody, *México y La Revolución Cubana* (México: El Colegio de México, 1972), 91. Cárdenas rejected taking a salary for the Balsas River position. Cárdenas, *Apuntes, 1957-1966*, 270.

42 Zolov, *Last Good Neighbor*, 109, 137.

43 For more details, see Iber, *Neither Peace Nor Freedom*, 164–8. *Política* faced both harassment from the Mexican government and received subsidies from it, in an effort to steer the left. Zolov, *Last Good Neighbor*, 87–90.

44 Barry Carr, *Marxism and Communism in Twentieth-Century Mexico* (Lincoln: University of Nebraska Press, 1992), 227–8; Doyle, "After the Revolution."

45 On Lombardo Toledano see Daniela Spenser, *En combate: la vida de Lombardo Toledano* (Ciudad de México: Debate, 2018).

46 Heriberto Jara a Hugo Cuesta Jara, October 24, 1961, Heriberto Jara papers, box 47, folder 1522, AHUNAM; "Delegación Mexicana a la Conferencia de los Pueblos Latinoamericanos en La Habana, Cuba," January 23, 1962, file 11-6-62, gallery 1, AGN; Lázaro Cárdenas to Vicente Lombardo Toledano, July 9, 1962, Lázaro Cárdenas papers, section "Comité Mexicano por la paz, 1955–1963," roll 23, AGN. Carlos Maciel, *El Movimiento de Liberación Nacional: Vicisitudes y Aspiraciones* (México: Universidad Autónoma de Sinaloa, 1990), 143. "Declaraciones del Movimiento de Liberación Nacional sobre las posiciones del Partido Popular Socialista," June 18, 1962, Heriberto Jara papers, box 47, folder 1523, AHUNAM.

47 Circular, May 9, 1963, Heriberto Jara papers, box 47, folder 1523, AHUNAM; "El PCM ha hecho y seguirá haciendo sus mejores esfuerzos para vigorizar el MLN," n.d. [October 1963], PCM archive, box 48, folder 3, CEMOS; "El MLN reafirma su posición unitaria y denuncia la conducta provocadora de líderes del PC y del FEP," *El Día*, in PCM archive, box 49, folder 56, CEMOS. Cárdenas Solórzano, *Sobre Mis Pasos*, 61–3; Arnoldo Martínez Verdugo, *Historia Del Comunismo En México* (México: Grijalbo, 1985), 294–5. Memo, August 14, 1964, DFS archive, Cuauhtémoc Cárdenas Solórzano—versión pública, volume 3, AGN. The best guide to the MLN's internal fissures, precisely because it is an intensely partisan text, is Maciel, *El Movimiento de Liberación Nacional.*

48 Konder to LCR, May 2, 1961, LCR papers, section "Conferencia Latinoamericana y Tricontinental–2, roll 24, AGN.
49 Cárdenas, *Apuntes, 1957-1966*, 212. LCR to Fidel Castro, September 24, 1962 and LCR to Fidel Castro, September 25, 1962, LCR papers, section "Conferencia Latinoamericana y Tricontinental," roll 25, AGN.
50 "Comisión sobre la Conferencia Tricontinental," October 26–29, 1962, LCR papers, section "Conferencia Latinoamericana y Tricontinental–2," AGN.
51 The "Stalin Peace Prizes" were not technically issued by the World Peace Council, but were given by the Soviet government. The WPC handed out its own International Peace Prize until 1957 though a broadly similar list of people received the awards.
52 "Comité del pueblo chino por la defensa de la paz mundial," February 21, 1962, LCR papers, section "China," roll 26, AGN; Lázaro Cárdenas to Kuo Mo-jo, September 5, 1963, and "Puntos principles enunciados en el artículo titulado 'El origen y el desarrollo de las diferencias entre la dirección del P.C. de la URSS y nosotros," September 6, 1963, LCR papers, section "China," roll 26, AGN. See also Zolov, *Last Good Neighbor*, 256–65.
53 Bernal to LCR, December 14, 1962, LCR papers, section "Comité Mundial de la Paz," roll 23, AGN.
54 Representatives to Oscar Kambona, February 7, 1963, LCR papers, section "Conferencia Latinoamericana y Tricontinental–2," roll 24, AGN.
55 On the Brazilian conference, see "The Hemisphere: Where Did Everybody Go?" *Time*, April 5, 1963. (*Time*, as was typical of the time, was hewing close to official US government perspectives on the event.) Nkrumah to LCR, September 25, 1963 and LCR to Nkrumah, October 26, 1963, LCR papers, section "Conferencia Latinoamericana y Tricontinental–2," roll 24, AGN.
56 "Comité preparatario de la Conferencia de los Tres Continentes," El Cario, September 1–2, 1965," LCR papers, section "Conferencia Latinoamericana y Tricontinental–2," roll 24, AGN.
57 Quoted in Zolov, *Last Good Neighbor*, 264.

3

A Voice for the Yugoslavs in Latin America

Oscar Waiss and the Yugoslav-Chilean Connection

Agustín Cosovschi

Following its break with the USSR in 1948 and in the framework of a wider strategy to multiply its allies beyond the Eastern Bloc, socialist Yugoslavia set out in the early 1950s to establish relations with left-wing movements and governments in the non-European world. Latin America appeared then as a promising place to knit progressive alliances, especially due to the presence of a large Yugoslav diaspora in the countries of the Southern Cone and more generally because of the auspicious economic potential of countries such as Mexico and Argentina for the expansion of Yugoslav trade. Nonetheless, great physical distance and a general lack of knowledge of the Latin American setting constituted major obstacles for Belgrade's efforts, which made the hunt for strategic allies even more pressing. In that context, the unexpected development of relations with the Popular Socialist Party in Chile (*Partido Socialista Popular*, PSP) appeared as heaven-sent: after initial contacts in 1951, thanks to the Chileans' initiative, relations between the Yugoslav regime and the PSP developed spectacularly throughout the following decade, paving the way for Yugoslav endeavors in the region and also leaving a strong imprint on the history of Chilean socialism.

These and other similar stories notwithstanding, relations between Yugoslavia and Latin American countries have generally been disregarded by the existing literature. Authors working on Yugoslav foreign policy have often focused on Yugoslav relations with the United States, with the USSR and with African and Asian nations, especially through the lens of the Non-Aligned Movement (NAM) and the United Nations (UN) (Dimić 2014; Bogetić 2008; Mišković 2014; Rubinstein 1970; Jakovina 2011; 2003). Likewise, Yugoslav activities in Latin America have remained by and large disregarded by authors working on the Latin American Cold War, which has for the most part focused on the influence of the United States in the region, only secondarily analyzing the part played by the USSR and more rarely touching on connections with the Third World or NAM (Harmer 2011; Rabe 2012; Rupprecht 2015; Pettinà 2018; 2016; Hershberg 2007; Gleijeses 2002). Two remarkable exceptions are a recent article by Johanna Bockman concerning the influence of Yugoslav Marxism on Chilean and Peruvian economic thinking (Bockman 2019), and Joaquín Fernández's analysis of the

PSP's ideological transformations during the 1950s, which underlines the influence of Yugoslav thought on the ideas of Chilean socialists (Fernández 2017).

And yet, relations between Yugoslavia and Latin American countries can tell us much about the history of the Cold War. Particularly, Yugoslav efforts to foster connections with Latin American left-wing movements and parties can be most revealing. First, these relations shed light on unexplored aspects of Yugoslav foreign policy beyond the classic narratives of nonalignment. Second, they can also reveal largely unexplored dimensions of the history of the Latin American Marxist left, showing uncharted networks beyond the United States and the Soviet bloc, and involving actors that often lay outside of the scope of the state. More remarkably, these relations are also telling of the nature of the Third World as an international and transnational project: knitted on the basis of a yearning for political, social, and economic models that stepped away from both American hegemony and Soviet-type socialism, many of these connections, and the ideas that lay behind them, were essential for the rise of Third-Worldism after Bandung in 1955 and for the foundation of the Non-Aligned Movement in Belgrade in 1961.

In this chapter, I examine the development of connections between socialist Yugoslavia and Chilean socialists during the 1950s. For that, I mainly draw from Yugoslav archival sources, also relying on the writings of Chilean socialists and on the existing literature. My central claim is that the development of these relations was functional to the internal needs of the Chileans, as much as to the geopolitical aims of the Yugoslavs, which essentially attests to the decentered and plastic nature of Third World and nonaligned solidarities.

For the Yugoslavs, relations with the Chilean socialists offered an entry to the Latin American continent through one of the most active Marxist parties in the region, giving Belgrade not only a foothold in Latin America but also valuable information and contacts in a mostly unexplored region. In turn, for the Chileans, relations with Belgrade offered a Marxist model that stepped away from Soviet hegemony and integrated elements of nationalism and early Third-Worldism, thus allowing them to support their claim that the construction of socialism in Chile should not mechanically follow orthodox blueprints established by Moscow. This was especially important during the late 1940s and early 1950s, when Chilean socialists entered a process of radicalization following their disappointment with the conservative turn of the previous years and started to look for a model that lay in between American and Soviet schemes. Yugoslavia would in many ways fulfill those ideological, theoretical, and geopolitical needs, and it would remain a powerful point of reference for many socialists during the following years, particularly in the context of wider strategic discussions within the Chilean left.

In my analysis, I especially underline the figure of Oscar Waiss. A Marxist intellectual of Trotskyite background who was also inspired by Latin American nationalist and anti-imperialist thinking, Waiss was a leading figure in the formation of Chilean socialism and a key agent in the development of connections with the Yugoslav regime. His curiosity and sympathy toward the Yugoslav experience, as well as his traditionally critical stance vis-à-vis Moscow's foreign policy, made him a perfect instrument in the articulation of these networks. I especially focus on his book *Amanecer en Belgrado* (*Dawn in Belgrade*), published in 1956 and based on his experiences during a journey in Yugoslavia together with socialist senator Aniceto Rodríguez the previous year, which became one of the first and most exhaustive works about the Yugoslav socialist experience available to Latin American readers in Spanish language. Oscar Waiss's praise for the Yugoslav partisan struggle against fascism, his admiration for the Yugoslavs' courage and independence vis-à-vis the USSR and his strong advocacy for socialist self-management turned him into a voice for Yugoslav ideas in Latin America. Thus, I seek to underline the central role of intellectuals in the construction of rising nonaligned solidarities, as well as the importance of books and other cultural artifacts as instruments to disseminate the ideas, values, and images on which these networks were built.

Drawing from Waiss's writings, from Yugoslav sources concerning his sojourn in Yugoslavia and from his letters with Yugoslav representatives, I argue that this role as a spokesman for the Yugoslavs was much in tune with the Yugoslavs' geopolitical needs and also allowed him to underpin an original Marxist discourse that responded to his radical, anti-authoritarian, and anti-Soviet leanings. I also claim that his admiration for the Yugoslav model was especially meaningful in the context of the internal struggles of Chilean socialism in the late 1950s, when Waiss advocated for radical and popular revolutionary politics against the increasingly peaceful strategy of Chilean socialism.[1]

Hence, by analyzing the creation and development of these connections and emphasizing their usefulness not only to the Yugoslavs' geopolitical goals but also to the Chilean socialists' internal political necessities, I attempt to show the two-sided appeal of international and transnational connections that were at the basis of the creation of Third-World and nonaligned solidarities. Contrary to authors such as Guy Laron who have interpreted the "Third World" as a ruse by semi-peripheral countries to profit from peripheral countries (2014), I contend that shifting and widening our focus to actors laying outside the sphere of the state shows that Third World and nonaligned solidarities were efficient precisely because they had effects beyond the domain of pure economic and geopolitical interest. This story suggests, on the contrary, that these networks of solidarity, and the ideas, discourses, and values that lay behind them, responded to the overlapping necessities of the diverse actors involved, however unequal or asymmetric.

Crossing Paths: The Yugoslavs Meet the Chileans

After the split with the USSR in 1948, facing not only economic isolation but also the immediate threat of a Soviet invasion, Yugoslavia set out to develop an autonomous foreign policy mainly with the aim to secure political, economic, and military assistance from Western powers and particularly from the United States (Jakovina 2003; Rajak 2014). In parallel, Belgrade started to develop its first systematic contacts with recently decolonized Asian and African nations on the basis of a nascent neutralism, thus setting the grounds for an international network of alliances that would later lead to the creation of the Non-Aligned Movement (Rajak 2014; Mišković 2009; Jakovina 2011). In that context, Yugoslavia's policy of establishing wider and stronger connection with governments and progressive movements in the non-European world also reached Latin America, a region of special interest not only because of its economic potential but also due to the presence of a large Yugoslav diaspora (Pajović 1995; Rubinstein 1970: 94).

In spite of growing interest for the region, after having sent two official delegations to the continent in 1946 and 1949 in an attempt to broaden political and economic relations and having also appointed a new ambassador to head the cherished delegation in Buenos Aires,[2] Yugoslavia's ambitions in Latin America found numerous obstacles. On the one hand, the great physical distance that divided both regions, as well as the general lack of knowledge of the local context, posed logistical and economic obstacles to Belgrade's plans. On the other hand, the strong supremacy of Moscow-oriented communist parties in left-wing politics, and the weakness of many social-democratic parties such as the Argentine Socialist Party, made it that the Yugoslavs would not have it easy in finding local partners to develop their actions. And yet, an encouraging sign came in the early 1950s from the distant Chile, where a group derived from a split within the Chilean socialists, the Popular Socialist Party, approached the Yugoslav diplomatic representation in Santiago with the intention to develop closer relations.

In many ways, Chilean socialists constituted almost an ideal partner for the Yugoslavs. The product of a year-long political construction dating back to the times of the ephemerous Chilean Socialist Republic of 1932, their party had a history of active institutional participation through the Popular Front governments of the 1930s and a fairly good electoral record. However, with the conservative turn of the 1940s, the party had lost much of its drive and its support in the ballots and had also become riven with internal divisions. As a result, the Socialist Party had even lost its official denomination to a lesser right-wing faction that decided to support president Gabriel González Videla' anticommunist laws in 1948, having now to operate under the name of Popular Socialist Party (*Partido Socialista Popular*, PSP). Later on, under the leadership of younger and more radical Raúl Ampuero, the party's decision to support the populist leader Carlos Ibáñez del Campo for the 1952 elections in exchange for the suppression of anticommunist laws and with the hope of attaining more progressive economic policies also provoked significant detachments from the party, among others that of Salvador Allende, who would become the presidential candidate for the parallel Social Party of Chile (Walker 1990; Drake 1992).

Unsurprisingly, this time of crisis also brought ideological changes in the party's ranks. The disappointment caused by the conservative ramifications of the Popular Front experience during the 1940s led to a redefinition of the PSP's ideas in increasingly radical terms. The party launched then a strong criticism of the *etapismo* advocated by the communists, which posited the historical need to carry out the tasks of the democratic-bourgeois stage as a precondition to the socialist revolution and therefore promoted an alliance with bourgeois forces such as the center Radical Party (Casals Araya 2010; Rubio Apiolaza 2003). Concurrently, as analyzed extensively by Joaquín Fernández (2017), the PSP's discourse started including significant nationalist overtones: faced with the rise of nationalist popular governments in neighboring Argentina and Brazil, and assessing positively developments in Guatemala and revolutionary Bolivia, the party increasingly insisted on the need to imprint a national and anti-imperialist character to Latin American revolutions and compete with populist forces for the support of the masses. As stated then by leading party intellectual Oscar Waiss in his seminal work *Nationalism and Socialism in Latin America*, published by the party's press in 1954:

> One cannot lead a crusade of such a magnitude, nor can one inspire trust in the masses, if one does not recognize the dynamics of the movement. And the most important task of these parties (and the hardest one) consists in recognizing with precision the national and popular tendencies to interpret them objectively, in the most adequate moment and with voices of order, that is, chants of struggle that represent the true desire and real necessities of the working masses.[3]

In this context of ideological and political reorientation, the PSP's shift to nationalist positions included the adoption of early forms of Third-Worldism and strong expressions of solidarity toward movements of national liberation in Asia and Africa. As underlined by Fernández, "the socialists manifested their support for movements that were waging wars of decolonization in Algeria and South Asia, as well as for Nasserism in Egypt" (Fernández 2017: 36). Thus, the party conceived the emancipation of Latin America and its struggle for socialism as a process that was inextricably linked to struggles for national liberation and socialism in other geographies of the rising Third World. As stated by Waiss:

> The struggle of the Latin American peoples for their liberation is a part of the world struggle of workers for socialism, and there will always exist a necessary bond between those who fight for the same cause to find a common revolutionary language. . . . In this sense, the agreements of the Rangoon conference in Asia, the achievements of the workers' state in Yugoslavia, or the revolts in our continent, they are part of a whole, which is the struggle for socialism.[4]

But the socialists' solidarity with national liberation movements in Asia and Africa was a symptom of a larger quest for political inspiration abroad. The party was especially interested in foreign revolutionary experiences that offered alternative paths to socialism, away from solutions championed by Moscow. As stated by Drake in a classic study on Chilean socialism, "during Ampuero's reconstruction [of the party], socialists were restlessly seeking for a model between the Radicals and the Communists, between the United States and the Soviet Union" (1992: 264). In this context of ideological and political reorientation, the Yugoslav experience started to elicit much interest among Chilean socialists, who not only expressed their support for Yugoslavia after the break with the Soviets in 1948 but also drew much inspiration from Yugoslav ideas during the following years, among other things publishing texts by Yugoslav authors such as Edvard Kardelj and Boris Ziherl in their party press, praising the national character of Yugoslav socialism and acclaiming Belgrade's autonomy from Moscow. Hence, in the early 1950s, when the time became ripe for the Yugoslavs to explore Latin America in their quest for extra-European alliances, the Chileans' interest for the Yugoslav experience became the basis for a strong partnership that would extend for years to come.

According to Yugoslav sources, the first contacts between the Yugoslav regime and the PSP took place in August 1951, through the Yugoslav delegation in Santiago. In a note to Belgrade, Yugoslav representative Lazar Lilić described his meeting with Ampuero and stated that the Chileans had not only expressed their admiration "for the stance of our party leadership in their defense of our country's independence," but also their wish to "become better acquainted with the theoretical and practical work of the KPJ [Yugoslav Communist Party]."[5] Initial contacts elicited much interest among the Yugoslavs, who saw here an opportunity to expand their endeavors in Latin America. As underlined some time later by the Yugoslav delegation in Santiago, cooperation with the PSP could lead to a strengthening of Yugoslav influence in the region. This was stated in a note to Belgrade from 1953, where it was suggested that formal ties should be established between the PSP and the Socialist Alliance of the Working People of Yugoslavia (SSRNJ). Successor to the Popular Front, the SSRNJ was an umbrella organization of the communist regime that grouped Yugoslav sociopolitical organizations in the country but which with time became also responsible for establishing links with progressive forces abroad. As recommended by the Yugoslav authorities in Chile, collaboration could start with a visit of the PSP delegates to Yugoslavia. Such a visit could be very useful for the development of Yugoslav positions not only in Chile but more generally in South America:

> I hold that the experience that the members of the PSP could take from our country would have particular importance, and that it would surpass the limits of Chile, considering that socialists in Bolivia are very weak, that in Argentina they are heavily pursued, but that the leadership of the PSP shows an indebted socialist solidarity towards movements in neighboring countries. Even more reason to do it as it seems that now, with the growth of the PSP, conditions have emerged to establish contacts with leading movements in Latin America as those that exist with movements in Europe and Asia.[6]

The relation with Chilean socialists was thus seen as having key importance for the Yugoslavs, as it had the potential to pave the way for them to jump into a region that had until then remained rather unknown and inaccessible.[7] The next year, when a Yugoslav mission headed by Jakob Blažević visited Chile and the PSP's members were invited to dine at the Yugoslav embassy, arrangements were made for Veljko Vlahović, the president of the Commission for International Relations of the SSRNJ, to travel to Latin America to visit the PSP. The proposition came from the Chilean socialists themselves, and the Yugoslav representation in Santiago insisted that the travel should be settled directly between them and the SSRNJ.[8] As evoked by Oscar Waiss in his memoires, the PSP leaders were delighted by the numerous ideological agreements that they found with the Yugoslavs:

> We had in common the most severe condemnation of Stalinism and its methods of fraud and intimidation, the aim not to recognize any ideological dogmas, opposition to sectarianism and a humanist awareness to deal with the most diverse aspects of social reality, from art to revolutionary action. The more we delved with

Blažević into the analysis of the historical process, the more agreements we found between his thinking and ours.[9]

In late 1954, Veljko Vlahović finally came to Chile in a tour that was announced as a general visit to the country in order to avoid any suspicion or conflict and which also extended to Argentina, Uruguay, and Brazil.[10] In conversation with other leading members of the SSRNJ after his return, Vlahović recalled his conversations with the socialists in Chile and he underlined the many virtues of the PSP, claiming that the Chileans were "the most interesting [political force] in Latin America," and that their strength and character were astonishing. He also commended their discipline, and much like Waiss, underlined the many ideological coincidences that bound them to Belgrade, claiming that "their views are absolutely identical to ours."[11]

As attested by archival sources and as described by Waiss in his works, Vlahović's visit helped to strengthen this blossoming friendship between the Chileans and the Yugoslavs. But more specifically, these first meetings also encouraged Belgrade to develop plans for a follow-up in Yugoslavia. Accordingly, Aniceto Rodríguez, back then secretary general of the PSP, and Oscar Waiss, party intellectual and responsible for the development international relations in the organization, would travel to the Balkans the following year in a visit that would turn out to be not only a significant step for Yugoslav policy in Latin America but also a fascinating episode in the political and intellectual history of Chilean socialism.

Socialist Self-Management from Within: Oscar Waiss Visits Yugoslavia

After Veljko Vlahović's visit strengthened contacts in Chile, the Yugoslavs were persuaded of the need to increase their efforts in Latin America. A letter sent to the Yugoslav delegation in Chile in early 1955 attests to this objective: weeks after Vlahović's return to Belgrade, it informed the delegation that "the Commission [for International Relations of the SSRNJ] has discussed the necessity and importance of establishing firmer relations with socialist parties and workers movements in Latin America," and discussed the idea of inviting a delegation of Chilean socialists to Yugoslavia, covering part of their expenses.[12] Time had come thus for the Chileans to visit Yugoslavia, and senator Aniceto Rodríguez and party intellectual Oscar Waiss were the ones chosen to tour the country in 1955.

In Chile, the context could not have been better for such a visit. After breaking with the Ibáñez administration in 1953 because of its increasingly conservative leanings, the PSP had taken an ever more radical turn in a trajectory that scholars such as Walker have labeled as its "Leninization" (1990). Conducting a critical revision of their earlier strategy of alliances and openly denouncing centrist political forces such as the Radical Party, the popular socialists adopted the idea of building a "national revolutionary state" and started rejecting collaboration with bourgeois forces, taking a path toward a redefinition of Chilean socialism's identity in increasingly radical terms (Fernández 2017; Rubio Apiolaza 2003; Drake 1992: 278). In this process of ideological transformation, Yugoslavia was seen as a novel and unorthodox experiment that could offer new and original inspiration.

Moreover, party intellectual Oscar Waiss was an ideal participant for such a trip. A Marxist thinker of Jewish background and earlier Trotskyite leaning, Waiss was a lawyer and a journalist. Traditionally very critic of the Soviet brand of centralized socialism and Soviet foreign policy, as well as sensitive toward Latin American forms of popular nationalism, he was wary of all that reeked of bureaucratism.[13] All of this made him particularly sensitive and open to Yugoslav ideas of workers' self-management, and his acquaintance of Veljko Vlahović in 1954, with whom he started to share an intense epistolary exchange,[14] made him a perfect instrument for the articulation of relations between Chilean socialists and the Yugoslav regime.

Waiss and Rodriguez's visit to Yugoslavia is thoroughly described in the book *Amanecer en Belgrado*, written by the former during his stay at a prisoners camp in Pisagua where he was sent by the Ibáñez administration after his return from Europe and published in 1956 by Prensa Latinoamericana, the PSP's press.[15] The book would become one of the main works on the Yugoslav experience for Latin American audiences and an influential piece in the political thinking of Chilean socialism (Fernández 2017). Moreover, Yugoslav sources contain considerable information about the Chileans' sojourn in Yugoslavia, showing their conversations with leading members of the Yugoslav regime throughout their stay. These talks reveal the strategic value that the Yugoslavs attributed to these guests as an entry door and information source not only to Chile but to the whole of Latin America. They also show the extent to which Waiss and Rodriguez were interested in, and inspired by, Yugoslav self-management, and how much of Waiss's book was almost a straight translation of their conversations with the Yugoslavs under a drive of strong enthusiasm for the Yugoslav socialist model.

Already during the first days after their arrival in Yugoslavia, Rodríguez and Waiss had talks with Yugoslav leaders in which they discussed the history of the PSP and its current situation. In conversation at the SSRNJ headquarters, they informed the Yugoslavs of the particularities of the Chilean political, economic, and social context, and also responded to their questions concerning the Latin American landscape. Waiss especially commended then the policies of the Bolivian nationalist revolutionary government, particularly its land policy, which he praised in opposition to what he perceived as a failed and shattered revolutionary experience in Mexico.[16] Moreover, the Chileans underlined the hegemonic role of American capitals and the concentration of the property of land in Chile. They also underlined that for them, the Yugoslavs' dictum about each country having to create its own path to socialism was most valued: Chile too, they claimed, had to conduct its own socialist experience without attempting to copy foreign revolutionary models, not even the Yugoslav one.[17]

Despite Waiss's initial insistence on the need to avoid copying foreign models, his book suggests that his fascination for Yugoslav socialism was sheer and that his experience in Yugoslavia marked a fateful moment in his ideological trajectory. The Chileans' activities during the trip and their impressions are thoroughly described in *Amanecer en Belgrado*, which remains until today one of the most extensive testimonies of foreign left-wing militants' experiences in socialist Yugoslavia. In these pages, Waiss describes their month-long sojourn in the Balkan country as one of wonder, full of fascinating encounters and cultural discoveries, but also of surprise and enlightenment, as the Chileans were eager to learn about self-management as a more open, democratic, and yet also efficient form of socialism.

The visitors were interested in learning about self-management as it was applied in the cities and in the villages, in the industrial world as well as in rural production. The unique character of Yugoslav socialism, held Waiss, lay precisely in the dominant role of the *commune* as the primary economic and social cell of the nation, as it had been recognized first by Marx, and then by leading Yugoslav theoretician Edvard Kardelj.[18] Hence, during their visit, the Chileans were many times taken to visit self-managed communities and factories in the republics of Slovenia, Bosnia, Croatia, Serbia, and Macedonia, and spent much time in long and instructive conversations discussing the minutiae of the Yugoslav system with local representatives in cities such as Belgrade, Rijeka, and Split.

Waiss was fascinated by the ways of self-management in local communities, which he saw in action in places like Kranje in Slovenia and Rijeka in Croatia and by the intricacies of the delegate system of political representation.[19] As someone who was especially concerned about the peasant question in his home country, the author highlighted his experiences visiting rural communities in Lazaropolje in Macedonia and Zreče in Slovenia, where he lauded the success of joint collective agrarian enterprises, organizations that were socialist in nature and nevertheless gave their members the freedom to join the enterprise or remain apart.[20] For Waiss, the economic and social achievements of the system provided enough evidence of the superiority of self-management: "This is not dry theory on paper," he stated, "it is life, which we have been able to witness as it glides pleasantly."[21] The virtues of self-management, claimed Waiss, were especially important for Latin Americans, who lived in a continent where the trends toward centralization and bureaucratization were stronger than elsewhere. Hence the value of the Yugoslav model, which involved "enterprises that act freely but are still, nevertheless, under the command of the collective."[22]

During his tour around Yugoslavia, Waiss not only had the chance to visit the farms, the factories and the city halls, but he could also get acquainted with the schooling system and visit museums, old palaces, and monasteries. The journey also allowed him to engage in dialogue with the common people in the country and learn about the experience of Sephardic Jews in Sarajevo, partisan women in Kranje, and young students in Zagreb. The experience not only left an imprint on Waiss's memory by virtue of the institutional solutions that the Yugoslavs had developed for their social and economic challenges, but also because of what he perceived to be a remarkable moral and human dimension in Yugoslavs socialism, and in the Yugoslavs themselves. In the book, the author described long and deep conversations with the Yugoslavs, where he extolled their discipline and courage as great heroes molded by their fight against fascism, he also commended their warm temperament and their sense of humor, and he celebrated their character and their moral values. About Veljko Vlahović, for instance, he wrote:

Veljko Vlahovic [*sic*] is a Montenegrin giant who lost a leg fighting for freedom in Spain. As a young man, he was a great sportsman. He was in Chile in 1954 and left there unforgettable memories among the socialists by virtue of his culture, his theoretical honesty and his personal friendliness. He has a childish gaze that reflects a pure soul. It is men like this who have been able to forge a great nation on its way to the future.[23]

This quote is revealing in multiple senses. First, it shows the admiration caused by the Yugoslavs and their revolutionary ethics, which Waiss especially appreciated. Second, the reference to Spain is particularly meaningful here. As Kirsten Weld has shown (2018), the Spanish Civil War had a deep impact on the lives and imaginaries of Chilean socialism, with many socialist leaders and intellectuals having committed for the cause of the republic during the war and advocated for its exiles after 1939. Vlahović's life story, and, more generally, the fact that several of the leading members of the Yugoslav Communist Party had participated in the antifascist struggle in Spain, was repeatedly highlighted by Waiss in this and other writings, and was surely valued by the Chilean socialists as a testimony of Yugoslavia's commitment to internationalism. Complementarily, the quote is also telling of the Yugoslavs' success in fashioning an image of national unity before the world: Waiss's use of the concept of "nation" in singular, and also his praise for the peace and camaraderie that the Yugoslav peoples had forged in war, reveals that he accepted the official discourse of the communist regime concerning the intricate national question in Yugoslavia, which posited the common struggle of the Yugoslav nations against fascism as the basis for their "Brotherhood and Unity," the primary founding myth of Yugoslav socialism (Wachtel 1998; Haug 2012).

Toward the end of the book, Waiss also described their meeting with Tito in Split and celebrated him as a hero for the world, extolling Yugoslav socialism once and again as a democratic alternative to the Soviet system. He also underlined the ideological openness of the Yugoslavs and applauded their efforts to merge their struggle with progressive movements in the rising Third World, in opposition to the classic and orthodox views of the Soviets:

> The Yugoslavs know that their own socialist movement has developed in opposition to the concepts and rules advanced both by the Kominformists, as well as by the social-democrats, and that new currents of thought are sprouting in Asia and Latin America, not even mentioning the tendencies that arise among European socialist and communist parties.[24]

The Yugoslavs' efforts, claimed Waiss, were the most promising enterprise for the future of socialism around the world:

> Much like they strive to fight bureaucratic trends on the inside, they try on the international stage to end ideological hegemonism, so to encourage more favorable conditions for a regrouping of the working class in the world. In this task, as a result of their long experience, they will meet the support and the encouragement of men, groups and parties from all corners of the world, who will become more and more numerous, turning into an avalanche.[25]

As documented in Yugoslav sources, the Chileans held conversations with leading members of the Yugoslav regime again before leaving the country in order to ask some final questions and clear some of their doubts concerning self-management.[26] These conversations were crucial for Waiss and Rodríguez to gather useful and precise data, and they also show some of their final impressions after a thirty-day sojourn.

Remarkably, transcriptions show that much of the information that Waiss included in his book was taken straight from the Yugoslavs' statements, with almost verbatim passages. A good example is their conversation with Svetozar Vukmanović-Tempo, in which the Yugoslav leader talked to the Chileans about Yugoslav prewar dependency on foreign capitals, the calamitous state of their economy after the war and the great merits of industrialization under socialism, which is all reproduced with extreme closeness in the book.[27] Moreover, the general laudatory tone of the book and especially the fact that much of Yugoslav life was depicted in it through direct translations and paraphrases from the Yugoslavs themselves, together with images and descriptions that portray the Yugoslavs under an extremely positive light, make *Amanecer en Belgrado* seem almost as a propaganda material for Spanish audiences made for (and to a certain extent made by) socialist Yugoslavia. The value of such a material should not be underestimated: in the context of the 1950s, when the Yugoslav regime found itself in competition with the Soviets and other socialist powers such as the Czechoslovaks and the Chinese for influence over the rising Third World, Waiss's book could be extremely helpful to contest accusations of revisionism launched by Moscow and Beijing, and it could upgrade Yugoslavia's image among Latin American readers.

Yet, Waiss's advocacy for Yugoslavia should not be interpreted as the mere result of Yugoslav calculation, as the Chileans themselves were especially motivated by what they had found in the Yugoslav experience and were enthusiastic about the value of such a model for their own struggle in Latin America. In their final conversations with the Yugoslavs, the Chileans claimed that what had impressed them the most was the Yugoslavs' "trust in the masses" and "how easily you try one solution and then jump to the next if the first one does not work, and your drive to include the masses in that process."[28] Moreover, Waiss highlighted the common nature that united the Chileans and the Yugoslavs by claiming that they had encountered "a temperament that is similar to ours" in Yugoslavia. And most important, he especially underlined that getting to know the Yugoslav experience had allowed them "to reflect upon our own mistakes," and even more remarkably, that they had been able to "confirm our methods in action."[29] These were significant declarations in the context of the mid-1950s, when the PSP was going through a deep process of reflection and critical discussion concerning revolutionary strategies, models, and methods.

All in all, Waiss and Rodriguez's visit to Yugoslavia as depicted in the book and as reflected in Yugoslav sources appears as a moving experience through which the Chileans not only created closer strategic relations with the Yugoslavs but also seemed to find proof that a different kind of socialism was possible than the one implemented in the Soviet Union, with implications for their own political strategy. In particular, Waiss's words attest to his amazement with socialist Yugoslavia and his enthusiasm about a better and brighter future for the working masses in the world. The mechanics of socialist self-management seemed complicated, he understood, but he himself had seen the system working. "Since I came back from Yugoslavia," he said, "people ask me: but does all of that work? And the truth is that it works. They have achieved it. I don't know how, but they have."[30]

Looking Up to Belgrade: The Yugoslav Model and the Internal Struggles of the Chilean Socialists

During the following years, relations/the relation between the PSP and the Yugoslav regime developed impressively, involving further reciprocal visits and joint editorial endeavors through Prensa Latinoamericana, but also initiatives in cultural cooperation, frequent communication between both sides of the Atlantic, and partnership in the framework of the Non-Aligned Movement.

Leading representatives of the Yugoslav regime continued to visit Chile during the late 1950s. In January 1959, for instance, the Yugoslavs were invited to participate in the congress of the Chilean Trade Unions Youth and in the national conference of the United Confederation of Workers' (CUT, *Central Unida de los Trabajadores*). It was decided that Stane Kavčič, president of the Slovene Republican Parliament, would be sent as a delegate. He was accompanied by Stane Južnič, expert on Latin American affairs, to perform as a translator and guide.[31] The visit was later corresponded with the coming of a Chilean socialist leader Clodomiro Almeyda to the fourth congress of the Confederation of Trade Unions of Yugoslavia (SSJ, *Savez sindikata Jugoslavije*) in April 1959.[32] Later that year, a mission of goodwill was sent to tour Latin America, including leading members of the SSRNJ such as Vladimir Popović, Svetozar Vukmanović Tempo, and Asher Deleon, who were again accompanied by Južnič. Tempo was then the president of the SSJ, and Popović, much like Vlahović, was also a former fighter in the Spanish Civil War. According to the account of the Yugoslav delegates and the discussions that ensued in their meetings, the tour was very useful for the establishment of contacts with Latin American socialist movements and to continue cementing a bond with the Chileans.[33] Moreover, several leading figures of Chilean socialism visited Yugoslavia during those years, among others Secretary General Raúl Ampuero, who toured the country with his wife in 1957,[34] and the new secretary general, Salomón Corbalán, who came in April 1958 to attend the seventh Party Congress of the League of Communists of Yugoslavia.[35]

Moreover, the friendship between the Chilean socialists and the Yugoslav regime developed against the background of an expanding relation between Chile and socialist Yugoslavia in several domains. Among other things, this expressed itself in the rise of trade between both countries all throughout the 1950s, with Yugoslav exports to Chile increasing fourfold between 1955 and 1959, going from 34 million dinars to 139 million dinars.[36] During those years Yugoslavia also started to develop a stronger cultural policy abroad, especially through the work of the Federal Commission for Cultural Relations with Foreign Countries, which became attached to the Ministry of Foreign Education and Culture in 1958 and allowed for the Yugoslavs to develop a systematic policy of culture and propaganda.[37] The Yugoslav regime gave significant importance to Latin America in these endeavors, making Chile one of its more important aims in the region and attempting to make the most of their friendship with the socialists, as well as to take advantage of the presence of a large Yugoslav diaspora in the country. As a result, Chilean students would be among the most benefited by Yugoslav scholarships in Latin America, together with Bolivians and Mexicans.[38] Moreover, the Chilean-Yugoslav Cultural Institute in Santiago, an institution meant for the diffusion of Yugoslav culture among wider audiences and often involving Chileans of Yugoslav background, received significant financial support from Belgrade. The Yugoslav regime intended to use this cultural institution to facilitate its political goals and was thus glad to see Federico Klein, a socialist, appointed as its director in Santiago.

The friendship between Chilean socialists and the Yugoslav regime would develop well into the 1960s and 1970s, and a shared desire for resistance against both American and Soviet pressures, as well as a strong sympathy for Third World progressive movements, would become the basis for common positionings in the Cold War. Chilean socialists would be among the few Latin American participants to witness the creation of NAM, participating as a party under an observer status in the Belgrade conference of 1961. Chile would become an observer country in the Cairo conference of 1964, only to enter as a full member of the movement under Allende in 1973.

But in the meantime, the Chilean political landscape went through deep changes, with heavy consequences on the political configuration of Chilean socialism and a number of readjustments that had direct consequences on the fate of Oscar Waiss. In 1956, as a result of the Ibañez administration's increasingly repressive policy toward the workers' movement, the PSP and the dissenting Socialist Party of Chile joined the Communist Party and other lesser organizations in the Front of Popular Action (FRAP, *Frente de Acción Popular*). The merger of the Chilean left would go further with the Congress of Unity of July 1957 in which Allende's and Ampuero's factions would reunite, thus leaving behind a year-long history of division within Chilean socialism. In the presidential elections of 1958, Allende would end up second to Jorge Alessandri by less than three points, inaugurating thus a new and booming period in the electoral history of the Chilean Marxist left. This translated into the socialists' ever more open integration to the rules of the institutional system under the banner of the "peaceful road to socialism," a strategy primarily promoted by the communists, which the socialists criticized in theory, but accepted in practice (Casals Araya 2010: 84–6).

These transformations, however, translated into the increasing exclusion of Oscar Waiss and his positions from the party, as he remained overtly critical of the conciliatory strategy adopted by the Chilean left. Remarkably, sources show that his experience in Yugoslavia and his connections with the Yugoslavs played an important part in this story.

As Waiss himself wrote in his memoirs, his visit to Yugoslavia had been a meaningful moment in his political and ideological trajectory. His plead for a radical popular politics and his conviction that the socialist revolution needed to draw from nationalism and anti-imperialism, while at the same time preserving the leading role of the working masses, had been shaped by the socialists' experiences during the 1940s and by the rise of anti-imperialist struggles in the Third World. But these ideas were reinforced by what Waiss saw in Yugoslavia. According to him, he became ever more convinced of the need for radical politics after his return from Belgrade:

> The [socialist] party's program, approved in 1947 and written by a commission headed by Eugenio González, was not exactly Leninist, although it did already orient itself timidly toward the denunciation of reformist hesitations. I believe that the new orientation came from my ceaseless agitation in the party's press and from the concepts put forward in my book "Nationalism and Socialism in Latin America". . . . The final definition derived from the tour that we did with Aniceto Rodriguez in Yugoslavia. In my interventions during that trip I insisted that our party was different from all other fellow parties in other countries due to its Marxist revolutionary character, and this was underlined by Aniceto in each occasion that he had. From then onwards, the whole Central Committee held this position, which unfortunately was far from corresponding to the essence of the party and to the quality of its militants.[39]

During the following years, despite seeing himself as one of the PSP's ideological guides, Waiss found himself more and more in dissent with the party's official line. Already after his return from Yugoslavia, he was excluded from the Central Committee by Ampuero's initiative. Later, his support for Eugenio González as a secretary general against Salomón Corbalán and his criticisms against resolutions taken in the Congress of Unity would make him distance himself even further from the leadership, launching strong criticisms against Allende, Corbalán, and Ampuero in the following years.

In this context, Waiss would take ideological and symbolic refuge in Yugoslavia, which he saw as a true popular and revolutionary experience, and he would strive to keep afloat his friendship with the Yugoslavs in spite of his loss of support at home. In 1957, after the party congress that sealed the unity of the socialists, Waiss set off to Europe on a long trip, where he had meetings with left-wing leading figures such as Marceau Pivert and Michel Pablo, and also took the opportunity to visit Yugoslavia again.[40] He had arranged this trip beforehand through his regular exchanges with Vlahović, letting him know of his disappointment with current developments in Chile and expressing his need to take some distance from the party.[41] In one of the letters, he expressed with particular zeal his need to go back to Yugoslavia at this time of crisis, claiming:

> I do not think that I exaggerate if I tell you that, much like the Muslims do their pilgrimage to Mecca, this is for me a true pilgrimage to a country where the socialism for which I struggle is being built and, above all, put to practice.[42]

By 1960, Waiss position in the party had become ever more untenable. In spite of his long trajectory in the ranks of Chilean socialism, he was facing growing isolation. In this moment of disorientation, again, he could not help sharing his thoughts and concerns with Vlahović. In one of his letters, Waiss stated his persuasion that the socialist strategy in Chile was incurring in sectarian mistakes by aiming to conquer the workers through elections instead of seeking the revolutionary mobilization of the wider popular masses, "as it had happened in Yugoslavia," and more recently in Cuba. "They are centrists," he claimed about his comrades, and said:

> The Workers' Front, done like this, without any explanation, without any grounds and without a long-term strategy, reduced to a momentary tactic, allows them to show themselves as revolutionaries without [actually] reaching revolution, and in the meantime to keep some electoral positions.[43]

By the end of the letter, Waiss expressed his fears of being expelled from the party together with other dissidents. He ended his message with a remarkable expression of devotion for Yugoslav socialism: "At least, comrade, if you ever learn about my expulsion, you will know that I am not any old Đilas, but instead, a true Marxist who wants to live revolution, and not only talk about it."[44]

Vlahović responded to Waiss with some caution, claiming that it was the Yugoslavs' policy not to meddle in the internal affairs of other socialist movements. Nevertheless, he transmitted his concern and sorrow for these ongoing problems and he expressed his sympathy for the difficult situation that he was going through, encouraging him to be strong in face of such setbacks which were also part of the struggle for socialism. In his final lines, he expressed more clearly than ever his appreciation for a man that he himself considered to be a voice for the Yugoslavs in Latin America:

> For me personally, and for our workers' movement, you will still be the man who has collaborated with sincerity and carried out enormous efforts for our mutual understanding, so that progressive forces in your country, and not only in your country, know the reality of socialist Yugoslavia. I will always cherish this.[45]

Waiss responded to this letter with a new message to Vlahović, making clear that he feared for his position in the party, but that he had not been expelled from the organization.[46] The following year, however, his situation became ever more serious, finally leading to his expulsion in August 1961. From then onward, much like the Yugoslavs themselves had done in their darkest hour, Waiss would have to take an uncertain path to find a place under the sun.

Conclusions

In this chapter, I have examined the development of connections between socialist Yugoslavia and Chilean socialists during the 1950s. Drawing from Yugoslav archival sources and also relying on a number of writings and letters, I have shown that this Chilean-Yugoslav connection, developed initially by the Chileans' initiative, developed impressively during the 1950s and translated into reciprocal visits, joint cultural initiatives and collaboration in the framework of the Non-Aligned Movement during the following years. These efforts gave the Yugoslavs what was probably their most solid position in Latin America and also left deep imprints in the history of Chilean socialism during a time of ideological and theoretical transformation. In my analysis, I have especially focused on party intellectual Oscar Waiss and his transformative experience as a traveler in Yugoslavia in 1955, which attests to the impact that Yugoslav socialism had on Chilean left-wing politics and to the evolution of Yugoslav policy in Latin America. As I have shown Waiss's experiences in Yugoslavia constituted a fateful moment in his ideological trajectory, reinforcing a leaning for radical popular politics that drew inspiration from developments in diverse geographies of the rising Third World.

My central argument has been that relations between Chilean socialists and the Yugoslav regime thrived as a result of overlapping geopolitical and internal necessities. For the Chileans, socialist Yugoslavia provided a model that stepped away from Soviet hegemony and integrated elements of nationalism and early Third-Worldism, while simultaneously discrediting Soviet claims that there was an exclusive road toward socialism, and that the road necessarily followed Moscow's guidelines. For the Yugoslavs, the friendship with the Chileans not only gave them an entry to a continent where contacts were scarce but also provided them with valuable information concerning the local political landscape. Remarkably, the Yugoslavs found a particularly strong support in Oscar Waiss, whose radical stances and fascination with the Yugoslav model turned him into somewhat of a voice for the Yugoslavs in Latin America. As seen throughout the pages of his book *Amanecer en Belgrado* and in other writings, including his correspondence with Yugoslav leaders, Waiss found in socialist Yugoslavia not only a much looked-for model for radical and popular revolutionary politics but also a moral inspiration, which became even more significant in the context of the internal struggles of Chilean socialism during the late 1950s and early 1960s.

By examining the development of these connections, I have attempted to shed light on certain dimensions of Cold War political and intellectual history that have by and large remained uncharted. Moreover, I have attempted to shed light on the central role of intellectuals and books in the dissemination of the ideas, values, and images on which rising nonaligned solidarities were built. Perhaps more important, I have also attempted to show that the efficiency of the Third-Worldism and nonaligned politics was often based on the intersected elective affinities of diverse state and non-state actors involved in its construction, however unequal or asymmetric these actors may have been. Thus, the story of the Yugoslav-Chilean connection suggests that we must strive to analyze the history of the Third World project and NAM focusing not only on state-to-state diplomacy, nor exclusively through the lens of pragmatic economic and geopolitical interests, but rather as the dynamic product of entangled elective affinities, shifting ideological sympathies, and converging strategic needs that connected a wide variety of political actors on the ground.

Notes

1   This chapter is the result of a wider and ongoing research on Yugoslav endeavors in Latin America during the Cold War, conducted in dialogue and collaboration with several colleagues. I am especially grateful to Marcelo Casals and Joaquín Fernández

for having significantly informed and guided my work on Chile. I am also thankful toward Eugenia Palieraki for her counsel.

2 For the Yugoslav ambassador's memoires, see Petrović, Slavoljub Đera, *Sećanja i zapisi jednog borca i diplomate* (Belgrade: DTA, 2007).

3 Oscar Waiss, *Nacionalismo y socialismo en América latina* (Buenos Aires: Ediciones Iguazú, 1961 [Santiago, 1954]), 128.

4 Ibid., 165.

5 "Šifrovano pismo," August 27, 1951, Archive of Yugoslavia (AJ) 507, "Chile," IX, 21 / III-1.

6 "Šifrovano pismo," June 5, 1953, AJ 507, "Chile," IX, 21 / III-3.

7 For a longer and more detailed account of Yugoslav endeavors in Latin America during the 1950s, see Agustín Cosovschi, "Searching for Allies in America's Backyard: Yugoslav Endeavors in Latin America in the Early Cold War," *The International History Review* 43, no. 2 (2021): 281–96.

8 "Telegram," September 12, 1954, AJ 507, "Chile," IX, 21 / III-13. The Chilean proposal is also referred in in Oscar Waiss's memoirs. See Waiss, *Chile Vivo: memorias de un socialista* (Madrid: Centro de Estudios Salvador Allende, 1986), 109.

9 Waiss, *Chile Vivo*, 109.

10 It should be kept in mind that, as other leading members of the SSRNJ, Vlahović had fought in the Spanish Civil War, which might have also made him more sensitive to the particularities of Latin American context and certainly increased his prestige in the eyes of the Chileans.

11 "Zabeleška sa sastanka Komisije za međunarodne veze SSRNJ na kome je drug Veljko Vlahović podneo izveštaj sa svog puta po Latinskoj Americi," 1955, AJ 507, "Chile," IX, 21 / III-13, 1–4.

12 "Šifrovano pismo poslanstvu Čile (Bolivija)," February 22, 1955, AJ 507, "Chile," IX, 21 / II-4.

13 Waiss's biographical background is well told in his memoires. See Waiss, *Chile Vivo*.

14 Waiss's abundant exchange with Vlahović can be found in AJ 507, "Chile," IX, 21 / III.

15 Oscar Waiss, *Amanecer en Belgrado* (Santiago: Prensa Latinoamericana, 1956).

16 A celebration of the Bolivian revolution's achievements together with a critical assessment of the Mexican revolutionary experience can also be found in Waiss's writings. See Waiss, *Nacionalismo y socialismo en América latina*.

17 "Zabeleška o razgovoru sa delegacijom Socijalističke partije Čile, 16 augusta 1955 u sedištu Socijalističkog saveza radnog naroda Jugoslavije, August 16, 1955, AJ 507 "Chile," IX, 21 / II-4, IX, 21 / II-5.

18 Waiss, *Amanecer en Belgrado*, 34.

19 Ibid., 43–9.

20 Ibid., 70–3.

21 Ibid., 72.

22 Ibid., 80.

23 Ibid., 70.

24 Ibid., 151.

25 Ibid.

26 "Stenografske beleške sa razgovora između čileanske delegacije i članova Saveznog odbora SSRNJ u Komisiji za međunarodne," September 12, 1955, AJ 507 "Chile," IX, 21 / II-4, IX, 21 / II-5.

27 Waiss, *Amanecer en Belgrado*, 60.

28 "Stenografske beleške sa razgovora između čileanske delegacije i članova Saveznog odbora SSRNJ u Komisiji za međunarodne," September 12, 1955, AJ 507 "Chile," IX, 21 / II-4, IX, 21 / II-5., 16–17.
29 Ibid., 16–17.
30 Ibid., 76.
31 "Zabeleška: Poziv iz Čilea," AJ 117.
32 "Izveštaj o boravku delegata iz Čilea i Urugvaja," AJ 117.
33 "Stenografske beleške," November 7, 1959, Commission for International Relations of the CK SKJ and the SO SSRNJ, AJ 142, Fasc. 37.
34 "Zabilješka," AJ 507 "Chile," IX, 21 / II-6.
35 AJ 507 "Chile," IX, 21 / II-16.
36 Čehovin, Dušan, *Ekonomski odnosi Jugoslavije sa inostransvom* (Belgrade: Kultura, 1960), 117.
37 "Informacija o komisiji za kulturne veze s inostranstvom," AJ 559, Fasc. 1. 1–3.
38 "Izveštaj o radu 1965," AJ 559, Fasc. 23. 47–8.
39 Waiss, *Chile Vivo*, 121.
40 Ibid., 126.
41 AJ 507 "Chile," IX, 21 / II-9.
42 AJ 507 "Chile," IX, 21 / II-11.
43 AJ 507 "Chile," IX, 21 / II-53.
44 Ibid.
45 Ibid.
46 Ibid.

4

The End of Ideology and the Third World

The Congress for Cultural Freedom's 1955 Milan Conference on the "Future of Freedom" and its Aftermath

Daniel Steinmetz-Jenkins

Introduction: The Search for a Philosophy of Freedom after the Second World War

Although it has never been studied in full detail, the Congress for Cultural Freedom's (from hereon CCF) 1955 Milan conference devoted to the "Future of Freedom" might be considered one of the epochal intellectual moments of the second half of the twentieth century. In mid-September 1955, more than 140 scholars from all over the world took part in the six-day conference, the largest in the history of the organization. The key idea that guided the conference was the end of ideology. Although the notion had different formulations at the time, it was the French liberal Raymond Aron's version of the doctrine that set the agenda for not just the conference but the future of the CCF.[1] As Daniel Bell later explained, "In the last decade the Congress took the question of the 'end of ideology' and made it a central intellectual issue in the world community."[2] In this regard, the afterword to Aron's highly successful book L'Opium des intellectuels, published just months before the conference, named "The End of the Ideological Age," is of crucial importance.[3]

As the guiding inspiration for the 1955 Milan conference, Raymond Aron was given the task of writing the pilot paper that would establish the terms by which the Congress hoped to reconstruct the idea of freedom. The title of this pre-circulated paper was "De quoi disputent les Nations," which first appeared in the French journal Nouvelle Revue Française in 1954 and a year later in Encounter with the title "Nation and Ideologies."[4] This small article was later reformulated and placed in the afterword of The Opium of the Intellectuals. "We are becoming," Aron declares, ever more aware that the political categories of the last century—Left and Right, liberal and socialist, traditionalist and revolutionary—have lost their relevance. They imply the existence of conflicts, which experience has since reconciled, and they lump together ideas and men whom the course of history has drawn into opposing camps.[5]

In Aron's judgment, Western Europe was moving into a "non-millennial socialism and a non-reactionary conservatism"[6] that offered both peaceful governance and peaceful opposition. He viewed ideological controversies in Western societies to be fading since the welfare state had proven it could reconcile divergent demands and, in turn, deflect revolutionary passions. The best way to maintain the system, argued Aron, required political elites to engage in various "degrees and methods of compromise."[7]

The six-day Milan conference consisted of six sessions devoted to rethinking the idea of freedom and specifically according to Aron's notion of the end of ideology. What comes off, specifically from the Western representatives, is triumphalism: the end of ideology as *fait accompli* in the West. Michael Polanyi, for instance, observed that the conference room was filled with thinkers "diametrically opposed" but who nonetheless now believed they no longer occupied different political worlds. "Ideologies have noticeably failed," remarked Polanyi, "and political fury has subsided. . . . This probably means that political thinking is ready to consider a reform of political and economic thought guided by a taste for concrete interest."[8] Sidney Hook expressed similar optimism: "If all the nations of the world," Hook argued, "are free to accept a common method of settling the issues that divide them, their ideological differences, no matter how extreme, would have only peripheral effects on the political shape of things."[9] And British Labour MP Hugh Gaitskell bluntly rejected the notion that political freedom depends ultimately on economic freedom. "It is nonsense," Gaitskell proclaimed, "to speak as if the whole apparatus of government control and intervention, and the welfare state, which has existed in Britain since the war, and is now more or less a permanent feature of economy, it is nonsense to say that all of these things have in any way whatever interfered with, or altered the nature of British freedom."[10] He went on to suggest that there is no necessary connection between even a fully nationalized economy and the violation of political freedom. In other words, the British welfare state had made ideology obsolete.

For the Western participants at Milan, the future of freedom looked promising and hopeful. Indeed, a brief report of the proceedings written by the sociologist Edward Shils appeared in the CCF journal *Encounter* demonstrated the confidence that the Western participants at Milan exuded in their conviction that the end of ideological age had arrived. Shils noted that the general agreement of the participants over the waning of ideology, together with the belief that the Soviet Union was losing the cultural Cold War, gave the conference the feeling of a "post victory ball."[11] It took five years, but by 1955 the CCF had arrived at a constructive philosophy to carry out its mission of promoting cultural freedom. It would reach the shores of the United States in Daniel Bell's *The End of Ideology* (1960), which stirred considerable debate—and to some extent lives on today in the guise of Francis Fukuyama's notion of the "end of history."

The New Left in the United States criticized the end of ideology for being a smug doctrine of the liberal status quo that trivialized or ignored the harsh poverty of those excluded from its benefits—"the other America," as Michael Harrington described it. The argument of this paper is that much of this debate had already been prefigured in Milan, however by a rather different group of thinkers. Representatives from the "underdeveloped nations" naturally wondered how the end of ideology applied to their respected countries. They critically viewed the end of ideology through the lenses of bad faith: a philosophy of freedom now heralded by their former colonial masters, who had long prevented their own economic, cultural, and political freedom. As the writer Dwight Macdonald, who attended the event as an observer, aptly put it: "the Asian delegates came to find out what 'freedom' really means to people with white skins— and to present to these cultural representatives of their present or former masters a list of complaints."[12]

Just a few months before the Milan event in April 1955, the landmark Asian-African Conference had taken place in Bandung, Indonesia. The CCF took great interest in this event having financed Richard Wright's trip to Bandung to report on the event, which was published in book form in 1956 with the title: *The Color Curtain: A Report on the Bandung Conference.*[13] Bandung signaled a crucial moment for the CCF. It represented the Third World's emergence as a *diplomatic bloc* in the Non-Aligned Movement. The mid-1950s were thus a crucial time of strategic importance for the CCF, which coincided with peak optimism for American modernization theory, and the hope emerging states would follow "the western model of develop"; an optimism which the CCF did much to embody.[14] The significance of the Milan meeting, then, is not simply that it led to the American debate over the end of ideology during the 1960s. Rather, it was the second half of the conference that forced the CCF to take up a new problematic: the relationship between the end of ideology and the "underdeveloped world." As General Secretary Nicolas Nabokov noted in 1956, perhaps "the most urgent question discussed at the Milan conference concerned the economic development of technologically ill-equipped countries."[15] In this sense, 1955 marked the CCF's turning away from the fight against communism in Europe and turning toward its fight against global communism—a fight which lasted until the CCF's demise in 1966 due to revelations of its financial connections to the CIA. Given this diplomatic opening, the CCF sought to sway intellectuals and thought leaders from African and Asia away from neutrality and alignment with the Soviets and toward an acceptance of the "free world."

What has been explored in only passing detail is how the participants from the developing nations who attended the Milan conference specifically thought about the triumphalism over the end of ideology on display at the Milan conference.[16] There were thirty participants from South America, Asia, and Africa present at the event, and almost all of them either gave papers or offered comments—some of them were or became key representatives for the Congress at its various offices around the world.[17] What their comments reveal is a diversity of critical opinion and thought not only about the limitations of "Western" conceptions of freedom, but specifically concerning how to reconcile political freedom with rabid industrial modernization. It will be shown that many of the representatives from "new states" believed that it was absolutely necessary for the Western powers to commit themselves to a just economic and legal international order to ensure the development of the new states. This general sentiment is summed up in the paper that the development economist Arthur Lewis's gave in Milan: "The Western democratic nations have a moral duty to help the underdeveloped countries substantially, just as within each nation most of us now agree that there is a moral duty to tax the rich, to help the poor."[18] Alternatively, an economic order rigged to the unfair economic advantage of the West, they reasoned, would lead to resentment and, in turn, make the Chinese and Soviet models of development appealing. To what degree Western states were obligated to assist the economic development of new states, the paper shows, led to a heated debate at Milan, one which helped set the agenda of the CCF for years to come. In turn, it raised the question of whether new states should even seek to advance along the lines of the "Western model" of development, especially given its particular cultural mores and values that the Asian delegates in particular judged harshly. The paper concludes by suggesting that Raymond Aron, the mastermind behind the end of ideology, was highly suspicious of using "the West's" own unique path to modernization as a model of development for the "Third World." In this sense, he sided with much of the critical sentiment expressed by many of the Congress' representative from Asia and Africa.

Culture and Freedom

For good reason the end of ideology is often criticized as the prime example of rule by technocracy. By denying the need for ideology, the assumption is that all political and economic challenges can be resolved through technocratic adjustments to liberal systems of governance. However, many of the end of ideologists associated with the CCF were Weberian-inspired sociologists, such as Daniel Bell, Raymond Aron, and Seymour Martin Lipset. Just like Weber made a genealogical argument for the origins of modern capitalism by seeing an elective affinity between it and Calvinist theology and values, these thinkers themselves recognized the role that Western culture and values played in the emergence of the end of ideology—as is perhaps most notably on display in Daniel Bell's famous book *The Cultural Contradictions of Capitalism* (1976).

The question of the historical and cultural conditions in the West that gave rise to the mid-twentieth-century vital center/consensus politics proved to be of essential importance at Milan as the title of numerous papers demonstrate: "Cultural Freedom in an underdeveloped economy" (Eric Da Costa); "Reason, Tradition and Freedom" (Theodor Litt); "Tradition and Freedom" (Michael Freund); "Tradition and Liberty: Autonomy and Interdependence" (Edward Shils). How, though, could the developing nations be put on the path for their own end to ideology given their different cultural values and tradition? As one participant put it: "many of these countries are underdeveloped because of their having experienced the influence of the Industrial Revolution without that of the Renaissance."[19] The industrial revolution without the Renaissance, according to this perspective, constituted the Soviet model of modernization, the very entity the CCF was established to resist. However, if certain cultural values are necessary for an end of ideology, this could also entail Western cultural imperialism.

A point in case where this tension appeared on full display in Milan can be seen in the intervention of Astad Dinshaw (A. D.) Gorwala who at the time was the director of the State Bank of India, Bombay. Gorwala was no doubt a fitting choice for the CCF event: a known opponent of Indian cooperation with the Soviet Union, he had blasted

Nehru's visit to the USSR in June 1955, which had taken place just months before the Milan conference. Yet, despite his critical views of the Soviet Union, Gorwala, who at the time wrote for both the *The Times of India* and *The Statesman*, proved to be the most outspoken critic of the naïve optimism he associated with the end of ideology, which he thought to be tone deaf to the economic realities of the underdeveloped world.

He first pointed out a tension between the Congress' defense of cultural and political freedom versus the kind of rapid industrialization underdeveloped nations would need in order to make the appeal of communism obsolete. "If they have to [industrialize] entirely from within themselves," observes Gorwala, "they will have to adopt some of the means, some of the means . . . the methods as have been adopted in the Soviet Union."[20] Therefore, to ensure real freedom, Western countries—"the richer brethren," as he called them—must be prepared to offer substantial economic assistance through international organizations.

The question here involved not whether some level of assistance should be given, everyone but specifically how much and in what manner. Gorwala believed that Western nations should be beholden to some kind of international organization, which he believed would ensure fair economic policies toward developing nations. Some of the Western contingent felt like this could all too easily lead to a kind of political blackmail, one in which colonial and postcolonial nations would support the Soviet Union if the Western nations did not offer radical economic assistance. The charge of blackmail was leveled by the conservative British historian Max Beloff who rebuked these representatives of the "backward" countries for simultaneously blaming the West "largely for their own backwardness," while asserting that a moral duty lies upon these same Western nations to preserve and extend freedom in their societies. They back this position, argued Beloff, by claiming otherwise these countries will go the way of communism. "Can there be a dialogue about equality and not merely a series of arguments with blackmail behind?"[21]

Gorwala's rejoinder to Beloff proved illuminating. "As to the gentlemen who talked about threats and blackmail . . . it is entirely a question of self-interest: our interest and his interest are the same."[22] But more important, accusations of blackmail, Gorwala argued, were fundamentally misguided since they wrongly assumed that such assistance demanded the living "standards of Chicago in every village."

> On the contrary, in the larger parts of Asia and Africa, we would feel somewhat tired of the standards of Chicago. We would be quite content with a few simple things: a house, and two meals a day, and a little breakfast, now and again, consisting of extremely simple food, just enough clothes to cover the body, a little house, opportunities for education for everybody, and a little public health. If that were available, we would consider that the standard in living is greatly advanced: and that is what we want. It is not a case of intellectually going astray and demanding suddenly that a Cadillac appear.[23]

Yet, even in rejecting crude Western materialism, Garwala, nevertheless insisted on the prioritizing of economic needs over cultural values. Garwala complained that giving culture such importance came at the expense of economic concerns that were far more pressing in India: "[They] propose," he says, "to start by education when many people in India do not even get one full meal a day. It's all well to talk of a cultural lag but when you are at the barest margin of subsistence, before thinking of higher values the least you can do is to meet those most elementary needs."[24] Garwala clearly thought the idea of a cultural lag had racist connotations. He viewed it as providing either a justification for either colonial rule, or, in the case of postcolonial states, dependency on the paternalism of the West.

On the last day of the conference, Garwala, along with George F. Kennan, Michael Polanyi, and a few others, offered closing remarks.[25] Garwala credited the West with having discovered democratic governance, which had given hope around the world for all those longing to be free. Yet he concluded: "a number of papers at this conference decry that hope. Only those of a certain tradition, almost of a certain race can, it is said, make democracy work. The rest, the lower breeds without the law, let them hang their heads in shame and note that this esoteric secret is not for them."[26] The only solution to this predicament, argued Garwala, would be for the Western nations to accept the establishment of an international and independent political body devoid of racism, and committed to the economic advancement of the developing world. Here, Garwala put his hopes in the United Nations, which in his eyes had the worldmaking power to resist the "tremendous odium of colonialism."

Third World Nationalism and the End of Ideology

Even if his tone was harsher, A. D. Gorwala was hardly alone in his criticism of the end of ideology being touted as a Western triumph. Such was made clear on the fourth day of the conference, which was entirely devoted to a panel titled "the role of nationalism in fostering and imperiling free societies; the influence of colonialism and racial conflicts."[27] Papers were given by the politician and sociologist, K. A. Busia; the Labour Party leader Denis Healey, the activist Rita Hinden, and academics such as Hans Kohn and Herbert Passin, and Germán Arciniegas, among others. Busia—who would become prime minister of Ghana in 1969—offered a paper titled "The Influence of Colonialism and Racial Conflicts on the Development and Maintenance of Free Societies."[28] To unpack his argument, it will be helpful to recall that a key element of the end of ideology thesis held that the nationalist movements associated with interwar fascism in Germany and Italy had been defeated on the battlefields of the Second World War. This kind of nationalism constituted a dangerous ideology, but nevertheless one which the postwar welfare state, along with expanding European political and economic integration, had now made obsolete. At the same, the Western contingent of the Congress recognized that many of the European nationalist movements of the nineteenth century were liberal reform movements seeking to root political authority in constitutions.

How the Congress should view nationalism, specifically as it relates to colonialism and emerging nations, therefore, presented a dilemma, since nationalism was historically a vehicle for both radical ideologies in Europe, and also liberal reform movements there. It is exactly here that Busia made a key intervention by suggesting this dilemma presumed that developing nations should be beholden to the Western political model: "Britain, America and the democracies do well," he observed, "to be proud of their political constitutions":

> But that pride must go with the knowledge that institutions that have served one country well may not be suitable in other . . . the adoption of Western institutions in Thailand has been twenty-three years of graft and corruption. . . . My plea is that the older democracies should not be doctrinaire, but empirical in their approach to constitutions and political institutions. It should be recognized that the principles and ends of democracy can be realized by other people through institutional forms different from those to which the West is accustomed.[29]

But insofar as the Congress was worried about a nationalist backlash in colonial and developing states, Busia paper sought to make one major intervention: European imperialism gives birth to the very kinds of nationalism for which the Congress feared most. In arguing this, he quoted in the affirmative a 1949 article by Sir Alfred Zimmern on nationalism in Southeast Asia, which stated that in nationalism there was the "inevitable reaction of people who had been living for generations under a humiliating sense of inferiority, in the face of the pride, the prejudice, and, too often, the crude biological fallacies of their white superiors."[30] In commenting on this passage, Busia argued that the same could be said of the British colonies in West Africa. "I speak with West Africa of which I have first-hand knowledge in mind," commented Busia:

> Their nationalism is more than the desire for modern constitutional forms or European technology to improve standards of living. It is the urge for self-expression, for national independence and cultural freedom; and above all for the recognition of their equality with other nations, and for opportunities to win international respect through cooperation and through contributing to the independent life of the international community of the 20th century.[31]

Busia sought to remind the Congress of what appeared to be its unrealistic idealism which assumed countries emerging from colonialism could develop economically, and at the same time develop parliamentary institutions within a nation-state framework that did not exist before the rule of the metropolitan countries.[32] It is here that Busia specifically brought up the naïve optimism over the end of ideology thesis expressed during the first half of the conference in Milan.

> I am very interested in the point made yesterday by Hugh Gaitskell that control of the economic plans of a country by the government, need not necessarily mean also the surrender of the political freedom; but you are speaking against the background of a country which already has standards of political freedom, respect of government for the views of the minority, and established parties. . . . We need to develop these at the same time.[33]

Busia, like with Gorwala, suggested that given these circumstances, only an international organization like the United Nations could provide sympathetic encouragement to those countries seeking to realize democracy through institutions in keeping with their own traditions and political experience.[34] Given the two World Wars, Busia viewed the United Nations as a symbol of a new kind of international life. This new internationalism, Busia concluded, demanded a kind of cooperation, in which certain countries, given their fortunate circumstances, are in a position to give more than others. "And that is the basis, I should have thought, of responsibility."[35]

Following Gorwala, the social activist Rita Hinden presented a paper entitled "Colonies and Freedom." Hinden, who was born in Cape Town, had founded the Fabian Colonial Bureau in 1940 and wrote a book on Fabian colonial policy during the war years titled *Plan for Africa* (1942). In frustration, Hinden resigned in the early 1950s from the bureau since it moved away from seeing development as a necessary prerequisite for independence due to growing fears it would be a significant financial burden for British citizens. At the time of the event, she was the editor of the London-based publication, *Socialist Commentary*, and defended a kind of ethical socialism in the tradition of the British moral economists and specifically R. H. Tawney[36]

Hinden's paper, which, in part, sought to point out the weakness of imperial justifications for not granting national independence to colonial states, sought to make one fundamental intervention. If the CCF aspired to understand the future of freedom, it would need to recognize that what the Western world understood freedom to involve something qualitatively different than non-Western conceptions of freedom.

For them the contrast between a free and an unfree society is not the distinction made in the Western world between societies which enjoy political liberties and those which do not. It is the distinction—this cannot be repeated too often—between societies which have their national independence and those which have it not.[37] During the question time, Hinden pressed the line of argumentation further. Insofar as freedom for colonial states meant national independence, personal liberties were of mere secondary importance, to the greater goal of overcoming imperialism. Therefore, she concluded that the only way the West could maintain stable relationships with colonial peoples would be to "talk in their language and not ours."[38] "We must understand their demands for national freedom," Hinden affirmed, "and not talk in terms of individual freedoms of democracy which sound false in their ears as long as they have not even achieved the national freedom which we have taken for granted."[39] Hence her contempt for the very kind of modernization that appealed so attractive to some members of the Congress, namely one predicated on colonial people emulating Western value schemes:

> Do not let us deceive ourselves thinking we can buy the friendship of colonial peoples with money or promises of economic advance. We can win it only by a deep and full recognition of their equality as human beings and an identification of ourselves with what is in fact important to them, and not what we think should be important to them.[40]

Hinden here is ultimately making a socialist ethical argument for finding common cause with colonial peoples based on what she describes as the universal need for "self-respect" and "freedom from contempt." The recognition of such needs would be realized in the independence of colonies and an "equal partnership" between all nations.

Unlike Gorwala and Busia's papers, very little is mentioned by Hinden in terms of the kind of international order she imagined for her vision of the free world. However, like with the Fabian Colonial Bureau, she rejected the argument of certain participants at the Congress who believed any radical redistribution of wealth on the global scale to help underdeveloped countries would lead to a decline of living standards in Western countries, as long as they continue along in their current levels of prosperity. "We, in Britain," she observed, "give something of the nature of £ 30,000,000 a year to the underdeveloped countries. We could give them ten times that figure and our consumption in standard of living, which is rapidly increasing, would still not fall."[41] Here, in a nutshell, was Hinden's vision of the future of freedom.

The Response of the Western Delegates

The criticisms of Gorwala, Hinden, Busia, and others were an indictment of the festive triumphalism that marked the Euro-American enthusiasm over its supposed end of ideology. What is most revealing about such discontent is the reaction that it provoked from the Western delegates. Some were quite naturally receptive to such criticism. Seton Watson, the British historian of Russia, admitted that the "Anglo-Saxon Westerners," as he described them, were in danger of falling into a kind of Victorian mental isolationism. By this he meant a tendency to think that the problems which have mattered in the last thirty years, in Europe and the United States, must be the ones which now must matter most in underdeveloped countries. And here he warned his North American and European colleagues of the dangers of transporting political doctrines that took centuries to evolve in Europe, to places where they have never existed in such form:

> In the underdeveloped societies, modern education, industrial development and modern political ideas, arrive suddenly together prefabricated, imported, ready-made. The political ideas, particularly liberalism, nationalism and socialism, which have been formulated in the period between the Reformation and the 19th century, arrive in underdeveloped societies . . . at a time when the social conditions to which these ideas were related have hardly yet come into at all.[42]

Given these conditions, Watson concludes that whatever path to development these countries take, it will not fit the familiar pattern of Western industrial society. What must be accepted by the West are different models of development. Echoing these comments was Nicolas Nabokov, the secretary general of the Congress, who, in embarrassment, expressed frustration that the attendees from the developed countries offer only a "torrent of words recommending freedom" and warnings about the Soviet Union, but prove so unhelpful in offering constructive assistance. "This is a very sad situation," he lamented, "and I very much regret that so many people here from the United States, from England were silent."[43] As an inner circle higher-up in the CCF, Nabokov's mission was to stymie impasses that would influence the non-Western delegates from taking neutralist stances. This was most certainly the case with the

Indian representatives at the conference, whose criticisms of Nehru's rapprochement with the Soviet Union, was key for the Congress mission of containing communism in the Third World.[44] In this sense, Nabokov statements suggest he viewed the conference as a failure.

On the other end of the spectrum were those Western representatives who saw the demands of the Asian representatives, in particular, to be self-righteous and hypocritical—the very kind of position that Nabokov feared most. British historian Max Beloff's comments concerning blackmail is a point in case, which we have already seen. But the biggest example of reaction proved to be the famed diplomat-intellectual George F. Kennan, someone regularly involved with CCF activities. Kennan's noted cultural conservatism was on display throughout the event. Early on in the conference, Kennan proved hostile to the end of ideology thesis and specifically as it had been argued in Daniel Bell's paper "The Ambiguities of the Mass Society."[45] Bell's paper suggested that given the rise in Western living standards, along with stable political governance, mass society should no longer be feared. Interestingly, many of the charges the New Left would level at Daniel Bell in the 1960s were articulated by Kennan in response to Bell's paper in Milan:

> I cannot share the hopefulness and complacency of Mr. Bell about the present state of American society.... The decay of local government, the chaotic disintegration in community life in many of our great urban centers, retrogression of our education system. Brutalization of a large portion of our teenage youth, the uncreativeness of recreational patterns.[46]

Kennan's list of social pathologies rambled on, but, unlike the New Left, the inspirations for his views are due to his cultural conservatism, one which viewed mass society, urbanization and industrializing processes as destructive forces underlying communities and local traditions.

Scholars have long dissected the racist dimensions of Kennan's brand of pastoral conservatism, which, in part, entailed his judgments over whether certain ethnicities are fit to politically govern.[47] Whether due to mere elitism, subterranean racist views or both, Kennan's closing remarks to end the conference, and later statements about the Milan event, were directed squarely at the representatives of the underdeveloped nations. He was, in particular, vexed by those speakers from the developing nations who reproached the United States for its failure, in comparison to the solidarity that communism offers, to present the world with some sort of cause or comradeship. The freedom it offered was materialistic and spiritually empty. Kennan stated that he could not accept this reproach, and that the conference revealed "the immense and tragic differences of mind and spirit between the western and non-European worlds."[48]

Two factors bear light on Kennan's comment regarding the conference's "non-European" representatives. First, they are immediately prefaced by Kennan's rejection of egalitarian democracy. "All men were born with equal dignity. . . . But they are far from equal in their powers of insight, and their ability to contribute usefully to the process of civilization. To be safe in freedom, peoples must have the courage to differentiate where nature has differentiated . . . God forbid we should ever be without an elite."[49] Kennan thus appeals to nature as an implicit justification for the disparity between the Western and non-Western worlds. But Kennan's implicit appeal to natural hierarchies in his closing remarks were made explicit a few months after the Milan event. Stephen Spender, the codirector of *Encounter*, reported in its pages that Kennan had relayed to him that some of the speeches made by the delegates from Asia had almost proven to him there was "little point in Americans attending conferences with Asians."[50] According to Spender, Kennon thought the speeches made it clear that whatever Americans did they were always thought to be acting from power-lusting, money grabbing, or war-mongering motives. In his luminous, enthusiastic way, Kennan went on to say that his objection applied not only to the Milan conference meeting with Asian delegates but to American apologias everywhere—in Asia, in South America, in parts of Europe even. He did not mean, he said, that material aid should be abandoned, but that Americans should assert bluntly that they only helped people because they wanted their 12 percent profit.[51]

Ultimately, Kennan's cultural superiority led him to the realist view that too many differences divided the United States from the underdeveloped countries and that a project for sponsoring global development would lead to failure. "This relation should lead to divorce," as he put it.[52] Whatever optimism the end of ideology might have heralded for the Western delegates was offset by it being a colossal hypocrisy in the eyes of the non-Western delegates. Little wonder why Dwight Macdonald titled his report on the conference: "No Miracle in Milan." For the next few years the CCF would sponsor numerous events in the attempt to resolve these contradictions. This proved to be a complete failure.

Conclusion: Raymond Aron and the End of Ideology after Milan

Raymond Aron's thinking about the end of ideology offers an illustrative way of showing how optimism over an end to ideology among the Western delegates at Milan eventually transformed into disillusionment with it. Aron was always quick to point out that when he wrote about the idea of an end of ideology in his famous *The Opium of the Intellectuals*, it appeared in the epilogue of the book, and as a question: "The End of the Ideological Age?" Unlike Seymour Martin Lipset, who bodily defended the notion, Aron viewed the end of ideology as a thesis at best. In fact, well before the end of ideology debate took off in 1960, the triumphalist and parochial overtones of the various CCF gatherings clearly bothered Aron.[53] If Milan signaled the CCF's turn toward development in the Third World, the follow-up conferences had, to Aron's consternation, reduced modernization to Westernization. A point in case involves Aron's response to a 1958 keynote address Edward Shils gave at the CCF conference in Rhodes, Greece, titled "Representative Government and Public Liberty in the New States."[54] The stated aim of the conference, which included representatives from Asia and Africa, concerned "problems of democracy in the new states and a discussion of the means by which free institutions can be sustained and strengthened."[55]

Shils's argued that "modernity entails democracy, and democracy in the new states must above all be equalitarian."[56] The one-to-one connection between modernity and democracy, argued Shils, demanded the dethronement of the rich and traditionally privileged from their positions of long-standing political power. It also required the breaking up of large private estates, progressive income taxation, universal suffrage, and the replacement of monarchies by republics. Shils also made the assumption that modernity entailed disenchantment with religion, which he believed stymied the sense of robust individuality so characteristic of Western societies.[57] Shils viewed the CCF as a training ground for these liberal values, which educated elites from the Third World would seek to establish in their respective countries.

At Rhodes, Aron clearly recognized that Shils's position assumed the imposition of Euro-American values abroad. But what works in Britain, stressed Aron, might not necessarily work elsewhere. As he put it, "if democrats are to try to make democracy work elsewhere, especially in Africa and Asia, can we afford to keep our attention focused exclusively on our attractive western features?"[58] Aron went on to suggest that the establishment of parliamentary democracy in the developing states, as things currently stood, was a utopian dream; a pluralistic party system assumed a level of national unity and general agreement that did not exist in the new states. Or, "some of the so-called 'new states' have emerged without the minimum of national unity which is necessary for democratic political controversy."[59] The contradiction, as he noted, is that liberal values presuppose liberal institutions to maintain them; in developing nations such institutions are typically ineffectual.

Upon hearing Aron's pronouncements at Rhodes, his colleagues wondered if he thought Western-style democracy even possible for the new states. The Swiss journalist Francois Bondy responded that emerging states in Asia and Africa "start at political democracy," which supposedly would lead them down the path to becoming full capitalist economies. "I wonder," Bondy asked, "is the process of starting with the latest model of democracy and then retrieving the early steps of capitalism possible?"[60] Aron's rejoinder to Bondy explicitly illuminates his skepticism regarding Shils's notion of transferring political democracy to the new states:

> What I would like to say is that the present experience is without parallel in world history. We take institutions which have grown up slowly in the West and we transplant them in countries where often neither the state nor the nation exist and where the tasks to be achieved are enormous, and were, in fact, never achieved in the West with constitutional procedures and party systems.[61]

Shils was asked for his thoughts concerning Aron's point, which he dodged by simply mentioning the political conditions of various developing states.[62] This was eventually followed by Aron's mysterious concluding remarks: "the most impressive fact, but perhaps depressive too, is that we intellectuals, coming from all parts of the world, all speak the same language. We use the same words, the same vocabulary; we work with the same concepts."[63] Aron thus sought to remind his colleagues of the linguistic particularities of what they took to be the universal political norm.[64]

Shils penned a summary of the conference proceedings, which conceded to Aron's critical conclusions: Rhodes had floundered where Milan had remained blind: those pleading for the democratic legitimation of public authority in the new states were forced to acknowledge the institutions necessary for such legitimation to be totally lacking. Hence, if spreading Western democracy to the Third World had any chance, it would have to violate its own liberal presuppositions:

> The paradox of Rhodes was this: It was agreed that strong government is necessary and that meant strong leadership by dominating personalities and a powerful and able civil service. The dependence on government to create a society which will be able to act independently of government naturally creates misgivings.[65]

Now almost sounding like Rostow, Shils suggests that such an arrangement would simply be a "transitional period," one that would provide the necessary ground conditions for cultivating both a liberal sensibility and networks of autonomous civic life no longer constrained by local religious traditions and tribal practices. From this would spring a desire to establish and participate in representative institutions. Shils concludes by acknowledging that Aron viewed such a scheme with pessimism.[66]

Aron commented that a major problem with the CCF meetings since Milan, particularly the 1957 Tokyo conference devoted to economic reform in the Third World, was their myopic focus on the Westernization of non-Western societies. The fact that the seminars were devoted to the problems of transferring Western institutions to the non-Western world compelled Aron to ask: "Shouldn't the West take a long hard look at itself?"[67] The post-Milan seminars assumed, he argued, that the West was sufficiently sure of itself that it could examine its possible universalization without at the same time examining itself. The problem, Aron continued, is that even as developing nation-states sought to appropriate American technology and economic models, it did not automatically follow that they wanted to accept American-style political institutions. Rhodes had floundered where Milan had remained blind.

In August 1963, Daniel Bell wrote a memorandum to the executive board of the CCF summing up the history of the organization's past while charting a path for its future. Bell first noted that the end of ideology constituted the fundamental doctrine of the CCF, the origins of which he traced back to Aron's *The Opium of the Intellectuals*. The concept proved so valuable to the CCF, observed Bell, since it swept away the illusions of rigid Marxism and to expose the emptiness of the old political tags. But the times had changed, observed Bell, necessitating that the CCF move beyond the notion: "We may ourselves feel that the theme is exhausted, that it was a reflection of the discussion of the fifties."[68] Just a few years earlier, the end of ideology had been heralded as the dawn of the new era at Milan. Less than a decade later, Daniel Bell, who had earlier proclaimed an exhaustion with ideology, had come to view the end of ideology using the same language. The CCF had never resolved the contradictions that presented themselves in Milan. The best strategy for the organization going forward was to simply move away from it.

Notes

1 For different versions of the end of ideology articulated during the 1940s and 1950s, see Chaim I. Waxman, ed., *The End of Ideology Debate* (New York: Funk & Waxman, 1968).

2 Daniel Bell, "Preliminary Memorandum for the Future of the Congress," *International Association for Cultural Freedom Records*, Box 85, Folder 10 (exact date unspecified). In this regard, the afterword to Aron's most well-known book, *L'Opium des intellectuels*, published just months before the conference, named "The End of the Ideological Age," is of crucial importance: Raymond Aron, *L'Opium des intellectuels* (Paris: Calmann-Lévy, 1955). For Aron's reassessment of the end of ideology after the decades-long debate it caused, see Raymond Aron, *The Industrial Society: Three Essays on Ideology and Development* (New York: Praeger, 1967), 92–143.

3 Raymond Aron, *L'Opium des intellectuels* (Paris: Calmann-Lévy, 1955). For Aron's reassessment of the end of ideology after the decades-long debate it caused, see Aron, *The Industrial Society*.

4 Raymond Aron, "De quoi disputent les nations?" *Nouvelle Revue Française* 22 (October 1953): 612–37; "Nations and Ideology," *Encounter* 16 (January 1955): 24–33.

5 Ibid., 24.

6 Ibid.

7 Ibid., 33.

8 Michael Polanyi, *International Association for Cultural Freedom Records*, Box 396, Folder 7 (September 13, 1954).

9 Sidney Hook, *Opening Address: International Association for Cultural Freedom Records*, Box 396 Folder 7 (September 13, 1954).

10 Hugh Gaitskell, *Opening Address: International Association for Cultural Freedom Records*, Box 396 Folder 7 (September 13, 1954).

11 Edward Shils, "Letter from Milan: The End of Ideology," *Encounter* 20 (November 1955): 54.

12 Dwight Macdonald, "No Miracle in Milan," *Encounter* 27 (December): 74.

13 Richard Wright, *The Color Curtain: A Report on the Bandung Conference* (New York: World, 1956).

14 For the CCF's role in promoting modernization theory, see Nils Gilman, *Mandarins of the Future: Modernization Theory and the Cold War* (Baltimore: Johns Hopkins Press, 2007), 1–23; 113–54.

15 Nicolas Nabokov to Sune Carlson, *International Association for Cultural Freedom Records*, Box 402, Folder 11 (November 19, 1956).

16 See, for instance, Margery Sabin, "The Politics of Cultural Freedom: India in the Nineteen Fifties," *Raritan* 14, no. 4 (Spring 1995): 45–65; Roland Burke, "Real Problems to Discuss: The Congress for Cultural Freedom's Asian and African Exhibitions, 1951–1955," *Journal of World History* 27, no. 1 (2016): 53–85.

17 For the list of participants, see *International Association for Cultural Freedom Records*, Box 397, Folder 2.

18 Arthur Lewis, "Is Communism Necessary for Rapid Growth in Under-developed Countries?," *International Association for Cultural Freedom Records*, Box 398, Folder 10.

19 *International Association for Cultural Freedom Records*, Box 398, Folder 11.

20 *International Association for Cultural Freedom Records*, Box 395, Folder 1.

21 *International Association for Cultural Freedom Records*, Box 397, Folder 9.

22 Ibid.

23 Ibid.

24 Ibid.

25 See *International Association for Cultural Freedom Records*, Box 397, Folder 5.

26 *International Association for Cultural Freedom Records*, Box 398, Folder 7.

27 See *International Association for Cultural Freedom Records*, Box 397, Folder 5.

28 Ibid.

29 See *International Association for Cultural Freedom Records*, Box 398, Folder 5.

30 Ibid.

31 Ibid.

32 See his comments in *International Association for Cultural Freedom Records*, Box, 396, Folder, 9.

33 See *International Association for Cultural Freedom Records*, Box 398, Folder 5.

34 Ibid.

35 Ibid.

36 For a short biography of Hinden, see the entry for "Hinden, Rita" available in: *The Oxford History of National Biography*, https://www.oxforddnb.com/view/10.1093/ref :odnb/9780198614 128.001.0001/odnb-9780198614128-e-59962.

37 Quoted in *International Association for Cultural Freedom Records*, Box 398, Folder 8.

38 Quoted in *International Association for Cultural Freedom Records*, Box 398, Folder 1.

39 Ibid.

40 Ibid.

41 Ibid.

42 Quoted in *International Association for Cultural Freedom Records*, Box 397, Folder 9.

43 Ibid.

44 On the CCF's various initiatives in India during the 1950s, see Eric D. Pullin, "Money Does Not Make any Difference to the Opinions that We Hold": India, the CIA, and the Congress for Cultural Freedom," *Intelligence and National Security* 26, no. 2–3 (April-June, 2011): 377–98.

45 *International Association for Cultural Freedom Records*, Box 398, Folder 5.

46 *International Association for Cultural Freedom Records*, Box 397, Folder 11.

47 Most notably, see the relevant passages in his diaries: George Kennan, *The Kennan Diaries* (New York City: Norton, 2014), 507; 606–7.

48 *International Association for Cultural Freedom Records*, Box 398, Folder 9.

49 Ibid.

50 Stephen Spender, "Notes from a Diary," *Encounter* 27 (December, 1955): 54.

51 Ibid.

52 Ibid., 55.

53 One way to grasp the differences between Shils and Aron comes by way of an assumption made by the American intellectual historian Nils Gilman. In *Mandarins of the Future*, Gilman argues "that the end of ideology hypothesis emerged directly and specifically out of comparative reflections upon the differences between the 'developed' and 'underdeveloped worlds.'" Leaving aside that the "end of ideology" has a deeper history that preceded the CCF, Gilman is correct to note that representatives from "developing" nations at the 1955 event pushed the "western members" to construct global understandings of modernization. Gilman prefaces these observations by stating that Aron's version of the end of ideology, which really is a subsidiary element of his thinking on industrial society, was much more subtle and complex than that of his American counterparts. Proponents of the end of ideology

in the United States, argues Gilman, "would not resonate [with the] call for political temperance, which had been Aron's main point in promoting the phrase in France." See Gilman, *Mandarins of the Future*, 59.

54 For the Rhodes conference papers, see *International Association for Cultural Freedom Records*, Box 409, Folders 1–5.

55 The author of the conference announcement is not given: "Rhodes Conference to Access Democracy in New Nations," *International Association for Cultural Freedom Records*, Box 408, Folder 1 (n.d.).

56 Edward Shils, "Political Development in the New States," *Comparative Studies in Society and History* 2, no. 3 (April 1960): 266.

57 Ibid., 286.

58 Ibid.

59 "A Round Table Discussion of the Differences between East and West," *International Association for Cultural Freedom Records*, Box 409, Folder 4 (October 1958, exact date unspecified), 3.

60 Ibid.

61 Ibid.

62 Ibid., 4.

63 Ibid., 6.

64 The American thinker who seemed to be most affected by the celebratory mood of the Milan proceedings did not actually attend any of the post-Milan CCF seminars: the political sociologist Seymour Lipset. See in particular his: *Political Man: The Social Bases of Politics* (London: Heinemann, 1959), 403, 406. Although Lipset would deny that he ever intended the end of ideology to signify the end of class struggle in the West or to prop up the status quo, it is easy to see why some of the triumphalist statements of *Political Man* were understood in exactly this manner. In this regard, *Political Man*'s concluding chapter is telling. In a mere three paragraphs Lipset opines on the relationship between the end of ideology and the coming world order. He claimed that if the leaders of the Third World were to ever establish Western forms of governance, it would be necessary for them to be "irresponsible and demagogic in the early stages of the development." See Lipset, *Political Man*, 406. Lipset's thesis, observes Gilman, "sanctioned support for non-democratic developmental regimes in the name of establishing the 'economic preconditions for democracy.'" See Gilman, *Mandarins of the Future*, 62. In this sense his thinking differed little from Rostow's.

65 Edward Shils, "Old Societies, New States," in *Democracy in the New States: Rhodes Seminar Papers*, ed. Prabhakar Padhye (New Delhi: Congress for Cultural Freedom, 1959), 21.

66 Ibid., 25.

67 See the responses to Aron by George F. Kennan and Asoka Mehta in *World Technology and Human Destiny*, 56, 122–39.

68 Daniel Bell, "The Seminar Program of the Congress: A Preliminary Memorandum," *International Association for Cultural Freedom Records*, Box 86, Folder 5 (August 1963, exact date unspecified), 2.

5

Latin American Network in Exile

A Communist Cultural Legacy for the Third World

Marcelo Ridenti

This chapter seeks to show how, in the circumstances of the Cold War, some Latin American communist authors in exile took part in a circle that helped diffuse their work in various countries and languages, as well as to establish links with the audience beyond the communist sphere. Initially from Paris, they had access to an international network of resources and support by taking part in the Soviet system of large-scale cultural diffusion after the Second World War. If this fact stigmatized them as communists, later distension between the superpowers opened space for them to be accepted by the Western noncommunist market as well, as in Jorge Amado's typical case, in addition to opening an international dialogue, especially in the orbit of the so-called Third World.

The insertion of Latin American artists and intellectuals in communist networks would contribute to the idea of national liberation and the Third World, by imagining alternatives for a social, economic, political, and cultural organization in which nations would emerge free from colonial or imperialist rule. The social and emotional ties, generated particularly among the writers in exile, would contribute to creating new transnational solidarity that would go beyond the polarization of the Cold War, although involved in it. In other words, they took part in a kind of cultural prehistory in the constitution of the Third World imaginary in Latin America, without which it is not possible to understand it well.

Latin American communist artists and intellectuals had a strong presence at the peace congresses and the World Peace Council (WPC), where they arrived mainly through the cultural sector of the French Communist Party (FCP). The latter was responsible for coordinating the movement in the West, under the leadership of the writer Louis Aragon from the late 1940s. The exile in Paris helped the approach to the Peace Movement. They fled from persecution in their countries at the beginning of the Cold War. The most notorious cases were those of Chilean senator and poet Pablo Neruda and Brazilian deputy and writer Jorge Amado. They had their mandates revoked and were very well received in Paris by the comrades of the FCP, then at the height of its popularity, due to its prominent role in the Resistance, having obtained almost a third of seats in the Legislative Assembly in the first election after World

War II. The party opened especially its cultural reviews to Latin Americans, who had prominent space in *Les Lettres Françaises* and *Europe*.

At the beginning of the Cold War, the celebration of popular culture and realism was present in the articles about Latin America by the French communist cultural press, in addition to the mystique surrounding peoples from a distant continent. It gave space for socially and politically committed artists, in tune with the FCP's programmatic line, to value national and popular sources in culture, in contrast to cosmopolitan formalism, supposedly allied with imperialism.

Among Latin American artists who lived in Paris and belonged to Aragon's circle, we can mention the Cuban poet Nicolás Guillén, Argentine writer Alfredo Varela, and Chilean novelist Volodia Teitelboin (a communist leader too). They also joined the international movement, as well as Venezuelan artists Adelita and Héctor Poleo, Guatemalan writer Miguel Ángel Asturias, Paraguayan poet Elvio Romero and his fellow countryman, the composer Assunción Flores. Other names were the Uruguayan novelist Enrique Amorim, Haitian poet René Depestre and Brazilian painter Carlos Scliar. At the World Peace Council, Neruda, Amado, and Guillén acted as leaders, and soon won the Stalin International Peace Prize, intended to be a counterpoint to the Western Nobel Prize. The prize would take Lenin's name from 1957 onward, after the political changes in the Soviet Union. Amado won the award in 1951, Neruda in 1953, and Guillén in 1954. The three of them were close to the Soviet writers and intellectual leaders Ilya Ehrenburg and Alexandre Fadeyev, the successor of Andrei Zhdanov, formulator of socialist realism as a state cultural policy.

Latin American Exile: Pablo Neruda and Jorge Amado

The May 1948 issue of *Europe* contains an example of the highlight for Latin American artists by the communist press. The journal opened with Neruda's poem "Chronicle of 1948 (America)," in which he dedicated verses to various countries from Latin America, with fragments also published by *Les Lettres Françaises*; poems by the Chilean author and articles about him frequently appeared.[1] Neruda remained on the wave throughout the 1950s, for example, his famous poem *Canto General* was published, and an interview with him by Jean Marcenac featured on the cover of *Les Lettres Françaises*, which emphasized the theme of peace in the context of the communist "international struggle for peace."[2]

Neruda joined the Chilean Communist Party effectively in July 1945 but claimed to have become "a communist before myself during the Spanish war" (Neruda, 1974, pp. 135, 174). He served as Chilean consul in Barcelona and soon afterward in Madrid, from 1934 to 1937. Neruda met and became friends with many left-wing artists in Spain, including the Argentine painter Delia del Carril, his future wife, and a convinced communist militant. He lost his great friend and writer Garcia Lorca, assassinated by Francoists. Ardor for the republican cause motivated him to write the book *España en el corazón* (*Spain in My Heart*), whose first edition was made precariously by soldiers in the middle of the fighting (Neruda, 1974, p. 123).

After being removed from the consular post by the Chilean government, due to his support for the Republicans, he spent a period in Paris, where he met the communist poets Paul Éluard and Louis Aragon, friends for life. Together, they prepared a large international congress of antifascist writers to be held in Spain in July 1937, including the presence of many Latin Americans. Further on, with the election of a popular front government in Chile, the poet ambassador would again be sent to Europe to organize a ship trip that would take to Chile 2,000 Spanish refugees arrested in France, on the mission he considered the most relevant of his life (Neruda, 1974, pp. 124–30, 144–7; Feinstein, 2004, pp. 126–9).

Back in Chile, Neruda began to prepare his *Canto General*, which he would later consider his most important book. The plan was to make a long poem in homage to Latin America, grouping "historical incidents, geographical conditions, lives and struggles of our peoples," in the words of Neruda (1974, pp. 139, 176). His experience as a consul in Mexico from 1940 to 1943 also inspired the book. He got involved with the local artistic and intellectual milieu marked by ideas from the left, such as the muralists Orozco, Rivera, and Siqueiros. Neruda became friends with all of them, especially Siqueiros, whom he helped escape to Chile after an unsuccessful attempt to kill Trotsky, then a refugee in Mexico (Neruda, 1974, pp. 155–7; Feinstein, 2004, pp. 150–70).

Due to a disagreement with the new Chilean government, whose guidelines he considered reactionary—for example, the refusal of visas to Africans, Asians, and Jews—Neruda gave up his diplomatic career in 1943. Before returning to his country, he made a long trip to Peru, especially enchanted by the ruins of Machu Picchu, to which he dedicated a poem that would become part of the *Canto General*. The book was the result of the antifascist political environment during the Second World War, which resulted in Neruda's election as a senator in Chile in March 1945. With the escalation of the Cold War, which caused the loss of Neruda's mandate, he had to flee his country to avoid being arrested, after a long period of hiding in which he had time to write new poems for the *Canto General*, finally concluded. The book was progressively written and published in 1949, with wide dissemination by the communist press from Paris, where he took refuge after a spectacular escape from Chile, crossing the Andes with the aid of communist militants (Neruda, 1974, pp. 164–93; Feinstein, 2004, pp. 171–235).

In turn, Jorge Amado was the favorite Brazilian artist of the communist publications, especially in 1948 and 1949, when he was exiled in Paris, integrated to the French and also international communist milieu, which had in the city one of the main points of convergence of their intellectual networks. *Europe* published an excerpt from *The Knight of Hope*, Amado's famous book about Luís Carlos Prestes, the general secretary of the Brazilian Communist Party.[3] In the same issue, the writer Pierre Gamarra made a brief complimentary comment on the French translation of *Dead Sea* (*Mar Morto*). According to him, the novel would be "full of lyricism and songs, yet realistic, which proves once again that dignity is on the side of 'simple people.'" The note ended up lamenting that Amado had to leave France since the government suspended his stay visa.[4]

Amado had already faced persecution in Brazil, after the withdrawal of his mandate as a constituent federal deputy by Sao Paulo. It was a result of the ban on the activities of the Communist Party of Brazil. In agreement with the party leadership, he would leave the country in January 1948. The aim was to denounce in Europe the democratic setback in Dutra's administration, taking advantage of the fact that Amado was already a well-known writer in Brazil and abroad. His translated works had given him visibility and credibility. In France and other countries, Amado helped organize events to accuse the Brazilian government and eventually took a central place in the international articulation of pro-Soviet artists and intellectuals.

Amado originally planned to live in Italy with his wife Zélia and their newborn son. However, the electoral defeat of the Italian Communist Party led them to settle in Paris, where they lived until they had to leave the country in 1949. During his time in France, Amado became one of the leaders of the world Peace Movement, which mobilized communists from around the globe. He made numerous trips, especially to Eastern European countries, in a context in which the Soviet Union was threatened by the Cold War atomic escalation at a time when only the United States had the nuclear bomb (the first Soviet artifact would come in August 1949). Some Brazilians from Amado's close group of communist artists and intellectuals, as well as Neruda and other Latin Americans, also had to withdraw from France for political reasons. Amado would not be allowed to return to the country for sixteen years.

In exile, Jorge Amado and his wife Zélia Gattai were supported by an extensive network of communist solidarity, from neighborhood committees in countries such as Italy and France to the high cultural summit in Eastern Europe, making contact with renowned artists and leaders of the international communist movement. They visited factories, schools, workers' clubs, as well as high artistic circles.

The couple accepted frequent invitations to visit communist countries, usually for free. They were on vacation or business in the Soviet Union, Czechoslovakia, Poland, Hungary, Romania, East Germany, Bulgaria, always staying at the best locations, with interpreters and guides at their disposal. The authorities of the artistic and cultural world, and even politicians in the strict sense, welcomed them, given Amado's role in the international Peace Movement. All communist countries had their Writers' Union. Their artists enjoyed several relative perks if they were in tune with the regime, such as international travel, accommodation in good hotels, large-scale publications, participation in parties and festivals—film, music, theater, literature, and so on. Writing retreats in prime locations were also available, such as Dobris Writers' Castle, 40 kilometers from Prague, where the Amado couple would later live after their expulsion from France, attesting the internationalist solidarity in the circles in tune with communist regimes.

The honors and mutual references between Latin American artists, intellectuals, and politicians, sewn by the French communist press, can be observed, for instance, in Jorge Amado's text entitled "Message of Hope," a cover story for *Les Lettres Françaises*. Amado wrote it as soon as he arrived in France, entitled to a large photo, in which the Brazilian communist leader Luís Carlos Prestes appeared between Amado and Neruda.[5] It was an express tribute to the Brazilian Communist Party general secretary, who had been outlawed, in connection with similar articles being done in France to greet Maurice Thorez and, on an international scale, to praise Stalin. In the same issue, also called cover, an interview with "the great Brazilian novelist Jorge Amado" was published.[6]

Perhaps the pinnacle of Jorge Amado's presence on the pages of *Les Lettres Françaises* has been the publication of his novel *Les Chemins de la Faim (Seara Vermelha, Red Field)*, with illustrations by Carlos Scliar, a communist painter from Southern Brazil, also living in Paris at the time. It included a series of episodes from number 246 to 273, in 1949 and 1950.

The Impact of the Experience Abroad

Les Lettres Françaises also published many articles on and by Nicolás Guillén, Cuban, Black, and communist. The poet lived in Paris, where he would not be allowed to stay from the late 1950s (Guillén, 1985, p. 131 et seq.). With the victory of the Cuban Revolution, Guillén returned to the island, where he would preside over the Cuban Union of Writers and Artists from 1961 until he died in 1989. The Guatemalan writer Miguel Ángel Asturias was a regular contributor too. His country had entered the left-wing wave with the Arbenz government, who suffered a US-backed military coup d'état in 1954. The French communist cultural press also highlighted some Mexican painters such as Siqueiros, Rivera, and Orozco.

The space offered by the French communist press was relevant to publicize the work of Latin American artists who were part of the communist network. Some of them became essential agents of the circuit in their countries, incorporating and spreading international practices, as Jorge Amado did by organizing the collection "People's Novels" for the Brazilian Communist Party after his return in 1952. The experience abroad also influenced the author's work, such as his novel *The Bowels of Liberty*. The Russian edition appeared in record time in 1954, praised in the Soviet Union as the first Latin American novel in the canons of socialist realism, according to Aguiar (2018).

Among Brazilians, Amado was the primary beneficiary of the integration into the communist cultural network, first in Paris, then in the Writers' Castle in Czechoslovakia. Published in several languages, winner of the Stalin Prize, he became a kind of communist cultural ambassador of Brazil. He always helped writers, painters, filmmakers, and other artists to project themselves and even win awards abroad, given his privileged position and contacts in the sociability of communist networks. Amado helped, for example, in awarding as young director the filmmaker Nelson Pereira dos Santos for his movie *Rio, 40 degrees* at a festival in Czechoslovakia in July 1956 (Salem, 1987, p. 122). Returning to Brazil in mid-1952, Amado consolidated his position as the leading communist artist. Without formally breaking with the party, he would become a traveling companion after Khrushchev's report against Stalin in 1956 but always continued in the international communist orbit. From that year to 1958, the novelist ran his independent journal called *Paratodos*, inspired by *Les Lettres Françaises*. His partner of adventure was the communist architect Oscar Niemeyer, who was building Brasilia, the new capital for the country. Kubitschek administration tolerated some activities of the communists, but the party remained outlaw.

The family letters sent by Jorge Amado as soon as he arrived in France attest that he quickly articulated the publication of all his books that he intended to see translated. The novelist obtained an advance on copyrights that would allow him to live in Europe for at least one year. In contact also with literary agents from other countries, he expressed in a letter to his wife a wish that he would achieve in the following years: "I have all my books negotiated here. And they are traded in other European countries" (Amado, 2012a, p. 43). On April 7, 1948, he wrote triumphantly: "I just didn't put the books I didn't want to" (2012a, p. 55). Two months in Paris were enough to pave the plan for the international diffusion of his work.

Although Amado left Brazil on a political mission to escape persecution after the loss of his parliamentary term—which allows configuring his extended stay abroad as an exile—the trip also served his personal and professional purposes. According to him, in a letter written at the time to his wife: "this trip will be infinitely useful, in all aspects. I tend to take it as long as possible, at least three years. With less time, it is impossible to see Europe" (Amado, 2012a, p. 36). But he warned: "For me, this trip is not a picnic, it is really a study trip and I hope to enjoy it as much as possible" (2012a, p. 55).

Meetings in Paris have helped to strengthen ties between communist artists from Latin America. The most noticeable approach from exile in France was between Jorge Amado, Pablo Neruda, and Nicolás Guillén, three celebrated communist writers in the intellectual milieu of their respective countries. They were friends and made many trips together through the communist circuit, as leading militants of the world Peace Movement.

To get an idea of the importance of staying in France for Guillén's friendship with Amado, suffice it to say that the Cuban poet recorded in his memoirs that he first met the Brazilian in Paris in 1949 after both were forced to leave their countries (Guillén, 1985, p. 121). He forgot that their first meeting was in Rio de Janeiro in 1947, in a recital of poems at the Brazilian Press Association (ABI), as Jorge Amado recalled (2012b, pp. 29–30). After presenting the guest in the event, Amado would have taken the poet to the hospital, where they went to meet the newborn son of the Brazilian writer.

Such imprecision of the memoirs would reveal that the vital thing for Guillén was knowing Jorge in the context of his exile in Paris, where they lived in the same hotel (Guillén, 1985, p. 221; Gattai, 2009a, p. 335). Amado's alleged precision, on the other hand, would express the importance he attached to contacts with the celebrated intellectuals he received, to the point where he was hosting one of them when his first child with Zélia was born. Besides, the episode was expressive of the rapid personal approach that Amado sought to establish with artists he admired.

Nicolás Guillén was an assiduous character in the memoirs of Jorge and Zélia, who appeared more moderately in the Cuban's autobiography. He made a brief but warm reference to the couple, not by chance centered on their friendship in Paris (Guillén, 1985, pp. 121–2). The poet's recollections of his four trips to Brazil from 1945 to 1961 involved other Brazilian artists. He was especially impressed by the person, life, and work of the famous communist painter Cândido Portinari, to whom he dedicated several pages (Guillén, 1985, pp. 115–28). Not surprisingly, the French communist cultural press received well Portinari's exhibitions in Paris.[7]

Pablo Neruda dedicated a poem to his friend Jorge Amado in the journal *Europe*. The theme was another Bahian writer, "Castro Alves do Brasil."[8] Several passages of the memoirs by Zélia Gattai and Jorge Amado remember Neruda, in episodes all over the globe, including Neruda's home in Chile and Amado's in Brazil. Their stay in France had strengthened their relationship (Gattai, 2010, p. 309).

Mentions of the Brazilian couple were affective but scarce in Pablo Neruda's memoirs, for example, when he related their journey together to Asia in 1957 (Neruda, 1974, p. 233 et seq.). Their peers and communist friends Emi Siao, Ting Ling, and Ai Qing[9] formed the "reception committee" in China, despite the ongoing persecution against them in the country, already after the termination of Stalinism in the Soviet Union. Both Neruda and Amado revealed a discomfort in the face of the situation (Amado, 2012b, pp. 354, 355, 409; Neruda, 1974, pp. 233–241). The episode generated anguish: "they disappeared before we boarded back" (Amado, 2012b, p. 409). Both Amado and Neruda have since then maintained a criticism of the Chinese line. Neruda wrote: "I could not swallow, for the second time, that bitter pill," the cult of the leader's personality. He left China "with a bitter taste in the mouth, that I still feel today" (Neruda, 1974, p. 239, 241).

Neruda did not mention Amado in his recollections of the Stalin Peace Prize, in which both played a significant role, although Neruda's was more central. Perhaps the reason was that Amado moved away from communist militancy, unlike the Chilean, who always ranked first in international prestige. He also had the first place in the relationship between Latin American intellectuals and communists abroad, as can be seen by the priority references to him at the French communist cultural press.

According to Neruda, "the revelations about the Stalinist era had broken Jorge Amado's spirits." He reported that they were old friends, shared years of banishment, identified "in a common belief and hope." But he thought himself less sectarian than the Brazilian, who "had always been rigid." After Khrushchev's report at the 20th Congress of the Soviet Communist Party, the Bahian novelist would have become quieter and soberer by "writing his best books, starting with *Gabriela, clove and cinnamon*, a masterpiece." A novel already distanced from a "direct political character" (Neruda, 1974, p. 237).

The book made an instant success in Brazil, it sold almost 200,000 copies in two years, a national record. In the time of *détente*, it became a hit both in the USSR and the United States. The Soviets ran an original print of 100,000 copies in 1961. The American edition appeared in 1962, by Knopf; the book remained among the top ten on *The New York Times* around a year. It was the second published novel by Amado in the country of his friend Michael Gold. *Violent Land* (*Terras do sem fim*) had been the first in 1945. The State Department had sponsored the edition as part of the good neighbor policy at the end of the Second World War. Published also by Knopf, the novel did not sell much. American market ignored Amado during the worst years of the Cold War; as a communist, he was not allowed to enter the country from 1952 onward (Aguiar, 2018).

Amado's French season, in which he joined the world Peace Movement, enhanced the diffusion and repercussion of his name and work. The process followed in Czechoslovakia, and also during the constant travels through Europe, especially the communist countries. Some of his books had already appeared in France, Italy, Eastern Europe, and Spanish America in the 1930s and 1940s. However, few works were translated and edited in more significant numbers.

As Zélia Gattai said, referring to Romania—something that could be seen in other countries too—Amado's prestige "also came, and above all, from his role in the fight for peace, because of his position of responsibility as a member of the Bureau of the World Peace Council" (Gattai, 2009a, p. 370).

In 1948, Jorge Amado traveled from Paris to Warsaw to attend a meeting to prepare the World Peace Congress of Intellectuals, held in August. It became known as the Wroclaw Congress, which attracted to Poland participants from around the world. Amado was elected one of the vice presidents of the Congress. At this Congress, Pablo Picasso made a passionate intervention in defense of the fugitive poet Pablo Neruda (Feinstein, 2004, p. 237). His drawing of the peace dove became a symbol of the world Peace Movement (Utley, 2000).

The success of the Wroclaw Congress led to the organization of the First World Peace Congress at the Salle Pleyel in Paris, in April 1949. Jorge Amado actively participated in the organization of the Congress, alongside Frenchmen like Aragon, Vercors, Laffitte, and Frédéric Joliot-Curie, as well as many foreigners, including Soviet writers such as Ehrenburg and Fadeyev. The surprise of the Congress was the sudden appearance of Pablo Neruda, much welcomed by everyone. The World Peace Council (WPC) resulted from this Congress, initially named the World Committee of Partisans for Peace. The new organization would have its base in Prague; personalities from around the world were elected in Paris to lead the new institution (Iber, 2015). Jorge Amado became a member of the Executive Committee of the Council. This position would guarantee him a special bond with politicians, intellectuals, and communist artists on a planetary scale (Gattai, 2009a, p. 314 ff.).

The WPC opened the way for the foreground projection of Jorge Amado's name in the international communist media, especially in the Soviet Union and Eastern Europe. When he arrived in France, Amado already had books published in Spanish, French, English, Italian, and Dutch. Between 1949 and 1955, the period of his militancy at the WPC, they reached eighteen other languages, according to Josélia Aguiar (2018). His correspondence with the Soviets shows that Amado was trying to publish his books in Russian as early as 1934. Still, he only managed to fulfill his dream when he became one of the WPC leaders. His prominence led the author to win the Stalin International Peace Prize in December 1951. He would personally receive the award in Moscow, where he was warmly welcomed at a solemnity at the Academy of Sciences of the Soviet Union in January 1952. The ceremonial greetings came from his friend, writer, and diplomat Ilya Ehrenburg, who had been on the jury (Gattai, 2009a, p. 234; Gattai, 2009b, p. 186 et seq.).

The prize was so relevant at the time that Jorge Amado stated in his memoirs to be proud of receiving it, even after abandoning Stalinism and the Communist Party:

I was a Stalinist of irreproachable conduct, underboss of the sect, if not bishop at least Monsignor. I discovered the mistake, which cost labor and suffering. I left the Mass in the middle and slipped away quietly. I became aware and left the herd, but I've never hidden or denied having received, on day of glory, with incredible honor and emotion, the International Stalin Prize [. . .] culminating moment of my life. (Amado, 2012b, p. 446)

These words give an idea of the importance for Amado of his role in the World Peace Council, as well as for other communist artists who felt rewarded and consecrated by receiving the prize. Speaking of the subject at the beginning and the end of his memoirs, which is fragmented and out of chronological order, Amado symbolically reiterated the relevance of this "culminating moment."

In Paris, the Brazilian had approached the writer that would become his greatest Soviet friend: Ilya Ehrenburg. In addition to being a well-known writer, he was, at the time, "a kind of Soviet government spokesman" on foreign policy, according to Amado (2012b, p. 107). He would later engage in the official de-Stalinization campaign, publishing works critical of the earlier period, such as the 1954 pioneer *The Thaw*, a name that would qualify Khrushchev's policy from 1956. But at the turn of the 1940s for the 1950s, he remained a faithful Stalinist ally with Jorge Amado's other Soviet friend and protector, Fadeyev, who would kill himself in 1956 after the denunciation of Stalin's crimes.

Heaven and Hell

Jorge Amado wrote that he had his first doubt about communism when he learned—in a bar talking with friends in Budapest in 1951—that comrades were tortured by the Hungarian government's political police during the Rajk trial, in an inner reckoning of the ruling summit (Amado, 2012b, p. 36). That same year, the novelist received the Stalin Prize, and his book *The World of Peace* was published in Brazil by the editorial Vitória that belonged to the Communist Party. The text praised communism and omitted his doubts: "unconditional Stalinist, I silenced the negative aspects as it was appropriate" (2012b, p. 184).

In turn, Zélia recalled that doubts about communism arose when they learned in Moscow about the prison of their friend Artur London. The Czechoslovak communist leader was arrested in 1951. During the Slansky trial, the accusation against him was of being a Trotskyist-Titoist-Zionist conspiracy, along with fourteen other leaders, eleven of whom were executed later. They were mostly Jews like London, who got life in prison, but would be pardoned and released in 1955 (Gattai, 2009b, p. 133 et seq.). Jorge Amado supposed at the time that the renegades deceived London, for "it would be impossible for Zélia and me to believe that Gerard [London's war name], a hero of Spain and the Resistance, the most loyal of the communists, is a traitor" (Amado, 2012b, p. 190).

Zélia Gattai recounted the uneasiness at the Writers' Castle with the persecuting atmosphere. It was the "time of fear and loneliness," which, however, did not shake faith in Stalin nor prevented them from regularly following the Peace Council meetings and make frequent travels with artists and intellectuals involved with the council. Their daily life went on at the castle of Dobris, where one day Zélia and Jorge opened their doors to welcome their friend Lise, wife of the persecuted London, and their children, under the disapproving gaze of other residents.

During a stay in Budapest, while he was still living in Paris, the Hungarian authorities granted Amado's request to visit Lukacs, with whom the Brazilian had made contact at the Wroclaw Congress. By the time the renowned communist philosopher had fallen in disgrace. Later, in Bucharest, Amado was allowed to visit novelist Zaharia Stancu, who was removed from the position of general secretary of Romanian writers. In those "unhappy weeks and months" at Dobris Castle, according to Amado, doubts and sleepless nights grew, he and Zélia contemplated each other with "a lump in the throat, a desire to weep" (Amado, 2012b, pp. 190–2; Gattai, 2009a, p. 361 et seq; Gattai, 2009b, p. 86).

Dobris Castle was still open for less controversial visits by communist artists such as Anna Seghers, animating the daily life of Zélia and Jorge. Celebrations were held there, including the lay christening of Paloma Gattai Amado, born in Prague. It was a "big party" with caviar and vodka brought from Moscow by Ehrenburg, the godfather of the girl next to Neruda and Guillén. Besides sandwiches and cakes, the champagne went to the Lafitte couple, who once had advised Zélia not to get involved in the internal affairs of the Czechoslovak Party. At the same time, the daughter of Chilean painter Jose Venturelli was "baptized." She received the name Paz (Peace). The girl had several godfathers, including the mighty Soviets Fadeyev and Korneichuk, as well as the president of the Czech Union of Writers Jan Drda, and the Turkish poet Nazim Hikmet, all of them Amado's friends (Gattai, 2009b, p. 169 et seq.). Neruda and Guillén had already been godfathers at the most modest celebration of "baptism" of the little João Jorge, held at the hotel where the Amados lived in Paris, having as their "priest" the writer Alfredo Varela, who would receive the Lenin Peace Prize of 1970–71 (Gattai, 2009a, pp. 137–139; Guillén, 1985, pp. 121–2).

In that "time of fear and loneliness" in late 1951, Jorge Amado won the coveted Stalin Prize, as it turned out. It was also then that he and his wife received from the Union of Chinese Writers the "dream invitation" to know China (Gattai, 2009b, p. 173). Living in paradise, they saw the hell a few steps away, reserved for dissidents. At that time, Amado wrote *The Bowels of Liberty*, considered the pinnacle of socialist realism in Brazil (Gattai, 2009b, pp. 13, 121 et seq; Gattai, 2011, pp. 42–3, 104).

Jorge Amado's militant activities took up too much time, taking his literary production to a slow pace, sacrificing his writing career "to fulfill political tasks," as Zélia Gattai pointed with a hint of outrage (2009b, p. 179). "For a writer who lives of literary work, running eight years without a new book in bookstores is a disaster" (Gattai, 2011, p. 42). Indeed, Amado's production—which had been a new novel every year or two from 1933 to 1946—fell sharply in his most active period of communist militancy from 1945 to 1955. Eight years passed between the publication of *Red Field* in 1946 and *The Bowels of Liberty* in 1954. In the intermission, *The World of Peace* appeared in 1951, a narrative of Amado's travels through the communist bloc. The book was in such a line with Stalinism that the author later vetoed the reprint. At the time, most of his writings were directly related to his political activity, including the novel *The Bowels of Liberty*.

If Jorge Amado's literary production had slowed down, he got a compensation: the visibility that his work gained from the political and cultural contacts which he made especially abroad, expanding his fame and the diffusion of his increasingly translated books into several languages. His insertion in the communist cultural and political network and his role in the Peace Movement involved a loss of autonomy as a writer.

However, at the same time, it established or deepened the international contacts that would allow Jorge Amado to be the most known Brazilian author, published worldwide, a best seller. His captive audience increased, and he guaranteed recognition among the peers that would last after leaving the Communist Party, without fanfare, not to harass former comrades in Brazil and abroad, nor his left-wing audience, let alone the Soviet Union. He would remain attached to the Peace Movement and successfully edited in communist countries while gaining autonomy and consecration as a writer in capitalist nations as well.

In 1962, ten years after the return of his extended stay abroad with his family, Amado had already become a member of the Brazilian Academy of Letters. He also was an outstanding personality of the cultural establishment, with international circulation on all fronts, as can be noted, for example, by the content of his family correspondence (Amado, 2012a). Metro-Goldwyn-Mayer bought the right to transpose the novel *Gabriela, Clove and Cinnamon* to the cinema, paying enough for the purchase and renovation of a beautiful house in Salvador. His books were increasingly translated and disseminated also in Western countries and all over the world. He could afford to refuse invitations not only to symposia in the United States and West Germany but also to the Soviet Union and Cuba. Invited to be part of the Casa de las Américas prize jury in Havana, he nominated the Brazilian friend and novelist Dalcídio Jurandir to take his place (Amado, 2012a, pp. 139–49). Such success in a conflicted world involved political ability, revealed, for example, in a letter to Zélia in October 1962. He gave justifications for refusing an invitation: "having not gone to the USSR, I also do not want to go to the USA" (Amado, 2012a, p. 146). Later, in 1971, he felt safe for a seven-month stay as a visiting professor at Pennsylvania State University, without giving up bonds with communist countries (Amado, 2012b, p. 380).

Toward the Third World

The dissemination of Latin American artists by the French communist press—and later by the World Peace Council on an expanded scale—would contribute to building solid ties between them. The bonds would last for the following phases of the Cold War and help the construction of a Latin American culture articulated with the emergence of the Third World, especially after the Cuban Revolution of 1959.

In a way, the communist conception of revolution for Latin America had already brought elements to what would later be called the Third World, the set of nations that the communists regarded as colonial or semi-colonial. Since the 1928 Congress of the Communist International, Latin American communist parties considered that their societies would be at the democratic-bourgeois stage of the revolution, since they were dependent on imperialism, with expressive feudal remnants in the countryside, similar to the so-called colonial and semi-colonial societies.[10] There would still be no objective conditions for carrying out a socialist revolution. Class struggle and the contradiction between capital and labor were in the background, given the priority task of joining progressive forces for national development, hampered by the associated interests of imperialists and large landowners. Then, workers, peasants, students, and petty-bourgeois sectors should ally with the national bourgeoisie to build independent peoples and nations, free to develop their productive forces. Only in the second stage, a properly socialist revolution could be possible.

Therefore, according to the communists, the revolution would have an anti-imperialist, anti-feudal, national and democratic character in Latin American countries, and could be achieved peacefully, or by weapons, if necessary. Artists and intellectuals linked to the party should play an essential role in the awareness and organization of the people, in addition to occupying spaces in their professional fields and cultural production, in favor of national development. In practice, an intense rapprochement between the communists and nationalist ideas was in progress. It gained force by the victory of the Chinese Revolution in 1949 and the Cuban Revolution ten years later, as well as others, such as the late liberation of the Portuguese colonies in Africa in the 1970s, spearheaded by movements that claimed to be Marxist-Leninist.

Amid this ideological conception, at the beginning of the Cold War, Latin American writers were incorporated by the French communist press, which welcomed them as persecuted by oligarchic tyrannies in their countries. As we have seen, they appeared on the pages as authentic representatives of national and popular cultures, oppressed by American imperialism and its allies in each nation. They would soon come to play a role in the world Peace Movement, which opened up unprecedented possibilities for building international networks that would not stay within the limits of the Cold War.

Eminent communist artists in the postwar period and the first half of the 1950s helped constitute a kind of prehistory of Third World ideals, which would gain strength in Latin America, especially after the victory of the Cuban Revolution. Many of them continued to operate, perhaps without the same prominence, given the emergence of new generations. Let's take the example of the three writers most committed to the World Peace Council in the region, who had been exiled in Paris and highlighted by the communist press. Guillén completely aligned himself with the Cuban Revolution, Neruda remained faithful to the rearticulated Soviet positions after the death of Stalin, while Jorge Amado moved away from them. However, the Brazilian stayed in the so-called progressive field, assuming moderate and conciliatory positions. Each of them inserted themselves in the Third World wave of which they were precursors.

Three Aspects of the Communist Cultural Legacy for the Third World

The new Third World ideological construction in Latin America was indebted to the previous communist moment in the intellectual sphere at least in three senses: (1) the institutional one, for example, with the legacy of the communist congresses in which Latin Americans took part, notably those promoted by the World Peace Council; (2) the diversified continuity of personal commitment of the old generation to the construction of a Latin American identity with intense nationalist colors, in coexistence with new characters and ideas in the cultural and political scene; and (3) the influence of the work of these artists for the new Third World generation, who appropriated it regardless of the authors' intention.

In the institutional aspect, the construction of a Latin American identity as part of the Third World has a link with the WPC and other initiatives of the Soviet bloc, such as international youth congresses, film and theater festivals, and so on. As Patrick Iber has already noted, "few saw Latin America as part of the Third World at the end of the 1950s." Latin American countries had ceased to be colonies more than a century ago, unlike several nations in Africa and Asia, characterized by recent or ongoing decolonization. However, the WPC had already mobilized nationalist, noncommunist sectors in the 1950s, as in the case of the movement around former Mexican president Lázaro Cárdenas, with more considerable momentum soon after the Cuban Revolution (Iber, 2015, pp. 145–73).

Indeed, the advent of the Cuban Revolution would change the situation: the ancient struggle in the region against underdevelopment and imperialism came to be associated with more intensity to that of other peoples against colonialism and for national liberation. For example, leftist movements engaged in the construction of a Tricontinental Conference that took place in Havana in January 1966, with representatives from Latin America, Asia, and Africa. Soon after that, Che Guevara's call to build "two, three, or many Vietnams" would echo around the world. This conference and others "had their origins in discussions and planning supported by the World Peace Council, but under very different leadership they created very different movements that in neither case acted precisely in the interests of Moscow" (Iber, 2015, p. 172).

The construction of Third World ideals in Latin America—and the very idea of Latin America understood as *América Nuestra* (Our America)—matured with the Cuban Revolution and its internationalizing institutional initiatives, such as the above-mentioned Tricontinental and the Latin American Organization of Solidarity (OLAS), gathered in Havana in August 1967. The revolutionary internationalist policy had strong cultural expression in institutions such as the *Instituto Cubano del Arte e Industria Cinematográficos* (ICAIC—Cuban Institute of Art and Film Industry) and *Casa de las Américas*. They sought to bring together writers, filmmakers, artists, and intellectuals from Latin America, open as well to other Third World countries, identified with anti-imperialism, anticolonialism, and national liberation struggles.

Regarding the second aspect (the diversified continuity in new terms of the personal commitment of writers in the construction of a Latin American identity as part of the Third World), we saw that Guillén became president of the Cuban Writers and Artists Union. He managed to balance himself in power until the end of his long life. In that prominent institutional position, he participated in the international initiatives promoted by Havana. He always sided with Fidel Castro in the veiled or expressed conflicts not only with the United States but also the Soviet Union and sectors of Cuban and Latin American artists and intellectuals. That could cost the price of wear and tear with old friends from the time of exile in Paris and the movement for world peace. It was the case with Neruda, who faithfully followed the political trajectory of the Soviet Union and the Chilean Communist Party in the post-Stalinist phase, in uneasy coexistence with the Cuban allies.

In his memoirs, Neruda referred in passing to the so-called international boom of Latin American literature in the 1960s, expressly citing the "names of García Marques, Juan Rulfo, Vargas Llosa, Sábato, Cortázar, Carlos Fuentes, the Chilean Donoso." He expressed admiration for their books "increasingly essential in the truth and the dream of our Americas." But a certain distance from the new generation became evident when he referred to it with a dose of poison: "It is also common to hear that they form a self-promotion group" (Neruda, 1974, p. 290). García Marques and Cortázar were among the friends who went to dinner with Neruda in Paris after the poet received the news of the Nobel Prize awarded to him (1974, pp. 304–5).

A similar ambiguity appears concerning the Cuban Revolution and its leaders, Fidel Castro and Che Guevara, with whom Neruda had personal contact after the triumph in the Sierra Maestra. He boasted that he was the first poet to write an entire book to exalt the Cuban Revolution, entitled *Canción de Gesta* (Neruda, 1974, p. 325). But he was disappointed that they did not give due weight to the book in Cuba, according to his biographer Adam Feinstein. In November 1960, Neruda made his first visit to revolutionary Cuba, with which "there would be a whole string of misunderstandings and antipathies" (Feinstein, 2004, p. 325–6). Neruda supported the Cuban Revolution in public, but took a distance from it privately, such as the criticism of Che Guevara's youthful voluntarism and the cult of the personality of Fidel Castro (Feinstein, 2004, pp. 325–6, 347).

Neruda was flattered to learn that Guevara read excerpts from *Canto General* to guerrillas on nights in Sierra Maestra. Also, when he knew that it was one of the two books that the revolutionary carried in his backpack when captured in Bolivia (Neruda, 1974, p. 320). But the poet expressed a political distance, critical of militarism, by declaring himself surprised to have found Guevara in a military uniform in full exercise of bureaucratic activities in the Cuban Ministry of Finance. Then, the Chilean heard from the leader that "we cannot live without war." Neruda disagreed with stupor since he considered war "a threat, not a fate" (1974, pp. 320–1). He identified himself more with the *détente* taken over by Soviet foreign policy than with the armed struggle proposed by the Cubans for the Third World, although sympathetic in defense of Cuba against American imperialism.

Neruda would soon be involved in a conflict. In an open letter, Cuban artists and intellectuals accused him of having accepted an award from the Peruvian government—then an enemy of Cuban policy and local guerrillas. They also complained that Neruda had attended a world Pen Club congress in the United States, in a supposed capitulation to Yankee imperialism. The critics ignored that the poet defended anti-imperialist positions and read committed poems to huge American audiences.

Neruda got hurt and never complied with the accusations of "submission and betrayal," made against him by the writers Roberto Fernández Retamar, Edmundo Desnoes, and Lisandro Otero, but also signed by dozens of others, including his friends Nicolás Guillén, Alejo Carpentier, and Juan Marinello in July 1966. They proposed to speak "on behalf of all the peoples of *América Nuestra*, all the hungry and humiliated peoples of the world," assuming the identity of Latin Americans and "men of the Third World." For them, "the trail of true coexistence and the real settlement of war (cold and hot), passes through national liberation struggles, passes through guerrillas, not through impossible reconciliation," which they attributed to Neruda's position.[11] Feeling wronged, Neruda never went to Cuba again, nor did he forgive the signatories of the letter. He received solidarity from the Chilean communists, who interpreted the episode as an attack by Cubans on their political line (Neruda, 1974, pp. 321–5; Feinstein, 2004, pp. 342–58).

Neruda would return to attend a Pen Club meeting in New York in April 1972, when he was the ambassador for the Allende government in Paris (Feinstein, 2004, p. 386). He spoke about the influence received from the work by Walt Whitman, the problems of Latin America, particularly his country, also seeking to find "hopes for the total extinction of colonialism in Africa and Asia" (Neruda, 1973, pp. 11–2). But the poet did not pronounce the term "Third World," perhaps believing that the Soviet side contemplated the topic. Many years before, in 1950, the World Peace Council sent Neruda as a representative to India, where he had already been when he served as a Chilean diplomat in Asia early in his career. The aim was to strengthen the local Peace Movement and negotiate with the government of Nehru, whom he met personally. The poet was received coldly, at the limit of hostility, by the authorities who imposed bureaucratic difficulties that much irritated him. Nevertheless, he saw his efforts bear fruit five years later, in the context of the organization of the Third World. Nehru received the Stalin Peace Prize with Neruda's vote, "consecrated as one of the champions of peace" (Neruda, 1974, pp. 202–7).

In turn, Jorge Amado would also make his contribution to the Third World when he was no longer a communist. He was friends with authors from Spanish America, Africa, Asia, and Brazil itself. It was the case of the filmmaker Glauber Rocha, originally from Bahia, like him. In the past, Amado had been the main star of the Brazilian left on the international stage. Later, Glauber became the most worldwide renowned Brazilian artist in defense of national liberation struggles. In the 1960s and early 1970s, he approached ideas by authors such as Frantz Fanon and Che Guevara, highlighting the need to use violence by the oppressed peoples of the Third World, with whom he had a particular identification. With the film *Antonio das Mortes*, Glauber won the award of best director at the Cannes festival in 1969. The following year he got European funding to shoot a movie in Congo, *Der Leone Have Sept Cabeças*. The title was an attempt to "achieve a synthesis of historical myths of the Third World through the national repertoire of popular drama" (Rocha, 1997, p. 43). According to Ivana Bentes, "each word in the title indicating a colonizer: German, Italian, Anglo-American, French, Portuguese" (In Rocha, 1997, p. 44).

In 1971, Glauber traveled to Northern Africa and filmed in Morocco. Next, he lived in Cuba from November 1971 to December 1972 (Pierre, 1996, p. 68). He was very friendly with the director of ICAIC, the Cuban Alfredo Guevara, with whom he had frequent correspondence since 1960 (Rocha, 1997). Glauber helped organize the aesthetic and political project of creating a new Latin American cinema. The task was shared with filmmakers from Cuba, Argentina, Chile, and Brazil, in search of building "*América Nuestra*," in the context of the affirmation of the Third World, seeking to articulate a series of national cinematic movements in a project of continental dimension (Villaça, 2002). Glauber has also visited Allende's Chile and Alvarado's Peru, which he considered allies in the struggle to liberate Latin America from imperialism.

He wanted to be a "tricontinental filmmaker," a revolutionary both in politics and aesthetics (Rocha, 1997, p. 43). He also filmed moments of the carnation revolution in Portugal, participating in the documentary *As Armas e o Povo* (*The guns and the People*), made by a collective of cinematic workers between April 25 and May 1, 1974.

From that year on, Glauber Rocha began to publicly express opinions that indisposed him with most of the left. He bet that the government of General Geisel could become "revolutionary militarism that would bring about the changes that the left did not know how to do or could not do," in the words of Ivana Bentes (In Glauber, 1997, p. 50). Many interpreted his position as adherence to the government policy of slow, gradual, and secure opening to democracy in Brazil. Glauber found support from Jorge Amado, a friend who was the subject of his short documentary film *Jorjamado no cinema*, from 1979. The novelist—who cultivated friends across the ideological spectrum—was one of the chief negotiators for the Geisel government to accept Glauber's return from exile in 1976. Amado would visit the young friend in the last days of the filmmaker at a hospital in Lisbon, before returning to die in Brazil. The novelist was present as well at Glauber's funeral in Rio de Janeiro in 1981 (Amado, 2012b, pp. 82, 118). Both shared a Brazilian and Bahian identity, united in this period by the solidarity of artists who saw themselves as heretics in the left.

Attesting his old friendship with Glauber Rocha, Jorge Amado did not remember if he was the one who recommended the filmmaker to read *One Hundred Years of Solitude* or vice versa. Amado would be introduced to García Marques at a meeting of Latin American writers at the Frankfurt fair in 1970, in a context involving publishers and literary agents. Later he was with the Colombian in Cartagena, Paris, and Havana, where they had dinner with Fidel Castro (Amado, 2012b, p. 261). This brief passage from Amado's memoirs could well illustrate the triangle formed in the period by literature, market, and revolution, in the terms of Claudia Gilman (2003, p. 21).

Jorge Amado was friends with other authors from the boom of Latin American literature, such as Vargas Llosa. He helped the Peruvian a lot in 1979, by facilitating contacts in Brazil when the fellow went on a research trip to write the famous book on the Canudos episode in the hinterland of Bahia, entitled *The War of the End of the World* (Amado, 2012b, pp. 302–3). The Brazilian author has also often been with Julio Cortázar, whom he met many times, the last one on a television talk show in Germany, where they denounced the tortures perpetrated by the dictatorships of their countries. The Brazilian would write a tribute text to the Argentine after his death, published in Sandinista Nicaragua, at the request of Minister Tomás Borge. As a jury member of the international prize Pablo Neruda, promoted by the Soviets, Amado gave his vote to the award winner poet Ernesto Cardenal, another Nicaraguan minister, a Catholic priest of Liberation Theology (Amado, 2012b, pp. 393–4). These episodes attest to the proximity of the old Amado to the young Nicaraguan government, which closed the cycle of revolutions in the Third World in 1979, the same year of the Iranian Revolution. The cases also reiterate the permanence of his influence and prestige abroad, as well as his political and intellectual bonds involved in awarding prizes.

Like Neruda, Amado supported the Cuban Revolution. Still, he did not always hide criticisms of Fidel Castro, not to mention Che Guevara. The latter is remembered in his memoirs only twice, in brief excerpts that mock the youthful worship devoted to the commander by Amados's son, João Jorge (2012b, pp. 186, 281). It did not prevent him from visiting Cuba in 1962 and other times, and from being with Fidel, with whom he discussed the need to open up his regime to the Black religious culture of *santeria* on a visit in 1986 (Amado, 2012b, pp. 189–90).

Concerning the third aspect—the influence of the work by these old writers for the new Third World generation—it is possible to find appropriations beyond the original circumstances and limits of their production. That is evident in Che Guevara's use of Neruda's *Canto General* during the guerrilla struggle to motivate his group, particularly in Bolivia, in a way that the poet considered politically wrong, despite the heroism and good intentions.

Similarly, there was a remarkable impact of the novels by Jorge Amado—especially from his former communist phase—on the writers and anticolonial activists of Portuguese Africa in the 1960s and 1970s. It is evident in the testimony of the renowned Mozambican writer Mia Couto, whose father was a poet and gave the name of the Brazilian to two of his sons, one called Jorge and the other one Amado. As stated by Mia Couto, "Jorge Amado was the writer who had the greatest influence on the genesis of literature in African countries that speak Portuguese." The "immediate and lasting" influence of the Brazilian novelist in Angola, Mozambique, Cape Verde, Guinea-Bissau, and São Tomé and Príncipe would be due to three factors, according to Couto: first, the literary quality of the text; second, the existential familiarity with African Brazilian culture presented by Amado's novels, which allowed to foresee the possibility of building new nations in Africa, independent of the Portuguese cradle; and finally a third reason, which can be called linguistic, showing the potential of speaking and writing a different kind of Portuguese in the former colonies in search of their own identity. All these factors, it may be added, are linked to the circulation of Amado's work in African anticolonial circles, much facilitated by the communist network that spread Amado's novels, often underground. Thus, "Mozambican and Angolan nationalist poets raised Amado like a flag," in the words of Mia Couto (2012, p. 193).

When he met Jorge Amado in Luanda in 1979, the Angolan writer Luandino Vieira told the Brazilian that he decided to sell his blood in a hospital in the 1950s, in order to get money to buy the novel *The Bowels of Liberty*, the communist saga of Resistance to the dictatorship of Getúlio Vargas, written by Amado in his exile at the Writers' Castle (Amado, 2012b, pp. 208–9). Luandino, sentenced to fourteen years in prison at the Tarrafal Concentration Camp in 1964, "sent a letter beyond the bars asking for the following:—Send my manuscript to Jorge Amado to see if he can publish it there in Brazil," on the report of Mia Couto (2012, p. 192).

Many other African writers, artists, and activists mirrored Jorge Amado's work to form their own identity in the pre-independence context. They paid particular attention to the committed novels of the first phase, such as *Jubiabá*, *Sea of Death*, *The Violent Land*, and *Captains of the Sands*, as demonstrated by Carla Cordeiro (2017). Not by chance, another writer of influence in Africa during this period of the national liberation struggle was also a communist: Graciliano Ramos "revealed the bone and stone of the Brazilian nation. Amado exalted the flesh and the feast of that same Brazil," in the words of Mia Couto (2012, p. 190). Ultimately, Jorge Amado, who had become moderate and conciliatory in the 1960s and 1970s, saw his works from the communist phase gain new breath and meaning in the context of national liberation struggles in Portuguese-speaking Africa.

As can be seen, the formulation of Third World political and cultural alternatives, not only in Latin America, had an essential link with the immediately previous communist struggles, particularly in the internationalization of artists and intellectuals, such as the writers Pablo Neruda and Jorge Amado. In turn, they had their bonds with the utopias defeated in the Spanish Civil War, which referred to the triumph of the Russian Revolution of 1917. The historical process spanned the entire twentieth century, involving artists committed to political projects, imagining a new world, to which they would contribute with their affective and creative ties, as well as their disputes and rivalries.

Notes

1   *Europe*, n. 29, May 1948, 1–9. *Les Lettres Françaises*, n. 202, April 1, 1948, 5.
2   *Les Lettres Françaises*, n. 351, January 22, 1951, 1 and 8.
3   *Europe*, n. 47–48, December 1949, 151–66.
4   *Europe*, n. 49, January 1950, 105–6.
5   *Les Lettres Françaises,* n. 197, February 26, 1948, 1 e 3.
6   Ibid., 4.
7   See, for example, *Arts de France,* n. 9, 1946, 3–16. *Les Lettres Française,* n. 664, March 28, 1957, 12.
8   *Europe*, n. 67–68, July–August 1951, 36–7.
9   The poet Ai Qing was father of the famous dissident of our day, the artist Ai Weiwei, born that same year of 1957.
10 See, for example, the classic book by Caio Prado Jr. (1966).
11 Full text of the letter, https://www.neruda.uchile.cl/critica/cartaabierta.html, consulted on May 1, 2020.

6

Radical Scholarship and Political Activism

Walter Rodney as Third World Intellectual and Historian of the Third World

Andreas Eckert

Between Reflection and Action

The year "1968" has acquired a status of youthful rebellion against established powers. Mainly associated with places in the North Atlantic realm such as Berkeley, (West-) Berlin, and Paris, it is increasingly seen as a moment of truly global resonance, even sometimes as the first global rebellion that simultaneously reverberated in many regions of the world.[1] While 1968 is still predominantly a symbol of left-wing activism, the year itself was rather contradictory in political terms. In the United States, it was marked by the assassinations of Martin Luther King and Robert Kennedy and the election of Richard Nixon. In Eastern Europe, it was the year when Soviet tanks crushed the Prague Spring. In China, it was the beginning of the end of the mass movement phase of the Cultural Revolution. And even in France, only a month after the supposedly revolutionary May 68, the Gaullist right captured power winning more than three-quarters of the seats of the National Assembly. In 1968 Ayi Kwei Armah published his novel *The Beautiful Ones Are Not Yet Born*, in which he evoked the disillusion of young Ghanaians who had been captivated by the idealism and dynamism of the new postcolonial state, only to see their contemporaries and families caught up in the greed and corruption of the new order. And finally, in the summer of that year, audiences around the globe were shocked when newspapers and TV stations confronted them with photographs of starving children in the secessionist Republic of Biafra in Nigeria. "Biafra" became the epitome of a humanitarian crisis and a key episode for the restructuring of the relations between "the West" and the "Third World."[2]

However, the Congress of Black Writers that was convened in early October 1968 in Montreal was without any doubt a gathering of firmly left intellectuals, talking revolution to an engaged and sometimes combative crowd. The event was organized by a group of Caribbean and Black Canadian students and members of Montreal's wider Black community.[3] Despite the absence of speakers from the African continent, Latin America, and the non-Anglophone Caribbean, the Congress was a crucial Black international event that bridged generations and political perspectives. Among the participants were representatives of an older generation of pan-African and Black radical figures—most notably C. L. R. James[4], as well as younger radicals, for instance, Stokely Carmichael, the Trinidadian-born African American, "prime minister" of the Black Panther Party and at the time of the gathering, where he gave the closing address, at the height of his popularity. The debates were not free from conflicts, due to a combination of intragenerational political dynamics, differences, and divergent ideas on how to address anti-Black racism. A striking feature of the Congress was the total absence of women's voices. Even Miriam Makeba, the famous exiled South African singer, only appeared as companion of her husband, Stokely Carmichael.

The Congress of Black Writers also ushered a young scholar onto the world stage as an historian of Africa and an emerging political voice. Walter Rodney, born in Guyana, a PhD from the School of Oriental and African Studies in London, had a brief teaching stint at the University of Dar es Salaam in Tanzania and had recently been appointed professor at the University of Mona in Jamaica when he appeared at the Montreal meeting. He delivered a much-noticed talk on "African History in the Service of Black Liberation" in which he argued that "African history must be seen as very intimately linked to the contemporary struggle of black people. One must not set up any false distinctions between reflection and action."[5] In a nutshell, the second sentence reflected his lifelong credo. Montreal 68 brought Rodney into contact with some key figures of the Black Power movement in the United States and marked the beginning of his trajectory as a foremost Third World scholar-cum-activist, a mobile and restless existence that ended with an early and violent death.

Rodney was merely thirty-eight years old when in 1980 Guyana's government had him murdered in the capital Georgetown in a politically motivated assassination. At this young age he had, however, already left a mark on an entire field of research and stirred debate beyond strict academic confines, a feat achieved by only few historians and generally only after much longer careers. Published in 1972 by Bogle l'Ouverture, a small publishing house founded by exiled Guyanese in London, in cooperation with the Tanzania Publishing House based in Dar es Salaam, Rodney's book *How Europe Underdeveloped Africa* (HEUA) was an engaging account of the role played by the slave trade and colonialism that revealed Europe's role in fomenting the dismal state of affairs in Africa borrowing heavily from Latin American dependency theory.[6] Rodney was an important voice among those critics who, in the 1960s and 1970s, have emphasized the other, ostensibly real functions of "modernization": to win the newly independent nations for the "free world" while at the same time securing unfettered access to their considerable natural resources and using the decolonized regions as a social scientific laboratory without having to bear responsibility for their experiments' effects. His provocative arguments inspired generations of Africa scholars and activists, and some argue that this study "was the 20th century's most important book on African history."[7] *HEUA* has been translated into numerous languages, French, Portuguese, and German among them. For instance, three years after the first English-language edition, the leftist publishing house Wagenbach brought out a German translation entitled *Afrika*.

Walter Rodney

AFRIKA

Die Geschichte einer Unterentwicklung

Politik 56   DM 14,50   Wagenbach

Figure 6.1 German edition of *How Europe Underdeveloped Africa* [www.abebooks.com].

Die Geschichte einer Unterentwicklung, which became one of the few academic books on Africa in German to sell copiously during the 1970s and early 1980s[8] (Figure 6.1).

Born in Guyana, Rodney was a professor of history at the University of Dar es Salaam in Tanzania when his most influential book was published. He was a man engaged in a broad set of activities: he was an author of academic books and articles, a university professor, a political activist, but also a "man of the people" who debated with the slum dwellers of Jamaica and Guyana, and tried to find appropriate ways of transmitting African history in collaboration with village teachers in Tanzania.[9] In his 1993 Reith Lectures, Edward Said describes an intellectual as someone who is

> neither a pacifier nor a consensus-builder, but someone whose whole being is staked on a critical sense, a sense of being unwilling to accept easy formulas, or ready-made clichés, or the smooth, ever-so-accommodating confirmations of what the powerful or conventional have to say, and what they do. Not just passively, unwillingly, but actively willing to say so in public. . . . There is no question . . . that the intellectual belongs on the same side with the weak and unrepresented.[10]

Although Said does not refer to Rodney, but very likely first and foremost to himself, these lines capture much of Rodney's spirit. In many instances Rodney emphasized the importance of blending his academic and political work: "As an academic," he wrote, "and for as long as I remain an academic, I must strive to provide the most important political service during the many hours in which I teach, research or engage in other activities related to my life as an academic."[11] Ultimately, merging his political activism and research is what initially cost him his source of livelihood in Guyana and, later, his life.

In the years following his violent death, the image of Rodney remained more or less that of a "scholar activist," a perspective that was partly blind to his rigorous social history studies and interpreted his academic oeuvre to a large degree as merely an instrument of political struggle.[12] Moreover, while one fraction of authors claimed Rodney mainly for the Caribbean cause, others emphasized his crucial role in rewriting (pan-)African history. Eventually, however, the growing interest in the "Black Atlantic" gave way to a new interpretation of Rodney's work as an intellectual and activist, as someone whose writings and political activities linked North America, the Caribbean, Africa, and Europe in ways that only very few of his generation managed to do.[13] The strong political inclinations of his writings, his focus—at least at times—on social history, and in particular his specific political work with the "wretched of the earth" set Rodney apart from later generations of postcolonial intellectuals.[14] Current important scholars associated with this line of thought, like Achille Mbembe, remain, notwithstanding their sharp-tongued, critical analyses, mostly limited to sweeping ideological criticisms, which hardly provide concrete recipes for political action.[15] The strands of global history, too, that analyse the questions that interested Rodney concerning the role played by the slave trade and slave-based production in the global rise of capitalism remain very cautious with regard to their political implications.[16]

Walter Rodney's trajectory reflects both the openings and closures of the Third World project as we approach the 1970s. As C. L. R. James stated, he himself, Aimé Césaire, George Padmore, W. E. B. Du Bois and others

> were faced with a particular challenge. As we grew up and went along, we had to fight the doctrines of the imperialist powers in order to establish some Caribbean foundations or foundations for the underdeveloped peoples. Walter did not have to do that. The aforementioned works were written before he was born. Walter grew up in an atmosphere where for the first time a generation of West Indian intellectuals were able not only to study the revolutionary and creative works that had been created in Europe but also benefit from and be master of what had been done in the same tradition in direct reference to the Caribbean. . . . To be born in 1942 was to have behind you a whole body of work dealing in the best way with the emerging situation in the Caribbean and the colonial world.[17]

It was the foundational, opening work of James and others that enabled Rodney to be a crucial figure in giving the Third World its own historiography. At the same time, the spaces he could navigate became increasingly constrained. Somehow, ironically, while his influence grew in North America and in parts of Europe and Africa, he was made a pariah by postcolonial governments and political elites in those places he most affiliated with, Jamaica and Guyana.

The Making of a Third World Intellectual

Walter Rodney's intellectual and political development was closely tied to two connected historic developments: first, the wave of national liberation movements that swept through the European colonies following the Second World War, and, second, the US civil rights movement, which gave significant momentum to pan-African movements globally. During his childhood, Rodney confronted harsh realities of racism and colonial exploitation. Only a few streets away from where he would later be assassinated, he and his five brothers and sisters were raised in precarious conditions. His parents were involved in the anticolonial and socialist "People's Progressive Party." Already at the age of eleven, Rodney began to take part in party meetings and handed out leaflets. This, as he called it in hindsight, "profound commitment to socialism" never left him. As a high-achieving pupil and excellent athlete, he earned scholarships that allowed him to attend secondary school and later study history at the University of the West Indies in Mona, Jamaica.[18]

As a founder of the Students' Democratic Party, he and some other students visited Cuba and the Soviet Union in the early 1960s. In Moscow, he was "amazed at the number of books they sell—in the streets, on the pavement, all over. In my society, you have to search for a bookstore and be directed and told that *the* bookstore is down *that* street, as if it's an alien institution. And even in America, one can buy hot dogs and hamburgers on the sidewalks, a lot of nice things like that, but not books."[19] Unsurprisingly, Rodney and the other students soon caught the attention not only of Jamaica's secret service but also the CIA. The Jamaican government reckoned that Rodney's contacts in Cuba extended to the highest level. "There is reason to believe," they claimed, "that whilst in Cuba Rodney and his companions were visited in the hotel by Castro himself." In any case, the student delegation returned to Jamaica with a "considerable amount of Communist literature and subversive publications of the IUS, including Che Guevara's Guerilla Warfare." Customs officials, probably tipped off by the intelligence services, temporarily seized the material and would later send their reports to US authorities that attempted to track Black power in Jamaica and elsewhere in the Caribbean and, in cooperation with local authorities, combat its influence.[20]

For his PhD, Rodney won a fellowship at the School of Oriental and African Studies in London, which at the time was one of the premier centers for the study of African history in the Anglophone world.[21] Looking back, Rodney described the PhD seminars there as "led by all these deans of knowledge on Africa, who had this tremendous flair for keeping everybody at a lower level."[22] The history PhD student from Guyana chose other audiences and regularly spoke at London's famous Speakers' Corner in Hyde Park. He also put in a regular appearance at discussion circles organized by C. L. R. James and his wife Selma James. James, as Rodney would later note, taught him to see the pan-African perspective and the ability to analyze historical situations.[23] Rodney was equally inspired by the work of Eric Williams. While he criticized him as the then president of Trinidad and Tobago, Williams's classic study *Capitalism and Slavery* (1944) provided Rodney with important insights into the connection between plantation slavery in the Caribbean and the rise of capitalism in Europe.[24] Finally, a less explicit but, nevertheless, important source for Rodney's thinking was W. E. B. Du Bois, whose argument that the enslavement of Africans was a key to the rise of Europe and to the development of global capitalism found considerable resonance in Rodney's work.[25] On the other hand, he found it difficult to relate to the British Left. Rodney felt that the intellectuals at the London School of Economics and from the milieu of the *New Left Review*, while radical in their words, were no more than a trend of the times, caught up in a tradition that was mainly concerned with appearing particularly clever. He decried their latent racism and open paternalism.[26]

In 1966, shortly after receiving his PhD, Rodney took up a teaching position at the Faculty of History in Dar es Salaam (USDM), which at the time had an excellent international reputation where precolonial African history as well as resistance against European colonial rule were at the center of teaching and research.[27] "I would have preferred to go to West Africa, which was my special area of research," Rodney stated later.[28] However, the military coup that overthrew Nkrumah in 1966 had led to both the forced and voluntary exodus of African American and Caribbean activist-expatriates from Ghana. The country ceased to be the leading independent state committed to global African emancipation. The kind of politics being developed in Nigeria, where the civil war had just started, did not appeal to Rodney either. And he felt that Guinea, as a former French colony, would place too many restrictions on his academic research and political activities due to differences in language and history, despite its president Sekou Touré being still widely regarded as an important fighter against neocolonialism.[29] Tanzania offered an obvious alternative. Even if not everybody shared the views of President Julius Nyerere on traditional African socialism (*Ujamaa*), the socialist experiment being shaped in the country and the general excitement of a new beginning brought many left-wing researchers in the humanities and social sciences from across the world to East Africa. Moreover, during this period Dar es Salaam was an important hub of global political activism, fuelled by multiple political strands.[30] Nyerere's repeatedly expressed emphasis on the importance of African history spoke directly to Rodney's professional aspirations as an historian, as an intellectual, and as a pan-Africanist.[31]

Just after Rodney's arrival in Dar, "the National Service Crisis" put the University in turmoil. Around four hundred students dressed in red caps and gowns took to the streets and marched from the main campus to the State House downtown to protest against the compulsory national service for students after their exam introduced a few months before. The idea behind this scheme was to require students to "pay back" the free education they had received through the building of needed infrastructure or teaching at schools. The students considered this an affront: "Let our bodies go. But our souls will remain outside the scheme, and the battle between the political elite and the educated elite will perpetually continue," they claimed, and on some of their posters one could even read "Colonialism was better."[32] Nyerere, apparently caught by surprise, reacted furiously and expelled two-thirds of the protesting students from university. He combined this measure with general (self-)criticism of the national elite ("a class of exploiters") that was echoed a few months later in the famous Arusha Declaration of February 1967. The declaration proclaimed the building-up of a socialist state as central goal of the governing party TANU and emphasized the particular importance of agriculture and agrarian development.[33] Nyerere also presented a new vision of an education system that would fully integrate students in the life of the dominant, rural community. According to him, education "must ensure that the educated know themselves to be an integral part of the nation and recognize the responsibility to give greater service the greater the opportunities they have had."[34]

Socialist staff members at the University including Rodney took the National Service Crisis as an opportunity to turn the university into a "people's institution." A collective of mainly expatriate scholars, among them Rodney, John S. Saul and Giovanni Arrighi, known as the "Group of Nine," handed in a proposal to alter the introductory course which was compulsory for students at USDM. Their paper was based on the conviction that "socialists do not grow on trees but have to be formed through (often painful) experience and study." Their recommendations, which strongly shaped the curriculum of the Institute of Development Studies founded a few years later, blended international socialist thought, dependency theory and Tanzania's *Ujamaa* experience. Large part of the curriculum focused on dependency paradigms and especially on theories of underdevelopment and formed a crucial context for Rodney's HEUA. Africa was always conceptualized as a whole, which marked a notable contrast to the overwhelmingly nationalist framework of much scholarship and teaching at USDM, for instance, in the history department.[35]

After less than two years in Tanzania, Rodney took up a position at his Alma Mater in Mona, Jamaica, where he established a Caribbean and Africa studies programme. At the same time, he became embroiled in politics and soon established himself as a harsh critic of the government and as one of the most visible faces of the Jamaican Black Power movement. In Jamaica, the components of Black power—ranging from Rastafarians of various lines and religious rebels to urban youths, university students, and radical intellectuals—remained rather uncoordinated. Both Black power activists and the government attributed to Rodney the potential to unite the fractions.[36] As Rupert Lewis observed, at the time an undergraduate student at Mona, "Rodney came to embody the aspirations of politically aware young people from the middle and lower classes who were alienated socially, economically and politically . . . [he] was so unlike the posturing and radical chic behaviour of some campus radicals."[37] Rodney deliberately lived off campus. While he continued to publish work on African history,[38] he increasingly developed "grassroots connections" and developed the praxis of "grounding." This term designated a space of self-determination and has its origins in the self-activity of slaves who sought to assert their own autonomy against various forms of oppression.[39] Rodney would accept invitations from a variety of groups such as Rastafarians, high school students or community organizations, where he would talk about African and Caribbean history and politics or discuss the Black power and civil rights movements in the United States.[40]

In October 1968, following his much-noticed talk at the Congress of Black Writers in Montreal, the Jamaican authorities barred Rodney from returning to the country. One pretext was that Rodney posed a threat to the tourism industry, crucial to Jamaica's economy. Fierce protests, which became known as the "Rodney riots," erupted the next day. Nothing of the sort had been seen in Jamaica since the colonial era, in the 1930s.[41] The "Rodney riots" highlighted the growing exchanges between Black Power in the Caribbean and on the North American mainland. The emergence of Black nationalist factions in Canada, particularly among West Indian students, provided a critical focal point for Caribbean intellectuals as well as a link to more prominent movements in the United States. Caribbean governments moved to cut those ties, including banning the works of US-based radicals, along with the radicals themselves. "But the genie could not be returned to the bottle; protests continued, including by Caribbean students in North America, most notably in Canada."[42]

After short stints in London and Cuba, Rodney was offered to return to Dar es Salaam, where he then spent five highly productive years raising his profile as a radical historian of Africa and the African diaspora.[43] His expulsion from Jamaica had received wide publicity in the Caribbean, North America, England, and Africa. The publication of his Jamaican lectures and speeches under the title *Groundings with My Brothers* further shaped his political reputation as the region's most important intellectual-activist.[44] During his second stay in Tanzania, he became even more the subject of increased international interest, not least in the United States, from both academics and activists.

Writing African History as Third World History: The Dar es Salaam Years

Rodney's dissertation, *A History of the Upper Guinea Coast, 1545-1800*, published in 1970 by Clarendon Press in Oxford as well as thematically related articles he wrote for renowned academic journals and handbooks, caused a great stir in the debate on slavery and the slave trade in Africa. Unlike established schools of thought within academia, Rodney vehemently defended the argument that slavery in Africa had foremost been the result of external demand and intervention. He also framed his first book within Marxist vocabulary such as "ruling class" and "superstructure," and emphasized the "cleavage" of class inequality. The main point of the study was that the Upper Guinea Coast should be seen as a place that underwent profound changes because of its incorporation into the larger trans-Atlantic economy via the slave trade and European "proto-colonization." These factors, Rodney argued, make untenable any description of West African societies as "traditional." His conclusions echoed widespread attempts to counter myths of a stagnant African continent "without history": "Yet far too often there has been a ready acceptance of reports on West Africa in the eighteenth and nineteenth centuries as representing certain timeless institutions, and it is even assumed that field studies of 'indigenous' African societies in the twentieth century disclose a fundamentally unchanged pattern."[45] His dissertation was critically received especially by North American specialists, something which Rodney explained as follows:

> It was very clear from some of the reviews that certain American scholars just felt hurt or wounded that anybody should dare to even begin to suggest that there was something like class analysis, or that when we are dealing with slavery in Africa, we must put it in the context of capitalism and not just see two abstract sets of bodies [Europa and Africa] meeting with each other.[46]

In *HEUA*, he would then expand the insights from this initial case study to the entire continent. In this book, Rodney sought to identify the underlying roots of poverty shared by Africa and other Third World regions located on the "periphery" of the world capitalist system. His text was crucial in shifting the terms from a neoclassical emphasis on "development" to an exploration of the deleterious effects of Africa's incorporation in the world economy. Although Rodney stressed the dialectical relationship between growth and development in Europe and stagnation and underdevelopment in Africa, it is important to note that he did not simply reduce Africans to victims. Throughout his narrative, he explored the role of local social forces that benefited from capitalist penetration, the slave trade, colonialism and neocolonialism, as well as of those who sought to blunt the European advances.

His positions earned him once more the fierce criticism of a number of his colleagues in academia, who emphasized, for instance, important regional differences in Africa and pointed out that even before the onset of the European slave trade, slavery had been an established practice on the continent. Obviously, the majority of his critics nonetheless did concede that the slave trade brutalized and enormously expanded this practice when Europe began trading in African slaves.[47] Immanuel Wallerstein, who was a vocal supporter of Rodney's work, noted that the book "is not based on archival sources, has no footnotes, and offers short annotated notes instead of a bibliography. It is openly didactic, and its intended audience is clearly university students and educated persons generally in Africa, and their friends and counterparts elsewhere."[48] Wallerstein's remark gets to the heart of some of the most widespread criticisms of the book: the way how evidence is used to substantiate the arguments. For instance, in the discussions about the role of slavery in distorting West African economic and social development, Rodney raised the issue of the profitability of slavery, a controversial debate within the relevant historiography. Instead of providing instances of how the profitability of slavery has been understood in scholarship, he dismisses the point right away, along with any who might suggest otherwise: "A few bourgeois scholars have suggested that the trade in slaves did not have worthwhile monetary returns. . . . This kind of argument is worth noting more as an example of the distortions of which white bourgeois scholarship is capable than as something requiring serious attention" (HEUA, 83). Similarly, in his discussion of the role of population loss as a factor in the underdevelopment of West Africa, a hotly debated topic characterized by significant numbers games and demographic models, Rodney made a moral, rather than a scholarly argument and failed to offer much concrete information. As the specialist on West African slavery Martin Klein noted in his review, in reference to Rodney's analysis of the disastrous effects of colonialism for Africa's development, such moralism, although it served Rodney's polemical purposes, tended to put off numerous academic historians: "For Africanists, most of whom do not defend colonial rule, much of this is like thrashing a dead dog."[49]

In spite of the criticisms received from his colleagues, Rodney's book explaining "underdevelopment" south of the Sahara struck a chord among fellow academics and the general public.[50] In the early 1970s, there was growing disillusionment with Africa's future potential. The young nations on the continent faced gigantic political and economic challenges. The first generation of African leaders seem to have been inclined to dismantle the structures of civic participation achieved during decolonization precisely because they had witnessed and benefitted from its success in making claims against colonial rulers. Now in power, they realized that to fulfil these claims might be even harder for them than it was for colonial rulers.[51] As far as the international community was concerned, the continent of hope had descended to widespread crisis incapable of producing the promised development, and at best an object of sympathy and recipient of aid.[52] Historiography increasingly reflected this development. More and more, instead of following up the roots of nationalism, the focus of analysis became the roots of underdevelopment. Frustration over the fruits of independence gradually shifted the focus onto the external determinants of Africa's economic and social problems.[53]

For these analyses, dependency theory provided an adequate theoretical framework. Instead of pointing to the alleged underdevelopment of the South as the primary cause for the unequal distribution of opportunities in life, the theory interpreted development and underdevelopment as two sides of the same coin, or, more precisely, as the global expansion of capitalism, which, according to the theory, entailed the unequal allocation of its benefits at a global scale. A later extension of the dependency theory was the world systems theory, as proposed in particular by Wallerstein, with its heavy focus on the international division of labour: free wage labor in the capitalist core found its counterpart in forced labor, slavery, and debt bondage in the periphery.[54] Rodney built on these insights to develop his vivid analysis of the history of economic ties between Africa and European capitalism. Even though he focussed heavily on the colonial period, it nonetheless became apparent early on that the nexus between the slave trade and the integration of Africa into an unequal and exploitative global economy would form the center of his analyses. During this phase, the continent had, according to Rodney, suffered an "irremediable loss of opportunities to develop." The forced migration of young men in particular and the import of Western products and technologies had suffocated the continent's innovative capacity. The heyday of the dependency and world systems theories remains firmly in the past. And more recent research on slavery and the slave trade has led to a more differentiated take on, or even refutation of, many of Rodney's findings. However, the rise of global history and the rekindled interest in the interdependencies of the capitalist world, as well as the role played by slave-driven production in the Atlantic region, have led to his insights and theories becoming relevant again.[55]

In his acknowledgements in HEUA (xiv), Rodney wrote: "contrary to the fashion in most prefaces, I will not add that 'all mistakes and shortcomings are entirely my own responsibility.' That is sheer bourgeois subjectivism. Responsibility in matters of these sorts is always collective, especially with regard to the remedying of shortcomings." Here Rodney was not only referring to one of the core clichés of the genre of acknowledgment writings that claims "all credit goes to my mentors, all mistakes are my own."[56] He also pointed to his efforts in Dar es Salaam to undermine the power structures of the profession. So he especially thanked "comrades Karim Hirji and Henry Mapolu," two undergraduates in the history department. The fact that Rodney referred to the students as comrades seemed to signal his attempt to overcome the student-teacher distinction based on authority and status, and to emphasize their shared and egalitarian ideological ground.[57] After his return to Tanzania, Rodney closely cooperated with the "University Students African Revolutionary Front" (USARF) and published in their journal "Cheche." At a USARF's seminar in December 1969, Rodney presented a paper entitled "The Ideology of the African Revolution" in which he followed Frantz Fanon's arguments by putting his fingers on the inability of anticolonial nationalists to attack capitalism and imperialism once formal independence was achieved. Moreover, he described "African socialism" as a curious creature that has turned out to be neither African nor socialist. The TANU government responded with an editorial in the "Nationalist" with the headline "Revolutionary Hot Air." Rodney's position was labeled as "completely unacceptable," especially as coming from a foreigner who seemed to have abused "the hand of friendship" extended to him by the government after his ban from entering Jamaica a year before.[58] In a comparatively mild form, Rodney had become a target of state repression in Tanzania as well, although in the following years he was sparred direct intervention from government or party authorities. However, after the Arusha Declaration the government increasingly exerted political control over teaching, research activities, and statements of scholars. The university now was part of the state apparatus and obligated to pursue the project of nation-building and the development goals as formulated by the government.

While Rodney continued to teach and write on pan-African topics, emphasizing the need to think Africa and the African diaspora together, he became increasingly impatient with the development of political pan-Africanism.[59] In preparation of the sixth Pan-African Congress to be held in Dar es Salaam in 1974—and for which he ultimately withdrew his support—Rodney criticized once more that during the process of national independence, African political leadership had accepted the "Balkanization" of the continent in exchange for the solidification of their own power.[60]

> Throughout the continent, none of the successful independence movements denied the basic validity of the boundaries created a few decades ago by imperialism. To have done so would have been to issue a challenge so profound as to rule out the preservation of petty bourgeois interests.... The neutrality and unity of nationalism is illusory . . . particular classes or strata capture nationalist movements and chart their ideological and political direction. Pan-Africanism today has to recognize such a situation, if it is to be a brand of revolutionary nationalism and if it is to be a progressive international force.[61]

He stated that African leadership did not fundamentally transform the effects of colonialism. One of the most practical manifestations of the challenges noted by Rodney involved who would be invited and recognized to participate in the proceedings of the Congress. Heads of State would be celebrated as formal delegations, but the degree to which various anti-government or nongovernment organizations and movements would receive the same treatment was unclear. Rodney's intellectual and political mentor C. L. R. James ultimately boycotted the Dar es Salaam meeting after it became apparent that leftist groups—particularly of the Caribbean—would be marginalized. In the end, the sixth Pan-African Congress became synonymous with "the triumph of ministry over movement and statecraft over struggle."[62]

Back to Guyana: Political Work,
Academic Mobility, and Death

In 1974 Rodney returned to Guyana to take up a professorship in history. When Tanzanian friends appealed to him to reconsider this move, Rodney responded: "No, comrades, I can make my contribution here, but I will never be able ever to grasp the idiom of the people. I will not be able to connect easily. I have to go back to the people I know and who know me."[63] During his stay in Dar es Salaam, Rodney mentioned several times his incapability to relate to Tanzanians outside the university walls. "[O]ne must know that society, that environment," he explained in an interview after he had left Tanzania.

> One must have a series of responses and reflexes that come from having lived a given experience. One must be able to share a joke because of a nuance in language and pronunciation. One must be able to go to the marketplace in the case of Tanzania, and bargain in the Swahili manner without being perceived as an outsider. Now, when one thinks of all these factors it's virtually a lifetime task to master a language and then to master the higher level of perception which normally goes into a cultures. And I didn't believe that I could afford that. I believed that there is another culture from which I derived into which I could project myself with greater ease.[64]

Rodney also partly shifted his research interests and began to increasingly work on the Caribbean while he continued to employ a broader view on the Black Atlantic connections.

Upon his arrival in Guyana, however, he was informed that the government had blocked his appointment. Married and with three children to care for, Rodney nonetheless decided to stay, in spite of the great material insecurity this implied. Most notably, he also decided to continue his political work. The Working People's Alliance (WPA) he founded became a serious threat to the ruling clique backing Prime Minister Forbes Burnham (Figure 6.2). Rodney also did not halt his academic activities at this point. Quite to the contrary, he tirelessly went on speaking tours across the United States, the Caribbean, and Europe, accepted various guest professorships, not least to secure a livelihood. In spring 1978, for example, he taught at the University of Hamburg where he presented a course on "One Hundred Years of Development in Africa." The lectures were recorded, and full transcripts were produced a few years later, including the question-and-answer sessions with the students. Among other things, he explained the challenges to constructively link historical research with actual political processes. "Many historians are afraid to deal with living history and I can understand why, because sometimes it is dangerous, especially in Africa. The moment that the social scientist begins to reflect too closely on the present, he or she is a subversive in the Third World. It is safer to be with the mummies and bones"[65].

During this phase he wrote articles and manuscripts on the history of the workers of Tanzania and Guyana and focused more systematically on perspectives "from below." These writings underlined Rodney as a social historian who worked closely with his

Figure 6.2 Rodney and future WPA members exit the Ministry of Labour and Social Security, Guyana *c.* 1971 (*c.* Wikimedia Commons).

sources. In spite of his intensive and highly dangerous political work, he repeatedly spent long stints at Guyana's national archive, a decision which surprised numerous of his friends and colleagues. His most in-depth study would only be published after his death. *A History of the Guyanese Working People, 1881–1905 (1981)* offers an exhaustive and archive-based analysis of the history of African and Asian immigration to Guyana, the interactions between the different ethnic groups, the long shadow of slavery, British colonialism's influence, as well as the economic and political constraints against which workers were increasingly rebelling.[66]

Meanwhile, the political situation in Guyana turned grave.[67] The WPA representatives, and in particular Rodney as their eloquent spokesperson, increasingly became the target of the state. Members of the party received threats, were dragged to court, thrown in jail on spurious grounds, and even murdered in public. Allegedly, Prime Minister Burnham told Rodney it would be wise for him to make a will. In spite of being barred from traveling abroad, Rodney left for Europe and Africa in May 1980. Zimbabwe had recently achieved independence and he met Robert Mugabe there, at that time still considered a great hero by many Black intellectuals. Mugabe asked him to establish an African research center in Zimbabwe, which Rodney declined. He believed his role was in the political struggles of his home country. Shortly after, he was murdered.

Rodney's assassination was part of a whole series of political murders—from Lumumba to Allende—who shaped the project of the Third World. His trajectory was marred with rising disappointments, with parochial national visions taking over the spirit of a united Third World. What made him so dangerous in the eyes of his opponents who finally decided to end his life was not so much his intellectual work but his political activities. But it was exactly the fusion of the two realms that made him such a powerful champion of an alternative global history that insisted in revealing the connected histories of sufferings and agency of those who were often considered of not having a history.

Notes

1 See, among many others, Omar Gueye, *Mai 1968 au Sénégal. Senghor Face au Movement Syndical* (Amsterdam: Amsterdam University Press, 2014). For a comprehensive view, Chen Jian et al., eds., *The Routledge Handbook of the Global Sixties: Between Protest and Nation-Building* (London and New York: Routledge, 2018).

2 Lasse Heerten, *The Biafran War and Postcolonial Humanitarianism. Spectacles of Suffering* (New York: Cambridge University Press, 2017).

3 On the Congress, see David Austin, "Introduction: The Dialect of Liberation. The Congress of Black Writers at 50—and Beyond," in *Moving Against the System. The 1968 Congress of Black Writers and the Making of Global Consciousness*, ed. D. Austin (London: Pluto Press 2018), 1–76.

4 C. L. R. James (1901–1989) was a man of varied accomplishments. Born in Trinidad, he spent much of his life in the United States and especially in Britain. He was a protean twentieth-century Marxist intellectual, a leading voice of pan-Africanism, a novelist, playwright, and critic, and, not to forget, one of the premier writers on cricket and sports. His study *The Black Jacobins* (1938) examines the dynamics of anticolonial revolution in Haiti and continues to influence scholarship on Atlantic slavery and abolition and its connection to capitalism. On James, see Paul Buhle, *C. L. R. James. The Artist as Revolutionary*, New and Extended Version (London: Verso, 2017); Christian Hogsbjerg, *C. L. R. James in Imperial Britain* (Durham and London: Duke University Press, 2014); Frank Rosengarten, *Urbane Revolutionary: C. L. R. James and the Struggle for a New Society* (Jackson: University Press of Mississippi, 2008).

5 Walter Rodney, "African History in the Service of the Black Liberation," in Austin, *Moving against the System*, 128.

6 The book underwent several reprints. In 2018, a new edition was published with Verso in London.

7 Karim F. Hirji, *The Enduring Relevance of Walter Rodney's 'How Europe Underdeveloped Africa'* (Montreal: Daraja Press, 2017), xi. Members of the *Institute of Black World* based in Atlanta, with whom Rodney cooperated from the 1970s onward, remembered that *How Europe Underdeveloped Africa* "immediately struck an exciting and responsive chord among many in this country [the United States]. Among politically-oriented black people it played something of the same formative role as Frantz Fanon's *The Wretched of the Earth* almost a decade ago." Vincent Harding et al., "Introduction," in Rodney, *HEUA*, XXII. The new English edition of the book contains a foreword by the eminent US scholar and civil rights activist Angela Davis in which she portrays Rodney as a "resolute intellectual who recognizes

that the ultimate significance of knowledge is its capacity to transform our social worlds" (IX).

8   Interest in Germany for Rodney's work was partly linked to the fact that Tanzania featured very prominently not only in the country's Third World movements but also among Africanist scholars. Numerous social scientists from the Federal Republic spent time at the University of Dar es Salaam in the late 1960s and early 1970s as doctoral students or visiting professors, and some of them got to know Rodney rather well. Among those was the sociologist Michaela von Freyhold (later professor at the University of Bremen), who explicitly engaged with his work. See her "Walter Rodney und die afrikanischen Eliten," in *Afrikanische Eliten zwanzig Jahre nach Erlangung der Unabhängigkeit*, ed. Eva-Maria Bruchhaus (Hamburg: Helmut Buske, 1983), 6–27.

9   Rodney emphasized the need for critical intellectuals to maintain close ties with the grassroots level in, *The Groundings with My Brothers* (London: Verso, 2019) (orig. London: Bogle L'Ouverture 1969).

10 Edward W. Said, *Representations of the Intellectual* (New York: Pantheon Books, 1994), 22–3.

11 Walter Rodney, *Walter Rodney Speaks: The Making of an African Intellectual*, ed. Robert A. Hill (Trenton: Africa World Press, 1990), 35. Cf. Alan Isaacman, "Legacies of Engagement. Scholarship Informed by Political Commitment," *African Studies Review* 46, no. 1 (2003): 1–41.

12 Edward Alpers and Pierre-Michel Fontaine, eds., *Walter Rodney—Revolutionary and Scholar: A Tribute* (Los Angeles: UCLA Center for African-American Studies, 1983).

13 The only substantial biography about Rodney has been written by Rupert Charles Lewis, *Walter Rodney's Intellectual and Political Thought* (Kingston and Detroit: Wayne State University Press, 1998). The more recent study by Amzat Boukari-Yabara, *Walter Rodney: Un Historien Engagé (1942–1980)* (Paris: Présence Africaine, 2018), does not provide any particularly new insights. Horace Campbell, "Walter Rodney: A Biography and Bibliography," *Review of African Political Economy* 18 (1980): 132–7 contains concise biographical and bibliographical information. An instructive piece that includes personal memories of Rodney and assessments of his political and academic impact is Clairmont Chung, ed., *Walter Rodney. A Promise of Revolution* (New York: Monthly Review Press, 2012). Michael O. West and William G. Martin, "Contours of the Black International. From Toussaint to Tupac," in *From Toussaint to Tupac: The Black International since the Age of Revolution*, ed. West, Martin and Wilkins (Chapel Hill and London: University of North Carolina Press, 2009), 1–44 set Rodney's work within the context of the "Black Atlantic." The Robert W. Woodruff Library in Atlanta/Georgia holds the Walter Rodney Papers, which also contain unpublished lecture manuscripts, essay draft versions, and letters (walterrodneyfoundation.org). These archives could not be consulted for this chapter.

14 For an early and in parts surely polemic critique of intellectuals with this type of perspective, cf. Arif Dirlik, *The Postcolonial Aura: Third World Criticism in the Age of Global Capitalism* (Boulder: Westview Press, 1997).

15 See, for instance, Achille Mbembe, *Critique of Black Reason* (Durham: Duke University Press, 2017).

16 For a general assessment of the field of global history, see Sebastian Conrad, *What Is Global History?* (Princeton and London: Princeton University Press, 2016). There is no reference to Rodney in this book.

17 C. L. R. James, "Walter Rodney and the Question of Power," in Alpers and Fontaine, *Walter Rodney—Revolutionary and Scholar*, 134.

18 See Lewis, *Walter Rodney*, Ch.1.

19 Rodney, *Walter Rodney Speaks*, 17.

20 Michael O. West, "Walter Rodney and Black Power: Jamaican Intelligence and US Diplomacy," *African Journal of Criminology & Justice Studies* 1, no. 2 (2005): 1–50 (quotes from reports of Jamaican intelligence services: 7).

21 See Ian Brown, *The School of Oriental and African Studies: Imperial Training and the Expansion of Learning* (Cambridge: Cambridge University Press, 2016).

22 Rodney, *Walter Rodney Speaks*, 24. In retrospect at least, the SOAS dons mainly had good things to say about Rodney. According to their doyen Roland Oliver (*In the Realms of Gold. Pioneering in African History* (Madison: The University of Wisconsin Press, 1997), 245), Rodney "wrote an outstanding thesis." In his obituary for Rodney, published in the *London Times*, his supervisor, Richard Gray, described him "as one of the most significant Third World historians of his generation." Quoted in Lewis, *Walter Rodney*, 42.

23 Lewis, *Walter Rodney*, 37–8.

24 See Pepijn Brandon, "From William's Thesis to Williams Thesis: An Anti-Colonial Trajectory," *International Review of Social History* 62, no. 2 (2017): 305–27, which emphasizes the strong intellectual influence of James on Williams. Rodney commented that "Williams was making points about what slavery and capitalism were about, and that these were both intellectually and emotionally appealing. One could recognize one's self in that history." Rodney, *Walter Rodney Speaks*, 14–15.

25 See especially W. E. B. Du Bois, *Black Reconstruction in America, 1860–1880* (New York: Touchstone, 1995 (1935)). In general, Rodney could be situated within the Black radical tradition as analyzed by Cedric J. Robinson, *Black Marxism. The Making of the Black Radical Tradition*, 2nd ed. (Chapel Hill and London: The University of North Carolina Press, 2000). See also Anthony Bogues, *Black Heretics, Black Prophets: Radical Political Intellectuals* (New York: Routledge, 2003); Tunde Adeleke, *Africa in Black Liberation Activism. Malcom X, Stokely Carmichael and Walter Rodney* (London: Routledge, 2017).

26 Rodney, *Walter Rodney Speaks*, 31. In some ways, Rodney echoes here an observation made by Stuart Hall about the eminent leftist social historian Edward P. Thompson, "He was committed to the cause of colonial liberation, but I didn't feel that he had a sense of what colonialism was and how it operated. He was very English in his imagination, in the fibre of his being. He didn't connect with my preoccupation about racial identity," in *Familiar Stranger. A Life Between Two Islands*, ed. Stuart Hall with Bill Schwarz (London: Allen Lane, 2017), 264.

27 Under the dynamic stewardship of Terence Ranger, who had been expelled from Southern Rhodesia (today Zimbabwe) in 1963 because of his political activities and was subsequently offered the position of head of department of history in the newly founded university of Dar, the international group of historians working there soon became known as the "School of Dar es Salaam." It became an influential player in the new academic field of African history. See Terence Ranger, ed., *Emerging Themes of African History* (Nairobi: East African Publishing House, 1968). The volume contains the proceedings of a widely noted conference held in Dar es Salaam in October 1965. For a concise portrait of Ranger with some information on his time in Dar es Salaam, see Diana Jeater, "Terence Ranger, 1929-2015," *History Workshop Journal* 81 (2006): 306–15.

28 Rodney, *Walter Rodney Speaks*, 32.

29 See Seth M. Markle, *A Motorcycle on Hell Run. Tanzania, Black Power, and the Uncertain Future of Pan-Africanism, 1964–1974* (East Lansing: Michigan State University Press, 2017), 77.

30 Andrew Ivaska, "Liberation in Transit: Eduardo Mondlane and Che Guevara in Dar es Salaam," in Jian et al., *The Routledge Handbook of the Global Sixties*, 27–38.

31 In his opening words to the history conference in Dar es Salaam in 1965, Nyerere noted: "The vital thing is that we should be able to develop a really African history. . . . It is only when these things are looked at from Africa outwards that history will develop." Cited in Markle, *A Motorcycle on Hell Run*, 78.

32 Quoted in Andrew M. Ivaska, *Cultured States: Youth, Gender, and Modern Style in 1960s Dar es Salaam* (Durham: Duke University Press, 2011), 127.

33 On the Arusha Declaration, see, among many others, Cranford Pratt, *The Critical Phase in Tanzania 1945–1968. Nyerere and the Emergence of a Socialist Strategy* (Cambridge: Cambridge University Press, 1976); Priya Lal, *African Socialism in Postcolonial Tanzania. Between the Village and the World* (New York: Cambridge University Press, 2015).

34 Julius Nyerere, "Education for Self-reliance, March 1967," in *Nyerere, Freedom and Socialism/Uhuru na Ujamaa. A Selection from Writings and Speeches 1965–1967* (Dar es Salaam: Oxford University Press, 1968), 290.

35 See Immanuel R. Harisch, "Facets of Walter Rodney's Pan-African Intellectual Activism during his Dar es Salaam Years, 1966–1974," *Stichproben. Vienna Journal of African Studies* 20 (2020): 114–15; Ivaska, *Cultured States*, 147–8; John S. Saul, *Revolutionary Traveller. Freeze-Frames from a Life* (Winnipeg: Arbeiter Ring Publishing, 2009), Ch.1. Most members of the "group of nine," Rodney among them, subsequently contributed to a collective volume that discussed the history and future tasks of education in Tanzania. See Idrian N. Resnick, ed., *Tanzania: Revolution by Education* (Arusha: Longmans, 1968).

36 West, "Walter Rodney and Black Power," 20–1. For Rodney and the Rastafaris, see Horace Campbell, *Rasta and Resistance. From Marcus Garvey to Walter Rodney* (London: Hansib, 1985), 128–33. On Rodney's political activities during his stay in Jamaica, see Lewis, *Walter Rodney*, Ch. 5.

37 Rupert C. Lewis, *Walter Rodney. 1968 Revisited* (Mona: Canoe Press, 1994), 2–3.

38 Walter Rodney, "European Activity and African Reaction in Angola," in *Aspects of Central African History*, ed. Terence O. Ranger (Evanston: Northwestern University Press, 1968), 49–70.

39 See Bogues, *Black Heretics, Black Prophets*, 128.

40 Some of these interventions appeared in Rodney, *Groundings with My Brothers*.

41 Michael O. West, "Seeing Darkly: Guyana, Black Power, and Walter Rodney's Expulsion from Jamaica," *Small Axe* 25 (2008): 93–104.

42 West and Martin, "Contours of the Black International," 30. See especially David Austin, "All Roads Led to Montreal: Black Power, the Caribbean, and the Black Radical Tradition in Canada," *Journal of African American History* 92, no. 4 (2007): 516–39.

43 For an assessment of Rodney's intellectual influence in Dar es Salaam, see Horace Campbell, "The Impact of Walter Rodney and Progressive Scholars on the Dar es Salaam School," *Social and Economic Studies* 40, no. 2 (1991): 99–135; Harisch, "Facets of Walter Rodney's Pan-African Intellectual Activism"; Harisch, *Walter Rodney's Dar es Salaam Years, 1966–1974: How Europe Underdeveloped Africa, Tanzania's ujamaa, and Student Radicalism at "the Hill,"* unpublished Master Thesis (University of Vienna, 2018); Markle, *A Motorcycle on Hell Run*, Ch.3; Lewis, *Walter Rodney*, Chs. 6 and 7. For an insightful account on Rodney's role on campus, see Issa G. Shivji, "Rodney and

Radicalism on the Hill 1966–1974," in *Shivji: Intellectuals at the Hill. Essays and Talks 1969-1993* (Dar es Salaam: DUP, 1993), 32–44.

44 Lewis, *Walter Rodney*, 117.

45 Walter Rodney, *A History of the Upper Guinea Coast 1545-1800* (Oxford: Clarendon Press, 1970), 259. A good summary of the book is provided by Jeffrey D. Howison, "Walter Rodney, African Studies, and the Study of Africa," *Ankara University Journal of African Studies* 1, no. 1 (2011): 55–7.

46 Rodney, *Walter Rodney Speaks*, 27.

47 This point is made in what is arguably still the best synthesis: Paul Lovejoy, *Transformations in Slavery: A History of Slavery in Africa*, 3rd ed. (New York: Cambridge University Press, 2011). See also Sean Stillwell, *Slavery and Slaving in African History* (New York: Cambridge University Press, 2014).

48 Immanuel Wallerstein, "Walter Rodney: The Historian as Spokesman for Historical Forces," *American Ethnologist* 13, no. 2 (1986): 330. Rodney himself made explicit why he refrained from a scholarly apparatus. "It was to insure that that I didn't remain a victim of presenting material in a context and in a form where it was only accessible to certain kinds of people. And among several other things, this text was designed to operate outside the university. It might get into the university, yes. I hoped it would. But it was designed to operate from the outside in the sense that it would not be sponsored by the people who considered themselves, and whom many others considered, to be the ones at that time who had the last word to say on African history and African studies. The aim of this publication was to reach our own people without having it mediated by the bourgeois institutions of learning." Rodney, *Walter Rodney Speaks*, 26.

49 Martin A. Klein, "Review of 'How Europe Underdeveloped Africa,'" *International Journal of African Historical Studies* 7, no. 2 (1974): 327. See also Howison, "Walter Rodney, African Studies, and the Study of Africa," 59.

50 Over the years, Rodney received numerous fan letters. One early reader of the book from Lagos, Nigeria, wrote to him in 1973: "I have just bought your book *How Europe Underdeveloped Africa*, and I want to inform you that you are one of my heroes . . . I am just twenty and entering the University of Ibadan next September . . . So all I need is inspiration from you." Quoted in Leo Zeilig, "Walter Rodney's Journey to Hamburg," *Review of Political Economy Blog*, www.roape.net (assessed December 22, 2019).

51 Frederick Cooper, "Possibility and Constraint: African Independence in Historical Perspective," *Journal of African History* 49, no. 2 (2008): 172.

52 Paul Nugent, *African since Independence. A Comparative History*, 2nd ed. (London: Palgrave, 2012). Frederick Cooper, *Africa since 1940. The Past of the Present*, 2nd ed. (New York: Cambridge University Press), 2019.

53 A comprehensive analysis of the related literature and debates is offered by Frederick Cooper, "Africa and the World Economy," in Cooper et al., *Confronting Historical Paradigms: Peasants, Labor, and the Capitalist World System in Africa and Latin America*, (Madison: The University of Wisconsin Press, 1993), 84–201.

54 For the relations between the World systems approach and African Studies, see William G. Martin, "Africa and World-Systems Analysis. A Post-Nationalist Project?" in *Writing African History*, ed. John Edward Philips (Rochester: University of Rochester Press, 2005), 381–402.

55 See Toby Green, *A Fistful of Shells: West Africa from the Rise of the Slave Trade to the Age of Revolution* (Chicago and London: University of Chicago Press, 2019).

56 See Emily Callaci, "On Acknowledgements," *American Historical Review* 125, no. 1 (2020): 126–31.

57 Harisch, *Walter Rodney's Dar es Salaam Years, 1966–1974*, 51; Markle, *A Motorcycle on Hell Run*, 97.

58 Markle, *A Motorcycle on Hell Run*, 90–1. See also Leo Zeilig, *Frantz Fanon. A Political Biography, Introduction to the Second Edition* (London and New York: I.B. Tauris, 2021), xviii–xxi.

59 For Rodney's conceptualisation of pan-Africanism, see Robert A. Hill, "Walter Rodney and the Restatement of Pan-Africanism in Theory and Practice," *Ufahamu. A Journal of African Studies* 38, no. 3 (2015): 135–58; Harisch, "Facets of Walter Rodney's Pan-African Intellectual Activism."

60 On the conference, see Fanon Che Wilkens, "'A Line of Steel': The Organization of the Sixth Pan-African Congress and the Struggle for International Black Power, 1969-1974," in *The Hidden 1970s: Histories of Radicalism*, ed. Dan Berger (New Brunswick: Rutgers University Press, 2010), 97–114; Andrew Ivaska, "Movement Youth in a Global Sixties Hub: The Everyday Lives of Transnational Activists in Postcolonial Dar es Salaam," in *Transnational Histories of Youth in the Twentieth Century*, ed. Richard Ivan Jobs and David M. Pomfret (Basingstoke: Palgrave Macmillan, 2015), 188–210; Brenda Gayle Plummer, *In Search of Power: African Americans in the Era of Decolonization, 1956–1974* (Cambridge: Cambridge University Press, 2013).

61 Walter Rodney, "Towards the 6th Pan-African-Congress: Aspects of the International Class Struggle in Africa, America and the Caribbean," in *African Intellectual Heritage: A Book of Sources*, ed. Molefi Asanta (Philadelphia: Temple University Press, 1996), 729–40. See Howison, "Walter Rodney, African Studies, and the Study of Africa," 51–3.

62 West, "Seeing Darkly," 101.

63 Quoted in Lewis, *Walter Rodney*, 218.

64 Rodney, *Walter Rodney Speaks*, 42.

65 See *A Tribute to Walter Rodney: One Hundred Years of Development in Africa. Lectures given at the University of Hamburg in summer 1978* (Hamburg: University of Hamburg, 1984). The lectures were published as a mimeographed copy on the occasion of the Hamburg University Days 1984, devoted to "Hamburg and the Third World." I thank Eckart Krause (Hamburg University Archives) for having provided a copy. Parts of his lecture "Violence and Resistance in African History," held at the University of Hamburg in the spring of 1978, are published in German translation in: *Freibeuter* 5 (1980): 47–53. See also Zeilig, "Walter Rodney's Journey to Hamburg."

66 Another posthumously published study on workers was devoted to labourers in the Tanzanian Sisal Industry, *Walter Rodney/Kapepwa Tambila/Laurent Sago: Migrant Labour in Tanzania during the Colonial Period. Case Studies of Recruitment and Conditions of Labour in the Sisal Industry* (Hamburg: Institut fuer Afrika-Kunde, 1983).

67 For the following part, see Lewis, *Walter Rodney*, Ch. 9.

7

From London 1948 to Dakar 1966

Crises in Anticolonial Counterpublics

Penny M. Von Eschen

In 1948, the African American anthropologist, choreographer, and dancer Katherine Dunham, unable to keep her New York City dance school open, departed for an extended run at the Prince of Wales Theatre in London, continuing on to engagements in Paris and Germany in late 1948 and 1949. Dunham's sojourn, begun out of necessity, landed her within a world of migrants, exiles, and refugees and put her at the center of negotiations over the reshaping of anticolonial modernities. At stake in such named and unnamed negotiations were key questions: how best to resolve vexing challenges faced by postcolonial societies on questions of power and authority after inheriting colonial state structures? How might societies achieve political unity in the face of ethnic, religious, and linguistic diversity?

Dunham and a wider group of artists and intellectuals had long been engaged in antiracist projects that sought to overturn colonial and racial hierarchies. Yet, the collapse of global empires during the immediate postwar years radically redefined their projects. As Prasenjit Duara has argued, "decolonization was one of the most important political developments of the twentieth century because it turned the world into the stage of history." For Duara, questions of what replaces colonial governance after independence, and whether current historical approaches are adequate to describe the transformation of decolonization remain paramount.[1]

This chapter takes postcolonial London as its entry point to engage capacious and intersecting Third World projects and their collisions with new racial formations in the immediate aftermath of the enormous global upheavals of the Second World War. Between 1945 and the end of 1948, when the Universal Declaration of Human Rights (UDHR) was signed in Paris, possibilities of a postcolonial dispensation based on Human Rights were sharply curtailed by the partition of India and Pakistan, the Naqba (disaster) of the Palestinian people with the creation of the State of Israel, and the May 1948 election of the Nationalist government in South Africa that implemented the apartheid system. Moreover, as Aimé Césaire argued, not only did the Second World War failed to democratize metropolitan culture, but as the United States moved into formerly European colonial spaces, it's Cold War foreign policies and extractive labor regimes extended colonial hierarchies in unprecedented and unpredictable ways.

This chapter considers a crisis in anticolonial modernity, highlighting the collisions between creative Third World projects and new forms of racial subjugation through two moments. First, I introduce the broader problematic of the paper with a sketch of 1948 London, then turning to a friendship that began in 1949 between the prominent African American actor, singer and anticolonial and civil rights activist Paul Robeson, and the Assamese filmmaker, lyricist, and singer Bhupen Hazarika, a relationship that generated the transformation and circulation of anticolonial projects despite disruption by Cold War state repression. Second, I follow these architects of antiracist and Third World imaginaries—in their presence and sometimes absence—to the 1966 First World Festival of Negro Arts in Dakar, reading the festival, like 1948 London writ large, through David Scott's conception of a "problem-space," in the sense of a discursive context of rival views where "what is in dispute, what the argument is effectively about, is not itself being argued over."[2]

In a concrete sense, 1948 London itself constituted a problem-space, as the city absorbed the migrations of peoples fleeing postcolonial crises during 1947–9. Indeed, the UDHR document itself can be read as a "problem-space." A critical 1948 touchstone, marking the reshuffling of discourses on racial hierarchies, the UDHR is often noted to be a turning point in rights claiming and the question of who has the authority to define and claim rights and who gets to bestow them. In recent debates, scholars such as Samuel Moyn have judged the UDHR, in the words of Lydia H. Liu, as a minor episode of diplomatic penmanship. Liu, focusing on the process of creating the document, allows us to appreciate broader options for thinking about postcoloniality even if such options were later foreclosed.[3] Considering the UDHR through the prism of a group of antiracist and anticolonial artists and intellectuals, I contend that over the decades of transnational performance, these artists and intellectuals had collectively called into a being an antiracist counterpublic, without which the UDHR would not have been imaginable. And as we will see later, Hazarika invoked the UDHR in his 1952 Columbia University dissertation, both as way of establishing the authority of the Indian government's education project, and as a thinly veiled critique of US repression of freedom of speech. Yet, if the UDHR recognized that the nation-state was an insufficient guarantor of rights, the limitations of the document stem from the international community's lack of authority over questions of who has the authority or right to move; a lack of authority to secure rights for those rendered stateless by war and postwar partitions. And following Scott, "what is in dispute"—the new postwar racial formations—is evaded in document's abstract declaration of expanded rights.

Like Gary Wilder's work on Aimé Césaire, I am interested in exploring openings in the postwar order that were "foreclosed by nationalist logics of decolonization." I argue that these foreclosures were experienced by migrants and artistic and intellectual sojourners alike as a crisis in political and cultural authority. For example, as seen in Dunham's choreography based on cross-cultural fusion, or Paul Robeson's friendship and collaboration with Bhupen Hazarika, this generation had affirmed an expansive vision of ethno-linguistic diversity that was imperiled by the limitations of nation-building projects and by the conferral of rights as the province of sovereign states.

London is a particularly generative space for exploring questions about political and cultural authority in the postwar world, for reading the reshuffling of racialized hierarchies at this moment, and the relationship between texts generated and circulating in the different registers of performance, intellectual production, engagements with quotidian racial discrimination (the color bar), and the state. In my broader project, I seek to reconstruct a thick description of texts and lived experiences at singular moments of naming and contesting racial and colonial formations.[4] Following what I have elsewhere called a jazz methodology of reading, I pay especial attention to the breaks and discontinuities, "slipping into the breaks and looking around."[5]

Dunham's extended run in London overlapped with a remarkable array of Black American performers in including the composer, pianist, and band leader Duke Ellington (at the Palladium), the dancers and film stars the Nicholas Brothers, and world-renowned singer, actor, and activist Paul Robeson.[6] Like Dunham, these artists had been associated with popular front culture and were escaping the pall that McCarthyism had cast over the United States. Overlapping for six months in a bleak and severely war-damaged London, in an atmosphere of camaraderie and competition, Black American artists coped with racial segregation in housing. Dunham and her compatriots also found themselves in a world of exiles, refugees, and migrants. As Dunham performed with her company in London at the Prince of Wales Theatre, presenting her interpretation of Caribbean cultural forms in the music and dance revue *A Caribbean Rhapsody*, members of the company frequented such afterhours establishments as the Caribbean Club and the Piccadilly, mingling with American and British troops and encountering calypso, highlife, and Afro-Latin music through such groups as the West Indian All Stars. At the same time, when she addressed the Royal Anthropological Society in London, presenting her work on Haiti in "The State of Cults among the Deprived," she drew not only fellow anthropologists, but an extended group of colonial and foreign office officials, along with personnel from the US Embassy and various national embassy representatives who had also flocked to her performances.[7]

Dunham and her compatriots Paul Robeson and Richard Wright (who visited London from his residence in Paris) were under varying degrees of US (and British and French) surveillance, as they moved through London and between Europe and the United States.[8] State tracking of anticolonial artists and intellectuals, as they evaded Cold War repression in the States and sought more flexible spaces in the London of the liberal Attlee government, suggests a postcolonial reading of George Orwell's 1949 dystopian novel, *1984*. The view of London as an imperial problem-space suggests the relevance of the novel's totalitarian locutions of "doublespeak," "newspeak," and "thoughtcrime" for the social landscape of empire as well as the three distinct inflections of Cold War repression seen in Britain, the United States, and the Soviet Union. Thus, the US media's demonizing manipulation of Paul Robeson's criticisms of Cold War militarism and racism in Paris in 1949 illustrates a crisis of authority inherent in the surveillance, counterintelligence, and fabrication of "fake news" by Cold War security states.

Dunham and the artists and intellectuals she encountered in London were part of a generational nexus—whose performances over the earlier decades of the twentieth century had helped call into being a new public culture of anticolonial modernity.[9] The possibilities of the moment are exemplified in the movements of the body imagined and enabled by the precision of the Dunham technique in dance and the spectacular leaps in the tap dance modernism of the Nicholas Brothers and African highlife in the dance clubs. But new constraints and contingencies are discerned by trading how different bodies moved through the social geography of London, negotiating where African American performers, Caribbean migrants, and various communities of refugees could live and eat.

Indeed, in the aftermath of the war, artists and anticolonial activists confronted new possibilities and new limitations. In addition to the onset of the Cold War that ravaged the careers of some (including Paul Robeson) and forced new nation-based strategies for others (including Dunham), new borders and boundaries that reified colonial structures in the supposed aftermath of colonialism point to the way that postwar international structures diminished the range of possibilities of emancipation that had been imagined in earlier antiracist and anticolonial formations.

A further concern with movement vis-à-vis borders and state structures inform my reading of the rich possibilities and ultimate constraints in the friendship between Paul Robeson and Bhupen Hazarika; a relationship that offers a window into the international circulation and translation of anthems synonymous with US struggles for racial justice, and their reinventions by participants in anticolonial, nonaligned, and postcolonial movements. Despite harsh state repression, the circulation and reinvention of music that emerged from international Popular Front labor and socialist movements, with much of the US music evocative of folk traditions of Negro spirituals, retained their power and relevance in the context of ongoing Black struggles for justice and equality throughout the twentieth century and as the postwar moment evolved into the global Cold War.

Musicologist Ronald Radano's conception of music as a social formation provides a useful framework for considering the political and aesthetic interplay of words and sound and their particular place in the political movements that preceded, exceeded, and outlasted superpower conflict.[10] Such performances and productions constitute a counter-hegemonic aural archive at the intersection of colonialism and the Cold War, one of orally transmitted, broadcasted, and commercially recorded music that crossed oceans and national boundaries, and constituted a social formation of politically charged sound and content. Far from merely providing a soundtrack of global movements, in evoking, documenting, and linking past and present struggles, these songs became part of a movement culture, within which music forged meaning and communities of struggle.

Here, I offer a modest tracing of the nomadic life of two songs, "Ol' Man River" and "We Shall Overcome," associated with US popular front culture, that passed through various performance settings, including Broadway musical theater, rallies of activists in the Black freedom struggle, and the international anticolonial left. After spending several years during the 1950s in New York, where he established a friendship with Paul Robeson, Bhupen Hazarika, the Assamese filmmaker, lyricist, singer, and political activist, returned to India and translated Robeson's version of Jerome Kern and Oscar Hammerstein II "Ol' Man River" "into the Assam language, re-titled as *Bistirno Parore*" (Of the Wide Shores). Hazarika changed the Mississippi referred to in the song to the river Brahmaputra that flows through the Assam region of India. Hazarika also wrote Hindi and Bengali versions of the song that were equally popular, both addressed to the Ganges River.[11]

Born in 1926, Hazarika had already made a mark as a singer and actor when he was drawn to the Indian struggle for independence. In 1949, he went to New York to study Communications at Columbia University. Hazarika was influenced by Robeson, joining him at civil rights rallies. While my research is new, still investigating records of direct exchanges, the parallel interests of the two artists are striking. When they met in 1949, Robeson was one of the most prominent Americans who had been active in support of Indian independence. Like Robeson, the younger Hazarika had already worked as a singer and in film; and like Robeson, had found his way to politics and anticolonialism. As Hazarika negotiated the complexities of honoring the cultural heritage of his home state of Assam, while believing in the national integration of all of India's regions and twenty-two official national languages, Robeson's belief that folk cultural expressions held universal appeal inspired Hazarika in new and deeper directions. Hazarika showcased Assam folk music for the world as he sought to overcome divisive ethnic divisions within Assam and throughout India. Influenced by Robeson, in addition to "Ol' Man River," Hazarika adapted Black American spirituals in many of his compositions.[12] It is significant that Hazarika was in New York to witness the height of Cold War repression against Robeson and the Council on African Affairs, the anticolonial organization that Robeson had worked closely with in support of Indian independence. Indeed, Hazarika was in New York when Robeson had his passport seized and was called before the House Un-American Activities Committee.

In relative isolation after he lost his passport, Robeson worked on a theory of music that linked classical Western music to the pentatonic scales of folk music. Fluent in multiple languages and musical traditions, for Robeson, universally shared linguistic and musical structures provided a basis for communication, improvisation, and innovation across traditions. Robeson loved jazz. His son Paul recalled frequent outings to hear Duke Ellington in the 1940s. Robeson was particularly fond of be-bop and visited the home of Thelonious Monk to discuss music. His friends Monk and Dizzy Gillespie were among the sponsors and participants of the US campaign to return his passport.[13]

The deep resonances between the projects of Robeson and Hazarika, and Hazarika's brilliance in negotiating the problem-space of Cold War New York City, can be glimpsed in Hazarika's 1952 PhD dissertation at Columbia University's Teacher's College. Animated by the claim that "New India has a duty to bring to the understanding of rural adult that he is a living member of the community, the state, and the world," Hazarika merged the "one-world" vision of the Indian government and the poetry of Rabindranath Tagore with John Dewey's work on democracy and education and Harold D. Lasswell's work on mass communication.[14] Arguing for the fundamental role of communication in democracy and the critical role of the audiovisual in mass communications, Hazarika laid out his philosophical frame as well as the fundamentals of working with UNESCO to assure that radio transmitters and film are accessible to all people in his first chapter.

Hazarika opened his dissertation with an epigraph from Tagore: "Life is rebellious. It grows by breaking the forms that enclose it, the forms that give shelter only for a particular period and then become a prison, if they do not change."[15] Invoking Tagore enabled a reading of "the intellectual and spiritual wealth of the country" as in motion, unpacking a dialectic between historical particularity and ideas of "one-world," and world citizenship, elaborated by the Indian government and Indian minister of education Humayun Kabir, who worked extensively with UNESCO with the goal of "bring[ing] the world to the community" through mass communication.[16] Tagore's poetry also served as the bridge to Hazarika's discussion of the critical role of Indian art, dance, and music in "symbolic communication," which Hazarika reads through a synthesis of Tagore and the American political scientist Harold D. Lasswell's work on mass communication. For Hazarika, in writing that the "universe talks in the voice of picture and gestures," Tagore has "expressed the aesthetic experience of symbolic communication." Asking if Tagore's pictures and gestures are "images of the rhythm that is pulsating through the ever-moving, ever-changing cosmic system?" Hazarika answers the question by elaborating the critical role of the audiovisual in mass communications.[17]

For Hazarika, democracy necessitates the "participation of every mature human being," and education must place citizens in the world. Drawing on Dewey, Hazarika argues:

> When we look at communication we must see it as a sharing process—sharing the intellectual and spiritual wealth of the country. Education will fail in its duty if it fails to make idea a common experience, a common possession, a common happiness. Democracy demands it today.[18]

Thus, the recommendations by UNESCO on the distribution of audiovisual and radio receivers (explaining the necessity of all five basic types of receivers to be accessible to all villages), practices already being implemented in India (though not nearly far-reaching enough), become a moral and political imperative.[19]

The principles of the Universal Declaration of Human Rights are critical to the implementation of the vision: "if one world thought is to be implemented it is essential that the written documents of liberty and equality signed by the voluntary association of cooperative nations" be presented "so that even the unlettered citizen can feel their impact and come to understand the documents themselves."[20] Hazarika again invokes Tagore's emphasis on constant change in a world in motion, in his critique of the incomplete application of the UDHR and the urgency of redress: "Community habits in terms of the Charter on Human Rights of the United Nations should be subject to constant evaluation and redirection." Democratic conditions of "living and thinking . . . cannot tolerate unchanging attitudes."[21]

Hazarika draws particular attention to the nineteenth article of the Universal Declaration of Rights: "Everyone has the right to freedom of opinion and expression; this right includes freedom to hold opinions without interference and to seek, receive and impart information and ideas through any media and regardless of frontiers."[22] For Hazarika, this was especially important "in the field of controversial subjects, international or national, instructional materials from both sides many contribute to academic freedom, which is an important element of democracy." Here, constrained by the "problem-space" of New York, in the very moment that the United States has revoked of the passports of Paul Robeson and W. E. B. DuBois precisely because of their effectiveness in communicating with the anticolonial world, Hazarika's invocation of the principles of the UDHR serves as a critique of the repression of free speech in the United States.

Returning to India in 1953, Hazarika worked with the left-wing Indian Peoples Theater Association.[23] Hazarika's adaptation of "Ol' Man River" built on modifications that Robeson had introduced into his own renditions. Between 1936 and 1938, first in concert and then in recording, Paul Robeson changed the words, fundamentally altering the song's meaning. Instead of the racist lyrics that were part of the original production of Showboat, "Niggers all work on de Mississippi, /. . .," Robeson later took ownership of the song, substituting "There's an ol' man called the Mississippi, / That's the ol' man I don't like to be . . ." Robeson's version condemns the river as indifferent to human suffering. ("What does he care if the world's got troubles, what does he care if the land ain't free?") Robeson's additional changes transform the song into a protest anthem. Replacing the original "Tote that barge! / Lift that bale! / You get a little drunk, / An' you lands in jail . . .," Robeson sang instead, "Tote that barge and lift that bale!/ You show a little grit / And you lands in jail. . . ." Robeson's most dramatic alteration shifts the song's mood from defeat to defiance. Instead of "Ah gits weary / An' sick of tryin'; / Ah'm tired of livin' / An skeered of dyin', . . ./," Robeson sang "But I keeps laffin'/ Instead of cryin' / I must keep fightin'; / Until I'm dyin', But Ol' Man River, / He jes' keeps rolling along!"

Hazarika's Hindi version, a reimagining rather than a translation, likewise admonishes the river for its indifference to human toil and suffering:

Ganga baheti ho kyun? (Hindi adaption of Old Man River)

Vistar hai apar, Praja dono par
Kare hahakar, Nishabdha sada
O Ganga tum, Ganga baheti ho kyun?

Naitikta nashta hui, Manavata bhrashta hui
Nirlajja bhav se baheti ho kyun?

Ganga why do you flow?

the spread is immense and
subjects on both banks are in turmoil
always quietly O Ganga, Ganga why do you flow?

morality stands destroyed, humanity stands corrupted
Why do you flow shamelessly?

Chorus: The call of history, roars
O stream of Ganga
turn powerless people into forceful strugglers
marching forward
Why don't you?

illiterate people, unlettered
innumerable people, without food
sightless, why are you silent seeing this?

individual stays self-centered
entire society characterless
lifeless society why don't you abandon?

Why aren't you the listener anymore?
you are definitely not animate
why don't you fill inspiration in life
exhilarated earth has become Kurukshetra (a battle ground)
Ganga, O mother, in modern India
Why don't you give birth to
a victor, a son like Bhishma (whose loyalty lay with the state)

Here, Hazarika's plea for a strong state implies a critical attitude toward the weakness of the postcolonial state and its inability to halt the communal, inter-ethnic violence that plagued the state of Assam, as well as other Indian states in the aftermath of partition. As journalist Bikram Bora has argued, "Hazarika's imagination brought together the components of an existing potential national identity and visualized it in his songs." This imagination had three strands. First, opposing caste and class hierarchy, and second, a revolutionary disregard for societal conventions, as reflected in the song *Auto-rickshaw Solau Ami Duyu Bhai* (We two brothers drive auto-rickshaws). Bora explains, the song "tries to do away with middle-class insistence on white-collar jobs—the very essence of middle-class consciousness," and the negative connotations associated with rickshaws. This, Bora argues, successfully resonated via the song as he sang, "It is a rule to break all rules." The third strand tried to transcend ethno-linguistic divides. As Hazarika put it, "[f]rom the banks of Brahmaputra since 1947, I have dreamt of an emotionally integrated India, a land of aesthetic opportunity for all ethnic groups."[24] But the war with superpowers (China, 1962) or adversaries born of colonialism and supported by superpowers (Pakistan, 1947, 1965, 1971) posed violent and costly distractions from goals of self-determination, democracy, and development.

"We Shall Overcome," the most recognizable anthem of the US civil rights movement, also found an important place in Indian culture and politics. Originating as a Negro spiritual, "We'll Overcome (I'll Be Alright)," was sung by striking Black women tobacco workers in North Carolina in 1945. One of the strikers, Lucille Simmons, led the strikers in a gospel version of the song at the end of each day of picketing. Union organizer Zilphia Horton, wife of Myles Horton, the cofounder of the Highlander School, learned the song from Simmons. It was recorded on Highlander's *People's Songs* in 1948 as "We Will Overcome." The folk singer Pete Seeger learned Horton's version in 1947 and changed the lyric from "We Will Overcome" to "We Shall Overcome." Additional verses were collectively written by activists who had trained at Highlander as they faced police raids and jail terms in 1959–60. The song was taught at the founding meeting of the Student Non-Violent Coordinating Committee in Raleigh, North Carolina, in 1960, and rapidly caught on to become a nationally known civil rights anthem.

Adopted widely as a song and slogan in multiple parts of the globe, including its invocation by the Northern Ireland Civil Rights Association, the song received both literal translations and inspired reimaginings. Pete Seeger has recounted the story of being stunned as he was booed in Prague in 1964 when he criticized the US war in Vietnam, but then winning over the crowd with his rendition of "We Shall Overcome."[25] The song was sung at rallies in Wenceslas Square during the tense days of the Velvet Revolution of 1989.

Like "Ol' Man River," "We Shall Overcome" resonated with audiences in India. Renowned Indian poet Girija Kumar Mathur contributed a literal translation in Hindi, "Hum Honge Kaamyab." Regularly sung by school children in India during the 1980s, the multilinguistic song has been described as an unofficial national anthem. A literal translation in Bengali, "Amra Karbo Joy," was composed by the folk singer Hemanga Biswas, and also recorded by Bhupen Hazarika. Another Bengali version, "Ek Din Surjyer Bhor," by Shibdas Bandyopadhyay ("One Day the Sun Will Rise"), was recorded during the 1971 Bangladesh War of Independence, when West Pakistan's invasion of East Pakistan (Bangladesh) with substantial US military support from the administration of President Richard Nixon, resulted, in the words of the US consul in Dacca, to "the mass killing of unarmed civilians, the systematic elimination of the intelligentsia, and the annihilation of the Hindu population."[26] The dynamics of the war cannot wholly be attributed to Cold War dynamics. But the war is a tragic example of how superpower ambitions intersected with colonial histories and highjacked the ambitions of decolonizing countries. The war would not have developed as it did, nor would the slaughter have reached such horrific proportions, without the US military support of Pakistan dating from the partition. At that fateful moment, Pakistan became a vital part of the US northern perimeter defense zone aimed at containing the Soviet Union. With consistent US hostility to the nonaligned politics of India, in 1970, the year before West Pakistan invaded the East, the United States supplied $40 million worth of weapons to Pakistan. Recorded by the Calcutta Youth Choir (in the Bengali region of India) and arranged by Ruma Guha Thakurta, "We Shall Overcome" became one of the best-selling Bengali records. Beloved by the first Bangladeshi prime minister Sheikh Mujibur Rahman, it was sung at public events after Bangladesh gained independence. Underlining the left-wing, popular front aesthetics of Robeson and Hazarika, who believed that folk music held a universal appeal that transcended cultural and political differences, the song was also adopted in the 1970s by the largest student organization in India, the Students Federation of India (SFI), based in the Indian state of Kerala, the country's area of greatest communist strength that had the first democratically elected communist state government. N. P. Chandrasekharan, an SFI activist, used the original melody and translated the song into the regional language of Malayalam, with the title "Nammal Vijayikkum."[27]

The multiethnic and multilinguistic affinities imagined in Hazarika's reimaginings, reinventing, and improvising across harmonic, rhythmic, and melodic traditions, and their resonances with Robeson's rejection of hierarchy in musical forms, were sharply challenged in the cultural politics of nationalism.

By the time of the 1966 First World Festival of Negro Arts in Dakar, Senegal, Robeson had retreated into seclusion from all but a few trusted allies. But the problem-space of Dakar—marked by tensions between attempts to reify purportedly authentic

African cultures on the one hand, and new forms of modernity on the other, would have been both vexing and familiar to Robeson. Like the new racial formations of 1948, the context of the festival was marked by superpower conflicts—violently etched onto decolonizing landscapes.

Hosted by Senegal's president Senghor, renowned as a poet and a major exponent of Négritude, the festival was cosponsored by the United Nations Educational, Scientific, and Cultural Organization (UNESCO). Celebrating Senghor's idea of the unity of African and Black diasporic literature, art, and culture, and asserting its universal appeal, the festival showcased decades of the circulation of Black culture.[28]

As US officials celebrated recent civil rights reforms and promoted an inclusive, color-blind vision of American liberalism, African American artists, many of whom had pursued Afro-diasporic aesthetic visions for decades, affirmed perspectives of Black global modernity informed by histories of prior struggles for democracy. Their projects concerned the recovery of Black global modernity, evoking a continuum of the New Negro (Harlem) Renaissance; Négritude, the Francophone literary movement devoted to assertions of a distinctly Black expressive culture, and popular front and wartime flows of Black cultural traffic; anticipating the literary and cultural nationalism and recovery of African heritage associated with the Black Arts Movement. In a pivotal, if fraught, moment, the festival announced a new era of independent global Black cultural production and modernity. Haunted by an earlier and arguably more expansive anticolonial cultural politics that had been integral to the lives and careers of such participants as Dunham, Langston Hughes, and Ellington, the uneasy, unacknowledged presence of a broader anticolonial cultural politics and an urgent sense of the unfinished struggle against racial injustice is evident in the challenges faced by Dunham, as well as in the boycott of the festival by Harry Belafonte and James Baldwin. The intrusion of unresolved histories and liberation struggles erupted in significant controversies within the festival itself and in charges leveled against the festival by outside critics.[29]

Critics indicted the United States and Senegal for their prompt recognition of the post-Nkrumah military regime in Ghana (two months prior) and their tepid protest against Rhodesia's unilateral declaration of independence (UDI) as a white minority government. Novelist James Baldwin and singer Harry Belafonte boycotted the festival, lambasting Senghor for everything from the concept of Négritude to the US-friendly politics of Senegal. Ralph Ellison and actors Ossie Davis and Sidney Poitier also boycotted the festival. Belafonte had visited Guinea several times as a cultural advisor to President Ahmed Sékou Touré and had criticized Senegal for failing to break off relations with Britain over Rhodesia's UDI, as Guinea had done.

Apart from artists, American attendance ultimately consisted of a delegation of 183 people from the American Society of African Culture (AMSAC), a cosponsor of the festival. Critics of US foreign policy suspected the organization—correctly, as later reports showed—of accepting Central Intelligence Agency funding. Thus, AMSAC's sponsorship of the festival associated it with US foreign policy and made it suspect. Indeed, many American participants were firmly in the pro-Senegalese and anti-Nkrumah/Touré camp. Just months before the festival, Nkrumah, Ghana's president, had been overthrown in a military coup widely (and correctly) perceived to have been backed by the United States.[30] Debates over the relative merits of pan-Africanism and Négritude as ideologies of African liberation reflected a moment of crisis in the evolving, uneasy relationship between race, modernity, and an increasingly globally assertive US liberalism.

At the festival, Katherine Dunham was unique among American participants in that she was invited directly by Senghor to serve as his advisor. Dunham had met Senghor at the height of her international success and acclaim during her first tour of Paris in 1949, immediately following her time in 1948 London. Disturbed that on opening night there were no Black people in the audience, Dunham went to the Sorbonne to locate African students and provided free tickets to her performances. There, she met Senghor, along with Sekou Touré, future president of Guinea.[31] But by 1966, Senghor and Touré were locked in a bitter political feud, much of which concerned Touré's scathing criticism of Négritude as synonymous with Senghor's politically retrograde leadership of Senegal.[32]

For over two decades, Dunham had toured internationally with her company, for much of that time engaging in fierce battles with the US State Department over its refusal to support her tours. When Dunham's company disbanded in 1965, just a year before the Dakar Festival, she welcomed the opportunity to join Senghor in a celebration of the evolving Afro-diasporic forms she been bringing to international audiences for decades. Indeed, by 1966, Dunham had spent more than half of her life on tour, performing in over fifty countries throughout Europe, South and East Asia, South America, and Africa.[33] Five years after her last rejection from the State Department, with her company defunct, Dunham received a six-month grant from the State Department in 1965, following her personal invitation from Senghor to work on the festival.[34] This token recognition did nothing to ease Dunham's resentment of her treatment by the State Department over the years.

Throughout her career, Dunham had been a robust critic of ideas of racial authenticity. Against a modernism that looked to so-called primitive peoples as a way of seeking physical and emotional liberation from the strictures and provincialism of late Victorian society, Dunham was committed to an aesthetics of cultural fusion, seeking to remake modernity by demonstrating the universality of rhythm and the equality of expressive cultures. Indeed, Dunham mocked ideas of authenticity. In her first visit to Paris in 1948, she found productions by African choreographers lacking in "theatricality and flair." She later recounted that she had created *Afrique* "almost tongue in cheek" intentionally invoking clichéd gender stereotypes and characters "to poke fun at her fellow choreographers and the thirst for authenticity among audiences."[35]

As Dunham sought to dissociate herself from exoticized images of the primitive, her most significant strategy of legitimation involved invoking her authority and expertise as an anthropologist. Dunham was invested in what she saw as the value of scientific truth claims of anthropology for debunking racism as well as for legitimating her projects. Throughout her decades of international touring, she appeared frequently as a lecturer at universities and public halls, discussing the relationship between ethnography and theater. Both were integral elements in her project of challenging racial hierarchies and essentialisms, as Dunham believed that her artistic adaptations of Afro-diasporic dance forms could at once inspire audiences to appreciate the dignity and accomplishment of these forms, while honoring the integrity of anthropological investigation in pursuit of the "truth."[36]

Ultimately, Dunham insisted that her work as a dancer and choreographer was essentially that of a creative artist, explaining that "it would be a sacrifice for a creative artist to present theatre in a purely ethnographic form." For Dunham, "in theatre, the relationship between form and function *is made*" (my emphasis).[37] Dunham reinforced this idea of creative adaptation and innovation with the example of her staging of the Brazilian Choros. Even though "Choros is not danced that way in Brazil," the instruments, music, clothing, and underlying rhythms were Brazilian.[38]

Yet, at the festival, Dunham retreated from her nuanced discussion of the relationship between anthropology and choreography, offering a functionalist view of dance incompatible with her discussion of performance as a transformative space, which in *making* form and function generates new possibilities for performers and audiences alike.[39] Dunham startled some festival participants when in a public lectures she stated that "dance is not a technique but a social act" and discussed the need to "return dance to where it first came from, which is the heart and soul of man, and man's social living."[40] Her statement generated a great deal of controversy, as many objected to what they heard as a defense of tradition over change and modernity. The anthropological thought that had previously worked in productive tension with Dunham's creative process now plunged her into conflict with friends and colleagues.[41]

As Dunham turned to a focus on anthropology, critics and audiences alike questioned the dance program that Dunham had put together, charging a neo-traditionalist staging of rural dance forms. The dance scholar Hélén Kringelbach has argued that "in many the ways the emphasis on reimagining rural practices for the stage, on timelessness, and on the selection of particular ethnicities to stand in for emerging national identities was in continuity with the late colonial politics that followed the Second World war."[42] As participants, such as Alvin Ailey, forcefully spoke out against an idea of Négritude that presupposed essentialist ideas of natural rhythm among Blacks and Africans, as Kringelbach argues, the:

> dance program magnified the dissonance between Senghor's version of Negritude and the Senegalese audience's appetite for cosmopolitanism; while Senghor and the festival organizers focused on the neo-traditional genre, people moved to Cuban rhythms and high life . . . and the performers who attended the Festival were enthralled by Ailey's *Revelations*.[43]

Responding to critics, Dunham acknowledged among "certain participants, a kind of mistrust, a *méfiance* at the likelihood of a reversal to the traditional that might serve to inhibit 'modernization.'"[44] Skeptically placing modernization in quotes, Dunham sought to assure her audience of her commitment to combining traditional and contemporary forms, and her belief that art must be original. "Influence," she declared, "is inevitable but nothing that is copied is true art."[45] But even in light of Dunham's affirmation of creativity and "modernization," as her biographer Joanna Dee Das has argued, in attempting to insert her anthropological definition of dance into the festival's dance programing, Dunham "came across as a paternalist American interventionist."[46]

When Dunham asked that dance be returned to the place from which it came, *from where* did she want to return it? Did she want to wrest it from the influence of the State Department patronage and its deep entanglements with the dance patronage network? Dakar was a moment of profound unease for Dunham, making it difficult to negotiate the distinct discursive fields that had always mediated her approach to dance. In a telling moment in African American filmmaker William Greaves's documentary of the festival, made for the US Information Agency (USIA), Dunham is filmed speaking with several people after the colloquium. At one point, she catches the camera out of the corner of her eye and turns away abruptly, refusing to engage the camera as if it were a mere annoyance, suggesting her refusal to endorse the USIA.[47] The triumphant presence of Hughes, Ellington, and Ailey, and Greaves's filming—all underwritten by the State Department—were perhaps a painful affront to Dunham just a year after her company had disbanded for lack of funds. During an address delivered at the festival, in an implicit but obvious comparison to Ellington and Ailey, Dunham reminded the audience that her school and company was "unsubsidized."[48] Throughout her life, Dunham would express anger over her exclusion from the tours, once referring to the 1963 Ellington State Department tour as an extravaganza.

The celebration of Hughes as the African American poet laureate at the festival and in Greaves's film must also have been challenging for Dunham. With his deep ties to the Caribbean and Latin America and his extended travel through and writing on Soviet Central Asia, perhaps no artist, apart from Paul Robeson, had been more in sync with Dunham's exploration of cross-cultural fusion than Hughes. Dunham had paid a high price for her commitments. Although Hughes had been hauled before the House on Unamerican Activities, in Dunham's eyes, Ellington, Hughes, and her male counterparts remained comparatively unscathed.[49] Hughes had been able to maintain his career as a writer. Dunham had lost her company, her artistic independence, and her livelihood.

Dunham's turn to claims about African authenticity was also symptomatic of a crisis in anticolonial politics. Senghor's claims of unity were belied by turns to ethnically based populist appeals and authoritarianism among some leaders in the face of internal and external challenges to their power. In several African countries, heads of state turned away from pan-African linkages to increasingly narrow populist appeals. With Nigerian culture and dance especially foregrounded in the festival's programming, the festival had been bookended by the first military coup in Nigeria in January 1966—and a second coup in July of that year, both—leading up to the 1967 Biafra war—a civil war.[50]

In the middle of such political fissures, for Dunham, Dakar forced a reckoning with the loss of an earlier popular front-inflected anticolonial milieu that Dunham, Hughes, and Robeson had at once created and thrived in. As many abandoned discourses that recalled popular front politics, the Cold War dynamics that marginalized Dunham and destroyed Robeson's career and health also narrowed the vocabulary and ground of inquiry for exploring such urgent issues for postcolonial states as appropriate development models, state-building, and ethnic divides.

Belafonte's boycott of the festival must have been particularly difficult for Dunham. Belafonte's wife, Julie, had been a dancer in Dunham's troupe. Julie and Harry Belafonte would later play a key role in rescuing the legacy of Dunham as well as their friend Paul Robeson from obscurity. As Belafonte established working relations with such exiled South Africans as Miriam Makeba and worked with Sékou Touré, his civil rights activism maintained the deep ties to global antiracist struggles. At a pivotal moment between Dunham's work in dance and her later activism challenging dictatorship and imperialism in Haiti, the particular fissures of the conference may well have been a catalyst for her ensuing break with strategies of pursuing government support and her later activism as a militant critic of US imperialism in Haiti.

Fissures in anticolonial modernity at its intersections with state power are further illustrated in the experiences of Greaves. In 1966, the USIA commissioned Greaves to direct a film on the Dakar Festival. The film not only stands out as a unique document of the festival, but it also became the most popular US Information Services film throughout Africa over the next decade, further marking a departure from earlier didactic films produced under the auspices of the USIA.

Born in 1926 in New York City, Greaves produced more than two hundred documentaries before his death in 2014. Known for his Public Broadcasting Service documentaries on Ida B. Wells, the African American journalist and leader of the early twentieth century anti-lynching campaigns, and Ralph Bunche, an African American political scientist and United Nations diplomat who won the Nobel Peace Prize in 1950, Greaves's relationship with the USIA began in the early 1960s when George Stevens Jr., then head of the USIA film division, was seeking a Black director and contacted Greaves about doing a film on dissent in America. The agency deemed Greaves's plans for the film too controversial, including his intended inclusion of the atheist Madalyn Murray O'Hair, a leader of the movement to ban prayer in public schools.[51] With the agency urging Greaves to change the film's focus to "freedom of expression," the resulting 1964 film *The Wealth of Nations*, typical of USIA propaganda on race relations throughout the 1950s and early 1960s, proclaimed: America is great because it allows its citizens to "do their own thing." With Martin Luther King's 1963 "I Have a Dream" speech featured in the film, along with shots of architects and creative artists at work, scholars Charles Musser and Adam Knee have argued that King's speech suggests "a purely personal vision rather than the expression of a larger political movement."[52] This promotion of color-blindness, with implicit or explicit erasures of the structural racism actually invoked by King in his famous speech, was typical of USIA radio and print propaganda.[53]

Amid Dakar Festival planning, the USIA approached Greaves and asked him to produce a five-minute newsreel on the event. Welcoming the opportunity to focus on Afro-diasporic and African cultural production, upon arriving in Dakar, Greaves immediately realized the value of a longer film, and he and his cameraman began shooting as much footage as possible.[54] The resulting forty-minute documentary was largely shot without synchronous sound. Greaves edited the sound and footage together by structuring the film around the poetry of Hughes and the music of Ellington. Opening with a sequence of Hughes walking on the beach with a voice-over of his poem "The Negro Speaks of Rivers," the film's oceanside setting and poem evoke a somber narrative of return, the Middle Passage of enslaved captives, and layered histories of enslavement, resistance, and emancipation linking Africans and

African Americans. Throughout, the film features prominent artists and performance ensembles as well as narrative commentary on the cultural contributions (especially dance) of new African nations.

Multiple ironies stand out in the film's positioning of cultural authority. James Baldwin, who had boycotted the festival, nonetheless appears through the filming of the festival's book exhibit, where his 1961 *Nobody Knows My Name: More Notes of a Native Son* and his 1963 *The Fire Next Time* are conspicuously displayed. The prominence of male artists Hughes and Ellington juxtaposed to Katherine Dunham's shadowy presence in the film—she is named only once as she sits behind a conference table—virtually erases her central role in organizing the festival. In this sense, the film mirrors the gender politics of state sponsorship that had infuriated Dunham. The film also captures the discrepancy between Dunham's programming of traditional dance and the modernist, cosmopolitan choreography of the Alvin Ailey Company. Following a series of traditional dance performances from multiple African countries, the film cuts directly from traditional dance of Chad to the modern choreography of Ailey.

Another central irony of production and distribution concerns Greaves himself, underlining the fraught negotiation of Black representation in a moment of ascendant US liberalism. Reflecting on the importance of the film for his own career, Greaves recalled: "You have to realize that the reason why I went into motion pictures was to make films like *The First World Festival of Negro Arts*. It was the first opportunity I had to make films that expressed a Black perspective on reality. Until then, I had not had access to financing which would permit that."[55] The USIA provided Greaves an unprecedented opportunity in his career. But the strict USIA ban on distribution of USIA materials within the United States meant that Greaves was unable to show or distribute his film within the United States and to Black American audiences. It would be nearly three decades after the film's production that Greaves was able to obtain distribution rights.

Greaves's 1968 experimental hybrid fiction-documentary film Symbiopsychotaxiplasm can be read in part, as a commentary on Greaves's inability to distribute his Dakar film in the United States. Shot in New York City's Central Park during the summer of 1968 and engaging the public by filming unscripted encounters of passersby with the film crew, Symbio presents an extended meditation on the creative process. Greaves appears in the credits for Symbio as an actor as well the director and producer. The actor/director William Greaves provokes and taunts his actors and crew through portraying a character—an overbearing and misogynist director named after himself—who proclaims that the film is about sexuality and then insists on continually reshooting a melodramatic breakup scene in which a woman angrily accuses her husband of being homosexual. With actors and crew alike mystified by the film's premise and expressing frustration during the seemingly endless retakes of the scene in different settings, the rebelling film crew films itself complaining about Greaves. They debate whether he is a bad director, has no idea what he is doing, or is simply crazy. As crew members contemplate various forms of mutiny, the film becomes an extended meditation on the possibilities and limits of artistic freedom and control; one crew member declares, "We are *not* trying to take this film away from Bill Greaves."

The issues of gender, sexuality, and the interrogation of the power dynamics within collaborative creative process between actors, director, and crew foregrounded in Symbio, echo tensions at Dakar over male authority and neo-traditional versus modern controversies over the dance programing. Greaves's embrace of the opportunity to foreground Black cultural production and the Dakar film's departure from didactic, pro-American narratives marks a shift that parallels changes in USIA and State Department programming, as US officials met with increasing criticism and resistance to US foreign policy, a departure that undoubtedly opened possibilities for multiple readings among African audiences.

Indeed, for all of these artists, the 1966 Dakar Festival represented both a vortex of the political and cultural contradictions of Black modernities and a pivot to a new cultural moment that both transcended and remained burdened by the problematics of colonial and Jim Crow hierarchies, defining a new global cultural scene of African, African diasporic, and anticolonial modernity.

Notes

1 Prasenjit Duara, *Decolonization: Perspectives From Then and Now* (London: Routledge, 2004), 1; Prasenjit Duara, "Transnationalism and the Challenge of National Histories," in *Rethinking American History in a Global Age*, ed. Thomas Bender (Berkeley: University of California Press, 2002), 30.

2 David Scott, *Conscripts of Modernity: The Tragedy of Colonial Enlightenment* (Durham: Duke University Press, 2004), 3–4.

3 Lydia H. Liu, "Shadows of Universalism: The Untold Story of Human Rights Around 1948," *Critical Inquiry* 40 (Summer 2014): 385–417; Samuel Moyn, *The Last Utopia: Human Rights in History* (Cambridge, MA: Harvard University Press, 2010).

4 Edward Said, *Orientalism* (New York: Pantheon Books, 1978), 19–21.

5 Penny Von Eschen, *Satchmo Blows up the World: Jazz Ambassadors Play the Cold War* (Cambridge, MA: Harvard University Press, 2004) 25.

6 The extent scholarship on Dunham, from my own "Made on Stage" to Johanna Dee Das's 2017 biography *Katherine Dunham: Dance and the African Diaspora* (Oxford: Oxford University Press, 2017) note Dunham's time in London as a pivot to two decades of international touring; none do more than touch on the overwhelmingly positive critical reception of the company. "Made on Stage: Transnational Performance and the Worlds of Katherine Dunham from London to Dakar," in *Biography Across Borders: Transnational Lives*, ed. Desley Deacon and Penny Russell (London: Palgrave Macmillan, 2010), 156–67.

7 Marc Matera, *Black London: The Imperial Metropolis and Decolonization in the Twentieth Century* (Oakland: University of California Press, 2015); Kennetta Hammond Perry, *London is the Place for Me* (Oxford: Oxford University Press, 2015); Jim Godbolt, *A History of Jazz in Britain* (London: Northway Books, 2010).

8 My broader project explores state records to ascertain whether the official monitoring of Dunham was limited to embassy reports, or whether it had been as extensive as surveillance in the cases of Wright and Robeson.

9 Michael Warner, *Public and Counter Publics* (Cambridge, MA: MIT Press, 2002).

10 Ronald Radano, *Lying Up a Nation: Race and Black Music* (Chicago: University of Chicago Press, 2003).

11 Thank you to Gyan Prakash for my first exposure to these reimaginings in 1995.

12 Prasanta Mazumdar, "Bhupen Hazarika: A Nomad's Journey Echoes on," November 6, 2011, DNA, Mumbai, http://www.dnaindia.com/india/report_bhupen-hazarika-a-nomads-journey-echoes-on_1608171.

13 Paul Robeson Jr., *The Undiscovered Paul Robeson: Quest for Freedom, 1939–1976* (Hoboken: Wiley, 2010) 65, 107, 232.

14 Bhupendra Kumar Hazarika, *Proposals for Preparing India's Basic Educators to Use Audio-Visual Techniques in Adult Education, Submitted in Partial Fulfillment of the Requirement for the Degree of Doctor of Education in the Advanced School of Education, Teachers College* (Columbia University, 1952), 3.

15 Ibid., 1.

16 Ibid., 33.

17 Ibid., 16.

18 Ibid., 15–16.

19 Ibid., 31–3.

20 Ibid., 31.

21 Ibid.

22 Ibid., 32.

23 Asjad Nazir, "Bhupen Hazarika Obituary: Inspirational Indian Singer, Lyricist, and Political Activist," *guardian.co.uk*, November 6, 2011, http://www.guardian.co.uk/world/2011/nov/06/bhupen-hazarika, retrieved on June 9, 2012.

24 Bikram Bora, "Bhupen Hazarika: The Sub-Nationalist Imagination of a Universalist," November 12, 2011, http://kafila.org/2011/11/12/bhupen-hazarika-the-sub-nationalist-imagination-of-a-universalist-bikram-bora/#more-10340.

25 Pete Seeger, *In Prague, 1964* (album).

26 Quoted in H. W. Brands, *India and the United States: The Cold Peace* (Boston: Twayne, 1990), 130.

27 http://fahaddreams.wordpress.com/2010/07/17/hum-hongen-kaamyaab/, retrieved on June 10, 2012.

28 The literature is vast, bit see, Brent Hayes Edward, *The Practice of Diaspora* and Harry Justin Elam Jr. and Kennell Jackson, eds., *Black Cultural Traffic: Crossroads in Global Performance and Popular Culture* (Ann Arbor: University of Michigan Press, 2005).

29 Small portions of this essay have appeared in a modified form in Penny M. Von Eschen, "Soul Call: The First Word Festival of Negro Arts at a Pivot of Black Modernities," *Nka: Journal of Contemporary African Art* 42–43 (November/2018): 124–35; and Von Eschen, "Made on Stage."

30 On the coup and its political and cultural ramifications in Africa and its diaspora, see Kevin K. Gaines, *American Africans in Ghana: Black Expatriates and the Civil Rights Era* (Chapel Hill: University of North Carolina Press, 2006).

31 Von Eschen "Made on Stage," 160.

32 See, Diawara, *In Search of Africa.*

33 Robert Schnitzer to Katherine Dunham, May 6, 1960, Dunham Papers, Box 27, Folder 4.

34 Dunham refers to the six-month funding in another funding application to the Ford Foundation.

35 Joanna Dee Das, *Katherine Dunham: Dance and the African Diaspora* (Oxford: Oxford University Press, 2017). 132.

36 "Notes on Open Forum," 4.

37 "Notes on Open Forum Held by Miss Dunham for Anthropological Students from University of Auckland," 1, March 30, 1957, Auckland, New Zealand, Papers of Katherine Dunham, Box 22, Folder 3, University of Illinois, Carbondale.

38 In a talk given to anthropology students at the University of Auckland, New Zealand, Dunham described her greatest anthropological influences as coming from her teacher Robert Redfield, a "great acculturation expert" and the functionalist school of Radcliffe Brown. Ibid.

39 Von Eschen, "Made on Stage."

40 Katherine Dunham, "The Performing Arts of Africa," in *Proceedings, Primier festival mondial des arts négres: Colloque/ First World Festival of Negro Arts: Colloquium* (Dakar: Éditions Présence Africaine, 1968), 478–9, quoted in Eugene Redmond, "Cultural Fusion and Spiritual Unity," in *Kaiso!: Writings by and about Katherine Dunham*, ed. Vévé A. Clark and Sara E. Johnson (Madison: University of Wisconsin Press, 2005), 560.

41 The scholar Vévé Clark has argued that Dunham's writing on Haiti relies on a form/function structuralist analysis of dance, whereas her choreography belongs to a narrative, modernist tradition. Clark's point is insightful for analyzing the uncharacteristic position Dunham took at the festival. Vévé A. Clark, "Performing the Memory of Difference in Afro-Caribbean Dance: Katherine Dunham's Choreography, 1938–1987," in *Kaiso!*, ed. Clark and Johnson, 320–40.

42 Hélén Neveu Kringelbach, "Dance at the 1966 World Festival of Negro Arts," in David Murphy, *The First World Festival of Negro Arts: Dakar 1966* (Liverpool: Liverpool University Press, 2017), 82.

43 Ibid.

44 Katherine Dunham, "Address Delivered at the Dakar Festival of Negro Arts," Senegal, April 3, 1966, reprinted in *Kaiso!*, ed. Clark and Johnson, 416. See Julia L. Foulkes, "Ambassadors with Hips: Katherine Dunham, Pearl Primus, and the Allure of Africa in the Black Arts Movement," in *Impossible to Hold: Women and Culture in the 1960s*, ed. Avital H. Bloch and Lauri Umansky (New York: New York University Press, 2005), 89.

45 Dunham, "Address Delivered at the Dakar Festival of Negro Arts," 415.

46 Das, *Katherine Dunham*, 168.

47 *The First World Festival of Negro Arts*, 1966, a film produced and written by William Greaves, http://www.williamgreaves.com/catalog.htm.

48 Katherine Dunham, "Address Delivered at the Dakar Festival," 416.

49 Langston Hughes, *A Negro Looks at Soviet Central Asia*, Langston Hughes papers, Beinecke Library, Yale University Library, New Hartford, CT.

50 See, Michael Gould, *The Biafran War: The Struggle for Modern Nigeria* (I.B. Tauris, 2013).

51 Adam Knee and Charles Musser, "William Greaves, Documentary Filmmaking, and the African-American Experience," in *Cinemas of the Black Diaspora: Diversity, Dependence, and Oppositionality*, ed. Michael Martin (Detroit: Wayne State University Press, 1995), 393.

52 Ibid.

53 Von Eschen, *Race against Empire: Black Americans and Anticolonialism, 1937–1957* (Ithaca: Cornell University Press, 1997), 128–34.

54 Knee and Musser, "William Greaves," 394.

55 Ibid.

8

Francis Newton Souza's Black Paintings

Postwar Transactions in Color[1]

Atreyee Gupta

Francis Newton Souza's (1924–2000) exhibition *Black Art and Other Paintings* opened in London's Grosvenor Gallery in the summer of 1966. The exhibition included a selection of works from a series of monochromatic black canvases that Souza—a South Asian artist from Goa who was then based in London—had painted between 1964 and 1965.[2] No photograph of the 1966 exhibition can be located. However, based on a 2013 re-hang by the Grosvenor Gallery, we can imagine that, upon entering the space of the white cube in 1966, the viewer encountered the artworks—black rectangles of different sizes—as an immersive whole whose austere uniformity invoked the transcendence and universalism promised in postwar abstraction. But this was only the surface; underneath lurked landscapes and portraits whose smidgeons became vaguely discernible only after the eyes adjusted to blackness. Seeing through blackness necessitated a kind of funambulist opticality whose demand was bodily: to see the figures embedded in black paint, the viewer had to assume a range of difficult postures and hold them until both the light and the angle of vision were suitable for the act of viewing to finally begin.

Even as Souza compelled his audiences to bend and lean sideways in a way that altered the very conditions of seeing, the clandestine imagery hidden behind black pigment did not necessarily depend on the viewer's cooperation in order to become representation. Rather, the images had an existence independent of the viewer's bodily contortions (Figure 8.1). If anything, the complex calisthenics involved in viewing Souza's black paintings only confirmed the impossibility of any unmediated transparency in cognition while simultaneously organizing visual exegeses around corporeal, rather than transcendental, color fields. In 1966, Souza's black paintings shocked his audiences.[3] For such an approach to color pushed, on the one hand, against the vexed associations between blackness and primitivism inherited from prewar European modernism and, on the other hand, against debates on color and transcendentalism that were unfolding across the north Atlantic worlds after the Second World War.[4] What meaning did black, as a color, have for Souza? Why did he wish to amplify an embodied particularity over the alleged universality of vision as

Figure 8.1 F. N. Souza, *Mystical Ebony*, 1965, oil on canvas, 60 × 24 in., artwork on display at Kiran Nadar Museum of Art, New Delhi, photograph by author. © Estate of F. N. Souza. All rights reserved, DACS/ARS 2021.

evinced in the discussion around abstraction and color on both sides of the Atlantic in the 1960s? What prompted him to dialogue with, and dissent from, the dominant discourses of postwar art? And what did the color black have to do with any of this?

Born in 1924 in Portuguese Goa, Souza began his career in British Bombay. Described in 1989 by the cultural critic Geeta Kapur as "an enfant terrible, all the more dangerous because he belonged to the oppressed races," Souza was considered by many of his contemporaries in India and Britain—where he had lived from 1949—to be one among the most noteworthy living artists.[5] As a mark of protest against the prescriptive dictates of the Bombay Art Society—the colonial-era institution which was still the primary forum for artists in the city in the late 1940s—Souza had formed the Progressive Artists Group (PAG) in 1947 with a cohort of young artists.[6] The alliance between the PAG and leftist politics in India was forged by Souza, who started reading Marx sometime around 1944 and identified with leftist cultural movements even after severing ties with the Communist Party due to a series of disagreements with the politburo regarding the subject matter proper to revolutionary art.[7] However, rather than attenuating his initial revolutionary fervor, Souza's separation from the Communist Party served to consolidate an artistic imagination that not only sublimated politics into aesthetics but also transformed the notion of political autonomy into a creative ideal.

Souza came of age as an artist in London. The publication of his first oft-quoted 1955 autobiographical essay in the influential literary magazine *Encounter* corresponded with the opening of his first major solo exhibition at Gallery One, an art gallery established by the Surrealist poet and art dealer Victor Musgrave in Soho.[8] This brought him to the attention of leading Marxist art critics such as John Berger, who authored a substantial review of Souza's exhibition in the *New Statesman* in 1955.[9] In 1964, when Norman Read, the then director of the Tate Gallery, accessioned his 1961 painting *Two Saints in a Landscape* at art historian and Victoria and Albert Museum curator W. G. Archer's suggestion, Souza also became one of the first South Asian artists to be represented in the permanent collection of any major modern art museum on either side of the north Atlantic.[10] Although Souza's "foreignness" was often commented upon—"his painting smells of brimstone and betel-nut," the art critic Nigel Gosling wrote[11]—the prodigious amount of critical literature published on the artist by his European contemporaries signaled his burgeoning international reputation. Still, Souza struggled with the impact that his "foreignness" had on his career in Europe; having left his native country at the age of twenty-five, he had become something of an "outsider" there as well.

Souza eloquently narrated his sense of dislocation in a series of autobiographical essays published between 1955 and 1959.[12] Replete with ekphrastic power, the autobiographical tracts served as a primary source of information on the artist and, for long, have substantively shaped retrospective critical interpretations of his work as well.[13] The overemphasis on the autobiographies, however, have left crucial pictorial questions unanswered. For instance, although the South Asian artist was preoccupied with the color black and returned to it repeatedly with a seemingly obsessive persistence from 1954 to 1965 when he completed a series of over fifty paintings that he called Black Art, art historians are yet to examine the resonances that the color had for Souza. Likewise, the overemphasis on autobiographical exergy has offered little critical perspective on larger world historical issues that Souza's pictorial practice both insistently absorbed and repeatedly thematized. Only more recently has a somewhat more multifarious perspective on Souza's oeuvre emerged, one that places him in dialog with his British contemporaries such as Lucian Freud and Francis Bacon and highlights his importance as a precursor to the Black Art movement and practice of institutional critique by diasporic African, Caribbean, and South Asian artists in post-1980s Britain.[14] Souza's sustained engagement with the color black in the mid-decades of the twentieth century further nuances this picture.

I argue in this chapter that Souza's darker paintings not only advance our understanding of the artist's oeuvre as a whole but also demand a rethinking of the politics and poetics of color in postwar art more broadly. As such, this line of enquiry vitalizes concerns of pictorial representation with pressing questions of political representation. As a number of historians have argued, decolonization accrued tremendous intellectual force and a wide affective reach after the Afro-Asian conference at Bandung, Indonesia, which inaugurated the Third World project in 1955.[15] In the mid-1950s, thinkers of decolonization such as Aimé Césaire and Alioune Diop already began to describe Bandung as foundational for a Third World practice.[16] Third World intellectual consciousness deeply affected diasporic thinkers in London as well, according to Souza's contemporary Caribbean novelist Samuel Selvon.[17] The political implications of the Non-Aligned Movement, including its connections with the Civil Rights movement in the United States, have been explored in more recent scholarship.[18] In contrast, we know far less about the ways in which such processes of decolonization activated artistic vision. I do not aim to posit Souza's creative imagination as coterminous with the entire cluster of political and intellectual movements described above. Neither do I want to suggest that the color black was Souza's sole artistic concern. Rather, I propose a conjunctural history that mobilizes the color black as a lens to unpack the intricate intersections between liberatory politics and artistic expression in the mid-decades of the twentieth century.

The Many Courses of a Fugitive Color

Blackness as a subject of representation in Francis Newton Souza's oeuvre is first intimated through figuration and color in the 1954 painting *Reclining Nude* (Figure 8.2). The odalisque-like reclining female figure occupies the entire pictorial surface that is otherwise shorn of any embellishment or prop aside from a deep red and maroon backdrop. The very presence of the figure—not because of its nudity or lascivious posture but because of color—breaks down imagined ideological, political, and social distances between the black body and its corporeal imprint in the history of art. As scholars have shown, even after the abolition of slavery in 1848 in France, the black female body remained configured as an attendant or subservient figure in the works of French artists such as Édouard Manet (*Olympia*; 1863), among others.[19] Souza—who received training in European academic art at the Sir Jamsetjee Jeejeebhoy School of Art in colonial Bombay between 1940 and 1945 and was introduced to French and German artists by the city's interwar diasporic Jewish intellectual community—was all too

Figure 8.2 F. N. Souza, *Reclining Nude*, 1954, oil on board, 23.6 × 47.2 in., private collection. © Estate of F. N. Souza. All rights reserved, DACS/ARS 2021.

conversant with this art historical trajectory. But having no access to African American art and literature, he could not have possibly known of the positive reconfiguration of the black body by artists and intellectuals of the Harlem Renaissance in the United States; he was surely unacquainted with the work of an African American artist like William H. Johnson, whose interwar oeuvre not only centralized the black female body but also endowed it with interiority and agency. How then are we to position such a radical uptake on black bodies by a South Asian artist whose intellectual formation occurred at a far remove from the historical crucible of the Black Atlantic or even the work of his African American contemporaries?

Souza, we may recall, had arrived in London in 1949 with a Portuguese passport. Souza's native Goa on the western coast of present-day India was at the time still a Portuguese colony and would remain so until it was ceded to India in 1961. Having once served as the capital of Portugal's Estado da Índia empire—a territory stretching from East Africa to Malacca in Southeast Asia—Goa remained connected to Indian Ocean Portuguese territories through the shared history of Catholic inquisitions, the continued movement of people, objects, and ideas across colonies in Asia and Africa, enduring debates on race and miscegenation, and the experience of ongoing colonial domination.[20] Colonized Africa, thus, did not figure in the cultural imaginary in British colonial or postcolonial India in quite the same way as it did in Portuguese Goa. For a Portuguese subject, the color black then had a very distinct meaning: "Under the oppression of the whites, the black man had cried out in blues," Souza wrote in his 1955 autobiographical essay *Nirvana of a Maggot*.[21] Painted two years later, the iconic blue-black figure placed upon the thick white impasto surface in Souza's *Negro in Mourning* echoed the tragedy of colonialism as recounted in the dialogic among whites, blacks,

Figure 8.3 F. N. Souza, *Negro in Mourning*, 1957, oil on board, 481 × 24 in., collection of the Birmingham Museums and Art Gallery, Birmingham, UK.

and blues in *Nirvana of a Maggot* (Figure 8.3). As if the dripping lines of paint were but streaming drops of tears—bodily secretions—embedded as marks of oppression in the viscous materiality of color pigment.

Notably, by the time *Negro in Mourning* was painted, the history of colonial oppression was becoming entangled for Souza with the lived milieu of post-imperial London where artists and writers from former colonies such as South Asia and the British West Indies found accommodation in crowded bedsits and cramped apartments in neighborhoods like Belsize Square and Notting Hill. Merely months after *Negro in Mourning* was painted, violence erupted in Notting Hill—not far from Belsize Square where Souza lived—when a white working-class mob led a week-long armed attack on West Indian migrants in the fall of 1958. "I painted 'Negro in Mourning' in London when the race riots flared. I personally think it is one of my best works—socialist realism maybe, Expressionism certainly. Moreover, 'Negro in Mourning' is close to the bone of man because it is about the colour of skin," Souza recollected.[22]

Negro in Mourning serves to employ the multimodal connotations that the color black accrued for the artist in the 1950s. As a sketch completed in the previous year indicates, the 1957 painting was based on a portrait of the African American jazz maestro Louis Armstrong, who had arrived in London in the summer of 1956 (Figure 8.4). We can assume that Souza was becoming more familiar with the African American Civil Rights discourses as these were being transposed onto the British cultural and political landscape through figures such as Paul Robeson, whose eventual exile to London indelibly intertwined blackness with questions about equality and enfranchisement posed by the still-unfolding processes of decolonization and anti-

Figure 8.4 F. N. Souza, *Louis Armstrong*, 1956, ink on paper, 10.5 × 8 in., The Darashaw Collection. © Estate of F. N. Souza. All rights reserved, DACS/ARS 2021.

segregation movements.[23] Simultaneously, through Musgrave, the Surrealist poet and proprietor of Gallery One in Soho which represented the artist from 1955 to 1963, Souza was being drawn into the heart of London bohemia. He spent evenings in the Colony Room club where artists, poets, and diasporic intellectuals gathered and took noctambulant rambles along Mayfair "at night or in the early hours of the morning."[24] Through these circuitous ambits, he found bonhomie with diasporic Caribbean intellectuals such as Selvon, whose 1956 novel *The Lonely Londoners* was an extensive mediation on racial blackness and the color black.[25] Indeed, in retrospect, it is easy to see how the 1957 painting *Negro in Mourning* connected the color black with the expansive web of intellectual affinities and political affiliations that Souza had developed by this time.

Herein also lay a confounding representational paradox, one that substantially concerned Souza in the period under consideration: color—which was often believed to be subservient to line, form, and composition—had remained conspicuously absent in postwar modernist art historical analysis until the 1970s, at least in the north Atlantic context.[26] But more than any other color, it was black that was caught in a condition of double erasure. Most theorists of modern Western art in the 1950s considered black to be a noncolor and, therefore, relevant only as a shadow, an obverse of true colors, or better still a negation of color. Consequently, black was neither included in color spectrums reproduced in academic treatises on painting nor was its use as an independent color part of art school education in Europe or its colonies.

The removal of black from the roster of colors occurred as early as 1665, with Isaac Newton's discovery of the color spectrum through experiments with light sieved through a glass prism. After Newton, a number of artists paid attention to the mechanics of perception and the effect that color had on the viewer.[27] Scholars have argued that this constituted a chromatic revolution. For within this new chromatic order, neither black nor white were considered true colors—black even less so than white, according to the historian Michel Pastureau.[28] While Newton's approach to color theory was positivist, the German philosopher Johann Wolfgang von Goethe also authored a popular color treatise in 1810, which laid stress on the subjective and emotive qualities of color. Arguably, Goethe's color philosophy was far more popular among artists. Neither Newton nor Goethe, however, allocated black the status of a color.[29] While the complexity within the art history of color is beyond the scope of this argument, it is worth reiterating that, by the nineteenth century, aside from Vincent Van Gogh and Paul Cézanne, the Impressionist painters with whose work Souza was perhaps the most familiar had eliminated the color black even from shadows, choosing instead to simulate the effect of darkness by combining blues, greens, and reds.[30] According to Souza, Pierre-Auguste Renoir disliked the achromatic color so much that he compared "a spot of black" to a "hole in the painting."[31]

At the other end was the history of European modernist primitivism, which implicitly collocated the color with the naïve, the infantile, the uncivilized, the savage, and the barbaric.[32] Originally attributed to any cultural artefact that did not belong to the Greco-Roman classical tradition or the Italian Renaissance, the word primitivism was, by the twentieth century, used specifically to describe Oceanic and African art. More pointedly, for artists such as Paul Gauguin and Pablo Picasso, the primitive served as a foil for the other of the white European and primitive cultural production, many have indicated, allowed for a critique of Western modernity.[33] The blackness that animated modernist primitivism thus had a double innuendo. As feminist art historians have argued, the tacit locus of European modernist primitivism "was the black female body, which became the harbinger for a savage sexuality that exceeded the limits of representation," while cultural objects, such as African totemic sculptures and masks, took on a central representational role in modern art.[34] Some of these ideas were taken up by Surrealists such as André Breton in the postwar years and were adopted, albeit with substantial inflection, by the artists and poets of the short-lived CoBrA collective, who, prompted by perceived limits of European humanism, sought to wield dialectical materialism to painterly atomism and creative experimentation in the aftermath of the Second World War.[35] Within prewar and postwar primitivism, the color black then signaled the body and pigment simultaneously. This was calibrated, of course, through the prism of race even as the agency of the color itself was rarely acknowledged.[36] It is this very elusive history of the color black and the racialized body of the other that Souza's 1954 *Reclining Nude* educes visually.

The belittlement of black in color theory, however, was sharply offset by its implacable prominence in a very different register of intellectual thought and practice. For the color black was already interpellated by the energies of decolonization. Initiated by Senghor, Césaire, and Damas in Paris, the Négritude movement had marshalled the negative energies implicit in a term like *nègre* to annunciate a new dialectic of black consciousness well before the beginning of the Second World War. Souza himself encountered Négritude in the early 1950s, not through Senghor, Césaire, or Damas, but through Jean-Paul Sartre.[37] When Souza first met Sartre in Paris, the English translation of "Black Orpheus"—Sartre's extended critical essay on Négritude written in 1948 as a preface to *Anthologie de la nouvelle poésie nègre et malgache*, the now-seminal anthology of African and West Indian Négritude poetry edited by Senghor—had just been published in the journal *Présence Africaine*.[38] "Black is a color," Sartre had affirmed, and "liberty is the color of night."[39] Sartre's delineation of the color black as the only viable praxis of revolution in the twentieth century was perhaps most generative for Souza, who separated from the Communist Party in 1948 but was progressively becoming more and more steeped in Marxist and anti-imperial intellectual movements. For Souza, the fugitive color—abound with achromatic pigmental materiality, controverted in art historical opacity, resonant with political potentiality—mattered.

Color Index in Colored Contexts

Several works from the 1950s reveal the ways in which the color black was becoming more and more central to Souza's palette, in turn fusing representational concerns with questions of race, imperialism, class, and, keeping the Goan context in mind, caste oppression. Souza's life-size 1959 painting *Crucifixion* now in the collection of Tate Modern, London, for example, depicted Christ, not in the form of a fair-skinned beatific icon, but as a misshapen black figure bearing marks of brutalization. In this instance, the coloration of the sacramental body was significant. For unlike the Iberian colonial worlds of Spanish America and the Philippines, where the Black Christ—Cristo Negro or the Black Nazarene—enabled indigenous communities to refashion Christianity in their own image, the color black was already internal to the dynamics of Hindu caste oppression in precolonial Goa.[40] As scholars have shown, Portuguese proselytization in Goa strategically assimilated such preexisting social hierarchies ordered around caste or *varna* (literally color), which historically allocated blackness to lower castes (*sudra*), slaves (*dasa*), and other purported enemies of the fair-skinned upper caste Aryans. In terms of liturgical practices, social hierarchies in Portuguese Goa translated into the institution of separate services for upper and lower caste denominations by way of endorsing existing caste-based conceptions of purity and pollution.[41]

That epidermal hierarchies reflected in representational registers is apparent in a seventeenth-century Goan oil painting, which shows Francis Xavier, the cofounder of the Society of Jesus, baptizing a low-caste Paravar fisherman (Figure 8.5). Not dissimilar to the representation of African bodies in contemporaneous European paintings, the figure of the Paravar also bears testimony to the circulation and reuse of representational conventions across colonial image worlds. As the art historian Victor I. Stoichita has argued, the black skin color "was considered to be the accursed mark of original damnation laid upon the lineages of Ham, the indecent son of Noah. Blackness as a visible sign of sin was also one of the fundamental *topoi* of discourses on the Fall and Salvation."[42] The operative conceit of epidermal darkness as a symbol of sin, Stoichita

Figure 8.5 Artist unknown, *St. Francis Xavier Baptizing a Paravar Pearl Fisher*, seventeenth century, oil on canvas, 29 1/4 × 22 3/4 in., private collection. Photograph © Sotheby's 2020.

elaborates, "insists on the universality of the Resurrection, whilst emphasizing the inevitable descent of 'black' spiritual bodies into the shadows of Tartarus."[43] The color black—a means of picturing subalternity—was then doubly charged. And Souza—who had received art training in childhood through art workshops conducted by the Jesuit clergy—was no doubt alert to the representational nuances of such chromatic arrangements.[44]

Crucifixion was one of the two paintings that Souza completed in the summer of 1959. The second painting, *Nyasa Negress with Flowers of Thorns*, was a direct reference to the ongoing liberation struggle in the British protectorate of Nyasaland (Malawi) in central Africa, as the title indicates (Figure 8.6). At the time Souza painted *Nyasa Negress with Flowers of Thorns*, the British governor of Nyasaland had just declared a state of Emergency. But rather than drawing on symbols with readily legible referents, Souza's painting assembled a series of vexed cultural associations. The dark Nyasa figure resembled totemic sculptures removed from the African continent by European explorers and housed in various museums across Europe. Thus, even as the title of the painting contextualized the figure within the geopolitical space of Malawi, the formal constitution of the figure simultaneously collapsed the distinction between the sociopolitical body and its cultural manifestation as image in a way that dispensed with any pretention of representational transparency. The bristling thorns emanating from the hair recalled talismanic African sculptures fitted with copper and iron nails and the

Figure 8.6 F. N. Souza, *Nyasa Negress with Flowers of Thorns*, 1959, oil on canvas, 51.5 × 38 in., private collection. Photograph © Christie's © Estate of F. N. Souza. All rights reserved, DACS/ARS 2021.

fetishization of such objects by modernist primitivists such as Picasso and others in the prewar years. Souza's paintings from the 1950s thus imparted a historical sensibility to pictorial surface by consolidating a range of critical concerns around the color black. His aesthetic philosophy, too, assembled discrete ideas drawn from seemingly disparate contexts—Négritude, Marxism, and the history of colonialism—to shape an aesthetic vocabulary that was entirely his own. British critics, however, failed to make note of Souza's unconventional approach to blackness, likely due to the ambiguous status of the color black in modern European art; for most, "the nailed Martyr with flanking potentates" was "most quelling."[45]

But the point did not escape German Jewish writer Ulli Beier, whose critical vision was, according to the art historian Chika Okeke-Agulu, singularly "most influential" in shaping Nigeria's postwar modernism in lines with the ideals put forward by the founders of the Négritude movement through venues such as the cultural journal *Présence Africaine* edited by Diop.[46] Notably, the impact of the Bandung conference had not only left a deep imprint in the pages of *Présence Africaine* but had also inspired Diop to organize the First International Congress of Black Writers and Artists in 1956. Intended to be a "cultural Bandung," the Congress had set out to challenge the idea that "the vocation of the universal is a virtue inseparable from Europe," as Diop wrote.[47] Like many of his contemporaries, Beier too was invigorated by the moment of Bandung and the very same ideals that excited Diop also catalyzed Beier's critical vision. When Beier stumbled upon Souza's *Crucifixion* and *Nyasa Negress with Flowers of Thorns*, among other paintings during a visit to an exhibition at Musgrave's Gallery One in London in 1959, he was astounded. Returning to Nigeria, he immediately published an important article on Souza in the *Black Phoenix*, the cultural magazine whose title, according to Okeke-Agulu, drew upon Sartre's "Black Orpheus."[48] Souza and Beier did not meet in person and we can assume that Souza's interest in Négritude was unknown to the critic when he, under the nom de plume Omidiji Aragbabalu, wrote: "Souza's art, bridging two worlds and two cultures, is of great significance to us in West Africa [. . .] from the ruins of our various traditions in Asia and Africa we are beginning the work of synthesis and reconstruction."[49] By drawing upon a wide array of historical sources, Souza, Beier argued, transcended both South Asian and European painterly conventions to develop a radically new language of expression that not only resonated across colonized and formerly colonized worlds but also centralized a critique of oppression as such. Going by Souza's painterly output, we can imagine that the artist would have fully agreed with the critic's assessment. Overall, the approach to color that emerged in Souza's practice in the 1950s had significant implications for the work that he began in the years that followed.

Black Art

Although Souza did not begin working on his monochromatic black canvases until 1964, the problem of the color black as the primary subject of representation already concerned him by the end of the 1950s. Yet, even as the artist marshaled a range of historical vectors that converged around the color black, the expressive potential of pigment still remained underexplored in his works, as Kapur commented in 1992.[50] A similar opinion had been expressed in 1957 by the British critic David Sylvester who observed: "I think Souza will have to get vibration and meaning into the strokes of his brush and into his color, use paint as *medium* of feeling, not as a way of ornamenting illustrations of it."[51] We can imagine that Souza, who was exceptionally sensitive to critical opinion, would not have taken this charge lightly. In a 1966 interview, he claimed to have finally resolved the representational dilemma presented by the color in his Black Art series with which I began this chapter.[52]

The color black was the subject of Souza's monochromatic Black Art series. But not all of Souza's monochromes are uniformly dark or monotonously matt. One canvas has a glossy reflective surface, another has a lighter matt black hue, a third is rendered with a minor black-brown tint, and a fourth reproduced in Figure 8.1 is a mixture of matt and gloss. Such variations withstanding, the color black was the portentous subject of the paintings. And it is in this sense that the entire body of works also appear at the first glance to be nonrepresentational mediations on color, thus seemingly confirming to the highly mediatic and ocular emphasis in formalist discourses that dominated critical lexica in the mid-decades of the twentieth century. This ostentatious mediatic focus, however, constitutes an elaborate subterfuge of the very same critical emphasis that the paintings appear to uphold. For the putative emptiness that meets the eye at the initial glance is but an ocular misapprehension as figural imagery lurk immediately beneath the seemingly ungiving black surface. Although the figurative renditions embedded under the black surface bear stylistic homology with the works completed in the previous years, there is a crucial distinction between Souza's previous experiments with the color black and the black paintings of the mid-1960s: figures had been presented as images ensconced within the limits of the canvas in the artist's earlier paintings. Their address to the viewer had also been primarily optical. It is not that the figures in the black paintings now refused such an address. It is just that the painter had become far less acquiescent of the viewing gaze.

There is one abstract canvas among Souza's black paintings (Figure 8.7). It is composed of a cluster of small squares that replicate grains of wood. The grid-like composition plays with the tension between the concreteness of architectonic modularity implied in the square and the limber manipulability of oil paint. The surface that is thereby conjured up has the appearance of flaking desiccated skin that is irregular in texture, cracked, and brittle to the touch, thus stretching the boundaries between abstraction and figuration, representation and the body. A nimble engagement with the ambivalent facticity of perception is at the core of the artwork's conception. The idea behind the work, after all, had emerged from an absurd exchange with the influential Paris gallerist Iris Clert recorded in a letter written to Musgrave several years ago: "By the way have you seen the photographs of my floor taken by Gerald Howson? Iris Clert thought it was my latest style and started raving. John Christoforou was with me. He then explained that it was my studio's floor and not my paintings. You should have seen her face fall."[53] Clert's optical error was simple enough. A supporter

Figure 8.7 F. N. Souza, *Untitled*, 1965, oil on canvas, 29 × 19 in., private collection. © Estate of F. N. Souza. All rights reserved, DACS/ARS 2021.

of abstract painters such as Yves Klein—another painter of monochromes—Clert had mistaken the linear grid of the black-and-white photograph of the studio floor for a nonrepresentational geometric composition. But for Souza, who subsequently reproduced this photograph without any commentary among his paintings in an exhibition catalog, both the image and the exchange with Clert set the context for imaginatively probing the limits of ocularity.[54] Not surprisingly, he returned to the same photograph and reconfigured the image into an abstract figuration—an anachronistic twist on the very terms of representation—in his black painting. This painting was one among his first monochromes.[55]

All other paintings in the Black art series are figurative. The black figures rendered in thick impasto strokes surface—as if out of their own violation—only under certain viewing conditions, when the angle of light and angle of vision are perfectly aligned. The circumstances of such an optical encounter necessarily involve significant discomfiture as the viewer's body has to contort itself into impossible postures difficult to hold long enough for a contemplative aesthetic experience to occur. That an aesthetic experience is distinct from all other forms of experiences had been

Figure 8.8 F. N. Souza, *Untitled*, 1964–5, oil on canvas, 42.5 × 67 in., private collection. © Estate of F. N. Souza. All rights reserved, DACS/ARS 2021.

underscored by art theorists such as Roger Fry and Clive Bell in the first decades of the twentieth century and shored up in the postwar years by prominent critics such as Clement Greenberg and Michael Fried. Yet, standing in front of Souza's black canvases, it is impossible not to be deeply aware of the discomforted body, desperately twisted as it is in the quest for vision. An aesthetic transcendence capable of reducing everything to the same formal universal is thus promised in the black paintings but then forever postponed. Furthermore, the artist had hidden a second multichromatic layer underneath the thick black surface of some of the paintings (Figure 8.8). This layer has become partially visible only recently, after some of the canvases have developed craquelure across the surface—the cutaneous exterior—as the black paint layers have aged and shrunk back to reveal a subterranean anthropomorphism. A body within a body.

The layered surplus implicit in the construction of the paintings is likely not intended to eradicate or erase optical experience but rather to lace the pictorial with an interplay of the sensual. Such tactics of deception, of course, were utilized by painters since time immemorial, so to speak. We need only to recollect the long history of trompe l'oeil and academic perspectival illusionism against which modernists like Souza had riled. However, in the black paintings, the specific method of embedding and layering the body—the body of the canvas conceptualized as both surface and depth, the body of color, and the colored body—perhaps derived from the technology of transparency and projection, which Souza had started using from the early 1960s onward and which made the process of mark-making striated. A 1965 photograph of Souza and his transparency projector shows the artist working on a sketch which is projected on a canvas in the background that contains markings that have already been covered up by the first layer of dark paint (Figure 8.9). This points

Figure 8.9 Tony Evans, *Souza in His Studio*, 1965, black-and-white photograph, size variable. Photograph Tony Evans/Timelapse Library Ltd via Getty Images. © Estate of F. N. Souza. All rights reserved, DACS/ARS 2021.

to the material and pictorial impact that layering and coating necessarily had on his painterly procedure. But foregrounded in other photographs is another equally important quality, one that pertains to a cautious employment of bodily comportment that distends from the otherwise processual engagement with transparency, projection, and layering (Figure 8.10). These are not only far more theatrical in terms of framing and the amplification of light and shadow but also evince a significantly more performative syntax. In one, Souza crouches on the ground arms extended for the benefit of the camera in a choreographed gesture that clearly has more to do with staging than it has to do with the pragmatics of painting. Souza returned to such documentary photographs of himself with insistent abandon as he began to cut and splice photographs in his sketchbooks in the early 1960s. As visible in one folio, he also refurbished such photo compilations with a serial structural logic that implicitly drew into the visual quotient his own body (Figure 8.11). The photographic compilation anticipated the chromatic seriality of the black paintings while the cover of the *Black Art and Other Paintings* catalog reenacted the structural logic of the photographic folio, the latter no doubt originally envisioned as a private exercise in photo collage (Figure 8.12).

Of course, there are some obvious differences in what the photographs actually show. The ones in the photo compilation record artistic process and thus belong to a documentary genre while the one on the cover of the catalog is a single black-and-white formal portrait of the artist now cut into sixteen uneven squares and laid on a rough grid. Aside from such distinctions, the primary additive element in the catalog is

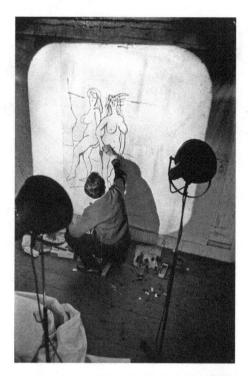

Figure 8.10 Crispin Eurich, *Souza*, 1964, black-and-white photograph, size variable. Photograph courtesy the Crispin Eurich Photographic Archive. © The Crispin Eurich Photographic Archive 1.

a seemingly bland silver coating that, if scratched away by an inquisitive viewer, reveals two dark figures fully covered in a glossy plastic polyvinyl chloride outfit flanking the artist (Figure 8.13). The cover of the exhibition catalog was designed by Souza, and, as such, it elucidates a peculiar dialogic between the ocular and the corporeal that the black paintings also instantiate. Precisely how this structural logic springs from the technology of transparency and projection is difficult to extrapolate as Souza did not expound upon this matter. But the connection can certainly be sustained by way of juxtaposition, as seen in the photo compilation folio and the cover of the exhibition catalog. In effect, the ocular-centric ontologies of the pictorial pregiven in modernism are rendered inadequate.

Such juxtapositions relentlessly return us to the body. The artist's own body, the cutaneous quality of the paintings, and the contorted body of the viewer. It is tempting to read into this insistence on the body an oblique reference to Souza's Paris-based Martinican contemporary Frantz Fanon, whose profound influence on contemporaneous intellectual thought and decolonial politics is now widely acknowledged. As others have noted, Fanon's delirious array of self-images in *Black Skin, White Masks* were all tethered to imperialist stereotypes of blackness: "I was battered down by tom-toms, cannibalism, intellectual deficiency, fetishism, racial

Figure 8.11 F. N. Souza, *Sketchbook*, 1963, black-and-white photographs on paper. Photograph reproduced from *Francis Newton and Maria Souza: A Life Partnership in Art* (New York: Christie's, 2014), 236. © Estate of F. N. Souza. All rights reserved, DACS/ARS 2021.

defects."[56] Such a sense of the corporeal, Homi Bhabha has written, could not be simply assimilated into the Cartesian distinction between the mind and the body or neatly "resolved in the epistemology of 'appearance and reality'"[57] as consciousness and cognition refracts, in Fanon's terms, in that returning gaze—"look a Negro"[58]— of the white European. The corporeal body was for Fanon the source of an impossibly fractured but critical crucible of a black consciousness that functioned through a making that was not quite its own. Certain threads of corresponding intellectual strands between Fanon and Souza have been alluded to by the artist Rasheed Araeen.[59] But, in essence, Souza's own mediations on blackness in the Black Art series refuses the gaze. For the pigmental opacity in Souza's black paintings categorically rejects any visual reckoning with the color black that proceeds from generalized dermatological assumptions. Moreover, Souza is not, strictly speaking, an artist of African descent. Then, what he insists upon in place of generality is, as performance studies scholar Fred Moten so wonderfully puts it in a different context, the "irremediable homelessness common to the colonized, the enslaved, and the enclosed."[60]

Figure 8.12 Exhibition catalog, *Black Art and Other Paintings* (London: Grosvenor Gallery, 1966). Photograph courtesy Grosvenor Gallery, London. © Grosvenor Gallery, London.

Conceivably, there is no simple way to communicate a chromatic schema that places color at the intersections of the social, the epistemic, the ocular, and the bodily except via the sociability of viewing. This sociability is how the black paintings work; in the absence of this contact, they retract into the inertness of monochromatic oversaturation, as if parodying the essentializing chromatic valence of the color black as a noncolor, negation of color, stasis, and absence. This language of negation is exactly what Ad Reinhardt, another postwar painter of monochromes, used to describe the color black.[61] But for Souza—an artist of color—black was fundamentally "kinetic"; the color black stood not for stasis but for the incalculable rhythm of movement that did not heed any critical protocol that distinguished aesthetic experience from the experience of the everyday.[62] Consequently, the obdurate opacity presented by the black paintings are not resolved but only conspicuously magnified in photography. When underexposed, the black figures retrocede into the black surface; when overexposed, the pictorial surface is distorted by refraction, thus inclining the color black toward white or gray.

Figure 8.13 Exhibition catalog with silver coating scratched out, *Black Art and Other Paintings* (London: Grosvenor Gallery, 1966). Photograph courtesy Grosvenor Gallery, London. © Grosvenor Gallery, London.

Even more impossible to see in a photograph than in person, the black canvases thus demand a moment of contact that is not only optic but also embodied. As his then partner Barbara Zinkant recalls, Souza placed lamps around the paintings in his studio and spent hours pondering over visual distillation, physical movement, and their relation to the angle of sight to choreograph the terms of relationality between the body of representation and the body of the viewer.[63] But this is also a kind of viewing that is impossible to maneuver when encountering the work as a photograph. We could perhaps then say that the body matters in the black paintings almost as much as the color black matters for Souza.

We may recall that monochromatic painting—of which Kazimir Malevich's 1913 *Black Square* was an early example—has been consecrated in art history as a tangible expression of the subliminal. In 1950s Paris, Souza's contemporary Klein had already adopted the idea "of pure realms of color and color as a spiritual realm."[64] In New York, the color-field painter Mark Rothko insisted on color's ability to express basic human emotions—"tragedy, ecstasy, doom, and so on"[65]—to precipitate a transcendental encounter with infinity. Rothko may have associated the color black with the absolute, and hence the emphasis on black in the murals that he completed between 1964 and 1967 for John and Dominique Menil's ecumenical chapel in Houston. Around the same time, Reinhardt—also Souza's contemporary—described his near-monochromatic black paintings as attempts to arrive at "a pure, abstract, nonobjective, timeless, spaceless, changeless, relationless, disinterested painting."[66] In hindsight, the association of the color black in postwar art with infinity, purity, spirituality, and transcendence may appear universal. But in insisting that his viewers twist, bend, and turn, Souza may have harbored an aspiration of a very different sort. Let us not forget that, when wielded by the disenfranchised in the second half of the twentieth century, the color black—the Négritude poetics of the color black, the black of the Black Panthers, the black flag of dispersed anarchist groups across the world—functioned as (a)chromatic contractions of resistance.

Notes

1   The illustrations for Chapter 8 are not included in the open access ebook edition owing to third-party rights restrictions. Images for this chapter are available in the print edition. A more extensive discussion on F. N. Souza's black paintings has appeared in *The Art Bulletin*, where the illustrations accompanying the present chapter have also been reproduced. See Atreyee Gupta, "Francis Newton Souza's Black Paintings: Postwar Transactions in Color," *The Art Bulletin* 103, no. 4 (2021): 111–37.

2   While no definitive catalogue raisonné of Francis N. Souza's oeuvre exists, fifty-one black paintings were located in various private and public collections and displayed in the *F. N. Souza Black on Black* exhibition at the Grosvenor Gallery in 2013. The lead essay by Zehra Jumabhoy in the catalog for the exhibition is the only published scholarly text until date to focus on this series. See Zehra Jumabhoy, "F. N. Souza: Dark Visions," in *F. N. Souza Black on Black*, exh. cat., ed. Grosvenor Gallery (London: Grosvenor Gallery, 2013), 7–13. The works in the 2013 exhibition included, but were not limited to, the black canvases that were displayed in the *Black Art and Other Paintings* exhibition of 1966. See the checklist in Grosvenor Gallery, *Black Art and Other Paintings*, exh. cat. (London: Grosvenor Gallery, 1966). No high resolution photographs of the re-hang could be located. For installation views, see https://www .grosvenorgallery.com/exhibitions/126/installation_shots/ (accessed April 28, 2021).

3   For example, see newspaper clipping "The Black Art in London," Name of paper not known, May 7, 1965. "Working notes, Articles, Exhibition Brochures and Some Correspondence on Francis N. Souza 1961–65," W. G. Archer Papers, Mss. Eur F236/164, India Office Records and Private Papers, British Library.

4   For a discussion on blackness and primitivism in prewar modernism, see Hal Foster, "The 'Primitive' Unconscious of Modern Art," *October* 34 (1985): 45–70. The literature on color and transcendentalism in postwar art is vast. For a synoptic summary, see Mark A. Cheetham, "Matting the Monochrome: Malevich, Klein, and Now," *Art*

Journal 64, no. 4 (2005): 94–109. In contrast, the question of color in modern South Asian art has remained largely underexplored with the exception of Natasha Eaton, *Colour, Art and Empire: Visual Culture and the Nomadism of Representation* (London: I. B. Tauris, 2013). My own arguments regarding color also draws on John Gage, who suggests that the problematic of color cannot be understood exclusively in relation to the history and theory of color in art history and color theory. John Gage, *Colour and Meaning: Art, Science and Symbolism* (Berkeley and Los Angeles: University of California Press, 1999).

5 Geeta Kapur, "Francis Newton Souza: Devil in the Flesh," *Third Text* 3, no. 8–9 (1989): 25–64, 32. For early art criticism published in India, see Hermann Goetz, "Rebel Artist Francis Newton Souza," *Marg* 3, no. 3 (1949): 34–9 and Albano Francisco Couto, "Two Goan Artists: Souza, Pepeira," *Marg* 8, no. 1 (1954): 26–34. For Souza's reception in London, see Pierre Descargues, "F. N. Souza," *Les Lettres Françaises*, July 15, 1954: 10; Author not known, "Portraits by Sculptors and Painters," *The Times*, November 22, 1957: 8; and G. M. Butcher, "The Image and Souza," *The Studio International* 162, no. 823 (1961): 176–9.

6 At the time of its inception, the members of the Progressive Artists Group included F. N. Souza, Maqbool Fida Husain, Krishnaji Howalji Ara, Syed Haider Raza, and Hari Ambadas Gade and the sculptor Sadanand K. Bakre. For a history of the Progressive Artists Group, see Yashodhara Dalmia, *The Making of Modern Indian Art: The Progressives* (New Delhi: Oxford University Press, 2001).

7 This is discussed in Edwin Mullins, *F. N. Souza* (London: Anthony Blond Ltd., 1962), 15–16.

8 See Francis N. Souza, "Nirvana of A Maggot," *Encounter* 4, no. 2 (1955): 42–8.

9 John Berger, "An Indian Painter," *New Statesman*, February 25, 1955, 277.

10 According to a letter from Norman Read dated November 18, 1964, the Trustees of the Tate Gallery had considered Souza's works on at least two prior occasions but were not sufficiently convinced to make a purchase. The accession in 1965 was made possible by a gift from Victor Musgrave of Gallery One. For the correspondence between Norman Read and Archer regarding the accession of Souza's painting by Tate, see Archer Papers, Mss. Eur F236/164. The correspondence spans November 1964 to January 1965.

11 Nigel Gosling, "East to West," *The Observer*, April 5, 1964, 24.

12 The autobiographical texts were collated and published in Francis N. Souza, *F. N. Souza—Words and Lines* (London: Villiers, 1959).

13 For example, see Mullins, *F. N. Souza*, 46–50 and Dalmia, *The Making of Modern Indian Art*, 90–1.

14 For the Black Art movement, see Eddie Chambers, *Black Artists in British Art: A History Since the 1950s* (London: I. B. Tauris, 2014). For studies that places Souza alongside his British contemporaries, see Gregory Salter, "Looking at Identity: Bacon, Souza, Freud," in *All Too Human: Bacon, Freud, and a Century of Painting*, ed. Elena Crippa (London: Tate Publishing, 2018), 42–53; Leon Wainwright, "Francis Newton Souza and Aubrey Williams: Entwined Histories at the End of Empire," in *Visual Culture and Decolonization in Britain*, ed. Simon Faulkner and Anandi Ramamurthy (Hampshire: Ashgate, 2006), 101–26; and Catherine Jolivette, *Landscape, Art and Identity in 1950s Britain* (Surrey: Ashgate, 2009), 82–7.

15 A third alternative to the bipolar politics of the Cold War, the Non-Aligned Movement generated a vast transcontinental network that cut across Asia and Africa and eventually extended to East Europe and Latin America. First conceptualized in

1955 at a meeting of African and Asian countries held in Bandung and formalized in Belgrade in 1961 under the leadership of Tito of Yugoslavia, Nasser of Egypt, Nehru of India, Nkrumah of Ghana, and Sukarno of Indonesia, the Non-Aligned Movement included over thirty newly independent nations who did not subscribe to the Cold War's seemingly hegemonic capitalist West/communist East binary. See Vijay Prasad, *The Darker Nations: A People's History of the Third World* (New York and London: The New Press, 2007).

16 Alioune Diop, "Discours d'ouverture," *Présence Africaine* 8/10 (1956): 9–19. Also see Aimé Césaire's speech delivered to the Action Committee of Intellectuals Opposed to the Conduct of War in North Africa in Paris in 1956, as quoted in Gregson Davis, *Aimé Césaire* (Cambridge: Cambridge University Press, 1997), 100.

17 Asked whether his consciousness of the Third World affected his writing, Samuel Selvon responds: "Yes, I think that is true. That happened to me when I went to England; perhaps it would not have happened to me if I had remained in the Caribbean." Peter Nazareth, "Interview with Sam Selvon," *World Literature Written in English* 18, no. 2 (1979): 420–37, 431.

18 For the effects of the Bandung conference on the American civil rights movement, see Brenda Gayle Plummer, *Rising Wind: Black Americans and US Foreign Policy, 1935–1960* (Chapel Hill: University of North Caroline Press, 1996).

19 Writing about the figure of the black maid in Manet's Olympia, T. J. Clark states that "the fiction of 'blackness'" lingered "as the sign of a servitude." T. J. Clark, *The Painting of Modern Life: Paris in the Art of Manet and His Followers*, rev. ed. (Princeton: Princeton University Press, 1999), xxvii. More recently, Darcy G. Grigsby has proposed that we see Manet's representation of Olympia's maid as "a newly enfranchised member of the working class." Darcy G. Grigsby, "Still Thinking about Olympia's Maid," *The Art Bulletin* 97, no. 4 (2015): 430–51, 432. For the broader context of such representations in nineteenth-century Western art, see Griselda Pollock, *Differencing the Canon: Feminist Desire and the Writing of Art's Histories* (London: Routledge, 1999), 246–315, and Denise Murrell, *Posing Modernity: The Black Model from Manet and Matisse to Today* (New York: Columbia University Press, 2019).

20 The early modern history of Catholicism in the Estado da Índia is extensively discussed in Ines G. Županov, *Missionary Tropics: The Catholic Frontier in India* (Ann Arbor: University of Michigan Press, 2005). For twentieth-century transnational anticolonial connections, see Margret Frenz, "Transimperial Connections: East African Goan Perspectives on 'Goa 1961,'" *Contemporary South Asia* 22, no. 3 (2014): 240–54.

21 Souza, "Nirvana of A Maggot," 24.

22 F. N. Souza Files, Archives of the Birmingham Museums and Art Gallery.

23 See Sean Creighton, "Paul Robeson's British Journey," in *Cross the Water Blues: African American Music in Europe*, ed. Neil A. Wynn (Jackson: University Press of Mississippi, 2007), 125–44.

24 Souza, "My Friend and I," in *F. N. Souza*, 22–7, 26. For Souza's interactions with the London bohemian circle, see Darren Coffield, *Tales from the Colony Room: Soho's Lost Bohemia* (London: Unbound, 2020).

25 Samuel Selvon, *The Lonely Londoners* (Essex: Pearson, 1956).

26 For a detailed historical survey of the color black in Western art and art history, see Michel Pastoureau, *Black: The History of a Color* (Princeton: Princeton University Press, 2008). Also see John Gage, "Color in Western Art—An Issue?" *The Art Bulletin* 72, no. 4 (1990): 518–41.

27 See Henry Guerlac, "Can There Be Colors in the Dark? Physical Color Theory before Newton," *Journal of the History of Ideas* 47, no. 1 (1986): 3–20.

28 Pastoureau, *Black*, 144–8.

29 See Frederick Burwick, *The Damnation of Newton: Goethe's Color Theory and Romantic Perception* (Berlin: Walter de Gruyter, 2012).

30 See Philip Ball, *Bright Earth: Art and the Invention of Color* (New York: Farrar, Straus and Giroux, 2001), 168–96.

31 Souza, quoted in Author not known, "Paint it Black," *The Observer*, Sunday, May 15, 1966, 23.

32 For a critique, see James Clifford, *The Predicament of Culture: Twentieth-Century Ethnography, Literature, and Art* (Cambridge, MA: Harvard University Press, 1988), 129–214. The epistemological implications of such assignations are addressed by Césaire when he writes: "From the psychologists, sociologists et al., their views on 'primitivism,' their rigged investigations, their self-serving generalizations, their tendentious speculations, their insistence on the marginal, 'separate' character of the non-whites, and—although each of these gentlemen, in order to impugn on higher authority the weakness of primitive thought, claims that his own is based on the firmest rationalism [. . .]. Aimé Césaire, *Discourse on Colonialism* [1950], trans. Joan Pinkham (New York: Monthly Review Press, 1972), 56.

33 For example, see Hal Foster, *Prosthetic Gods* (Cambridge, MA: The MIT Press, 2004), 3–8.

34 Maria J. Guzman, "'Pull up the Bumper': Fashion and Queerness in Grace Jones's *One Man Show*," in *Imagining the Black Female Body: Reconciling Image in Print and Visual Culture*, ed. Carol E. Henderson (New York: Palgrave Macmillan, 2010), 79–94, 88.

35 See Karen Kurczynski and Nicola Pezolet, "Primitivism, Humanism, and Ambivalence: Cobra and Post-Cobra," *RES: Anthropology and Aesthetics* 59, no. 1 (2011): 282–302.

36 These ideas implicitly inflected Souza's reception in Europe. Consider, for instance, the following words penned by the art critic Anita Brookner, "F. N. Souza, the Indian Painter who Mingles Reminiscences of Bacon, Buffet and Clav4, with Colour that Apparently Goes Back to the Fauve Dufy (Gallery One, North Audley Street). He is against the Bomb (he will have to do better than this), and appropriately his style has a liveliness that teeters over into violence, like *a child throwing a tantrum at his own party.*" Anita Brookner, "Current and Forthcoming Exhibitions," *The Burlington Magazine* 103, no. 705 (1961): 522–5, 525, emphasis mine.

37 Transcript of unpublished interview between Souza and Archer on March 28, 1962 at the Victoria and Albert Museum. Archer Papers, Mss. Eur F236/164. Souza's ongoing interactions with Sartre is referenced in a letter to his first wife Maria Souza dated May 14, 1984, where he writes: "I have always appreciated the way you have rooted for my art [. . .] when I and you moved to London, Husain and the other Indian artists, some of them living in Europe, like Raza and Padamsee, would drop in, and you would go to Paris to visit them (and on Bastille Day, Sartre would dance with you)!" Cited in Maria Aurora Couto, "Memories," in *Francis Newton and Maria Souza: A Life Partnership in Art* (New York: Christie's, 2014), 19–20, 19.

38 Jean-Paul Sartre, "Black Orpheus" [1948], trans. S. W. Allen, *Présence Africaine* 10/11 (1951): 219–47.

39 Ibid., 230.

40 This is discussed in Alexander Henn, *Hindu-Catholic Encounters in Goa: Religion, Colonialism, and Modernity* (Bloomington: Indiana University Press, 2014), 126–58.

41 For a detailed discussion, see Henn, *Hindu-Catholic Encounters in Goa*, 83–125.

42 Victor I. Stoichita, *Darker Shades: The Racial Other in Early Modern Art*, Samuel Trainor trans. (London: Reaktion Books, 2019), 54–5.

43 Ibid., 54–5.

44 Souza, "A Fragment of Autobiography," in *F. N. Souza—Words and Lines*, 7–11, 8.

45 Nevile Wallis, "Rooms with a View," *The Observer*, November 8, 1959, 24.

46 Chika Okeke-Agulu, *Postcolonial Modernism: Art and Decolonization in Twentieth-Century Nigeria* (Durham: Duke University Press, 2015), 132.

47 Cited in Nancy Jachec, *Europe's Intellectuals and the Cold War: The European Society of Culture* (London: I. B. Tauris, 2015), 92.

48 Okeke-Agulu, *Postcolonial Modernism*, 133.

49 Omidiji Aragbabalu, "Souza," *Black Phoenix* 7 (1960): 16–21, 21.

50 Kapur, "Francis Newton Souza," 57.

51 David Sylvester, "A Goan Painter," *New Statesman*, December 14, 1957, 6–7, 7.

52 Barrie Sturt-Penrose, "Profile: F. N. Souza," Name of paper and date not known. Archer Papers, Mss. Eur F236/164.

53 Letter from Souza to Musgrave, Barcelona, June 11, 1958. Gallery One Correspondence File, TGA 8714/3/24.

54 Gallery One, *F. N. Souza* (London: Gallery One, 1959). Tate Archives, TGA 8714/5/5.

55 Statement by Barbara Zinkant dated June 2013 in Grosvenor Gallery, *F. N. Souza Black on Black*, 34.

56 Frantz Fanon, *Black Skin, White Masks*, trans. Charles Lam Markmann (London: Pluto Press, 1986), 112.

57 Homi Bhabha, "Foreword: Remembering Fanon," in Fanon, *Black Skin, White Masks*, vii–xxv, xii.

58 Fanon, *Black Skin, White Masks*, 112.

59 Rasheed Araeen, *The Other Story: Afro-Asian Artists in Post-war Britain* (London: Hayward Gallery, 1989), 23.

60 Fred Moten, "The Case of Blackness," *Criticism* 50, no. 2 (2008): 177–218, 187.

61 See Ad Reinhardt, "Black as Symbol and Concept," in *Art as Art: The Selected Writings of Ad Reinhardt*, ed. Barbara Rose (Berkeley: University of California Press, 1975), 86–8.

62 Souza, quoted in Author not known, "Paint It Black," 23.

63 Statement by Zinkant dated June 2013 in Grosvenor Gallery, *F. N. Souza Black on Black*, 34.

64 Rebecca Solnit, "Yves Klein and the Blue of Distance," *New England Review* 26, no. 2 (2005): 176–82, 178.

65 As Rothko stated: "I'm interested only in expressing basic human emotions—tragedy, ecstasy, doom and so on—and the fact that lots of people break down and cry when confronted with my pictures show that I communicate those basic human emotions. . . .The people who weep before my pictures are having the same religious experience I had when I painted them. And if you . . . are moved only by their color relationships, then you miss the point!" Mark Rothko quoted in "Notes from a Conversation with Selden Rodman, 1956," in *Writings on Art: Mark Rothko*, ed. Miguel López-Remiro (New Haven: Yale University Press, 2006), 119–20.

66 If Reinhardt conceived of the blackness of the black paintings as infinity itself, then his
    black paintings were, in Rosalind Krauss's words, "the vehicle for the staging of this
    'it' that one could not keep track of, except to acknowledge the infinitely slow pulse
    of perceptual change, to take account of the fact that perception is the registration of
    pure difference." Rosalind Krauss, "Overcoming the Limits of Matter: On Revisiting
    Minimalism," in *American Art of the 1960s*, ed. John Elderfield (New York: Harry
    Abrams and Museum of Modern Art, New York, 1991), 123–41, 123.

9

Listening to the Cold War in Bombay

Naresh Fernandes

In 1951, Indian moviegoers were swaying in their seats to a sound that they'd never quite heard before. The hit film that had captivated them was *Albela*, the tale of a poor man who dreams of making it big on the stage. A large part of the film's appeal was contributed by the lively soundtrack. Among the most popular tunes was one called *Deewana Parwana*, which featured swinging clarinets, jazzy drums, and a catchy trumpet solo.[1]

The screen versions of most Hindi film songs feature extras miming at playing their instruments. But unusually, *Deewana Parwana* featured members of the band that had actually recorded the tune. It was headed by the famous Bombay leader known as Chic Chocolate. *Albela* became so popular that Chic's band, the Music Makers, began to wear those costumes for their performances at clubs and hotel ballrooms too.[2]

In the 1940s and 1950s, Chic—whose real name was Antonio Xavier Vaz—seemed to be everywhere: at the Taj Mahal Hotel in downtown Bombay, at hotels like Hackman's in the Himalayan resort town of Mussoorie during the summer season. Known as "India's Louis Armstrong," he played the trumpet and tried hard to develop a gravelly singing style like that of his African American hero from New Orleans.[3]

The appearance of Chic Chocolate and the Music Makers in *Albela* was unusual, but the use of big band jazz rhythms and instruments was quite common in Hindi films by the late 1950s.

In the Hindi movies of the 1950s, as I have noted previously,

swing came to signify a bold modernity and often provided the backdrop for a plot in which young people fall in love without regard for the conventional arranged marriages their parents wanted to set up for them. But sometimes, these sounds were used disapprovingly, to remind audiences of the perils of forgetting India's ancient culture in the face of creeping Westernisation. To illustrate this, films often grafted on a 'cabaret scene' set in a nightclub, in which a "vamp"—a scantily clad woman (dressed only in balloons or in ostrich feathers or in a sequinned gown with a daring slit)—would shimmy to a sax-studded band playing in the background, as the hero pondered evidence of moral laxity: unmarried men and women dancing together, smoking cigarettes and drinking.

The vamp's jazzy song often bristled with aphoristic allusions to the dangers of forgetting Indian values.[4]

These songs were the soundtrack of Indian life. In the absence of a commercial music industry, it was tunes from the movies that put a bounce in India's step, offered advice to the lovelorn, provided solace in moments of grief, and lulled it to sleep on rainy nights. The audience wasn't stuck for songs to match its moods. India produced an average of 430 films a year in the 1950s, each with at least eight tunes. Between 1931 and 1954, the country produced only two Hindi films that didn't have any songs. As predicted, they were commercial failures.[5]

So how did swing and big band instrumentation come to find its way to Bollywood? For that we have to travel back to 1935. On stage in the ballroom of the Taj Mahal Hotel in Bombay is Leon Abbey, a violinist from Minnesota and his band.[6] Leon Abbey caused a sensation when he came to Bombay because he led the first African American ever to play in India. As jazz became popular around the world, it was only natural that it found its way to Bombay pretty soon. As a port city and the largest city in the British Empire, Bombay had sought out the latest trends from around the world since the 1860s, when the city made its fortunes trading cotton. Jazz had been heard in the city since at least the late 1910s: gramophone records with New Orleans ragtime were the rage among the city's upper crust. Pretty soon, local bands began to play this new syncopated music from America.[7]

When Abbey and his band arrived in town, Bombay was going through a construction boom—with a great many buildings coming up around town in the new streamlined Jazz Age style of art deco. To the Grecian and Egyptian motifs that characterized the style in other parts of the world, Bombay added its references from Indian mythology.[8]

Though Bombay's upper classes welcomed the chance to foxtrot to the music that had caught the fancy of their counterparts in many other parts of the planet, they complained that the change was too rapid.

"His style was so new when Leon first played for us that many of the die-hards insisted on simpler tunes and popular numbers," *The Times of India* reported. Abbey's boys were forced to make some adjustments. "Their quicksteps have slowed from Paris speed—the fastest in all the dancing world—to Bombay speed," *The Times of India* reported. "They have toned down their 'hotting' to meet the less sophisticated taste of Bombay." But *The Times* seemed to approve of Abbey. The band "is teaching us in Bombay what rhythm means," it wrote. Abbey seemed amused by the controversy. One old-timer recalled him chuckling, "First they swore at my music, then they swore by my music."[9]

Abbey's visit opened the floodgates. Over the next few years, other American jazz musicians followed him, notably a trumpet player named Cricket Smith and piano player Teddy Weatherford. Both of them ended up staying in India for several years. These musicians didn't only perform songs they knew from America. They started to write music when they were in India.[10]

These African American journeymen played a vital role creating a jazz culture in India. Though Indian musicians had been playing swing music since the mid-1920s,

Figure 9.1 American pianist Teddy Weatherford and his band in 1938, featuring both American and Indian musicians.

they had learnt to play the music by reading the music scores and by listening to records. Having these African American musicians in town completely energized the scene. Both Cricket Smith and Teddy Weatherford recruited Indian musicians to play in their bands and taught them how to jazz the American way (Figure 9.1).[11]

For many musicians in colonial-era India like Chic Chocolate, this was wasn't just another style of music: jazz was a quest for freedom, both artistic and political. Its emphasis on improvisation allowed them to escape the structural rigidities of the Western classical music they had grown up playing. And in that musical freedom were resonances of political freedom too as anticolonial campaigns British India and Portuguese India grew stronger (Figure 9.2).

By the 1940s, Bombay had a vibrant jazz scene. In 1949, two years after India's independence from the British, a concert program carried a list of bands available for hire in Bombay: there were more than sixty, starting with the Alexandra Band and ending with the Zoroastrian Symphonians.[12]

Among their members were musicians who were trying to take jazz out of the confines of the ballroom and to less-affluent audiences than those to be found in luxury hotels.

At the forefront of this effort was the Bombay Swing Club, formed in 1948. One of its early brochures claimed: "Swing music attracts people of all classes, races and creeds—typist, millowner, surgeon, mechanic, intellectual and low-brow, all keenly enjoy the exhilarating effervescent quality in swing music."

Figure 9.2 Trumpet player Chic Chocolate—the Louis Armstrong of India—and his band in Bombay, *c.* 1948. © Chic Chocolate Family.

But it wasn't all fun and games in Bombay at the end of the 1940s, especially for jazz musicians. Prohibition had gradually been introduced in Bombay, a reflection of the Gandhian austerity so valued by the Indian state. Going dry reduced revenues for hotels and made them less enthusiastic about hiring bands. In addition, there was a growing suspicion of cultural forms that were considered colonial hangovers—and jazz was certainly among them.[13]

That's when the movies came to the rescue. Quite by coincidence, technological developments in that period allowed sound in the films to become more sophisticated. Until 1931, Indian films had been silent. In the early years of the talkies, the music was recorded by only a small group of musicians. But to effectively convey the drama unfolding on the screen, film soundtracks actually need large orchestras, all playing together to emphasize the urgency of a car chase, to highlight the suspense of an impending murder, or to serenade a sweetly developing romance.

This was a challenge. Indian music is melodic—the main performer plays a single melodic line and everyone in the ensemble else reiterates that line. On screen, this sounds very thin. But Western music is harmonic—the musicians in a band or orchestra play notes of related pitches, which makes the sound much fuller.

Most of the composers of Hindi film scores, who are known in India as music directors, were trained in Hindustani music. They had an admirable talent for creating memorable melodies. But to be translated into effective screen music, these melodies had to be harmonized to be played by a large orchestra.[14]

Here's where the Indian jazz musicians came in. A large number of them were from the Portuguese colony of Goa, south of Bombay. They had received their musical training in the Western classical tradition, in schools that had been set up by the Portuguese—who continued to rule Goa all the way until 1961. These Goan jazz musicians were among the few communities in India who knew about harmony. So the composers of film music began to hire these musicians as assistants to help them with their scores.[15]

The producer would organize a "sitting" at which the composer (most often a Hindu), the lyricist (often an Urdu-speaking Muslim), and the assistant would flop down on comfortable cushions to listen to the director narrate the plot. When the director indicated the point at which a song was necessary, the composer would hum out a melody or pick it out on his harmonium. It was the assistant's task to note down these fragments, which the composer would later piece together into an entire song, adding parts for the banks of violins and cellos, the horn sections, the piano, and the percussion.[16] In the West, the assistant would have been called an arranger: he arranged the parts for the various instruments.

But the assistant wasn't merely taking dictation: it was his job to craft the introductions and bridges between verse and chorus. Drawing from their bicultural heritage and their experience in the jazz bands, the Goan arrangers gave Bollywood music its promiscuous charm, slipping in slivers of Dixieland stomp, Portuguese fados, Ellingtonesque doodles, cha cha cha, Mozart, and Bach themes.

In addition, the majority the musicians in the film studio orchestras were members of swing bands. That's because they could read (and write) musical notation, a feature that was absent in Indian music, which uses an oral, memory-based system of instruction. While the musicians playing the Indian sitars and sarods had to keep rehearsing their parts until they'd memorized them, the jazz musicians simplified the recording process by simply reading the music off the scores. Soon, the orchestras in the film studios weren't looking very different from the bands playing at the Taj.[17]

Ironically, even as the instrumentation and the spirit that animated many Hindi film tunes drew their inspiration from American swing, the lyrics of the songs and the plot lines of the movies were suffused with the socialist idealism of Nehruvian India. Many of the lyricists were members of the Progressive Writers Association, dedicated to the idea of using their pens to eradicate social injustice and creating a more egalitarian society.

It all came together in a truly appealing way. To Victor Paranjoti, an Indian composer in the Western classical tradition, the Hindi film music of the period truly reflected the soul of the newly independent nation. "Maybe it is crude, maybe it is born out of wedlock . . . but it is vital and dynamic," he wrote. Though many serious musicians turned their noses up at the hybrid sounds emerging from the film studios, Paranjoti refused to join the chorus of snobs. He declared, "In Art and Culture, there is no birth control."[18]

As a consequence, a miscegenated music born in the ghettos of New Orleans that had found a niche in India's luxury hotels traveled back to the streets in a form that Louis Armstrong and his friends would never have imagined.

*   *   *

By the late 1950s, another layer was added to the Bombay jazz scene—against a rather more tumultuous backdrop of the Cold War.

In an attempt to win hearts and minds across the Third World, the US Congress in August 1956 approved an initiative called the President's Special International Programme. In essence, the United States decided to send artists around the world to demonstrate that American culture was vibrant and attractive—and far superior to anything that the Soviets could offer. The US program was intended to showcase a whole range of American art forms: classical music, Broadway musicals modern dance, such as Martha Graham's company.

But jazz quickly became the program's centerpiece. Jazz, after all, was the only home-grown art form the United States could boast of. Just as important, it was an African American art form. At a time when many people in the newly independent world were appalled by the segregation faced by Blacks in the US South, dispatching jazz musicians around the world gave Washington the chance to show that African Americans weren't being treated all quite so badly after all.[19]

Already, jazz was being broadcast to several parts of the world via the Voice of America's Music USA programme, which continued for more than thirty years. It was hosted by Willis Conover, whose knowledgeable baritone eventually drew in an estimated 100 million listeners. Conover was certain that jazz could ignite revolutions.

"Jazz is a cross between total discipline and total anarchy," he told *The New York Times*. "The musicians agree on tempo, key and chord structure but beyond this everyone is free to express himself. This is jazz. And this is America. . . . It's a musical reflection of the way things happen in America. We're not apt to recognise it over here, but people in other countries can feel this element of freedom. They love jazz because they love freedom."

Though his show was aimed at listeners behind the Iron Curtain, Indian fans also tuned in—though it was scarcely convenient to do so. Because of the time difference, "Music USA," which was relayed from Tangier, came on in India at 3.30 in the morning. Fans would wind up their alarm clocks, press their ear to the radiogram in the living room so as not to wake up the rest of the family, and go back to sleep an hour later.[20]

In larger Indian cities, the United States Information Service offices organized jazz listening sessions. Some of the reactions to this activity reflected the challenges US foreign policy was facing in India. Because of the suspicion that the American "foreign hand" was pulling a great many strings, some people believed that these jazz appreciation workshops were a sort of CIA puppet theater. These critics included the weekly Bombay tabloid *Blitz*, which ran a piece in the late 1950s accusing the USIS of breeding a traitorous Sixth Column.

"Exploiting the weakness of the average Indian for wine, women and a damned good show—any show, are the plethora of American social functions, the musical soirees, the gramophone record afternoons and a whole plethora of tricks," it thundered.

Blitz was very impressed by the efficiency of these tactics. It claimed that "no Indian attending these whoopees returns home without feeling that the Americans are their blood brothers and Washington is their spiritual home."[21]

When the Indian Congress for Cultural Freedom—the local affiliate of the Central Intelligence Agency-backed International Congress for Cultural Freedom anticommunism advocacy group—held its first session in Bombay in 1951, it acknowledged that music, art, literature, and painting were crucial weapons in the battle against the Left.

"The film industry deserves mention," a report on one session noted. "American influence is clearly visible in theme, film effects and jazzy music. Painting, music and literature (particularly the drama and the story) have close connections with it and it gives a welcome supplementary income to artists and writers, often their main source of economic independence."[22]

Not leaving anything to chance, though, American organizations—as Frances Stonor Saunders has extensively documented in *The Cultural Cold War*—acted decisively to fund literature. They granted writers visiting fellowships to initiatives such as the Iowa Writers Programme and supported Indian journals, such as the general interest *Imprint* and the rather more literary *Quest*.

Quest's output was of variable quality—when John Kenneth Galbraith saw a copy after becoming US ambassador in 1961, he commented that it "broke new ground in ponderous, unfocused illiteracy"[23]—but it provided a forum for new writers who would later blossom to produce work of great significance.

All this helped spawn a new literary culture, exemplified by poets like the bilingual writer Arun Kolatkar. In Anjali Nerlekar's rigorous study of the milieu, *Bombay Modern*, she notes that the poetry created by Kolatkar and his contemporaries embodies "a new way of knowing the urban space—not nativist, not internationalist, not global, not national."[24]

That could indeed have described the sound that some of Bombay's jazz musicians were aiming to create, though never quite achieved.

*   *   *

By the late 1950s, jazz had burst out of the ballrooms and city hotels. Several cafes and restaurants in the affluent South Bombay area featured trios and quartets that often started playing at tea time. But nurturing an interest for the music took some effort.

The challenges faced by fans in newly independent India are evident from the pages of *Blue Rhythm*, a short-lived jazz magazine published in Bombay in the early 1950s. Some articles described the agony of being unable to buy the latest records in a country that had restricted imports to conserve foreign currency. Others attempted to explain why jazz was a valid passion to follow in a country that was attempting to fashion a bold new national culture.

"Some people often ask why one should take an interest in jazz when Indian classical music is easily available," wrote Niranjan Jhaveri, one of the editors of *Blue Rhythm*. "They point out that jazz is a foreign music and anything foreign should not be encouraged where there is an Indian substitute." To this, the writer had a simple reply: "Personally, my main defence is that I just happen to like jazz a great deal. It has now a great hold over me and I like it that way."

The writer went on to invoke the ethic of internationalism that was so much an ideal in the New India. Jazz, he claimed, was the most global of all music. "From a confused birth in the slums of New Orleans, its vitality and power have today swept it around the world. Anything that is so pure and diverse must be shared by all the peoples of the world."[25]

That vision of internationalism is what the State Department played to in its Jazz Ambassadors programme. And the first musical envoy to visit India, Dave Bruckbeck who visited with his quartet in 1958, performed his role admirably. In addition to playing concerts in cities big and small, he spent time jamming with local performers, both jazz musicians and those who played in the Indian classical tradition. He even got one promising Bombay pianist a scholarship to study at the Berklee School of Music—a gesture that has since become part of city lore.

The next year, the impeccably coiffed Dixieland trombone player Jack Teagarden was sent to the subcontinent with his septet. Though Teagarden's style was a little dated, his Indian jazz fans were "passionately devoted," recalled the group's trumpet player, Max Kaminsky.[26]

In Madras, John Wiggin, the public affairs officer of the USIS, reminded Jack Teagarden's men that they were playing an important role in helping defeat communism in India. "Jazz," he told them, "was a great tool in helping save the country from the Reds."

But the trumpet player Kaminsky was skeptical. He believed that the differences between India and the United States were much more fundamental, as was obvious from their divergent approaches to music. Indian music "which is unwritten and is played by ear and from memory, does not have any harmonic system to speak of," the trumpet player said. "In the West, we built a whole musical civilisation on the basis of the harmonic system—and a political one on the same principles of order, structure and compromise." John Wiggin and the United States, Kaminsky concluded, "has a tough job, trying to get the Asians on a more harmonious kick."

Despite this warning, the United States was quite unwilling to give up the battle for Indian hearts, minds, and ears. More tours followed. In 1960, the cornet player "Red" Nicols did his tour of duty. Three years later, the Americans seem to have decided that the future of the free world would be imperilled unless they presented a really large surprise. They deployed one of the most charming musicians in their arsenal, the dashing Edward Kennedy Ellington—known universally as the Duke.

Ellington was not only the composer of some of the best-known tunes in the jazz songbook, he also had the ability to leave a long trail of friends wherever he went. Many of Ellington's sidemen were stars in their own right, so it was no surprise that they were mobbed by autograph seekers when they arrived in Bombay in October 1963.

Almost immediately, the 64-year-old Duke realized how tricky the business of cultural exchange could be. Installed in a split-level honeymoon suite at the Taj Mahal, Ellington rang for room service and asked the waiter what food was available. "I begin by reciting my favourites and get all the way down to chicken but he responds to every item by shaking his head side to side," Ellington wrote in his memoirs. "Although I am right here on the sea, he shakes his head again when I mention fish. Not knowing any better, I wind up eating lamb curry for four days, after which I discover that shaking the head from side to side means 'Yes.'"[27]

Like Brubeck before him, Ellington and his sidemen jammed with local musicians. After they returned to the United States, both turned the sonic impressions of their tours into albums.

In 1958, the Dave Brubeck Quartet's recorded a musical travelogue titled *Jazz Impressions of Eurasia* (Figures 9.3 and 9.4). The six tunes weren't intended to be fusion music. Rather, as the pianist explained in his liner notes, he "tried to create an impression of a particular location by using some of the elements of their folk music within the jazz idiom." The album included a piece called *Calcutta Blues*, which Brubeck described as an "oriental rag."

In 1966, Ellington distilled the sounds he'd heard on his trip into a work titled *The Far East Suite*. Like Brubeck's work, Ellington's suite wasn't trying to create a fusion. "I don't want to copy this rhythm or that scale," he wrote later. "It's more valuable to have absorbed things while there. You let it roll around, undergo a chemical change, and then seep out on paper in the form that will suit the musicians who are going to play it." The suite contains a tune called *Agra*, the city in which the Taj Mahal is situated and another called *Bluebird of Delhi*, which features Jimmy Hamilton's clarinet mimicking the mynah bird that inspired the tune.

Figure 9.3 Dave Brubeck jams with Abdul Halim Jaffer Khan in Bombay. © Jehangir Dalal.

Figure 9.4 Indian pianist Lucila Pacheco with Duke Ellington.

For Bombay's jazz musicians, these albums were an affirmation of a project some of them had embarked upon two decades earlier. Since the late 1940s, they had been composing tunes that gave jazz an Indian flavor, playing at Bombay Swing Club events and other forums. To hear American greats adopt the same strategy was a satisfying gesture of validation.

In the end, though, these experiments stayed confined to the concert hall, the scope of their ambition recognized by a sliver of elite listeners, some of whom now pay hundreds of dollars to buy the handful of records cut during that period.

The swing-inflected Hindi film tunes, though, set hearts racing around the subcontinent—and across the world. YouTube is filled with recordings of people from Nigeria and Russia, Kazakhstan and China singing and dancing to 1950s Hindi film music. In Bombay's mid-century film music, they hear an echo of their triumphs and disappointments, their hopes and failures and the possibilities of freedom, both trivial and momentous.

*   *   *

On the evening of Sunday, February 12, 1978, a group of enthusiastic fans filed into the Rang Bhavan amphitheatre in Bombay's Dhobi Talao neighbourhood for the inauguration of a music event of the sort the city had never witnessed before. The tiny classified ads that had appeared in *The Times of India* in the previous fortnight had promised "seven days of mind-blowing music" by the "greatest musicians in the world."

Gita Mehta, the writer from New York, was at Rang Bhavan looking for material for a book that she would later title *Karma Cola*, and she seemed rather amused by everything she witnessed. The auditorium was ringed on three sides by the gray-stone neo-Gothic buildings of education institutions such as St. Xaviers College, which had been constructed at a time, she would later write, when dreaming spires and higher learning were more or less synonymous in the British mind. India, on the other hand, was represented in the flora and fauna. "Large banyan trees broke through the cultural pretensions, leaves obscured by tattered kites, roots overrun by Bombay rats scurrying in and out of the event," she wrote.[28]

But despite the rodents and the odorous toilets, the ambition of the event was unmistakable. It was called the Jazz Yatra, the journey of jazz, and an unmistakable indication of the path it intended to take was to be found on the cover of the smudgy programme. A tagline described the Yatra as a "festival of Indo-Afro-American music."

Over the next three decades, the festival would, at two-year intervals, bring some of the biggest names in the jazz world to India.

The legends would include Max Roach, who had in the 1950s revolutionized the way the drum kit was played, transforming the drummer from being a mere time keeper into an instrumentalist as vital and creative as any other in the ensemble. There would be the saxophonist Staz Getz, whose wispy tone was instantly recognizable, especially when he played his most famous hit, *The Girl from Ipenama*, which was the result of an innovative collaboration with Brazil's best musicians in the 1960s. Violinist Stephane Grapelli would put a smile on everyone's face with his warm infectious tone, recalling the time he and the gypsy guitar player Django Reinhart had given jazz a deliciously French twist at the Hot Club of France in the 1930s.

But inviting American and European innovators to India was only one part of what the organizers intended to do. Also performing at the Jazz Yatra over the decades were cutting-edge musicians from Brazil and South Africa, Turkey, Sri Lanka, Yugoslavia and beyond—many from countries where jazz cultures had been enlivened by American Cold War jazz tours and by listening to Willis Connover's radio show.

The event was organized by the men who, as college students, had edited the jazz magazine *Blue Rhythm*. Now, as businessmen and as executives in leading firms, they were determined to showcase to the world their conception of jazz as a form that had profoundly been influenced by cultures from across the world—especially the Third World.

This endeavor was articulated explicitly in the program booklet of the 1980s edition of the Yatra. By the 1950s, wrote German jazz critic Joachim-Ernest Berendt, jazz musicians realized that there was "something colonialistic in their exclusive preoccupation with European music as though it were the only worthwhile music in the world" and began to seek out encounters with "Javanese, Balinese, Indian, Japanese, Arabian, Bedouin and other musical cultures and musicians from all over the world."

This was animated by a new political awareness, he noted, that encouraged interactions with "Third World music." He explained: "The discovery of world music and for that matter world culture by jazz musicians is one of the most important cultural aspects of Third World solidarity."

Where once such encounters had occurred almost exclusively in the metropolitan centers of the United States and Europe, Bombay and Delhi now became the venue for a variety of new collaborations. The Jazz Yatras helped shift the ground—literally—on which musicians were exchanging ideas, advancing, in some small measure, the contention that the Third World could help catalyze new conversations in jazz.

Notes

This article draws substantially from my previously published work, especially Taj Mahal Foxtrot, (New Delhi: Roli, 2012).

1 *Deewana Parwana* from the film *Albela* (1951), accessed on YouTube, https://www.youtube.com/watch?v=d7MUFKnYhq0.
2 From author interview with Ursula Fernandes, Chic Chocolate's daughter, and family photo album.
3 Author interview with Yvonne Gonsalves, Chic Chocolate's daughter.
4 Naresh Fernandes, *Taj Mahal Foxtrot* (New Delhi: Roli, 2012).
5 B. D. Garga, *So Many Cinemas: The Motion Picture in India* (Mumbai: Eminence, 1996).
6 Ralph Gulliver, "Leon Abbey," *Storyville* 73 (1977): 6–28.
7 H. J. Collet, "Thirty Years of Jazz in India: Our Top Bands Can Swing It with the Best," *The Illustrated Weekly of India*, August 22, 1948.
8 Navin Ramani, *Bombay Art Deco Architecture: A Visual Journey 1930-1953* (New Delhi: Roli, 2006).
9 Author interview with drummer Percy Dias.
10 Peter Darke and Gulliver Ralph, "Teddy Weatherford," *Storyville* 65 (1976): 175–90; "Roy Butler's Story," *Storyville* 71 (1977): 178–90.
11 Author interview with musicians Frank Fernand and Mickey Correa.
12 Bombay Swing Club brouchure, 1949.
13 Federation of Musicians (India) newsletter, various numbers, 1947–1949.
14 Gregory D. Booth, *Behind the Curtain: Making Music in Mumbai's Film Studios* (New York: Oxford University Press, 2008).
15 Mario Cabral e Sa, *Wind of Fire: The Music and Musicians of Goa* (New Delhi: Promilla and Co, 1997).
16 Author interview with musician Frank Fernand.
17 Author interview with musician Frank Fernand.
18 Victor Paranjoti, *On This and That* (Mumbai: Thacker and Co, 1958).
19 Penny M. Von Eschen, *Satchmo Blows Up the World: Jazz Ambassadors Play the Cold War* (Cambridge, MA: Harvard University Press), 2004.
20 Author interview with fan Jahangir Dalal.
21 E. J. Kahn Jr, "The Cominform at Work," *The New Yorker*, January 12, 1952.
22 *Indian Congress for Cultural Freedom*, Indian Congress for Cultural Freedom, March 28–31, 1951, The Kannada Press, 1951.

23 Joel Whitney, "How the CIA Sponsored Indian Magazines That Engaged the Country's Best Writers, *The Wire*, March 15, 2017, https://thewire.in/history/cia-sponsored -indian-magazines-engaged-indias-best-writers.

24 Anjali Nerlekar, *Bombay Modern: Arun Kolatkar and Bilingual Literary Culture* (New Delhi: Speaking Tiger, 2017).

25 *Blue Rhythm*, edited by Niranjan Jhaveri, August 1952–September and October 1953.

26 Max Kaminsky, *My Life in Jazz,* (New York, Evanston and London: Harper & Row, 1963).

27 Edward Kennedy Ellington, *Music Is My Mistress* (New York: Da Capo Press, 1976).

28 Gita Mehta, *Karma Cola* (New York: Simon and Schuster, 1979).

10

Imagining a Progressive World

Soviet Visual Culture in Postcolonial India

Jessica Bachman

In a letter from 1971, a young man from a village outside of Darjeeling—an Indian town located in the foothills of the Himalayas—wrote to the Soviet Union's largest foreign language publishing house, Progress Publishers, to praise the press' translation and publication work. He wrote: "In India your publications are huge in number, cheap in rates, and helpful to acquire a vast amount of knowledge on Marxism and Leninism."[1] But the letter writer, one Kamal Kumar Thapa, desired to consume more than just books from the USSR. He also wanted to obtain loose-leaf prints of the images he had seen in Soviet publications. "Please send the pictures of great leaders like Marx, Engels, Lenin, and Stalin to your Indian book agents, so that we can buy from them," he told the press, before concluding with this wish: "That your publications may spread all over the world and be admired by all the working people."

Thapa was far from the only Indian reader who desired to obtain loose-leaf copies of the images he had originally seen in Soviet books. Nor was he alone in his decision to write to the USSR in search of such images. Between the mid-1950s and 1970s, both Progress and the Soviet book export agency *Mezhdunarodnaya Kniga* (MezhKniga) received hundreds of requests for prints of the historical, political, and literary figures that inhabited the dust jacket covers and glossy page inserts of the Soviet books they had read.[2] While such prints were never made commercially available to foreign consumers, it was not uncommon for Progress and MezhKniga to cooperate and send readers the images they desired on an ad hoc basis.

This chapter traces the widespread circulation and consumption of Soviet texts-on-paper in India during the mid-twentieth century. It argues that richly illustrated Soviet books and magazines as well as the loose-leaf prints acquired through transnational correspondence with Soviet institutions functioned as significant enablers of progressive thinking, imagining, and self-becoming in postcolonial India. I use the term "progressive" here to denote a broad range of political and social commitments. These included (but were not limited to) commitments to social justice and the reorganization of Indian society along more egalitarian lines, socialist internationalism, anticolonial liberation movements, and technological and scientific development. Although the

Soviet print culture at the center of my analysis was certainly intended to produce an ideological effect, its ultimate reception was not predetermined. Indeed, I show how Indian consumers adopted, transformed, and repurposed Soviet visual materials to constitute themselves as modern leftist, internationalist, and cosmopolitan subjects in ways that could not have been anticipated or, on occasions, even desired by Soviet authorities.

Building on a body of scholarship committed to the construction of a "bottom-up visual history" of Indian modernity, this chapter situates the circulation and consumption of Soviet images in a framework that foregrounds the transformative potential of images to remake social, political, and ethical realities.[3] Studies of late colonial and postcolonial South Asian visual culture have brilliantly illustrated how anthropomorphized maps of Mother India, mass-produced "calendar art" images of Hindu deities and saints, posters of Bollywood icons, and prints of India's most famous freedom fighters have both produced and themselves been shaped by nationalist imaginings, different strains of religious and caste identities, and idealized performances of gender roles.[4] Other authors have begun to illuminate the complex relationship between the rise of left-wing political and cultural movements and changes in the field of visual artistic production in mid-twentieth century India, with Sanjukta Sunderason's recent work being an excellent example.[5] What this otherwise rich body of scholarship leaves unexplored, however, is the existence and flourishing of popular visual cultures that centered on materials and images originally produced and printed *outside* of India.[6]

It is well known that in the decades leading up to and following India's independence from Great Britain in 1947, domestically produced prints, photographs, and posters of political figures such as M. K. Gandhi, Bhagat Singh, Subhas Chandra Bose, and B. R. Ambedkar helped inspire new modes of thought, solidarity, and collective action in Indian society. But throughout the postcolonial period, the political imaginings of millions of Indian individuals were also fueled by foreign imagery that circulated on alternative circuits to mainstream "bazaar" networks. India's book market was one such circuit. In the 1960s and 1970s, decades marked by the ascendency of left opposition movements, trade union struggles, student activism, and anti-imperialist protest activity, a growing number of book outlets introduced eager reading publics to a wide range of foreign revolutionary texts, ideologies, and images. Many of these were imported from the USSR. By exploring the reception history of Soviet book imagery in India during this period, I take the study of India's postcolonial visual culture in a more transnational direction. Whereas other scholars have underscored the importance of India's working class, lower caste, and leftist movements to the changing iconography of Hindu deities and Bollywood heroes in the 1970s, this chapter traces the influence of imported Soviet images on the lives and identities of some of the individuals who aligned themselves with these movements and causes.[7]

The Soviet Union and its communist model of development have long loomed large in debates about India's postcolonial modernity. Jawaharlal Nehru, India's first prime minister, visited the USSR in 1927 on the cusp of the party-state's industrialization drive. Six years later, while serving time in jail for his leadership in the independence struggle, the nationalist leader praised the Soviet Union's economic system in a letter to his daughter, Indira Gandhi. Placing particular emphasis on the implications that centralized planning and state-led industrialization had for the Soviet state's achievement of self-sufficiency, he wrote: "The Soviet Government looked far ahead and decided to concentrate on these basics of heavy industries in the Five Year plan. In this way, the foundations of industrialism would be firmly laid, and it would be easy to have the light industries afterwards. The heavy industries would also make Russia less dependent on foreign countries for machinery or war material."[8]

After independence, Nehru, together with other state leaders, pursued a variety of strategies to overcome India's economic underdevelopment. On the one hand, they followed the Soviet blueprint with the establishment of a centralized state Planning Commission that funneled human and material resources toward large-scale industrialization projects and the creation of scientific research and development infrastructure.[9] The state embarked on the construction of steel plants, hydroelectric dams, nuclear energy facilities, electrical grids, and a network of elite engineering institutes. On the other hand, India used its centralized planning apparatus to pursue small-scale, bottom-up community development schemes.[10] Aside from serving as an inspiration and model for planned economic development, the USSR also provided India with direct material assistance; it dispatched technical advisors, industrial loans, military equipment, and grants-in-aid to the country from the mid-1950s through the end of the Cold War. This provision of development aid to the nonaligned country was central to the USSR's ideological competition with the United States for supremacy in the Third World, where it hoped to win newly formed nation-states over to socialist forms of economic and social development.[11]

But the project of showcasing Soviet modernity and securing India's goodwill was as much a cultural effort as it was an economic and diplomatic one. The deployment of development aid and the exchange of cultural artifacts and media technologies often went hand in hand and underwrote each other's success. The building of oil refineries, thermal power stations, and mines not only required the transfer of technology, financial resources, and technical experts to India but also the production of hundreds of technical books and engineering manuals in numerous Indian languages. In fact, at the same time as the USSR was engaged in the construction of the massive Bhilai Steel Plant in central India, it was simultaneously developing an eponymous Bhilai typeface, which was used to print books and magazines that celebrated these very forms of Indo-Soviet cooperation in Hindi's Devanagari script.

Cultural Diplomacy, Soviet Internationalism, and the Arrival of Soviet Books in India

The establishment of a popular Soviet visual culture and print sphere in India is linked to two parallel developments in the larger history of cultural interaction and exchange between the Soviet Union and India. The first of these developments concerns the USSR's establishment of mainstream cultural diplomacy ties with foreign, noncommunist governments in the immediate post-Stalin era. The second relates to the party-state's decision to provide material, logistical, and ideological support for a diverse range of anticolonial national liberation struggles and noncapitalist development programs. Following the death of Joseph Stalin in March 1953, the USSR abandoned its isolationist foreign policy and took a series of unprecedented steps to develop closer formal relations with not only countries of the capitalist West but also with a growing number of independent states in Asia and Africa. Between the mid-1950s and 1960s, it signed a flurry of bilateral cultural exchange agreements that called for the organization of artistic, literary, and academic exchanges with these states and the establishment of Soviet friendship societies. Nehru, whom Stalin had previously scorned and accused of being a lackey to British imperialism, reacted positively to Nikita Khrushchev's overtures for friendship and cultural cooperation. Following Nehru's heavily publicized visit to the USSR in June 1955 and a return visit later that same year by Khrushchev and Nikolai Bulganin, economic and cultural ties between the two states grew apace.[12] The USSR, in direct competition with the United States, began to provide India with the human, material, and financial resources it needed to industrialize its national economy. At the same time, the two countries began print and broadcast media exchanges. Many Bollywood hits and some Indian books and magazines traveled north to be screened and translated for Soviet audiences, while Soviet films, books, magazines, and radio broadcasts flowed south to the subcontinent.[13]

The driving force behind the Soviet Union's print propaganda program in India was Progress Publishers. Founded in 1931 and known as the Foreign Languages Publishing House between 1938 and 1963, Progress' official mission during the Khrushchev and early Brezhnev years was "to publish works that would serve to strengthen the Marxist-Leninist education of the masses abroad, to fight against bourgeois ideology, to expose the lies and the slander of the imperialist movement, and to widely propagandize the ideas of peace, socialism, and friendship of nations."[14] In the mid-1950s, Progress put this mission into action in Indian languages when it recruited nearly thirty South Asian translators to join its editorial team in Moscow. Tasked with translating Soviet literary fiction, sociopolitical literature, children's books, and classic works of Marxism-Leninism into the widely spoken languages of Hindi, Urdu, and Bengali, this first cohort of translators inaugurated what would soon become the press' largest and most successful language division. In 1957, the press released sixty-five titles in these three languages with a print run of 1.6 million copies. This not only surpassed the press' English-language print run of 1.3 million copies but also exceeded the number of copies it published in all other Western languages combined.[15]

Over the next decade and a half, a combination of official cultural diplomacy priorities and surging demand for Progress publications from readers on the ground prompted the publisher to translate books into twelve additional South Asian languages, ranging from Tamil and Telugu to Oriya and Assamese. This linguistic expansion helped fuel the publisher's phenomenal commercial success in India. By 1974, India was buying 2.3 million books a year (almost all of them Progress titles) from the export agency MezhKniga. Representing 20 percent of MezhKniga's global sales to capitalist countries, this trade volume made India the largest export market for Soviet books outside the Socialist Bloc (Figure 10.1).[16] The country would retain this status through the 1980s, when Progress began to publish more titles in higher

A view of the exhibition of Soviet books held at the Cannanore Town Hall.

Figure 10.1 Press clipping of a Soviet book exhibition held in Cannanore (Kannur), Kerala, 1979. In the 1970s, India became the largest global importer of Soviet books outside the Socialist Bloc.

print-runs in Indian languages than it did even in English, the language that had dominated the press' multilingual catalog since the early 1950s.[17]

The Soviet Union's internationalist commitment to the anti-imperial, emancipatory project of the Third World is reflected in the texts Progress chose to publish. In the late 1950s, amid the rapid decolonization of Africa, the press turned its attention to publishing books that treated the specific economic, social, and political realities of the Third World. It brought out a large number of edited volumes containing Lenin's writings on imperialism and commissioned Soviet area studies scholars to write histories of ongoing and past national liberation struggles and biographies of the African and Asian leaders of these movements. The press also fine-tuned its selection process for scientific texts and textbooks on industry and engineering in a bid to make this important genre category more responsive to the actual economic and scientific development needs of Third World nations.

At the same time, Progress was tasked with propagandizing the Soviet Union as a model for Third World development. At the behest of the powerful State Committee for Cultural Relations with Foreign Countries (GKKS), a de facto arm of the Communist Party's Central Committee, it created a new department of "original works" whose primary responsibility was to commission and publish "books on the Soviet Union." Books brought out in this clear-cut propaganda category covered everything from the history of Soviet industrialization and ballet theater to overviews of socialist public health and education systems. This "original literature" initiative grew out of GKKS' frustration with the press' traditional practice of presenting foreign readers with books that had previously been published by other Soviet presses. From the committee's perspective, the USSR's foreign propaganda needs, and in particular the need to showcase Soviet scientific and cultural achievements, were unique and could not be met with literature that was originally intended for a domestic Soviet readership. A more effective approach, as the GKKS chairman argued in a memorandum to the Central Committee in 1962, was to invest in the "preparation of books and brochures on the Soviet Union that are especially written for the foreign reader, paying particular attention to the release of such literature for the countries of Asia, Africa, and Latin America."[18]

"Books on the Soviet Union" as a publishing category covered not only union-wide achievements but also specific forms of progress achieved in the Soviet Union's Central Asian and Caucasian republics. From the earliest days of Bolshevik rule, these "eastern" Soviet regions played a critical role in helping the Soviet Union fashion itself as a "liberator and leader of all of its different 'Easts,'" which in the 1950s and 1960s came to encompass the decolonizing nations of Asia and Africa.[19] Thus, in addition to propagandistic works that covered the development of particular regions and cities in Soviet Central Asia, Progress also supplied its Indian readership with a steady stream of literary fiction from the Soviet East. Notable examples include Kyrgyz author Chingiz Aitmatov's novel *Jamila* (Figure 10.2), Turkmen writer Kayum Tangrykuliev's *The Golden Goblet*, and short story collections by the Chukchi novelist Yuri Rytkheu.

Many factors contributed to the enduring popularity of Progress books and magazines on the subcontinent, but among the most significant was their unique visual and material qualities. Progress was allied with the Soviet Union's most well-resourced and technologically advanced printing houses, ones that were equipped with offset printing presses, electronic engraving machines for the production of stereotypes, and photographic technologies for color separation.[20] The state guaranteed the press access to its limited, domestically produced reserves of high-quality typographical paper, coated fine paper, and photographic paper while also allocating it special imported paper and paperboard from Finland. The press' printing protocols, developed in order to maintain high, "export quality" standards, also called for the use of synthetic, fade-resident color inks (typically imported from abroad), high-quality metallic foils for embossing work, and liquid varnishes for cover materials.[21] These advanced printing technologies and high-quality materials, which only select Soviet presses had access to, allowed Progress to produce books and magazines that enchanted foreign readers. On the pages of Progress publications, Indian readers gazed at monochrome and color reproductions of photographs, illustrations, prints, maps, and drawings that exhibited finer lines, denser blacks, and significantly sharper tonal contrast than the reproductions they were accustomed to seeing.[22] Soviet publications also *felt* different in their hands. Books were bound in artificial leather and pigmented book cloth (buckram), featured metallic foil embossing on their covers, and contained strong, heavy-weight paper and smooth silver bromide paper inserts. Magazines were often produced with coated glossy paper. In the Indian context, where the letterpress dominated the printing

Figure 10.2 Second Urdu edition of Kyrgyz writer Chinghiz Aitmatov's novel *Jamila*. Progress Publishers made it a strategic priority to translate literary works from the Soviet Union's eastern republics for Indian audiences. *Jamila* was one of the most widely sold books from Soviet Central Asia in India.

sphere well into the 1980s, these distinctive forms, textures, and material features of Soviet print culture set it in a category apart from both domestic Indian and Western print publications.[23]

The theme of Soviet distinctiveness in the realm of printing finds expression in many letters addressed to the press. "It is doubtful," wrote one Abdul Khalim Khan from Bilaspur in 1969, "that you will find any publishing house in India that can compete with yours. Your books stand out for their sharp printing, beautiful, sturdy covers, and their affordability."[24] Another reader (who identified himself as a member of the elite Indian Administrative Service and assistant district commissioner of Guwahati, Assam) began his letter with the following introductory remark: "In content as well as in printing and binding I find it difficult to find comparisons to your books even in the West. Your workmanship is of a very high standard and I have bought several copies of quite many of your publications for presentation purposes."[25] Tellingly, this Soviet book consumer chose not to underscore his reading of the books (which he presumably did read) but rather his motivation to collect them "for presentation purposes." His remark illustrates the fact that Soviet books appealed to Indian readers for many reasons. They were not only read but also collected, admired, gifted, and (re)presented in contexts of the reader's own making. In the pages that follow, I pursue questions of visualization and the representation of Soviet imagery in more detail, examining the ways in which these images fueled dreams of scientific and technological development, the formation of progressive identities, and the solidification of Third-Worldist political affiliations.

Soviet Imagery and Development Imaginings in India

Both prior to and during his tenure as India's prime minister, Nehru insisted that the spread and adoption of a "scientific temper" would help liberate India and its people from restrictions imposed by religion and superstition. A scientific temper, he argued in his well-known *Discovery of India*, "is the temper of a free man."[26] This vision of a scientifically and technologically oriented India did not, however, imply the imitation of Western forms of industrial modernity. Rather, as Gyan Prakash has argued elsewhere, Nehru believed that India would draw on its rich philosophical history, cultural heritage, and collective traditions "to give a moral direction to science and technology," which Nehru saw as absent from the West.[27] In the first two decades after independence, the Indian state articulated this authoritative conception of Indian modernity through an array of practices that allowed its citizens to visualize a modern, developed India. The construction of hydroelectric dams, steel plants, factories, atomic reactors, and factory townships were not just monumental industrial undertakings but also forms of monumental visual propaganda that communicated Nehruvian ideals and state values to the public. These industrial and scientific undertakings were spotlighted in numerous state-produced documentary films, which, as Srirupa Roy argues, "locate[d] them in the contemporaneous time-space of the viewer with progress, modernity and development described not as idealized future horizons but as immediate, tangible substances."[28]

The widespread diffusion of Soviet imagery in Indian society added a critical international and internationalist dimension to these nation- and state-building processes which centered the ideas, practices, and display of development. With print runs and circulation levels that far exceeded even those of the National Book Trust (India's multilingual, state-run publishing house), affordably priced Soviet books and magazines enabled ordinary Indian citizens to incorporate visual manifestations of scientific, technological, and industrial modernity into the intimate spaces of their everyday lives in a way that could not be accomplished with monumental projects and state-sponsored displays, parades, and public film screenings. At the same time, these visual materials served as a reminder that many of the values, ideas, and norms promoted by the developmentalist Nehruvian state had strong socialist and internationalist affiliations. The use and creative adoption of Soviet visuals functioned for many readers as a sign of a shared global technical-scientific modernity.

A letter from one Fida Ali Ratlamwala of Raipur (a small city located close to the Soviet-funded Bhilai Steel Plant in central eastern India) supplies an excellent example of how Soviet images enabled Indian individuals to realize such global orientations. Ali opened his letter, which was addressed to the director of Progress Publishers, with a detailed description of his first encounter with Soviet books. During a sojourn in Calcutta in 1961, Ratlamwala paid a visit to the National Book Agency, located in the heart of the city's sprawling College Street book district. Once inside, he was approached by a Soviet magazine agent who sold him a two-year subscription to the Urdu-language edition of the magazine *Soviet Land*. As a bonus, the agent gifted him a calendar and English translations of *O narodnom obrazovanii* (On Vernacular Education) and *Sovetskii turkmenistan* (Soviet Turkmenistan) (Figures 10.3–10.4).[29]

Figure 10.3 Half title page of *Soviet Turkmenistan* (Moscow: Foreign Languages Publishing House, 1956).

The latter was particularly rich in visual content. It featured thirty photographic plates and illustrations that collectively represented Turkmenistan as land where industrial development and innovation had turned a formerly backward region into a prosperous socialist republic.

Using language that could have only pleased the recipient of the letter, Ali shared his delight with the books: "I read them with great satisfaction. I learned a lot of interesting things about your country, especially about the progress that has been achieved by the peoples of the Soviet Union."[30] But Ratlamwala tempered his enthusiasm in the second half of the letter when he wrote that although he found the overall printing quality and layout of *Soviet Turkmenistan* satisfactory, he remained troubled by the fact that the book's photographs were printed on both sides of the page. "If you want to cut out a photograph you like and put it in a frame," he remarked, "then you will inevitably destroy an equally good photograph printed on the opposite side."[31] For Ratlamwala, this was the book's biggest deficiency. He asked the publisher to rectify it in future publications.

What emerges from this account is an image of the simultaneous preservation and destruction of a Soviet, state-sanctioned model for the accelerated industrialization and cultural development of the Third World. On the one hand, Ratlamwala appears to embrace the interpretive line suggested by the producers of these propagandistic

Figure 10.4 Black-and-white photographs from *Soviet Turkmenistan* (Moscow: Foreign Languages Publishing House, 1956).

books. He identified the narrative history presented in both books as tales of collective "progress" and takes great interest in them. On the other hand, he wanted to take scissors to the book to decontextualize its pictures and reframe them to his own liking. We do not know precisely which images Ratlamwala planned to (or did) remove from the book for framing. But his frustration with the two-sided printing highlights the extent to which the reception of Soviet visions of development were literally and figuratively mediated by the creative energies of those who consumed them. This reader embraced the model of development presented in the book, but for the images to realize their full world-making potential for him, they would need to be set free from the confines of the book and incorporated into the everyday space of his home.

How widely Soviet visuals were appropriated and deployed for the purpose of technical and scientific self-realization in Nehruvian India is also seen in the numerous letters composed by Indian children and students interested in the realms of space exploration, astronomy, and astrophysics. Progress' 1961 release of *Earth and Sky*, an English-language translation of Aleksandr Volkov's original *Zemliya i nebo*, was particularly popular in this regard (Figure 10.5). After reading an acquaintance's copy of the book, one M. P. Joseph, a young student from Calicut, Kerala, wrote to the publisher to describe the effect it had on her perception of the solar system. In her 1962 letter, she remarked:

> Sir, the book *Earth & Sky* seems to be a very fine one in every aspect—the facts it contains about the earth and heavenly bodies, the painting and design . . . The imaginary trip to the moon is excellent. The reader really feels that she was really

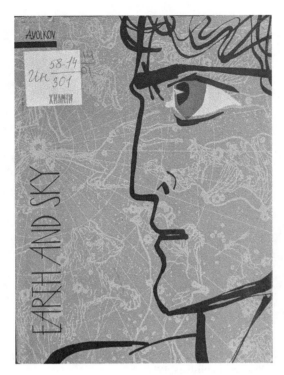

Figure 10.5 Aleksandr Melent'evich Volkov, *Earth and Sky* (Moscow: Foreign Languages Publishing House, 1961).

having an imaginary excursion to the moon! The beautiful picture of Saturn with the ring can never forgotten after seeing it! The descriptions and accounts of the Planets, Comets and Stars too are really of great educative value. I shall, therefore, be very thankful to you if you could possibly send me a copy of the book at your earliest convenience.[32]

One year later, in 1963, Progress editors received a similar letter praising the imagery found in *Life in the Universe*, the English edition of a book coauthored by Soviet biochemist Alexander Oparin and astrophysicist Vasily Fesenkov. The writer, who was a physics student living in a small provincial town in the state of Gujarat, asked the press to send him slide films of the photographs printed in the book so that he might incorporate them into a presentation for one of his courses. And finally, in another letter, a schoolboy from the state of Tamil Nadu requested a full-length, loose-leaf portrait of Laika, the space dog who was sent into orbit on Sputnik II in 1957. The boy had been introduced to Laika in the book *Rags, Borya and the Rocket: A Tale of Homeless Dogs and How They Became Famous*, but thought it was "unfortunate that the book did not include a full-size image of the dogs" (Figure 10.6).[33]

Taken together, these three letters elucidate the widening possibilities of scientific self-fashioning available to Indian students and youth during the Nehruvian period.

Figure 10.6 Photographic portraits of Soviet space dogs in M. Baranova and Konstantin Veltistov, *Rags, Borya and the Rocket: A Tale of Homeless Dogs and How They Became Famous* (Moscow: Progress Publishers, 1964).

They show how the tempering of scientific minds and the encouragement of positive attitudes toward India's economic development and scientific progress was not only a matter of domestic state policies, practices, and discourses but also involved the acquisition and creative use of visual and textual materials imported from the Soviet Union.

Soviet Portraits and the Making of a Progressive "Framing Picture" Culture

The photographic portraits that appeared in Soviet books and magazines brought a new heroic pantheon into popular circulation in India. It included a steady stream of the usual revolutionary suspects (Karl Marx, Friedrich Engels, and Vladimir Lenin) as well as icons of socialist realism, classic Russian authors, and pioneering scientists and cosmonauts: figures such as Maxim Gorky, Mikhail Sholokhov, Anton Chekhov, Ivan Pavlov, and Yuri Gagarin. In the 1960s and 1970s, this pantheon was widened even further as left-wing, revolutionary movements in the Third World began to capture the attention and support of Moscow. In response to this shift in Soviet foreign policy priorities, Progress brought out biographies of prominent socialist leaders from the Third World, including the Congo's Patrice Lumumba, Latin America's Che Guevara, and North Vietnam's Ho Chi Minh (Figures 10.7–10.9). As the readers' letters sent

Figure 10.7 *Patrice Lumumba: Fighter for Africa's Freedom* (Moscow: Progress Publishers, 1961).

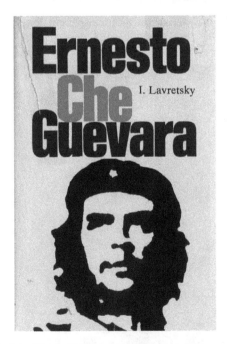

Figure 10.8a Dust jacket of the book *Ernesto Che Guevara* (Moscow: Progress Publishers, 1976). Scan courtesy of Thomas Mrett at the Internet Archive.

Figure 10.8b Portrait of Che Guevara on the frontispiece of *Ernesto Che Guevara* (Moscow: Progress Publishers, 1976).

Ho Chi Minh on the day of victory, 1954

Figure 10.9 Portrait of Ho Chi Minh from Yevgeny Kobelev, *Ho Chi Minh* (Moscow: Progress Publishers, 1989).

to Progress Publishers demonstrate, the portraits featured in these heavily illustrated biographies, novels, and propagandistic works came to form the backbone of a progressive "framing picture" culture in postcolonial India.

In the South Asian context, the term "framing picture" refers to any small, loose-leaf print or photograph that can be easily framed and displayed inside a home, shop, office, or other interior space. However, in academic discourse, the term has taken on a somewhat narrower meaning; it is typically used to designate cheap, mass-produced colored lithographs depicting Hindu Gods, saints, patriotic freedom fighters, and other nationalist heroes that were and continue to be ubiquitous objects of framing.[34] According to art historian Kajri Jain, framing pictures and other forms of Indian calendar art derive their meaning and significance from the vernacular cultural and commercial contexts in which they are produced and consumed. But it is important to recognize that not all of the mass-produced portraits used as everyday framing pictures in postcolonial India circulated in typical "vernacular" arenas such as the bazaar. Bound within the confines of books, Soviet imagery traveled along bookish circuits, appearing at bookshops, book fairs, libraries, schools, colleges, and reading clubs—venues frequented by educated and literate segments of the population. They were foreign in origin, foreign in content, and imbricated in a wider global literary sphere that Rossen Djagalov has aptly named the "Soviet Republic of Letters."[35] And yet, these alien portraits became desired objects of framing and display for Indians looking to visualize and venerate individuals who stood for radically more equitable social and economic structures and for international, anti-imperialist solidarities. Indeed, they were vernacularized through this very process.

As mentioned earlier, single-sheet prints of the figures who occupied the pages of Soviet books were not produced domestically in India. Nor did Soviet organizations and institutions export them for commercial sale or free distribution.[36] Even the Communist Party of India had a difficult time sourcing photographic images for important party congresses and often relied upon its artist cadres to draw portraits of communist leaders by hand (Figure 10.10).[37] To maneuver around this supply barrier, individuals turned to the pen and wrote directly to Soviet cultural institutions, including Progress Publishers, with requests for prints.

One of the most popular and widely sought-after framing pictures from the Soviet Union was the portrait of Maksim Gorky—the father of socialist realism. Gorky had been read in both English and vernacular Indian languages since at least the 1930s, when progressive political, cultural, and working-class labor movements became more active and widespread in colonial India.[38] But the audience for his works during the pre-independence period nevertheless remained circumscribed to several thousand communists, trade union leaders, and members of India's small, but influential, cultural left. After the USSR expanded its translation and book export program in the mid-1950s, a period that coincided with rising literacy rates in India, this readership rose into the millions. One of these readers was one Sayeed Akhtar, from rural Bihar. In his 1968 letter to the director of Progress, Akhtar thanked the Soviet Union for "introducing Indian people who speak the language of Urdu to Russian classics" before providing an overview of all Gorky and Chekhov novels he had read and enjoyed.[39] His list included every Gorky title that Progress Publishers had ever translated into Urdu: *The Birth of Man, Tales of Italy, Enemies,* Gorky's autobiographical trilogy, and

Figure 10.10 Hand-drawn portraits of Lenin and Marx appear on a backdrop used for the Communist Party of India's State Conference in Kollam, Kerala, 1975. Image courtesy of the AKG Centre, Communist Party of India, Thiruvananthapuram District Headquarters.

the writer's most famous novel, *The Mother*. His lengthy discussion of these works both cumulated in and lent credibility to a closing request for framing pictures in which Akhtar's already deferential and polished tone acquired an even higher level of obeisance. Referring to himself in the third person as *banda navāz* (lit. one who is bound in duty) and prefacing both authors names with *janāb* (honorable sir), Akhtar wrote: "If you could bear the inconvenience of sending me pictures of janāb Maxim Gorky and janāb Anton Chekhov, then this *banda navāz* would be much obliged."[40] Akhtar does not mention precisely which portraits he wanted, but most likely he had in mind one of the black-and-white bromide prints located on the frontispiece of the Indian language translations he praised (Figure 10.11).

If Akhtar's letter provides us with a sense of the deep appreciation Indian readers' felt for Gorky, still others can help us begin to answer more targeted questions: Why Gorky? What power did his autobiographical and fictional writings about the plight of the downtrodden, the greed of factory owners, and the political pursuits of the common man come to represent for millions of ordinary Indian individuals who read his work in translation during the 1960s and 1970s? And why was it so important for readers to get hold of his towering image?

The answer to these questions might be productively linked to the forms of individual and collective empowerment, self-respect, and historical relevance that Gorky offered his Indian readers at a time of immense upheaval in Indian society and the world at large. Beginning in the late 1960s, a series of overlapping struggles and mass movements were launched throughout India, including the Maoist Naxalite

Figure 10.11 Black-and-white plate of the Soviet author Maxim Gorky on the frontispiece of *The Birth of Man* (Bengali edition) (Moscow: Foreign Languages Publishing House, 1957). Image courtesy of sovietbooksinbengali.blogspot.com

uprising in the state of West Bengal, student and working-class riots across the states of Gujarat and Bihar, nationwide anti-Vietnam war protests, and violent clashes between communist-controlled trade unions in Bombay and the Marathi nationalist Shiv Sena Party.[41] Many of these movements and struggles were directed toward the pursuit of different forms of social justice that were left unresolved after Indian independence: land redistribution, rights and protection for urban laborers and landless peasants, and the eradication of political and economic corruption. In this context, Gorky's characters, who struggle with similar issues albeit in a different time and place, imbued Indian readers with the hope that progressive forces could one day triumph over reactionary ones, that unjust regimes could fall, and that the oppression of the masses would not last forever. But this hope hinged on the actions and choices undertaken by the common man and the self-sacrificing common woman who, in Gorky's works, were granted immense historical agency. They held the power to change their own lives, the lives of others, and the course of history through political enlightenment, selfless perseverance, and solidarity with the oppressed.

After reading Gorky's writings, both fictional and autobiographical, many Indian readers attempted to fashion themselves in a manner that reflected the writer's socialist values and the radical political commitments of his characters. For these acts of self-fashioning, readers deemed his portrait indispensable. "It is my hearty desire to have a photograph of Lenin and Gorky so that I shall build my career, my life, my work from Lenin and Gorky's life, idea, and inscription. So I honestly request you to send me the same as soon as possible," wrote one Arundhati Mukherjee at the end of a letter she penned to the USSR in early 1971.[42] Mukherjee, a student at a girl's college in the state of West Bengal (where the Maoist Naxalite movement had been on the rise since 1969), did not explain her request for Lenin's portrait. But she justified her affinity for Gorky when she wrote that she found the Bengali edition of *The Mother* to be "not only beautiful but useful as well." She explained further: "I firmly believe that it have [sic] immense possibilities for the future in the service of India, is it not? Please write to me your opinion." While Mukherjee's desire for a more in-depth dialogue with the Soviet publisher remained unfulfilled, her request for portraits was granted. Two months later, she received small, loose-leaf prints of Gorky and Lenin in the mail along with a short note that read: "We are happy to comply with your request."[43]

Looking at the previous example it becomes clear that these framing-picture requests were not sent willy-nilly. They were thoughtfully composed, open to dialogue, and reflective of sincere interest in the political affiliations and radical social commitments espoused by Soviet authors. This interest comes to the fore in another letter concerning *The Mother* from 1971. Addressing his letter to Maxim Gorky himself, one Bodh Rāj Gambhīr asked the author a string of questions about the fate of the book's heroes and villains. "What happened to Pavel, his mother, Andrei and all his comrades after they ran off to Siberia? Did they start a new party? Where did they live and hide? What happened to all the oppressed workers in his country? What became of the factory owners? All of this you absolutely must address in a future book. My comrades and I are waiting for it."[44] Gorky had died in 1936, but for this Delhi-based reader he was still very much alive and relevant to his understanding of how the toppling of a social order might proceed (Bodh Rāj had noted that the reason he had picked up the book in the first place was because it was supposedly based on actual historical events). The youthful urgency and restlessness with which the writer raised these questions is also echoed in the closing of his letter. "Collecting photos of writers is my hobby," he pronounced. "And I have created an album for them which I would like to see adorned with your photograph as well."[45]

While the towering figure of Gorky certainly played a leading role in the construction of a progressive Indian "framing picture" culture, readers also sought inspiration from the likenesses of Third World revolutionary leaders featured in Soviet books. One of these figures was Patrice Lumumba, the leader of the Congolese independence movement against Belgium and the nation's first prime minister. In 1961, one year after the African freedom fighter's assassination, Progress released a softcover biography of the leader entitled *Patrice Lumumba Fighter for Africa's Freedom* (Figure 10.12). In a letter sent to the USSR's embassy in Delhi that same year, one T. N. Kutty from Madras praised the USSR for its commitment to fighting for the freedom of people "under the colonial yoke." He wrote:

> First of all I must appreciate you to bring out such a useful book to the people in the world to know about the oppressed people of Africa and the great sacrifice of such a great man, the patriotic, revolutionary, and the emancipator of the Africans.

Patrice Lumumba speaks on arrival in Stanleyville, August 1960

Figure 10.12 One of many black-and-white plates in *Patrice Lumumba: Fighter for Africa's Freedom* (Moscow: Progress Publishers, 1961).

> Of course it is the U.N.O. and its General Secretary, Mr. Hammarskjold, who were responsible for the treacherous murder of Lumumba. I hope and I expect that the Soviet Union and other Socialist countries would be more precautious in taking action and keeping vigilant always against the imperialist oppression of the Colonial countries.[46]

Kutty ended his letter with a request for a framing picture of Lumumba, and the wording he used to express this desire is also worth quoting in full.

> The Photos depicting the life of Patrice Lumumba printed within the book and his portrait and the Photo that appeared in the front cover page of the above cited book have attracted me very much. I want to have the Photos to be framed and hung among the photos of the other leaders in my house. So, I shall be much obliged if you will arrange to send some printed copies of the above cited photos to my address. Yours fraternally, Kutty.

Kutty's request awakens us to the distinct possibility that, in some Indian homes, framed portraits of non-Indian Third World liberation leaders appeared alongside prints of domestic heroes and political figures. This possibility, in turn, not only leads us toward a more expansive understanding of what constituted everyday visual culture in India in the 1960s and 1970s but also directs our attention to the understudied role played by Soviet literary internationalism in the formation of internationalist and Third Wordlist identities in India.

Conclusion

This chapter has turned to archival sources in order to reconstruct a visual phenomenon for which little, if any, visual evidence survives. In making this unconventional methodological move, I have provided more nuance to our historical understanding of postcolonial visual regimes in India. Existing scholarship has largely treated these regimes as a domestic story, one grounded in the consumption of domestically produced Hindu, nationalist, and Hindu-nationalist imagery. But this chapter has shown that images originally produced for foreign audiences outside of India's borders also became important sources of identity formation and political inspiration in India in the decades after independence. The visuals contained within affordable and widely available Soviet books and magazines allowed readers young and old to carve out a variety of progressive, cosmopolitan, and socialist identities for themselves at a time when many Indians were looking outward to the world as much as inward at the nation.

Notes

1 Gosudarstvennyi arkhiv Rossiiskoi Federatsii (GARF), f. 9590, op. 1, d. 983, l. 165 (Letter from Kamal Kumar Thapa to Progress Publishers, December 21, 1971).

2 Between 1938 and 1963 Progress Publishers was known as the Foreign Languages Publishing House. But to avoid confusion, I will only use Progress Publishers in this chapter.

3 Christopher Pinney, *"Photos of the Gods": The Printed Image and Political Struggle in India* (London: Reaktion Books, 2004), 203.

4 See Pinney, *Photos of the Gods*; Kajri Jain, *Gods in the Bazaar : The Economies of Indian Calendar Art* (Durham: Duke University Press, 2007); Sumathi Ramaswamy, "Maps, Mother/Goddesses, and Martyrdom in Modern India," *The Journal of Asian Studies* 67, no. 3 (2008): 819–53; Kama Maclean, *A Revolutionary History of Interwar India : Violence, Image, Voice and Text* (London: Hurst and Co., 2015); See also many of the chapters in *Beyond Appearances?: Visual Practices and Ideologies in Modern India*, ed. Sumathi Ramaswamy (New Delhi: Sage Publications, 2003).

5 Sanjukta Sunderason, *Partisan Aesthetics: Modern Art & India's Long Decolonization* (Stanford: Stanford University Press, 2020); Sanjukta Sunderason, "Framing Margins: Mao and Visuality in Twentieth-Century India," in *Art, Global Maoism and the Chinese Cultural Revolution*, ed. Noemi de Haro García, Victoria H. F. Scott, and Jacob Galimberi (Manchester: Manchester University Press, 2019).

6 Sunderason's "Framing Margins" analyses Maoist imagery produced in India rather than imported imagery.

7 See Kajri Jain, "Muscularity and Its Ramifications: Mimetic Male Bodies in Indian Mass Culture," *Journal of South Asian Studies* 24 (2001): 197–224; and Priya Joshi, *Bollywood's India: A Public Fantasy* (New York: Columbia University Press, 2015).

8 Jawaharlal Nehru, *Glimpses of World History* (New York: Asia Publishing House, 1962), 854.

9   There is a substantial body of literature on economic planning and scientific and industrial development under Nehru. See Gyan Prakash, *Another Reason: Science and the Imagination of Modern India* (Princeton: Princeton University Press, 1999), chapters 6 and 7; Itty Abraham, "The Contradictory Spaces of Postcolonial Techno-Science," *Economic and Political Weekly* 41, no. 3 (2006): 210–17; Partha Chatterjee, *The Nation and Its Fragments: Colonial and Postcolonial Histories* (Princeton: Princeton University Press, 1993), chapter 10; see also Ramachandra Guha, *India after Gandhi: The History of the World's Largest Democracy* (London: Macmillan, 2007).

10   Daniel Immerwahr, *Thinking Small: The United States and the Lure of Community Development* (Cambridge, MA: Harvard University Press, 2015).

11   For a full treatment of India's pursuit and receipt of development aid from both the USSR and the United States during the Cold War, see David C. Engerman, *The Price of Aid: The Economic Cold War in India* (Cambridge, MA: Harvard University Press, 2018).

12   On the formation and evolution of Indo-Soviet diplomatic and trade relations, see Manu Bhagavan, ed., *India and the Cold War* (Chapel Hill: University of North Carolina Press, 2019); Vojtech Mastny, "The Soviet Union's Partnership with India," *Journal of Cold War Studies* 12, no. 3 (2010): 50–90; and Oscar Sanchez-Sibony, *Red Globalization: The Political Economy of the Soviet Cold War from Stalin to Khrushchev* (Cambridge: Cambridge University Press, 2016).

13   For more on the circulation and popular reception of Bollywood cinema in the Soviet Union during the Cold War period, see Sudha Rajagopalan, *Indian Films in Soviet Cinemas: The Culture of Movie-Going after Stalin* (Bloomington: Indiana University Press, 2008). Progress Publishers also translated many Indian works into Russian, but Soviet audiences showed considerably more interest in Indian film than in Indian literature. For a discussion of why translated Afro-Asian literature achieved only limited success in the USSR, see Rossen Djagalov, *From Internationalism to Postcolonialism: Literature and Cinema between the Second and the Third Worlds* (Montréal: McGill-Queen's University Press, 2020), 102–9.

14   GARF, f. 9590, op. 1, d. 386, l. 12.

15   GARF, f. 9590, op. 1, d. 351 (List of titles released in 1957). Despite large print-runs, the individual title count for Indian languages was still relatively low. In 1957 the press released 29 titles in Hindi, 22 in Bengali, and 14 in Urdu. The English-language title count was 152.

16   Rossiiskii gosudarstvennyi arkhiv noveishei istorii (RGANI), f. 5, op. 68, d. 1910, ll. 1–3. "Report to the Central Committee by Mezhdunarodnaya Kniga on Global Book Sales by Country, 1973-1974." India was classified as a "capitalist" country in Soviet records. Over half of the 2.3 million books MezhKniga sold to India belonged to the genres of literary fiction and children's literature. It is also important to note that India had been the largest importer of Progress Publishers' English-language books since the late 1950s.

17   Petr Petrov, *K istorii izdatel'stva "Progress"* (Moscow: Progress Publishers, 1987), 111. In the 1980s, Progress published books in more than fifty world languages.

18   RGANI, f. 5, op. 55, d. 210, l. 62.

19   Masha Kirasirova, "The 'East' as a Category of Bolshevik Ideology and Comintern Administration: The Arab Section of the Communist University of the Toilers of the East," *Kritika Explorations in Russian and Eurasian History* 18, no. 1 (2017): 8.

20   Progress books were printed at Leningrad's Printing House № 7, Moscow's "Red Proletariat" Printing House, the A. Zhdanov Exemplary Printing House №1, and

Printing House №3, among many others. Offset implies a method of printing wherein the printing image is first transferred from the plate surface onto a rubber roller or "blanket" and then "offset" or transferred onto the surface of the paper. On the formation of contracts and relationships between printers and publishers in the USSR, see Gregory Walker, *Soviet Book Publishing Policy* (Cambridge: Cambridge University Press, 1978).

21 GARF f. 9590, op. 1, d. 614, l. 111.

22 In India, offset printing did not begin to overtake letterpress printing and standard lithography until the 1980s. For a detailed discussion of the differences between photo-offset and older print reproduction processes, see Ruari McLean, "The Reproduction of Prints," *Print Quarterly* 4, no. 1 (1987): 40–5.

23 In the second half of the twentieth century, Indian publishers and printers faced numerous constraints on the adoption of such materials and technologies, including chronic paper shortages, limited access to chemicals needed to coat photographic paper, and low foreign currency reserves that prevented the importation of such materials and technologies from abroad.

24 GARF f. 9590, op. 1, d. 933, l. 28 (Letter from Abdul Khalim Khan to Progress Publishers, August 28, 1969).

25 GARF f. 9590, op. 1, d. 1038, l. 40 (Letter from Dhrubananda Das, IAS, Assistant Commissioner of Guwahati, Assam to Progress Publishers, July 3, 1972).

26 Jawaharlal Nehru, *The Discovery of India* (New York: The John Day Company, 1946), 524.

27 Prakash, *Another Reason*, 213.

28 Srirupa Roy, *Beyond Belief: India and the Politics of Postcolonial Nationalism* (Durham: Duke University Press, 2007), 47.

29 *Sovetskii turkmenistan* was originally published for a domestic audience in 1948 by the publishing house *Molodaya Gvardiya*.

30 GARF, f. 9590, op. 1, d. 501, ll. 14–17 (Letter from Fida Ali Ratlamwala to Progress Publishers, March 25, 1961).

31 Ibid.

32 GARF f. 9590, op. 1, d. 544, l. 28 (Letter from Miss M. P. Joseph to Progress Publishers, September 17, 1962).

33 GARF f. 9590, op. 1, d. 879, l. 3 (Letter from A. Nataranjan to Progress Publishers, December 28, 1968).

34 Daniel Smith, "Impact of 'God Posters' on Hindus and Their Devotional Traditions," in *Media and the Transformation of Religion in South Asia*, ed. Susan Snow Wadley and Lawrence A. Babb (Philadelphia: University of Pennsylvania Press, 1995), 24.

35 Rossen Djagalov uses the term "Soviet Republic of Letters" to describe USSR's own "ambitious projects for world literature," which operated according to very different "logic of textual circulation" than the "world republic of letters" theorized by Pascale Casanova. See Djagalov, *From Internationalism to Postcolonialism*, 21–22.

36 To the best of my knowledge, none of the Soviet cultural, diplomatic, and trade organizations with a presence in India distributed loose-leaf prints. These include *MezhKniga* (the Soviet book and media export agency), *Sovinformburo* (the Soviet Information Bureau), the Union of Soviet Friendship Societies (SSOD), and the cultural wings of the USSR's embassy and regional consulates. These organizations mainly sold and distributed books, magazines, pamphlets, brochures, films, and slides.

37 The Communist Party of India did have access to a limited number of photographic portraits from the USSR, but these were usually on permanent display in central and regional party offices.

38 Sunderason, *Partisan Aesthetics*, 65; Juned Shaikh, "Translating Marx: Mavali, Dalit and the Making of Mumbai's Working Class, 1928–1935," *Economic and Political Weekly* 46, no. 31 (2011): 65–73.

39 GARF f. 9590, op. 1, d. 828, ll. 21–2 (Letter from Sayeed Akhtar to the editor of Progress Publishers, October 23, 1968).

40 Ibid. The original sentence in Urdu is: "Agar āp janāb Maxim Gorky aur janāb Anton Chekhov ki ek tasveer irsāl karne ki zehmet gavara, to yeh banda navāz āp ki zarah navāzi kā hai."

41 For a detailed historical account of many of these movements, see Gyan Prakash, *Emergency Chronicles: Indira Gandhi and Democracy's Turning Point* (Princeton: Princeton University Press, 2019), esp. Chapter 3.

42 GARF f. 9590, op. 1, d. 983, l. 13 (Letter from Arundhati Mukherjee to Progress Publishers, February 7, 1971).

43 GARF f. 9590, op. 1, d. 983, l. 15.

44 GARF f. 9590, op. 1, d. 631, l. 23 (Letter from Bodh Rāj Gambhir to Progress Publishers, June 19, 1964).

45 In Hindi, the sentence reads, "Mujhe ek apna hastaksher sahit photo bhejiye kyonki mujhe lekhakon ke photo sangraha karne ka shauk hai aur main ne unki ek album banā rakhi hai jismen main āpka chiz bhi sushaubhit hota dekhna chahta hun to hun."

46 GARF f. 9590, op. 1, d. 631, l. 34 (Letter from T. N. Kutty to Progress Publishers, June 3, 1964).

11

The Battle of Conferences

Cultural Decolonization and Global Cold War

Monica Popescu

During the last week of June and the beginning of July 1979, Dennis Brutus, along with a suite of other famous African writers (Chinua Achebe, Ousmane Sembène, Mongo Beti, Camara Laye, Bessie Head, Ngugi wa Thiong'o, Wole Soyinka, Nuruddin Farah, Lewis Nkosi) participated in the (West) Berlin International Literature Days (BILT), an event scheduled as part of the larger First Festival of World Cultures, Horizons '79.[1] It gave him the opportunity to interact with fellow poets and novelists from Africa during a writers' workshop and also to meditate on the Berlin landscape, a divided city that, more than any other metropolis, was marked by the Cold War rift between the Eastern Bloc and Western polities.[2] It was not only the location that served as a perpetual reminder of the polarized cultural and political landscape. Whether deliberately or by chance, BILT was scheduled at the same time as the Sixth Conference of the Afro-Asian Writers Association (AAWA), which was unfolding in Luanda, Angola.

The overlap in targeted participants—writers from the former colonies—did not go unnoticed among each event's attendees, triggering questions whether the organizers in Berlin had deliberately attempted to commandeer distinguished authors who could have attended the rival conference in Luanda. In a review of the latter event for *Research in African Literatures*, Donald Burness and Geral Moser remarked that

> [i]n fact, except for the formidable representation from Angola and Mozambique, and the presence of Alex La Guma from South Africa, no recognized African writer of excellence was present. Many of Africa's most important writers were in Berlin attending another conference, a fact bitterly condemned on several occasions by the Afro-Asian Writers Union [*sic*]. It cannot be denied that the absence of such writers as Chinua Achebe, Camara Laye, Wole Soyinka, Ousmane Sembene, Ngugi wa Thiong'o and Dennis Brutus did affect the Luanda conference. Were these African writers suggesting that the writer must do more than echo pre-conceived thoughts? Or was it merely by chance that they were in Berlin rather than Luanda?[3]

The scholars' assessment conveys suspicion of ideological partisanship—a frequent feature of Cold War discourse. The implication that African literary celebrities would snub a conference that required writers to become ideological mouthpieces of the state is probably not an entirely accurate representation of the situation, especially as some of those present in Berlin had attended earlier AAWA conferences, were honored with the Lotus Prize for literature, and were generally in sympathy with the leftist principles upon which the association was built. Keeping in mind what we know today about the efforts the superpowers put into cultural diplomacy and swaying artists to their ideological camp, a more pertinent question could be whether the West German hosts had deliberately scheduled the festival to coincide with the competing event in order to secure the celebrities' presence in a Western capitalist country rather than in socialist Angola. Ultimately, the very suspicions raised by the parallel events, whether supported or not by the actual intentions of the organizers, highlight the reality of the polarized climate within which such meetings of artists took place.

If we see the conferences as rival events deliberately set up by the two Cold War ideological blocs, postcolonial writers emerge as the prized intellectual commodities over which the superpowers and their allies battled. These concurrent conferences are, therefore, much more than an example of an overabundance of cultural options available to Third World writers or an indication of the liveliness of the global literary scene. Various writers' reports on BILT and the AAWA conference, the stated aims of the events' organizers as reflected by brochures and leaflets, as well as a history of cultural diplomacy exerted by the superpowers and their allies through conferences, exhibitions, and competitions give meaning to and position these concomitant events on the map of the cultural Cold War.

Hot and Cold Conflict Forms

Participation in the two concurrent events speaks to the politics of organizing such large-scale conferences or festivals during the latter half of the global conflict: the distribution of names in the program suggests the organizers' desire to appear inclusive and comprehensive in the roster they put together, an aspect that would reflect well on the host countries. *Teses Angolanas*, the selected proceedings of the Luanda conference, offers a list of participants, comprising a rich array of countries from around the world, with a focus on Southern Africa (especially Angola and Mozambique), a large contingent of representatives from the USSR, but also from Afghanistan, Bangladesh, India, Iraq, Japan, Jordan, Mongolia, Palestine, Pakistan, Philippines, Thailand and Turkey. Some of the participants held prominent positions in the AAWA (Faiz Ahmed Faiz, Alex La Guma, Anatoli Sofronov); other attendees were famous writers and academics with strong Marxist credentials, such as the Hindi novelist Bhisham Sahni; the Hindi and Urdu poet Harivansh Rai Bachchan; the Indian Bengali poet Subhash Mukhopadhyay; the Bangladeshi academic and translator Kabir Chowdhuri; or the distinguished Palestinian poet Muin Bseiso, who had won the Lotus Prize conferred by the Afro-Asian Writers Association. Befitting the location, the largest group of participants was from Angola, and it comprised celebrated figures like Pepetela, Luandino Vieira, Manuel Rui, and the country's president, Agostinho Neto.[4]

In contradistinction, despite its inclusive name, the West Berlin-based First Festival of World Cultures (Festival der Weltkulturen) was focused on African and African diaspora cultural production, while its 1982 successor brought Latin America to the foreground. Aside from the writers mentioned earlier, other participants and events included notable musicians like Miriam Makeba and Hugh Masekela, West African griots, Caribbean steel bands and musicians from Brazil, photography of Malian architecture, a documentary on representations of the Third World in German children's books, and jazz concerts. However, the program rarely strays outside a rather narrowly understood African and African diasporic culture, with the notable exceptions of plays put on by a Syrian and a French theater company. While the total number of participating Black artists across the various film, literature, theater, traditional and modern music slots over the three-week program is truly impressive, the nagging perception of a spectacular array of African intellectuals on display for, rather than interacting with, the German public is difficult to shake off.

The pressure exerted by the host countries and their ideological overlords reminds us of the embattled nature of cultural production during the Cold War. Despite the decolonizing energy that the 1955 Bandung conference spurred, Third World nations' attempts to have a say in global affairs were often frustrated by the superpowers' continual efforts to expand their sphere of influence and the hardening of ideological fault lines that made nonalignment a difficult position to hold. While both the United States and the USSR claimed to support decolonization struggles, their aid was often tied up with self-interest. In fact, we can see the Cold War as a Second Scramble for Africa, and for the rest of the Third World, carried out this time in covert, neocolonial fashion. The repertoire of forms of influence exerted by imperial centers old and new ranged from direct involvement—proxy conflicts (Vietnam, Angola) and political and military interventionism (most countries in Central and Latin America)—to more indirect forms of cultural imperialism.

From the perspective of the former colonies, the conflict was notoriously hotter than its name announced: the superpowers used Third World countries as battlefields for proxy wars as well as strategic chessboards where military coups d'état and puppet dictatorships signaled the supremacy of either the West or the Eastern Bloc. This aspect is particularly relevant because the AAWA conference in Luanda unfolded while Angola was in the grip of one of the bloodiest and most protracted Cold War military conflicts, in which the Marxist government of the People's Movement for the Liberation of Angola (MPLA), with Cuban military and Soviet tactical support fought against the forces of the National Union for the Total Independence of Angola (UNITA), backed by the South African army and sometimes overt, other times covert support from the United States.[5] Yet, as David Caute pointed out, the Cold War differed from previous conflagrations due to the high profile accorded to cultural diplomacy and contests fought out by intellectuals and artists. The superpowers "dispatched their best ballerinas, violinists, poets, actors, playwrights, painters, composers, comedians and chess players into battle."[6]

In Africa and Asia, the late 1950s and the 1960s were dominated by the opposing cultural energies arrayed by the Congress for Cultural Freedom (CCF) and the Afro-Asian Writers Association (AAWA). Scholars have explored the various ways in which the CIA-funded CCF, with its offices in thirty-five countries, had "reshaped and refashioned the global literary landscape [. . .] and rendered those it supported more recognizable figures than others."[7] Aimed initially at luring Western European intellectuals away from Marxism and towards an US-friendly form of liberalism, the CCF soon turned its eyes toward the Third World. As much as their First World counterparts, African, Asian, and Latin American writers were being wooed with "over twenty prestige magazines," "art exhibitions," "a news and features service," and "high-profile international conferences."[8] The CCF's events for African writers include the watershed 1962 Makerere College conference in Kampala, the 1963 Dakar and Freetown conferences on the teaching of African literature in university, as well as the funding for the journals *Black Orpheus* and *Transition*.[9]

While in the past Cold War studies, based primarily within the disciplinary confines of political science and political history, presented a reductive bipolar view of the conflict that shaped the second half of the twentieth century, new directions in cultural history and literary studies have begun to present a much more complex view. Because the Cold War unfolded concomitantly with the struggle for independence in the so-called Third World, a global view of the conflict has emerged in landmark monographs such as Odd Arne Westad's *The Global Cold War* (2005) and edited collections like Andrew Hammond's *Cold War Literature: Writing the Global Conflict* (2006) and *Global Cold War Literature: Western, Eastern and Postcolonial Perspectives* (2012), Robert McMahon's *The Cold War in the Third World* (2013), and Giles Scott-Smith and Charlotte Lerg's *Campaigning Culture and the Global Cold War: The Journals of the Congress for Cultural Freedom* (2017). The conferences, magazines, and journals discussed in this chapter show not only the contours of cultural dynamics that spanned the First, Second, and Third Worlds but also bifurcations and fissures within ideological landscapes supposed to be unitary. The artists and intellectuals who participated in these discussions emerge as actors who shaped the direction of literary discourse and, as desirable subjects of the superpowers' competition for ideological and aesthetic dominance, they reveal the global scope of the Cold War.

West and East Berlin Notes

As a result of his attendance at the event in the West German capital, Brutus wrote a suite of vignette poems, "Berlin Notes," and a review essay, "The View from Berlin," that were published in the London-based magazine *West Africa* in 1979. He also produced a short essay, "African Publishing Houses: A Proposal" (1980), that took up a subject discussed at BILT and at the 1980 Frankfurt Book Fair, both of which showcased African literature.[10] The poetry he produced on this occasion as well as his notes reveal historical layers of German and European economic and cultural exploitation of other parts of the world, participation in networks of (neo)colonial domination, and a continuous demand for physical and affective labor that Africans have been asked to perform. While Brutus's criticism of West Germany comes as no surprise (the South African poet was an outspoken critic of arms deals between the host country and the apartheid regime), seemingly divergent yet disturbingly similar forms of domination appear in his reflections on East Berlin. In this chapter, I set Brutus's poetry and essays in dialogue with other African writers' reflections on West and East Berlin, drawing in particular on a letter Bloke Modisane sent from the GDR in the late 1960s. Through their writing, Berlin becomes one of the sites where the cultural Cold War is legible as a competition between forms of imperialism aimed at controlling Africa (and the rest of the Third World) rather than an ideological contest between the supporters of capitalism and followers of communism.

I have been unable to find any discussion of Brutus's participation in this festival in scholarly works dedicated to his poetry and activism. One might argue that it was a minor event, of lesser importance than his activism in support of the liberation struggle or for the expulsion of South Africa from the Olympic movement. However, given Brutus's keen interest in revealing the continually changing yet painfully present forms of racial and class discrimination in his country of origin and the United States, his reflections on Berlin clarify the intersection of several important political and cultural landscapes.

Brutus's poetry has been read from the perspective of the antiapartheid struggle and, on a larger scale, as contributing to the fight against colonialism and neocolonialism. This theoretical framework has led to an emphasis on African writers' interaction with Western cultural canons or the challenges of immigration to the Western world; only seldom do scholars attend to African writers' critical or appreciative reflections on the Eastern Bloc. The details in West and East Berlin that capture Brutus's attention reflect on African intellectuals' position as they navigated between the Scylla and Charybdis of the Cold War and the hidden forms of imperialism deployed by both sides.

The tenets of Brutus's criticism of West Berlin are in keeping with the larger themes of his leftist approach and, therefore, to a certain extent, unsurprising. For instance, he reads the 1970s conspicuous consumption in the West as the contemporary form of an economic system built on the material and cultural plunder of colonial domains. The dazzling array of exhibits in the Museum of Antiquities in West Berlin illustrates the forms of containment, decontextualization, and control of the cultural energy of African artifacts. In a vignette entitled "Nefertiti," Brutus reflects on the metonymic relation between the forms of storing and ostensibly protecting Egyptian works of art in Western museums and the sanitized distance at which African culture (whether literature or figurative art) is being consumed in the West:

Her presence is immense
her dignity overwhelming
this African queen
whose image stares down the ages
(an exact copy, they say,
of the one stored in the vaults)

unutterable elegance
of regal head and neck;
photography
marvelously
(no flashlights!)
is permitted.[11]

Brutus's focus on Nefertiti as an "African queen," a past leader who can be claimed by all inhabitants of the continent, works in contradistinction to disciplinary boundaries that separate North African (including Egyptian) civilizations from their sub-Saharan counterparts. His call to see the continent holistically and to understand its challenges in relation to global economic circuits and forms of exploitation is echoed throughout his work. Here the captive forms of African cultural capital, sequestered in the vaults or the displays of the museum, invites analogies with the African writers and artists paraded by the organizers of the Horizons '79 festival. Both Brutus and other literary workshop attendees remarked on the contradiction between the lavish funds spent by the West German state for putting African culture on display in Berlin and the minimal to nonexistent advertisement of the literary workshop to German authors and members of the public: "How then is a dialogue between North and South to materialize when the North is virtually absent," Dieter Riemenschneider asked, observing that only a few non-African participants were present.[12]

In his poem, Brutus identifies the transformation of forms of exploitation from direct oppression of Africans in Germany's colonial fiefdoms to the racist ideology developed during the Third Reich (traces of which surface in the West's covert disdain and condescending attitude toward contemporary African culture); and from forms of neocolonialism (West Germany's desire to strengthen its position of economic dominance in Africa) to the demands of affective labor (especially gratitude) made on the festival participants. Similarly, Brutus's prose bristles with irony as he points out the ideological and cultural capital derived by West Berliners, who spent more than 1 million marks for creating an exoticizing display of 400 African intellectuals and artists but made only half-hearted attempts at getting German writers to meet their African counterparts and even less effort to allow the participants to meet the press. Such apparently magnanimous spending is probed and exposed by the participants, who see the West German government's involvement "as a public relations exercise to win friends and influence people in Africa," a formulation reminiscent of the United States' "winning hearts and minds" program, and, therefore, an allusion to the cultural strategies deployed during the Cold War.[13]

Brutus's poetry creates a historical atlas, a system of mapping hidden power relations and subterranean deals crisscrossing the globe and also historical threads that connect one era to another, and one power configuration with its distant predecessors. In "Museum of Antiquities," a vignette suite entitled "Die Bildnisse des Augustus: herscherbild [sic] und politik im Kaiserlicher Rom" ["The Portraits of Augustus: Politics and the Image of the Ruler in Imperial Rome"] starts by describing the collection of statuary and canvas representations of the Roman Emperors—"dissolute Caligula," "manic Nero," "stoic Aurelius," and "the Prima Porta Augustus"—only to rapidly shift gears and historical eras in order to reflect on German-Southern African secret deals to build nuclear weapons:

4. (On a range in Zaire
even off limits to the Zairois
the children of Adolf Hitler
play with ghastly toys;

at Velindaba [*sic*]
they build nuclear bombs
for Apartheid and Nazism.)[14]

Posing as parenthetical information, the vignette in fact provides the key to reading the past through the present. In a poem concerned with the admiration contemporary cultures have for antiquity's dictators, this contemporary detour challenges the visitor's aesthetic pleasure in Roman artifacts by placing the emphasis on the political, financial, and human cost of such splendors. Brutus ruptures the safe distance at which imperial Rome is presented in museums by juxtaposing contemporary examples of autocratic or dictatorial regimes—whether Mobutu Sese Seko's Zaire or John Vorster's South Africa—which stood to benefit from Western powers' desire to secretly build nuclear arsenals despite official pronouncements condemning the arms race. He highlights economic pacts and deals between regimes that, in official documents, opposed and repudiated each other on moral grounds, yet covertly established military and economic pacts, a situation mirrored in other countries across the African continent. The threat posed by unregulated nuclear arsenals was particularly relevant when Brutus was writing his poems, only a few months after press allegations of a contract between West Germany and Zaire to test and build nuclear weaponry and revelations of South Africa's bid to enrich uranium at Valindaba, near Pretoria, and just days after SALT II concluded with a short-lived agreement between the USSR and the United States to limit strategic launchers.[15]

Confirming Brutus's reading of the festival as a watershed moment that illuminated contradictions between the Western world's munificent patronage of the arts and their economic interests in the Third World, other writers also treated BILT as an important event in their career. For instance, in an exchange with Litzi Lombardozzi in which he was making corrections to a biographical timeline, Lewis Nkosi observed with respect to the year 1979: "Missing here is a very important event which preceded my departure for Africa. 'Horizonte '79' in Berlin to celebrate African culture."[16] As he would do with the Frankfurt Book Fair the following year, Nkosi does not record the event only as a reunion of important African writers but as a forum for continuing the debate on African literary aesthetics and the relevance of political engagement to writers, a concern that occupies center stage in Brutus's reflections as well.

Despite the lack of proper organization, the writers' workshop extended existing dialogue among African authors or took the discussion in new directions.[17] The debated topics included the influence of politics on the forms and genres of writing produced in Africa; authors' commitment to sociopolitical issues; the relation between literary language, aesthetics, and literary themes; the potential elitism of literature in English and French and its intended audience; the necessity of promoting an African language like Swahili as a literary language; the political aspects of publishing and distribution networks for African literature; and, last but not least, the political and economic aspects of hosting a festival of African cultures like Horizons '79.[18] As with other conferences of African writers, the imprint of the Cold War was seen in the continued debates on the influence of aesthetic versus political principles in African writing.[19]

According to Nkosi, the workshop was also the scene of an "infamous confrontation" between himself and the Guinean author Camara Laye.[20] This occurred when Laye took as criticism remarks that Nkosi made about the latter's experimental writing—such as the Kafkaesque *Le regard du roi* [The Radiance of the King, 1954]—which were actually intended as a defense of such writing against the criticism of others. While the incident reflected a recurring misunderstanding between English- and French-speaking African writers, as meaning and good intentions oftentimes became lost in translation, Nkosi was continuing a long-standing debate about political commitment and experimental literature, an earlier instantiation of which took place at the 1967 Stockholm conference of African and Scandinavian writers.[21] As another example, while *The Radiance of the King* was embraced by Toni Morrison as "having accomplished something brand new . . . in fresh metaphorical and symbolic language," it was denounced by other writers as too European and, therefore, "imitative."[22] As Soyinka acidly put it "[m]ost intelligent readers like their Kafka straight, not geographically transposed."[23] This confrontation reminds us that the Cold War in African literature was oftentimes (yet not singularly) carried out as a battle between realism, seen by numerous leftist, politically committed writers as the only adequate form of representation of (neo)colonialism, and modernism, embraced as a form of artistic freedom and experimentation, universal in its appeal and unbeholden to political context.[24]

In his landmark essay "Postmodernism and Black Writing in South Africa," published in the decade after the end of the Cold War yet recapitulating observations Nkosi had repeatedly made during the previous decades, he evaluated the continued centrality of realism in Black South African writing as a "brittle" technique, insufficient for addressing oppression, and criticized the disappointing "prim disapproval of irony" that characterizes much of this fiction.[25] In his novels, such as the innovative *Underground People* (2002), he used irony to skillfully deflate both the grand claims of official apartheid ideology and the pompous solemnity of some of the leaders of the liberation movement. Satirical descriptions of redneck Boers and overbearing white landowners have never been lacking in the prose of Black South African writers, even though sometimes the brush strokes might appear too thick for today's tastes. What stands out in Nkosi's prose is his ability to distance himself from direct political affiliation and, while supporting the antiapartheid struggle, to expose the shortcomings of leaders in the liberation movement. Aesthetically, he argued for the dissociation of writing from political agendas.

As with earlier conferences and festivals that brought African writers together (Kampala 1962, Dakar 1963, Stockholm 1967), the debate over aesthetic freedom and political commitment, the latter perceived by writers like Alex La Guma and Ngugi wa Thiong'o as a rejection of Euro-American modernism and postmodernism in favor of realism and autochthonous literary styles, continued to divide the writers congregated in Berlin.[26] As a reviewer of the event observes, some of the Francophone writers were "hesitant and unwilling to discuss 'Politics and Exile' [one of the discussion topics] from a general political angle and preferred to draw attention to the personal plight of exiled writers."[27] This reluctance bespeaks the continuous presence of Cold War political fault lines that affected the artistic choices of these authors as well as their inclination or reticence to discuss political topics.

The divided Cold War world is crystallized in the topography of Berlin, a city partitioned by the Wall and the western part of which constituted an enclave in the middle of the German Democratic Republic. His poetry and conference ephemera attest that Brutus crossed into East Berlin and reflected on the differences between the two halves of the city separated by the Wall and the two global spheres of influence determined by the Cold War. However, he is not the only South African intellectual who reflected on the position of his country and of the antiapartheid struggle from both sides of the Iron Curtain. Along with the experiences of writers like Alex La Guma and Lewis Nkosi, Brutus's crossover from the West into the East offers a more complex, global view of forms of imperialism and neocolonialism during the second half of the twentieth century. Offering insight into the less glamorous or downright ugly aspects of both types of societies, Brutus's dual perspective from West and East Berlin also presents a more complicated view of the Cold War than the simplified communist versus capitalist binaries would suggest.

In the Cold War world, anticolonial writers were often likely to find a warmer reception in the Eastern Bloc, as these countries professed to support the decolonization struggles in Africa. Thus, South African intellectuals affiliated with the African National Congress and the South African Communist Party were often sent to study or to receive military training in Eastern Bloc countries.[28] For some of them, communist regimes served as potent symbols of equality and social justice and stirring examples for political mobilization and revolution. For instance, at the end of the travel book *A Soviet Journey*, in a rare lyrical outburst, Alex La Guma intimates the political and epistemological epiphany awaiting visitors in the Soviet Union, when first seeing the social transformations and technological prowess of the USSR: "One wanted to touch, to feel, to smell even, in that way one would, perhaps, *see*, admire the *sputniks*. It was the blind learning Braille."[29] In contrast to such wholehearted praise, Brutus's approach to the GDR, as seen on his visit to East Berlin, exhibits a much more qualified enthusiasm toward the promises of a socialist society.

One of the three vignettes dedicated to this part of the city is driven by the seemingly accommodating response to an implicit recital of faults a pro-Western speaker would find with the communist city:

> Yes, the streets are quieter
> and yes they seem deserted
> and yes there are fewer cars
> and fewer things in the drab shops
> and yes, on the deserted streets
> we see no winos and no prostitutes.[30]

The repetition of the affirmative "yes" suggests not so much the speaker's assent to the logic of such an assessment of East German society, but rather betrays his impatience with an approach that evaluates a regime based on the quantity of material goods on display. The final lines turn the compliant agreement into a positive social evaluation: the absence of prostitutes and winos might suggest a social system that precludes unemployment and exploitative labor.

However, the abrupt ending of this potentially positive evaluation and the transition in the next vignette to the displays in the famous Pergamonmuseum of antiquities (a stanza that mirrors Brutus's earlier reflections on the Museum of Antiquities in West Berlin), as well as the intimation that society, even there in the socialist world, seems driven by the same frenetic drive to destroy, suggest a more nuanced evaluation of the communist world. As in the West, the Pergamonmuseum elicits the poet's revolt:

> the immensity
> and splendour
> of this plunder
> overwhelms
> and appals.[31]

Nowhere in Brutus's work do we see the kind of enthusiastic endorsement of communism that permeates, for instance, La Guma's essays. In fact, Brutus was circumspect or downright critical of what he saw as negative influences of the Soviet Union on the antiapartheid struggle; for instance, he criticized the authoritarian top-down structures within the SACP and the ANC, which did not allow for deviations from the established party line.[32] His work suggests a much more nuanced attitude toward the reductive binaries that portray the Cold War ideological camps as the opposite of each other. Brutus implies that both types of society can produce exploitative structures and both can adopt arrogant attitudes toward African nations.

His circumspect view of East Berlin is mirrored by Bloke Modisane's account of the city. When in 1966 Modisane, a famous South African writer from the *Drum* generation decided to spend several weeks in Potsdam, in the GDR, for research purposes, the cosmopolitan-minded intellectual did not expect the lessons he was about to learn.[33] Writing to Margaret Legum, Modisane refers to his German adventures (both East and West of the dividing line) as a "safari" and locates the climax of this adventure, "in the sense of a re-education" in the GDR: "I've learned so much about my life by having been in Potsdam," the author observes, explaining that "[i]t was like being back in South Africa with the roles reversed in some kind of Kafka nightmare."[34] Life in Potsdam casts a new light on various forms of prohibitions under apartheid. The omnipresence of the police returns to him the hunted feeling he experienced in South Africa and which he dramatized in his 1963 autobiography *Blame Me on History*.[35]

Yet, as with Brutus's global perspective on power and oppression, for Modisane the GDR experience acts as a litmus text and clarification for experiences that he did not stop to question in South Africa: What does it mean to break the law to help those truly oppressed when you enjoy a position of relative security? Asked to purchase goods available in East Berlin at the Intershop, a store that sold otherwise unavailable Western goods to foreigners who had hard currency, Modisane found the emotional pressure to give away his coffee or chocolate to impoverished East Germans and the scrutiny of the police who monitored for illegal currency exchanges to be a painful reminder of the position in which he used to place his white friends in Johannesburg. Although he infuses the retelling with much humor, the most destabilizing experience takes place when a young woman offers sex in exchange for a marriage of convenience that would allow her to escape to the West. Modisane translates the tears in the woman's eyes following his refusal to the despair experienced by Black South Africans: "On the way home I moved the scene to Sophiatown. What if somebody could have helped me to get out of Sophiatown and did not? What thoughts would have turned in my mind?"[36] The experiences in the GDR activate a global perspective that connects seemingly disparate scenes, such as the oppressiveness of socialist dictatorships and apartheid totalitarianism.

As Simon Stevens observes, the value of experiences such as Modisane's lies in their ability to go beyond official discourses of solidarity. While anticolonial activists who traveled to the Eastern Bloc for training or official visits (such as Alex La Guma or Mongane Wally Serote) or even those who enjoyed leisure time (like Ngugi wa Thiong'o) barely interacted with the local populations, whose languages they did not speak, Modisane, who had spent four months honing his German skills in Bavaria, was actually able to interact with East Germans and came to understand the precariousness and fear that marked the life of citizens of this socialist country.[37] Thus, Brutus's and Modisane's visits to Berlin and their reflections on the Cold War ideological landscape could be used as a diagnostic tool for assessing under-explored cultural alliances and tensions during the latter half of the twentieth century. They also reveal the more subtle forms of cultural imperialism exerted by the superpowers during the Cold War.

Documents from Luanda

Regarding their presence in Berlin rather than Luanda, Brutus put out a trenchant statement:

> It should be explained, as Wole Soyinka stated in Berlin, that many African writers were unaware of the Luanda Conference and that others received invitations after they had already committed themselves to the Berlin International Literature Days (BILT). It would be useful to know how communications were so bad in this instance and how these can be avoided in the future."[38]

That Brutus went to the trouble of writing to *Research in African Literatures* to explain the reason for the writers' absence from Luanda highlights the importance of conferences as venues where the cultural Cold War was being fought and the significance he accorded the perception of African writers shunning the first Afro-Asian Writers Association (AAWA) conference south of the Sahara. The history of the AAWA reveals the complicated relations some of those present in Berlin had with their fellow writers in Luanda, due to ideological differences or disparities in their view about the relationship between artists and the state. While, based on their history of engagement with leftist organizations, Brutus, Sembène, and Ngugi would have likely regretted their absence from Angola, writers like Soyinka and Nkosi were more apt to give the socialist state a wide berth. Yet, this ideological bifurcation was the result of two decades of AAWA's existence within a polarized Cold War cultural field.

The Afro-Asian Writers Association had been conceived as a nonaligned cultural entity, a scion of the 1955 Bandung conference of African and Asian nations that had imagined a future when "the wretched of the earth" collectively could counter the harmful influence of imperial powers past and present, standing up to the emerging Cold War superpowers. The documents of the 1979 Luanda conference recapitulate the history of the association: the idea of creating a body representative of Afro-Asian writers was put forward at a 1956 writers' conference in Delhi, India. The birth of the AAWA occurred two years later, in Tashkent, the capital of the Uzbek Soviet Socialist Republic, where 204 writers from 37 Asian and African countries converged in 1958, setting up an association built on a progressive, anticolonial, and anti-imperialist platform.[39] The attendants included an array of distinguished and up-and-coming writers, from the nonagenarian W. E. B. DuBois to Mulk Raj Anand, Sajjad Zaheer, and Faiz Ahmad Faiz—the leading figures of the All-Indian Progressive Writers Association—and from soon-to-be-famous African writers like Ousmane Sèmbene and Efua Sutherland to the modernist Turkish poet Nazim Hikmet.[40] The following conferences took place in Cairo (1962), Beirut (1967), Delhi (1970), Alma Ata (1973), Luanda (1979), Tashkent (1983), and Tunis (1988).

While the association purported to be nonaligned, under the pretext of showcasing the rich artistic and intellectual traditions from its Central Asian republics, the USSR managed to steer much of the activity of the association. Three of the main conferences took place in this part of the Soviet Union and many more organizational meetings of the Writers Bureau—the coordinating body of the association—were hosted in Moscow, while *Lotus: Afro-Asian Writings*, the magazine published by the association, was printed in the GDR. In Djagalov and Christine Evans's apt formulation, the Uzbek and Kazakh Socialist Soviet Republics "synthesized the dual, if contradictory, role the Soviet state sought to play, [namely] a superpower offering a successful model of development and also the greatest Third-World country of all time."[41] The tension between these two Soviet masks inadvertently displayed the fissures between the USSR's official internationalist discourse, which pledged fierce support to anticolonial struggles, and its own imperialist agenda, aimed at expanding the Soviet state's global sphere of influence.

In his 1956 "Letter to Maurice Thorez," *Aimé Césaire* denounced not only the racial inequality within the French Communist Party and thereby left its ranks, but also the alternative masks of "brother" and "big brother" that the USSR had been donning.[42] It was one of the most eagle-eyed denunciations of a new world order that was forming in the aftermath of World War II, a bipolar structure within which the two new superpowers were beginning to exert new forms of imperialism. The shifting global configurations allowed other countries to take on the mantle of brotherly supporter of smaller decolonizing nations while also consolidating their position as regional power. China assumed this role beginning with the 1955 Bandung conference, when its presence created anxiety of a communist takeover of the nonaligned meeting.[43] Given the configuration of its economy as a mostly agrarian state, without a developed working class in the cities or an accelerated industrialization process that the USSR had undergone, China was able to play the Third World country card even more successfully than the Soviet Union. When the Sino-Soviet split transformed leftist fraternal bonds into acerbic enmity, both China and the USSR attempted to take over the Afro-Asian Writers Association and its larger umbrella organization, the Afro-Asian People's Solidarity Organization (AAPSO). In 1966, when part of the membership of AAWA decided to move its headquarters from Sri Lanka to the more Soviet-compliant Egypt and entrusted its leadership to the writer Youssef El-Sebai, China resolved to run a parallel and identically named association based in Beijing.[44] To clarify its ideological position, the China-based association published materials harshly condemning the USSR and the "grisly social-imperialist and social-fascist features of Soviet modern revisionism," which, they argued, "plotted and convened the bogus 'third conference' of Afro-Asian writers in Beirut, continuing their criminal activities of splitting the Afro-Asian writers' movement."[45] The vitriol contained within such pamphlets reveals the complex ideological Cold War landscape. By choosing to attend the events organized by one faction or the other, writers from the Third World shaped the cultural geopolitics of the Cold War.

Cuba is yet another socialist bloc country that saw itself and acted as a regional power. The Caribbean socialist state is of particular relevance for understanding the context of the 1979 Luanda conference because Angola was in the grip of a so-called civil war, which was in fact a Cold War hot conflict. As large numbers of Cuban soldiers served in Angola in the name of safeguarding former colonies from American imperialism, Tricontinentalism and internationalism were important discursive components of the political and cultural life in Angola. To further enhance ties between the two countries, a year before the conference the writers' unions from the two countries signed a cultural accord to promote each other's literature.[46]

Inevitably, expressions of solidarity in the anti-imperialist struggle took center stage at the AAWA conference in Luanda. The accomplished writer and president of Angola Agostinho Neto addressed the relation between nationally- and universally relevant themes and ideas.[47] Reminding those present of the political situation in Angola, under assault from South African military forces, he also pointed out the relevance of the anticolonial struggle to people beyond the boundaries of his country, whether in Zimbabwe, Namibia, or Timor-Leste. The conference participants also expressed solidarity through a general proclamation and resolution, forms that could be considered genres in their own right and potent instruments in the cultural Cold War. All the AAWA conferences and the principal meetings of the Permanent Bureau include such declarations and resolutions that are recorded in the "Documents" section of the journal *Lotus*. Whether in support of Vietnamese, Laotian, Angolan, Palestinian, or Zimbabwean peoples, these declarations trace the contours of a socialist world seemingly united against Western interference and imposition.[48] Yet, the genre of the declaration and resolution is not an attribute solely of leftist cultural organizations. The Congress for Cultural Freedom, the organization that ramped up the intensity and breadth of the cultural Cold War, was born in Berlin in 1950 at a conference that concluded with a manifesto.[49]

However, there were also clear differences in the handling of similar questions raised by conference attendees. As mentioned earlier, in Berlin, participants questioned the relation between politics and literature as well as the role of the writer within society: the issue of a writer's commitment had been a long-contested battleground. In Luanda, published documents presented a homogenous, orchestrated response: writers have responsibilities toward their societies. In keeping with the Soviet model, and similarly to writers' congresses in other socialist states, intellectuals were expected to participate in the transformation of society, as shapers of their fellow citizens' consciousness, ushering in a new worldview.[50] Even aesthetic concepts (such as the use of fantastic and dream elements in children's literature) are marshaled in order to enable social transformation.[51]

Within this highly fragmented cultural landscape, where enemies sometimes used similar genres and forms to formulate opposite goals, it is not surprising that writers questioned the bases upon which solidarity could be formed. In a highly metaphoric and nuanced speech—in contrast with the rather formulaic majority of the speeches given by participants at the conference in Luanda—Manuel Rui, a gifted novelist from the host country, posed questions about writers' relation to the majority of the population in their respective countries. Conveying his questions as an imagined interaction with an Angolan "nomad," Rui wondered whether an unlettered citizen who was otherwise immersed in the oral literary tradition would side with the global socialist cultural heritage or one based on racial identity.

> I asked for a reading of "Mother" by Gorki and of the poem the "Wall" by Guillén in the nomad's language. The nomad asked for explanations when he didn't understand. After that, he was content. We used to identify ourselves as "we" plural. Revolution! Now, we construct our identities by praising what Gorki and Guillén would say. However, if someone were to give a speech about what Marshal Idi Amin was in the nomad's language, the nomad might likely draw his bow and point his arrow at Amin, calling him a "Boer." And Amin was born in Africa. Gorki and Guillén were not.[52]

It is telling that the cultural networks evoked by Rui at the AAWA conference were those that the association had cultivated most assiduously, namely the relations with Soviet and Cuban culture (Maxim Gorky and Nicholas Guillén). Beyond the barrier of writing, beyond the distance of class (as the writer is a lettered person who moves in different social circles than the nomad), the two would agree on the value of socialist literature that conjures up the struggle against capitalist exploitation and imperialism. Poet and nomad would be united under the banner of revolution. However, the nomad would also have to recognize the dissimilarity between himself and a ruthless dictator like Idi Amin despite their racial identification. The slightly ambiguous formulation reminds us that Manuel Rui had been both a supporter of the MPLA and a nuanced critic of the new bureaucratic structures set in place in the young socialist state.

Indeed, ideological alliances were not the only types of connection during the Cold War. Numerous African writers fought ideological disunion by invoking a shared history of racial oppression, colonization, slavery, as well as similar cultural forms Black people from around the world inherited based on a putative biological unity. Negritude, a philosophy that became highly polarizing from the 1960s onward, especially in the formulation put forth by Léopold Sédar Senghor, the first president of Senegal, had galvanized the First Congress of Black Writers and Artists that took place in Paris in 1956. Yet, as with numerous other conferences and events to follow, the attempt to circumvent direct engagement with the superpowers had been unsuccessful at the Paris congress and in its aftermath.[53] Alioune Diop, one of the Congress' key organizers and the editor of the prestigious journal *Présence Africaine*, pondered whether he should attend the Afro-Asian Writers Association inaugural conference in Tashkent in 1958. The CIA-funded Congress for Cultural Freedom dissuaded Diop from participating, expressing concern about an event that happened under Soviet tutorship.[54] These highly partisan conference invitations illuminate the historical background against which the parallel conferences in West Berlin and Luanda unfolded in 1979.

The doubling of venues in 1979 proliferated even further. In February of the same year, a Workshop for Afro-Asian Writers took place in India. Those imagining that a known cast of characters frequently associated with the AAWA (among whom Mulk Raj Anand and Faiz Ahmad Faiz were the most prominent) had featured at this event, would be disappointed. Instead, government officials and representatives of Western institutions top the list of participants: Abul Hasan (books officer in the Indian Ministry of Education), Samuel Israel (former director of the National Book Trust, India), Dennis Gunton (Deputy Educational Advisor, British High Commission), Ravi Dayal (General manager of Oxford University Press), and Ka Naa Subramanyan (vice president of the Writers Guild of India). Nor were the participants from other countries drawn from the lists of progressive leftist writers featured in *Lotus*. Some of the participants went on to forge successful writing careers—for example, Shakuntala Hawoldar (Mauritius) and Marie Marjorie (Evasco) Pernia. Other participants include Mir Wali Nyham (Afghanistan), Kgogo Mudenge (Lesotho), Eno Bassey (Nigeria). Superficially, the goals of the workshop might appear closely aligned with its more than two decade-old counterpart. The workshop advocated "the importance of and role played by international workshops of this kind."[55] H. K. Kaul, introduced as the librarian of the India International Centre, described the role of writers in multilingual and multiracial societies and the hurdles created in the free exchange of ideas by the multiplicity of languages and suggested that the Afro-Asian countries should establish a Bureau of Afro-Asian Authors and Translators to combat all such problems.[56]

Speaking of literature that portrays "life and conditions of the lower middle class" and "social upliftment" instead of the familiar leftist critique of capitalism and imperialism in the pages of *Lotus*, the workshop ignored the well-established presence of AAWA in India.[57] Given the popularity of the fourth AAWA conference in 1970, which was inaugurated by Indira Gandhi, as well as the ubiquity of the journal *Lotus* among leftist intellectuals, the establishment of a parallel, similarly named organization, raises questions about its unstated origins, goals, and sponsorship. Overtly funded by the UNESCO Regional Center for Book Development, the Commonwealth Secretariat, Korean PEN, and a few governments of participating nations, the workshop and proposed organization might have been an attempt of Western or Western-leaning cultural institutions in India to counter the Soviet influence within Asian and African literary production, publication, and circulation.[58]

I have been unable to find any other documents about the proposed Bureau of Afro-Asian Authors and Translators. Yet, this is not an uncommon predicament. While in recent years a lot of research has focused on the global operations of the CIA-funded Congress for Cultural Freedom, which was launched in 1950 and folded in 1967 under the weight of the scandal of CIA funding for and ideological weaponization of American and international cultural institutions, and while the role of the Soviet-backed Afro-Asian Writers Association is beginning to be explored, most of the scholarship focuses on the 1950s and 1960s. There are obvious logistical obstacles to expanding this history into the 1970s and 1980s, as some archival repositories are sealed for fifty years. How did the cultural Cold War proceed after the 1967 revelations that numerous cultural organizations purporting to be independent and nonaligned had been sponsored by the CIA? This chapter has attempted to present a fragment of the global networks from the latter part of the Cold War.

Parallel conferences and cultural events like those from 1979 described above trace the contours of new cultural instruments the superpowers used in order to sway not only their own populations, but hearts and minds across the globe. More important, these events illuminate the determining contribution Third World writers had in shaping the cultural Cold War, whether by directly speaking against forms of imperialism, by promoting new aesthetic criteria, or even by inadvertently choosing to attend one event instead of another. Conference ephemera and short publications like the ones discussed previously do not only supply missing information about prominent Third World writers and activists but also interrogate why their work and that of other postcolonial authors has not been discussed more often in the context of Cold War research. Ultimately, focusing on this material means addressing why postcolonial studies and Cold War scholarship, although preoccupied with cultural phenomena that could be loosely seen as contemporaneous have not crossed paths more often.

Notes

A version of this chapter previously appeared as "The Battle of Conferences: Cultural Decolonisation and Global Cold War," in *The Palgrave Handbook to Cold War Literature*, ed. Andrew Hammond. (Cham, Switzerland: Plagrave, 2020), 163–82.

1 The festival took place between June 21 and July 15, 1979 (see *Horizonte 79 Magazin: Festival der Weltkulturen Berlin 21 Juni–15 Juli 1979* (Berlin, 1979); and Dieter Riemenschneider, "First Festival of World Cultures—Horizons 79, Berlin 21 June to 15 July 1979," *Kunapipi* 2, no. 1 (1980): 192–4).
2 The writers' workshop (June 25–27) was not advertised in the program and, as the organizer was absent, participating writers had to decide on a format and discussion topics (see Riemenschneider, "First Festival of World Cultures," 193).
3 Burness and Moser, "Sixth Conference of Afro-Asian Writers, 26 June to 1 July 1979," *Research in African Literatures* 11, no. 2 (1980): 235–6.
4 See Anon, "Lista de participantes, delegados e convidados," in *Teses Angolanas: Documentos da VI Conferência dos Escritores Afro-Asiáticos* (Lisbon: Edições 70, 1981), I, 190–5. The scale of the conference and total number of participants are difficult to gauge as most of the names in the proceedings are listed as 'head of delegation' for their respective countries.

5 For a more detailed representation of the complex Cold War dynamics in Angola, see Piero Gleijeses, *Visions of Freedom: Havana, Washington, Pretoria, and the Struggle for Southern Africa, 1976–1991* (Chapel Hill: University of North Carolina Press, 2013), 65–97, 393–420. Vladimir Shubin's *The Hot "Cold War": The USSR in Southern Africa* (2008) highlights the incongruity between the label "Cold War" and the devastating proxy conflicts fought by the superpowers in Africa, Asia and Latin America.

6 Caute, *The Dancer Defects: The Struggle for Cultural Supremacy during the Cold War* (Oxford: Oxford University Press, 2003), 5.

7 Andrew N. Rubin, *Archives of Authority: Empire, Culture, and the Cold War* (Princeton: Princeton University Press, 2012), 11.

8 Francis Stonor Saunders, *The Cultural Cold War: The CIA and the World of Arts and Letters* (New York: The New Press, 2013), 1. For further research on the CCF, see Giles Scott-Smith's *The Politics of Apolitical Culture: The Congress for Cultural Freedom, the CIA, and Post-War American Hegemony* (2002); Peter Kalliney, "Modernism, African Literature, and the Cold War," *Modern Language Quarterly* 76, no. 3 (2015): 333–67; Rubin, *Archives of Authority*; and Bhakti Shringapure's *Cold War Assemblages: Decolonization to Digital* (New York: Routledge, 2019). For an emerging history of the AAWA and its role in postcolonial studies and world literature, see Hala Halim, "*Lotus*, the Afro-Asian Nexus, and Global South Comparatism," *Comparative Studies of South Asia, Africa and the Middle East* 32, no. 3 (2012): 563–83; Duncan Yoon, "Our Forces Have Redoubled: World Literature, Postcolonialism and the Afro-Asian Writers' Bureau," *The Cambridge Journal of Postcolonial Literary Inquiry* 2, no. 2 (2015): 233–52; Monica Popescu's *At Penpoint: African Literatures, Postcolonial Studies and the Cold War* (Durham: Duke University Press, 2020); and Rossen Djagalov's *From Internationalism to Postcolonialism: Literature and Cinema between the Second and the Third World* (Montreal: McGill-Queen's University Press, 2020).

9 For further information on these conferences, see Chapter 1 of Monica Popescu's *At Penpoint: African Literatures, Postcolonial Studies and the Cold War* (2020); Es'kia Mpahlele, "Postscript on Dakar," in *African Literature and the Universities*, ed. Gerald Moore (Ibadan: Ibadan University Press, 1965), 80–3.

10 Dennis Brutus, "The View from Berlin," *West Africa*, August 27, 1979, 1558–9; "Berlin Notes," *West Africa*, August 27, 1979, 1559–60; "African Publishing Houses: A Proposal," *The Antioch Review* 38, no. 2 (Spring 1980): 233–6.

11 Brutus, "Museum of Antiquities," in Brutus, "Berlin Notes," 1559.

12 Riemenschneider, "First Festival of World Cultures," 193.

13 Brutus, "The View from Berlin," *West Africa*, August 27, 1979, 1559.

14 Brutus, "Museum of Antiquities," in Brutus, "Berlin Notes," 1559.

15 On the Valindaba uranium enrichment programme, see Anna-Mart Van Wyk, "Apartheid's Atomic Bomb: Cold War Perspectives," *South African Historical Journal* 62, no. 1 (2010): 100–20.

16 Nkosi, "Timeline for Lewis Nkosi," in *Letters to My Native Soil: Lewis Nkosi Writes Home (2001–2009)*, ed. Lindy Stiebel and Therese Steffen (Zurich: LIT, 2014), 184.

17 Both Brutus and Riemenschneider decried the lack of advertisement for the larger public and the poor organization of the workshop: as the official in charge did not show up on the first day, "[i]t was proof of the organizational skill of D. Brutus, N. Farah, L. Peters and others that a programme was charted out within a short time and that discussion on 'Politics and Exile' started soon after" (Riemenschneider, "First Festival of World Cultures," 193).

18 See Brutus, "View from Berlin," 1559; Riemenschneider, "First Festival of World Cultures," 193–4; and Bessie Head, "The Role of the Writer in Africa," *English in Africa* 28, no. 1 (2001): 33.

19 For further information on these debates, see Popescu, *At Penpoint*, especially Chapter 1.

20 Nkosi, "Timeline," 184.

21 See Wole Soyinka, "The Writer in a Modern African State," in *The Writer in Modern Africa: African-Scandinavian Writers' Conference, Stockholm, 1967*, ed. Per Wästberg (Uppsala: The Scandinavian Institute of African Studies, 1968), 14–36; and Nkosi, "Individualism and Social Commitment," in Wästberg, ed., *Writer in Modern Africa*, 45–58.

22 Morrison, "On 'The Radiance of the King,'" *The New York Review of Books*, August 9, 2001, 18; Wole Soyinka, "From a Common Backcloth," *The American Scholar* 32, no. 3 (1963): 388.

23 Soyinka, "From a Common Backcloth," 387.

24 While Soyinka himself was oftentimes criticized for his Euro-American modernist approach to writing, his criticism of Laye demonstrates that Cold War aesthetic battles were never a simple dispute between modernism and realism (see Georg M. Gugelberger, "Marxist Literary Debates and their Continuity in African Literary Criticism," in *Marxism and African Literature*, ed. Gugelberger (Trenton: Africa World, 1985), 2, 14).

25 Nkosi, "Postmodernism and Black Writing in South Africa," in *Writing South Africa: Literature, Apartheid and Democracy, 1970–1995*, ed. Derek Attridge and Rosemary Jolly (Cambridge: Cambridge University Press, 1998), 83, 77.

26 See Monica Popescu, "Aesthetic Solidarities: Ngugi wa Thiong'o and the Cold War," *Journal of Postcolonial Writing* 50, no. 4 (2014): 390.

27 Riemenschneider, "First Festival of World Cultures," 193.

28 See Constantin Katsakioris, "Creating a Socialist Intelligentsia: Soviet Educational Aid and Its Impact on Africa (1960–1991)," *Cahiers d'études africaines* 57, no. 2 (2017): 259–88.

29 La Guma, *A Soviet Journey: A Critical Annotated Edition*, ed. Christopher J. Lee, new edn (1978; Lanham: Lexington Books, 2017), 229. Here La Guma uses Sputnik, the first artificial Earth satellite, as a synecdoche for all Soviet technological inventions.

30 Brutus, "East Berlin," in Brutus, "Berlin Notes," 1560.

31 Ibid.

32 See Brutus, "Memoir: From Protest to Prison," in *Poetry and Protest: A Dennis Brutus Reader*, ed. Lee Sustar and Aicha Karim (Chicago: Haymarket, 2006), 36.

33 See Modisane, "Letter to Margaret Legum" (1966), The Colin Legum Papers, University of Cape Town Libraries, Manuscripts and Archives Department, B13.43. After several months of language training in West Germany, where he spent the last years of his life, Modisane went to the German colonial archives in Potsdam in order to do research for a book on the Maji Maji resistance (1905–1907) against German rule in East Africa (see Simon Stevens, "Bloke Modisane in East Germany," in *Comrades of Color: East Germany in the Cold War World*, ed. Quinn Slobodian (New York: Berghahn, 2015), 123). Margaret Legum was an antiapartheid activist and the wife of distinguished journalist Colin Legum.

34 Ibid., 1.

35 See Modisane, "Letter to Margaret Legum," 2–4.

36 Ibid., 3.

37 See Stevens, "Bloke Modisane in East Germany," 123.

38 Brutus, et al., "Letters to the Editor," *Research in African Literatures* 12, no. 1 (1981): 140.

39 See Anon, "VI Conferência dos Escritores Afro-Asiáticos: Documentos," in *Lavra & Oficina: Caderno Especial Dedicado à Literatura Angolana em Saudação à VI Conferência dos Escritores Afro-Asiáticos*, ed. União dos Escritores Angolanos (Lisbon: Edições 70, 1979), 132.

40 See Rossen Djagalov, *From Internationalism to Postcolonialism Literature and Cinema between the Second and the Third World* (Kingston: McGill-Queens University Press, 2020), 65. Based on Russian archive documents, Djagalov gives the number of attendees as "over one hundred" (ibid., 65).

41 Quoted in Ibid., 70.

42 Césaire, "Letter to Maurice Thorez," *Social Text* 28, no. 2 (2010): 149.

43 For perspectives on China's participation at Bandung, see Richard Wright, *The Color Curtain: A Report on the Bandung Conference* (Cleveland: World, 1956), 84–5, 90–2; and Yoon, "Our Forces Have Redoubled," 235–7.

44 See Yoon, "Our Forces Have Redoubled," 251–2.

45 Afro-Asian Writers' Bureau, *The Struggle between the Two Lines in the Afro-Asian Writers' Movement* (Place unknown: Afro-Asian Writers' Bureau, 1968), 2, 19.

46 See Don Burness, *On the Shoulders of Martí: Cuban Literature of the Angolan War* (Boulder: Lynne Rienner, 1995), 64.

47 Neto, "Discurso," in *Teses Angolanas: Documentos da VI Conferência dos Escritores Afro-Asiáticos* (Lisbon: Edições 70, 1981), I, 171–2.

48 See, for instance, the "General Declaration of the Fourth Afro-Asian Writers' Conference" (1971), which had taken place in Delhi in 1970.

49 See Congress for Cultural Freedom, "A Manifesto of Congress for Cultural Freedom," in *The Liberal Conspiracy: The Congress for Cultural Freedom and the Struggle for the Mind of Postwar Europe*, ed. Peter Coleman (New York: Free Press, 1989), 249–51. Jini Kim Watson has similarly theorized the role of resolution and conference documents with respect to PEN Asia events (see Watson, *Cold War Reckonings: Authoritarianism and the Genres of Decolonization* (New York: Fordham, 2021)).

50 See Comandante Ndalu, "Discurso de Abertura," in *Teses Angolanas*, 14.

51 See Maria Eugénia Neto, "Deve-se escrever para crianças empregando o maravilhoso?," in *Teses Angolanas*, 38–9.

52 Rui, "Entre mim e o nómada—A Flor," in *Teses Angolanas*, I, 32. I am grateful to Lanie Millar and Sara Hanaburgh for helping me with this translation. In the original Portuguese, Rui uses the term "Karkamano," which I have translated here as "Boer." Derived from the Italian words "calcare" and "mano," it is a slur suggestive of deceptive behaviour (pressing down the scales with the hand to tip them). In Angola, the slur is used to refer to white South Africans.

53 Cedric Tolliver points out the duplicity in Richard Wright's behavior in 1956 in Paris where, on the one hand, he expressed solidarity with the Congress' organisers and, on the other hand, informed the US Embassy on the conference events and distanced himself from those he perceived as having communist inclinations (Tolliver, "Making Culture Capital: *Présence Africaine* and Diasporic Modernity in Post-World War II Paris," in *Paris, Capital of the Black Atlantic: Literature, Modernity, and Diaspora*, ed. Jeremy Braddock and Jonathan P. Eburne (Baltimore: The Johns Hopkins University Press, 2013), 215).

54 For more details, see Horace Mann Bond Papers, University of Massachusetts, "American Society of African Culture, August 1, 1958–December 31, 1958," 49. I am grateful to Cedric Tolliver for bringing this letter exchange to my attention. Although Diop seems to have contemplated an invitation to participate at the inaugural AAWA conference in Tashkent, Rossen Djagalov points out Soviet cultural bureaucracies had decided against having him there (see Djagalov, *From Internationalism to Postcolonialism Literature*, 77).

55 Anon, *Workshop for Afro-Asian Writers, February 5–20, 1979* (New Delhi: India International Centre, 1979), 2.

56 Ibid.

57 Ibid., 9.

58 Ibid., 3. The India International Centre which spearheaded the project is, according to its website, a nonaligned institution which operates on the basis of grants from the Rockefeller Foundation.

12

The Death of the Third World Revisited

Curative Democracy and World-Making in Late 1970s India

Srirupa Roy

In recent years, there has been a surge of intellectual attention directed toward the mid-twentieth-century political project of the Third World.[1] As national parochialisms proliferate across the globe in the new millennium, sundering dense historical networks of international connection, the stories of an earlier age that witnessed nation-building as an international solidarity project, of a time when the national and the international related to each other as mutually enabling formations, hold a special attraction.

Unsurprisingly, the main narrative framework of the Third World story is that of nostalgia and loss.[2] Both critics and admirers of Third World internationalisms agree that this is a tale that belongs to the past: the time of the Third World is long over. The Third World project is invariably presented in linear terms: a birth, a flourishing, and then a death, bookended by two temporal markers, the 1950s and the 1970s.

Several scholars have nuanced this rather organicist perspective with useful reminders of the complex circumstances and tangled genealogies of the Third World, and have refuted the existence of a single birth-moment when a Third World project emerged fully formed. Instead, they argue, a series of distinct and even conflicting internationalist imaginaries that were sutured around varied geographies of connection (e.g., Third World, Bandung nations, nonaligned world, Afro-Asian solidarities, Tricontinental connections), and that activated different political horizons and goals (e.g., anti-imperialism, socialism, decolonization, nonalignment, racial fraternity of the "darker nations"), sedimented a new language and practice of international politics over time. The formation of the Third World has been reconceptualized as an ongoing set of historical processes rather than a singular and natalist act.[3]

This has also meant a move away from nation-statist and geopolitical "hard power" frames of analysis. In conventional accounts of how Third-Worldist and other allied political imaginations of international order gained legitimacy in the third quarter of the twentieth century, the actions and decisions taken by the leadership of new nations in the former colonial worlds of Asia and Africa have taken center stage. New scholarship on the subject offers a different perspective. By drawing attention to the cultural and informal political exchanges and encounters between individuals and groups that took place "outside geopolitical war rooms"[4]—transregional traffic that was both purposeful and serendipitous—scholars have pluralized and thickened accounts of Third World internationalisms as a set of socially rooted projects and processes.[5]

But these revisionist histories have a narrative limit. Most of the layered, processual, and socially located accounts of the Third World project engage its birth and life but not its death. The latter continues to be presented as a definitive *caesura*, a rupture in the late 1970s that is dramatically described as a moment and act of "losing utopia" or even an "assassination."[6] Moreover, unlike the pluralized and socially thick histories of how Third World internationalisms rose and flourished at a particular world historical conjuncture, the story of its collapse remains bound up in the register of nation-statist agency, Cold War geopolitics, and the macro-structural dynamics of global capitalist forces and relations. In available accounts, the main assassins of Third World internationalisms are choices made by national states and their leaders, and international geopolitical and economic forces, whether the shifting power dynamics of Cold War superpower rivalries or the new requirements of global capitalist expansion that manifested in the 1970s.

This chapter offers a different perspective on the transformations that took place at the end of the 1970s, looking *within* nation-statist orders to link the modulations of the Third World project (note that I term this a modulation rather than a loss, decline, or death) to a set of *domestically configured* social and political processes, events, and protagonists. I focus on the specific case of India, whose national leadership had played a pioneering role in sustaining and advancing Third World and allied imaginaries of internationalist nationalism in the postwar era.

I make two main arguments. The first relates to the exercise of transformative agency at the end of the 1970s, that is, the question of who killed the Third World, and how. Moving away from the usual focus on geopolitical dynamics, macro-structural explanations involving capital and the Cold War, and the decisions and actions of big men who strode the world stage (Nehru-Nasser-Tito-Sukarno-Castro),[7] I draw attention to a wide range of non-state social organizations, groups, and individuals that became influential within domestic political arenas in the late 1970s and contributed to the rise of a new national project that modulated prevailing Third World imaginaries.

The next set of arguments is about these modulations. What were the contours and concerns of the new national project that gained traction in India in the latter half of the 1970s, supplementing and eventually replacing the internationalist nationalisms of an earlier era? The late 1970s in India was a time when political democracy was restored following the end of the infamous national Emergency, a nineteen-month democratic gap in Indian political history (June 1975–March 1977) when the reigning Congress government under Prime Minister Indira Gandhi declared a constitutional emergency that suspended most democratic rights and freedoms and imposed centralized and authoritarian conditions of rule on the country. I argue that the political ferment that emerged at Emergency's end both reflected and advanced a significant normative shift, from the Nehruvian-era call of nation-building to the post-Emergency mission of democracy-rebuilding.

The idea of democracy-rebuilding introduced a new national diagnostics into public discourse, that is, a new way of identifying national problems and solutions. The prevailing decolonization paradigm was interrupted to target our own system rather than a foreign colonial state as the main problem at hand. Instead of declarations of independence from foreign colonial rule, calls to address self-created problems became increasingly vocal in the 1970s, particularly as the decade drew to an end. The focus was on the conditions of inequality, violence, deprivation, and misery that resulted from the failed promises and wrong leadership choices that we had made ourselves. The task at hand was not so much national liberation and development but rather the reform and cure of the damaged democratic system of independent India.[8] I term this the "curative democracy" project of the post-Emergency period, a distinctive normative and institutional formation that departed from the nation-building projects of the decolonization era in least two significant ways.

First, the idea of curative democracy was premised on and in turn shored up an opposition between electoral politics and morality, and defined democracy and popular sovereignty as specific kinds of moral "nonparty political" projects. The rise of a distinctive moral register of normative discourse in the late 1970s has attracted academic attention in recent years. For instance, in Samuel Moyn's global history of human rights, he describes how international relations were reconstituted around a new "moral utopia" of human rights that replaced the "political utopia" of decolonization in the late 1970s. Moyn is primarily concerned with the shifts in a globally articulated discourse. He maps the politics-to-morality normative transition in relation to international institutions and processes and highlights the leading role of individuals and organizations in First and Second World locations.[9] However, as the example of the Indian curative democracy project shows, institutions, processes, and actors located within the domestic political arenas of the Third World drove this transition as well.

For instance, in post-Emergency India in the late 1970s, a distinctive public language of antipolitics gained traction that linked political legitimacy and virtue to distance from electoral politics. Extra-parliamentary or non-electoral agents and institutions were authorized as the true representatives of the people, a collective subject defined in moral terms, whose representational needs were seen to elude and exceed the institutions and procedures of electoral democracy.[10] Along with the new moral rhetoric of international human rights discourses, the rise of "political outsiders" exerting moral authority in domestic political contexts, and increasing expressions of distaste and distrust for electoral politics within India, what Pierre Rosanvallon describes as the emergence of a "durable democracy of distrust," also shaped the global utopian transformations of the late 1970s.[11]

The second change brought about by the transition from national liberation to curative democracy was a recalibration of political scale. The horizons of political agency shifted in India in the late 1970s. The nation-building projects of the 1950s and the 1960s had engaged the territorial unit of the nation-state—the goals of liberation and development were to be realized at a national scale. The post-Emergency period of the late 1970s saw the contraction or involution of this national frame. The "local" and the "grassroots community" now joined the national masses as authentic loci of popular sovereignty, and political calls for decentralized, locally distinctive people's initiatives interrupted the prevailing centralized imaginaries of state developmentalism.

But as political horizons contracted, they also opened up in significant ways. The curative democracy projects of the late 1970s and the ideas and practices of popular sovereignty, moral antipolitics, and non-electoral representation that they introduced also created new geographies of international connection. In other words, the late 1970s did not witness the end of international nationalism as the various "death of the Third World" theories have announced, but rather the reworking of its affinities and pathways to create a different circuitry of international connection. Unlike the earlier moment of Third World solidarity projects, international affinities and exchanges in the late 1970s were not confined to state-made and state-sanctioned networks and pathways of international connection. Rather, they were often elaborated in explicit opposition to statist internationalisms; they activated new circuits and bypassed existing ideological binaries to produce new amalgams. The end of the Third World was equally a moment and process of world-making.

The remainder of this chapter fleshes out these arguments about curative democratic world-making in late 1970s India, a central episode in the story of Third World transformation. My specific focus is on the practices of new journalism after the Indian Emergency that played a key role in the transition from nation-building to democracy-rebuilding.

A New Democratic Normal: India after 1977

The 1970s were a tumultuous decade in India, marked by many dramatic political events. The decade began with an international war between India and Pakistan in 1971 over the liberation of Bangladesh. Student protests, strikes, militant left uprisings, and economic crises roiled the country in the early 1970s. The midpoint of the decade, June 1975, saw the abrupt overnight imposition of emergency rule by the incumbent prime minister Indira Gandhi of the Congress Party, citing unspecified internal threats to national security and stability. Elections and constitutional protections of citizens' rights were suspended. The country witnessed mass detentions of political prisoners, widespread press censorship, and the implementation of coercive policies such as slum demolition and the mass sterilization of male citizens in the name of population control.

The decade ended with the equally sudden withdrawal of emergency rule in the first quarter of 1977 and the subsequent restoration of Indian democracy. This was a process that involved many unforeseen developments and moments of high political drama as well, for example, the decisive electoral verdict that unseated the Emergency regime of Indira Gandhi and the Congress Party and brought a new political front, the Janata (People's) Party, to power in March 1977; the collapse of the Janata government within two years; the victory of Indira Gandhi in the elections of early 1980, the very individual who had until recently been publicly reviled as the architect of the hated Emergency. After all these eventful twists and turns, the 1970s ended just as they had begun. Indira Gandhi and the Congress were back in national office in 1980, and Indian democracy was back on track after what in hindsight was but a temporary episode of authoritarian experimentation.

Questioning this narrative of democracy's momentary disruption in the 1970s and the stark opposition between the democratic norm and the authoritarian exception that it presumes, the historian Gyan Prakash has recently drawn our attention to the historical lineages and precursors of the Indian Emergency.[12] Instead of a deviation from normal democratic logics, Prakash argues that the Emergency regime was connected to and enabled by many of the institutional and legal mechanisms of Indian democracy.[13] Prakash's historical and analytical insights on India's embedded and continuous emergency can also be extended to its aftermath or the period of the so-called democratic restoration that brought the 1970s to a close. In another ironic twist of history, many of the Emergency regime's institutions, policies, and ideas were unintendedly carried forward in the post-emergency years by efforts to reverse emergency authoritarianism and bring democracy back to India. Democratic normalcy did not return to some kind of *status quo ante* after 1977; you do not step in the same river twice. Instead of a restoration or return, the national democratic project was modulated and transformed after 1977, imprinted by the recent authoritarian past. The end of the 1970s saw the rise of a new normal in Emergency's shade.

Three features marked the political field of the late 1970s. First, faced with a crisis of legitimation and a pressing credibility dilemma in the aftermath of the Emergency, the new Janata government deployed a normative distinction between the legal-procedural rule of government and the moral sovereignty of the people. The Janata Party had won a clear electoral mandate in the 1977 elections. However, its political novelty as a politically untested coalition of ideologically diverse groups, and the visible escalation of factional infighting among senior leaders and ministers, saw media coverage and public discourse rapidly shift registers from euphoric support to skepticism and outright disapproval. The distinctive circumstances of the Indian Emergency's end also intensified the Janata's credibility dilemmas. Unlike other instances of regime change from around the world, the Indian transition from authoritarianism to democracy was not marked by a decisive institutional rupture. There were significant continuities in laws, policies, and especially in personnel across the 1977 watershed.[14] In this "past continuous" context, the Janata's electoral promise to provide true justice to the people and punish the perpetrators of the Emergency was soon sidelined by efforts to establish the procedural and lawful nature of governmental actions and prove that the rule-bound conduct of the new democratic government was substantially different from that of its authoritarian predecessor.

The proceedings of the Shah Commission of Inquiry that had been set up to look into the excesses of the emergency illustrate this shift.[15] As the commission's work continued through 1977 and the first half of 1978, it was charged with being politically motivated by opposition parties and the press, and establishing the procedural and lawful nature of its investigation became an urgent priority. The internal records of the commission reveal that its officials increasingly became concerned with questions of procedural correctness, and saw their work as manifestly incapable of providing the morality and justice that "the people want." Within less than a year of its establishment, the *limitations* of the Shah Commission and the fact that it could not bring the guilty to justice, became part of the official narrative that the Janata government—and the commission officials themselves—offered to prove that their work was lawful and rule-bound. The new democratic normal was structured around this divide, which opposed law and procedure to morality, justice, and the people. The credibility dilemmas confronted by the Janata government in the aftermath of the Emergency saw an officially sanctioned narrative about the "people outside" gain traction: how a representative government constrained by law and procedure cannot fulfil the expectations of popular sovereignty; how there is always and necessarily a popular gap at the heart of electoral representation.

The second notable feature of Indian democracy after 1977 was the expanded political presence and influence of non-electoral or extra-parliamentary actors and a surge in beyond-the-ballot claims of popular representation. Several new forms of political agency gained salience in the aftermath of the Emergency, and the theater of political action expanded beyond electoral politics. Contesting the representative authority and legitimacy of elected politicians (and of the bureaucracy they had installed), the media, the judiciary, academics, social movements, and nongovernmental organizations claimed that they could represent the interests and needs of the "real people" in more effective and authentic ways.

Finally, Indian democracy became increasingly mediatized in the late 1970s. Substantial changes in the political economy and technologies of Indian mass media amplified the social reach and presence of media in everyday lives. Technological innovations such as desktop and offset printing allowed newspapers to publish new local editions. There was a spurt in vernacular news publications, as computer-based print technologies offered cheap and efficient alternatives to the laborious hand-crafted production of individual metal typeface letters for non-Roman alphabets. Media growth was also fueled by the availability of new sources of capital. Many new entrepreneurs set up media businesses, eager to capture the expanding streams of advertising revenue generated by the growing consumer goods economy.[16]

Changes in the professional worlds of Indian journalism were also consequential. In the 1970s, a new postcolonial cohort of journalists born mostly after independence joined the ranks of journalists whose first-hand experience of colonial rule and the anticolonial struggle had reflected in the nationalist tenor of their journalism and their strong alignments with the Nehruvian national project. In contrast, the journalists who began their careers around the time of the Emergency had lived through student militancy and state repression; they were socialized in political and cultural milieus where in place of the optimism and hope sparked by mid-century utopias of national liberation and development, state-led projects attracted public critique, distaste, and fear.[17]

Journalists and media organizations began to assert their authority in political and public life. Casting aside the restrained registers of press discourse that had mostly aligned with state and national leadership in the first few decades after independence, journalists in the late 1970s took up increasingly critical and angry stances against the political system, and media publications frequently featured damning exposés of state violence, neglect, and failure.[18] In sum, the post-Emergency period saw a distinctive new media ideology and institutional-political identity emerge, of media as a political force in its own right. Diverging from the conventional liberal fourth-estate parameters of media as neutral providers of information and communication, journalists and media organizations became agents and authors of democratic politics who were actively involved in the legislative, policy, and even in the judicial work of the state.

Media and Curative Democracy

A powerful wave of investigative journalism swept Indian media worlds after 1977. The media revelations drew attention to a diverse range of concerns. For instance, the "Kamala story" about the sale of a woman in a north Indian town exposed the social practice of human trafficking, while the Bhagalpur exposé of the mass blinding of prisoners in the eastern state of Bihar disclosed a shocking account of police torture. Investigative journalism in the late 1970s also drew attention to incidents of political corruption, and several notable stories from the post-emergency period implicated prominent politicians in "scams" where political benefits were traded for personal financial gains. The Antulay cement scam was one such story broken by *Indian Express* editor Arun Shourie in the autumn of 1981. On the basis of documents leaked to him by an anonymous source, Shourie alleged that the chief minister of Maharashtra, A. R. Antulay, had extorted funds for the Congress Party's campaign from construction companies through the fictive sale of cement (hence the eponymous "cement scam"). Likened to the Watergate revelations in the United States, the story created a stir in the Indian parliament, and Antulay was forced to resign a few months later.

Although the specific issues of torture, trafficking, and graft that attracted media attention were quite different from each other, they were all represented in similar ways. India's new journalism after the Emergency had a distinctive style and idiom, and a few common themes were woven through all the media scandals that shook up public and political culture in the late 1970s and early 1980s. Let us take a closer look.

Implicating the Political System

First, all the post-emergency media exposés implicated the "political system" or the "political establishment." No matter the specifics of the incident at hand, journalists offered the same diagnosis, and elected representatives, bureaucracy, and police were invariably identified as the main cause of the problem. Often the culpability of the political system was not immediately clear,[19] and elaborate narrative explanations and moralized conclusions about the causes of specific incidents would be quite important to the genre of post-emergency investigative journalism. Media exposés offered up empirical details of events, but also provided preferred readings of them; what the story was really about was a very important part of the story. Another related theme was that of the unresponsive state. In many instances, the fallout of the media exposé, and the fact that after the revelations and the public outcry that followed the state still did nothing and nothing changed, were enfolded in the narrative to deepen the indictment of the system. This made the labor of investigative journalism present itself as all the more heroic, selfless, and even miraculous; an extraordinary act that persevered despite the odds stacked against it.

Wounded Citizenship

A second common theme is what I term "wounded citizenship," that is, presenting the generic citizen as an injured victim of the political system. In all investigative stories, if the unresponsive state and elected representatives were the villains, the citizen was the victim whose suffering and exploitation the media bore witness to.

The theme of suffering as such was not unknown to Indian political and public culture. Literary and cinematic texts of the post-independence period were suffused with dark and troubled representations of the contemporary Indian condition, and as I have documented in earlier work, the political discourse of the Nehruvian era was equally haunted by specters of an "Indian darkness."[20] In marked contrast to the triumphalist rhetoric of the twenty-first century that hails India's arrival on the stage of global recognition, official nationalism in the mid-twentieth century decades dwelled on the many difficulties and failures that confronted the newly minted Indian nation-state. In post-independence India, the figure of the impoverished, backward, and needy citizen was repeatedly evoked to legitimize the state-led project of national development; as long as there was misery and deprivation, nation-building policies had purpose and meaning.[21]

The official nationalist discourse of citizenship as victimhood did not uniformly encompass all Indians. There were specific victims who bore specific kinds of wounds. In Nehruvian India, wounded citizens were primarily specified as ascriptive minorities, that is, numerically small communities subjected to historical practices of discrimination and exploitation because they had been born into a particular identity group. Religion and caste were the main ascriptive identities that marked the terrain of wounded citizenship, and the Nehruvian state introduced a variety of constitutional and legal measures that recognized the distinctive concerns of religious minorities and caste groups at the lowest end of the caste hierarchy (the former Untouchables).[22] Moreover, as developmentalist discourse about the "hungry masses" and the "humble peasant" shows, statist concern about citizen-victims also had a strong class dimension in the early post-independence years. In the Nehruvian national imagination, economically marginalized citizens, religious minorities, and oppressed castes bore the wound of citizenship.[23]

These specifications would change in the late 1970s. Post-Emergency media narratives built upon and extended the theme of suffering and deprivation, but it was now increasingly presented as a general condition that affected *all* ordinary Indians in some way or another. Thus, while some post-Emergency media exposés continued in the Nehruvian vein and highlighted the extreme atrocities that the political system inflicted upon specific kinds of marginalized subjects (e.g., dalits, poor rural women, inmates of mental asylums, bonded labor, child labor), others took up a new cause, namely the suffering of urban middle-class citizens at the hands of the same system.[24]

In the late 1970s and beyond, the idea of the specific, historical wound borne by a particular, caste-class victim was generalized to include the entirety of the citizenry suffering at the hands of the political system. In post-Emergency political discourse, we were all repositioned as potentially wounded citizens: we the wounded people.

Media Crusades and Outsider Politics

Third, media exposés highlighted the heroic agency of the individual journalist and the role of media as the people's crusader.[25] The main protagonist of most media stories, particularly those that had involved undercover covert investigations, was the daring journalist who battled the system in the name of the people. His[26] interventions were presented as bold and dramatic acts that broke the fetters of bureaucracy and legal convention in order to respond to the higher moral imperative of democratic redemption.

Related to this was the theme of the media-judiciary partnership, or how journalists and courts could work together to redeem the people. For instance, the media revelations about the Kamala case led to a public interest litigation filed by the journalists who had covered the story, in which they petitioned the Supreme Court "qua citizens . . . to ensure that the executive takes steps to end the inhuman traffic in women."[27] This pattern of public interest litigation following media exposés would be repeated across a variety of different cases in the years to come.

Post-Emergency investigative journalism presented stories about representatives who failed the people and those who saved them. The elected representatives and government officials who did nothing to help the victims; the daring outsider journalist who battled the political system in the name of the people; the unresponsive state that remained unmoved but nevertheless the journalist persevered, enlisting the help of other like-minded political outsiders like the judiciary—these were the stock themes of investigative journalism after the Emergency, and they resonate with our contemporary present as well.

Across much of the world today, political discourse is framed by a triangular set of relations. The virtuous people are pitted against an indifferent, corrupt, cruel, and broken system until the redemptive political outsider—the third protagonist—restores the will of the people and cures democracy through his decisive and daring actions. As the example of India's new journalism shows us, this populist triangle associated today with the authoritarian specters of strongman politics was traced out several decades ago in the context of democratic restoration in the late 1970s, a time with a very different political and normative charge.

Concern Networks

The outsider politics of post-Emergency India was not only a normative discourse, but it was also a set of material practices and interventions. Many of the media exposés led to the formation of "concern networks": contingently assembled sets of individuals and organizations that came together out of a shared sense of urgent concern to undertake coordinated actions of democratic remedy and repair in the name of the people. Formed around media exposés and public interest litigations, concern networks flourished through the late 1970s and early 1980s, and the idea of the public interest came to be associated with a specific socio-legal ensemble comprising journalists, judges, civil liberties groups, and intellectuals.[28] What is significant for our purposes is that these concern networks drew their legitimacy and authority from their status as political outsiders, who claimed distance both from the temptations of personal profit and power that ensnared elected representatives and from the constraints of excessive procedural caution.

Through the post-Emergency period and beyond it as well, the interventions of investigative journalism and of "public-spirited" petitioners in public interest litigation were organized around the themes of distance from the constraints and corruptions of elected government, and the call for decisive, morally informed action that bypassed procedure, power, and personal profit. Amplifying the idea of popular sovereignty as a moral substance that eluded the formal institutional structures of representative government and electoral politics, concern networks enabled and legitimized representative claims made by self-appointed agents of the people, who acted on the grounds of their own conscience, motivated by their individual sense of public spirit and the concern that it ignited.

In sum, the transition from the nation-building paradigm of the post-independence era to the curative democratic project of the post-Emergency years saw a new principle and relation of extra-electoral political representation gain traction, where political outsiders to electoral politics (whether newcomers or strangers) were authorized as the authentic representatives of the people.

If electoral politics had failed to provide any effective mechanisms and structures to hold elected representatives accountable to the people who had elected them to office, outsider politics had a similar deficit. Accountability was turned into a matter of individual moral judgment and conduct on the part of "eminent citizens"[29] and other curative democrats who were moved, on their own accord, to act in the name of the people.

Political Horizons and World-Making

The late 1970s shift from nation-building to democracy-building rescaled the horizons of political agency and commitment as well. The effective reach of political action was no longer limited to the territorial confines of state sovereignty, as part of a nation-building project that was rolled out at a national scale. Instead, a new micro-political unit of the grassroots or local community came to define the ground and horizon of political engagement in the late 1970s and beyond.

Intimate Sovereignty and the Little People

Post-Emergency concern networks were formed around localized and small constituencies, for example, prisoners in Bihar's Muzaffarpur jail, pavement dwellers in

Bombay, construction workers in Delhi, women in a rehabilitation facility in the city of Agra, stone quarry workers in Faridabad, residents of a remote village in Himachal Pradesh who did not have access to roads.[30] The late 1970s and early 1980s have commonly been described in Indian political history as a period of intense social mobilizations that attempted to "avert the apocalypse."[31] It is worth remembering that these were all micro mobilizations, configured at a small and intimate scale, as so many *little* eruptions.

In tandem with the micro-scale remit of concern networks and the rise of media and socio-legal discourses about the "little people" as the authentic subjects of sovereignty, the post-Emergency period, particularly during the tenure of the Janata government (1977–80), saw new public and political languages of grassroots development and community empowerment take hold. Activating Gandhian conceptions of micro-scaled or decentralized sovereignty against the prevailing centralized national frames of Nehruvian and state socialist ideologies of development, a range of initiatives were undertaken by newly formed partnerships between state agencies, social action groups, and individual activists.

For instance, several scholars of Indian feminist history have documented how a distinctive configuration of "activism *with* the state" emerged in the late 1970s and early 1980s.[32] Entering the policy and administrative worlds of the state as advisors, consultants, and ad hoc employees, Indian feminists worked jointly with state officials to realize the goals of gendered empowerment by developing and implementing new policy frameworks in areas such as female literacy and education. As Malini Ghose and Aradhana Sharma have shown in their work on education and literacy initiatives in India, these involved small numbers of people in intensive, face-to-face interactions and had quite modest, and patiently incrementalist, aims and benchmarks of success.[33] In marked contrast to the monumentalist scale of high-modernist developmentalism— the "dams as temples of modern India" Nehruvian imaginaries that had linked national liberation and development to the grand ambitions of size and speed—these policy innovations were designed as micro-interventions in the everyday lives of rurally located communities of women.

The redirection of political concern toward small and intimate horizons, and the emphasis on decentralization and bottom-up modes of societal and political engagement drew inspiration from a variety of sources. These ranged from Gandhian vocabularies and programmatic initiatives of village republican self-sufficiency that gained a renewed salience during the Janata era to the rather unlikely provenance of Ford Foundation programs that encouraged various kinds of legal reform efforts geared toward grassroots legal access in India and other parts of the world at this time.[34]

In all of these legal, judicial, and activist initiatives, we see how ideas of democracy, empowerment, and popular sovereignty came to be associated with new measures of scale and magnitude. In marked contrast to the monumentalist ambitions of national liberation projects in the Nehruvian era, being smaller, modest, and localized in the late 1970s and beyond meant being more authentic, more democratic, and more connected to and expressive of the people's will. Media imaginaries were also shaped by similar kinds of downscaled orientations. As we have already seen, small and specific constituencies of wounded citizens, sometimes even just the plight of a single individual, were at the center of the media storms of the 1970s.

World-Making: New Circuits, New Amalgams

The preceding section described the rescaling of politics in late 1970s India, as various post-Emergency initiatives of democratic cure and restoration reoriented political concern from the sweeping national vistas of mid-century Nehruvian ideologies to the intimate and everyday worlds of the grassroots and local community and spectacles of individualized suffering. However, this did not mean an inward or parochial turn away from the expansive horizons of national internationalism as such. Rather, the curative democracy projects of the post-Emergency years drew on and fostered different kinds of international affinities and networks that often unfolded along new and unexpected lines. Although it is commonly described in the language of nostalgia and mourning, as the moment when international solidarities and connected horizons of decolonizing nationalisms were lost, the late 1970s decline of the Third World project in fact accompanied and enabled the rise of new worldly imaginations and acts of world-making. I end this chapter with a brief look at the other worlds that the political imagination of curative democracy made possible.

Two aspects of the networks and affinities that would traverse national borders in the late 1970s and beyond stand out for their marked difference from the international geographies of the Third World, nonalignment, Bandung, Afro-Asia, Tricontintental, and other decolonizing projects of an earlier era. First, they veered away from the well-worn grooves of state-produced and state-sanctioned internationalisms. In light of India's recent experience of the Emergency, the turn away from statist solidarity projects in the post-Emergency years was an unsurprising development. During the Emergency, authoritarianism on the domestic front coexisted with statist investments in Third World solidarity projects on the international stage. For instance, at the height of the Emergency in July 1976, the Congress regime strongly supported the establishment of an integrated Non-Aligned News Agencies Pool (NANAP) that would enhance the autonomy and accuracy of Third World information in a world media order dominated by the geopolitical and capitalist strength of First and Second World actors.[35]

Meanwhile, the same mechanism of an integrated news agency was used in the domestic political arena to advance media censorship and suppress informational autonomy. Within India, the *Samachar* news agency worked to create a pro-regime environment that shut out all dissenting media commentary; outside India, this institutional agent of authoritarian censorship was presented by the Congress regime as a shining beacon of Third World autonomy and sovereignty. After the end of the Emergency, when *Samachar* and other structures of emergency media were dismantled in the name of democratic restoration, it is not surprising that the enthusiastic advocacy for an integrated autonomous voice of Third World media died down as well.

In a similar vein, the prominent media attention on state-sanctioned geographies of international solidarity such as the Indo-Soviet Friendship treaty of 1971 or the Non-Aligned Movement summits in which national leaders like Indira Gandhi played a prominent role was diverted toward other imaginaries of international connection in the late 1970s and beyond. As the "West Asia" cover stories of *India Today* with their focus on the new possibilities of trade and business in this region showed,[36] these new connective geographies were formed and mediated by market rather than state forces that took the idea of the international beyond its investments in the Third World project of national liberation to engage new horizons of entrepreneurial and consumerist desires.

New non-statist geographies of international connection also restructured the epistemic communities and knowledge worlds in which curative democracy projects and their agents were located. Journalists, intellectuals, lawyers, and social movement and civil society activists encountered new kinds of international influences and ideas in the late 1970s that strayed from the officially recognized circuits of Third World exchange. For instance, the discoveries of the contemporary writings of Paulo Freire by several individuals who went on to play influential roles in social movement activism and policy advocacy circuits ensured that the Brazilian philosopher would be a key interlocutor and inspiration to India's curative democrats. Freire's distinctive ideas about "conscientization" and adult literacy inspired a range of popular scientific education and literacy movements across India, and made their way into governmental policy circles as well.[37] The biographies of other activists and intellectuals similarly document how the political imaginations of dissident scholarship and public intellectual writings from the Second World, by figures such as Václav Havel and Geörgy Konrád, resonated with Indian projects of a moral politics that rejected and transcended the institutional carapace of a statist order.

The distinctive intellectual currents that coalesced around and within the Centre for the Study of Developing Societies (CSDS) in this period, and the influential role that this intellectual hub would play in public and governmental circles as India's foremost interdisciplinary research center and think-tank of its times, exemplify the world-making impulses of the curative democracy project. As we will see, the new conceptions of the local and the grassroots were not confined within the territorial boundaries of the nation-state.

As intellectual biographies of CSDS and the memoirs of its founder Rajni Kothari have documented,[38] the main intellectual project of the center since its founding in the early 1960s was to make the case for a distinctive *Indian* modernity, and to do so via an empirical research program involving interdisciplinary field studies and surveys, in marked contrast to the formal and normative methods that dominated the political and social sciences in India at the time. Originally a research institution with close ties to the Congress government and Indira Gandhi herself (Rajni Kothari recalls several instances where Gandhi consulted him on political questions),[39] CSDS intellectuals reversed their allegiances during the 1970s and especially during the Emergency to come out in strong support of J. P. Narayan, the iconic leader of anti-Congress protest and subsequently of Emergency resistance.

In the late 1970s, researchers at the CSDS sharpened their intellectual focus on the idea of an indigenously rooted or vernacular modern. Developing wide-ranging critiques of top-down statist models of developmental modernity—both state capitalist and state socialist variants were targets of sustained critique—and the instrumental and power-serving calculations of party politics, Kothari and his colleagues advocated for a new and moral political order structured around "nonparty political formations" and "people's movements" that were organically embedded in and directly responsive and accountable to local contexts and communities. Explicitly eschewing models of revolutionary resistance, academics, activists, and the state were envisioned as partners in a new moral project of democratic renewal and expansion. These ideas found their way into the policy circuits of the government in the late 1970s and early 1980s,[40] aligning with cognate initiatives of decentralized governance (e.g., programs to revitalize *Panchayati Raj* institutions of decentralized village-level governance), community development and rural empowerment programs that paid special attention to gender concerns, and the encouragement of voluntary action by autonomous social action groups that partnered the state in joint implementation initiatives.[41]

CSDS intellectual conceptions of the grassroots and the indigenous as the authentic loci of popular sovereignty, and the emphasis on the moral charge of the nonparty political process, aligned with ideas and practices from other national contexts. Simply put, the idea of the indigenous/vernacular/local was very much a transnational idea that was developed in the context of Indian intellectual participation in international networks. It did not preclude, in fact it demanded, intellectual traffic beyond India. Thus, intellectual histories of CSDS show that the founding moment of this research institution in the 1960s cannot be thought outside the interactions between its founders and leading figures of American behaviorialism and comparative modernization such as Gabriel Almond. The distinctive empirical and behavioral turn of CSDS and the unique emphasis on survey studies and election studies was directly influenced by Kothari's engagements with the behavioralist paradigm of comparative politics in the postwar US academy in the 1950s–1960s.[42] The institutional life of CSDS also owed its existence, however, indirectly, to Cold War cultural and intellectual politics: Kothari set up CSDS as an autonomous research institute in 1963 with an individual grant of 70,000 rupees that he received from Richard Park, the director of the Delhi-based Asia Foundation, an organization subsequently documented as a recipient of funds from the CIA.[43]

Post-Emergency intellectual developments at CSDS also reflected broader global entanglements that exceeded the geopolitical confines of the Cold War matrix. The late 1970s and early 1980s ideas of grassroots democracy and nonparty political formations were fertilized in international networks such as the World Order Models Project (WOMP) of Richard Falk and Saul Mendlovitz, the United Nations University Programme on Peace and Global Transformations, and the intellectual exchanges that they made possible. Interactions with a diverse range of scholars and intellectuals— Mary Kaldor, Ali Mazrui, Richard Falk, and Charles Taylor are among the names of international visitors that feature prominently in CSDS archives. Circuits of international exchange that opened up outside statist geographies of internationalism,[44] ensured that the center's epistemic innovations were always open to, and nourished by, intellectual influences beyond India.

Along with their distinctive circuitry that enabled connections and exchanges beyond state-facilitated channels of international exchange and encounter, the networks that grew around the curative democracy projects of the late 1970s also stood out for their hybrid and ideologically ambivalent character. Muddying ideological distinctions of left and right, curative democracy projects drew on a range of influences and ideas from an eclectic range of sources. For instance, the institutional history of *India Today*, the news magazine that was one of the most important drivers of Indian new journalism shows that the influences that shaped the post-Emergency media field and the specific paradigm of investigative journalism that has been a focus in this chapter included new business models derived from US-inspired ideas about consumer-readers; ideas about "readable news" inspired by publications like *Time* and *Newsweek*; the consumer activism of Ralph Nader; and of course the investigative journalism of Robert Woodward, Carl Bernstein, and Jack Anderson.[45] The professional career of Arun Shourie, another prime agent of media activism in this period, reveals an even more curious amalgam of influences. A US-trained economist who worked at the World Bank for a decade prior to his return to India in 1977, Shourie has also been close to Hindu-nationalist organizations like the RSS and its political wing, the BJP.[46]

These and other examples suggest that the transition from nation-building to democracy-rebuilding, and the historical context of the late 1970s in which this took place did not so much involve the end of internationalist nationalisms as the inauguration and making of new ones. The Third World was replaced by other worlds in the late 1970s. Material and intellectual connections and affinities across national lines were produced in the very acts of affirming the indigenous-vernacular community as the locus of political engagement. To understand this process, we will have to look beyond and below the global structural determinations of geopolitics and capital to the strong and slow boring of hard boards within the arenas of domestic politics and social relations.

Third World Inside Out

The Third World is not a place, it is a project, Vijay Prashad reminds us in his riveting account of the varied political ambitions, imaginations, and agency of the "darker nations" that yielded the connected transnational "parallelograms"[47] of decolonizing solidarities in the third quarter of the twentieth century.[48] But what and where is the place from which to view this project? Prashad, like many of the revisionist historians who decenter conventional geopolitical accounts of the global Cold War, the Third World, and other international relations processes and projects, situates his account at an international level of analysis. He interrupts the Cold War superpower framing by bringing Third World nations and their strivings front and center, but the main theater of action remains the same. Other men enter the same global stage of history.

This chapter has offered a different view of the Third World, a view from inside out. Placing the Third World story within the domestic political and social arenas of national states (in this case, the Indian state), I have traced how in the late 1970s ideas of nation, democracy, freedom, and politics were shaped and contested by a diverse range of social actors and organizations that did not have an express interest or direct investment in international solidarity projects. Yet, it is precisely these non-cartographers of international space who, through their efforts to create a new national and local, opened new lines of connection and transaction beyond national and statist borders. Although they did not add up to a coherent international imagination that could neatly be captured by geographic, communal, or geometric metaphors—neither transregion nor community nor parallelogram was produced—these undoubtedly were acts of world-making as well.

As the 1970s came to an end in India, the promise of liberation and the geographies of international solidarity evolved away from the national state form that had anchored the mid-century Third World imagination. In many ways, these shifts were seeded and enabled by the Third World project itself. Three decades after the triumph of national liberation materialized the Third World, its impulse of resistance and critique was turned against the national states that had replaced their imperial predecessors, in the name of the freedom that they had failed to deliver.

When we look at the Third World project from places within, we see more a transmutation, a modulated evolution, than the finality of a death.

Notes

1 See, for instance, Itty Abraham, "Bandung and State Formation in Postcolonial Asia," in *Bandung Revisited*, ed. See Seng Ten and Amitav Acharya (Singapore: NUS Press, 2008): 48–67; Christopher Lee, ed., *Making a World After Empire* (Athens: University of Georgia Press, 2010); Vijay Prashad, *The Darker Nations* (New York: The New Press, 2007); Robert Vitalis, "The Midnight Ride of Kwame Nkrumah and Other Fables of Bandung (Ban-doong)," *Humanity: An International Journal of Human Rights, Humanitarianism, and Development* 4, no. 2 (2013): 261–88 for accounts of the transnational imaginaries and connections forged in the postwar conjuncture of decolonization.

2 As Antoinette Burton has succinctly summarized in her discussion of Afro-Asian connections, most accounts produce a "sentimentalization of solidarity" and present the connective imaginaries of decolonization as a "romance of overcoming" nation-statist order. Antoinette Burton, "The Sodalities of Bandung," in *Making a World After Empire*, ed. Christopher Lee (Athens: University of Georgia Press, 2010), 355, 352.

3 Recent scholarship has drawn attention to the "complex and uneven geographies of the postcolonial cold war world . . . its fitful, uneven, and aspirationally global territorialities." Ibid., 352–3.

4 "Inventing the Third World: In Search of Freedom in the Global South, 1948–1979," Workshop brief, SAS & Fung Programs Joint Symposium, Princeton University, February 28–29, 2020.

5 See Samantha Christiansen and Zachary Scarlett, eds., *The Third World in the Global 1960s* (New York: Berghan Books, 2012); Jim Pines and Paul Willemen, eds., *Questions of Third Cinema* (London: British Film Institute, 1989); Geeta Kapur, *When Was Modernism* (New Delhi: Tulika Press, 2000); Quinn Slobodian, *Foreign Front* (Durham: Duke University Press, 2012); Emily Wilcox, "Performing Bandung: China's Dance Diplomacy with India, Indonesia, and Burma, 1953–1962," *Inter-Asia Cultural Studies* 18, no. 4 (2017): 518–39.

6 On "losing utopia" see Samuel Moyn, *The Last Utopia* (Cambridge, MA: Harvard University Press, 2010), on "assassination" see Prashad, *Darker Nations*. Similar

views about the end of the 1970s as the end of the third world, and the attribution of causality and agency to national leadership choices and global structural forces are also expressed in recent books on the 1970s, for example, Niall Ferguson, Charles Maier, Erez Manela, and Daniel Sargent, eds., *The Shock of the Global* (Cambridge, MA: Harvard University Press, 2010) and Duco Hellema, *The Global 1970s* (Oxford and New York: Routledge, 2018).

7   The third world project, particularly its fabled origins in the Bandung moment, has mostly been described by "fraternal narratives" about a "Third World Brotherhood." Burton, "The Sodalities of Bandung," 358, 257. See Vitalis, "The Midnight Ride of Kwame Nkrumah" for an important corrective on the actual unfolding of the Bandung conference, including the accurate details of those who were actually present in Indonesia.

8   This was not just limited to India. Through the decade of the 1970s, logics of regime change that were not limited to decolonization—the transition from formal colonial rule by external colonial powers to sovereign statehood—manifested across the geographies of the third world. Iran, India, Pakistan, Argentina, Chile, Nicaragua, China, Angola, Mozambique, Vietnam, Cambodia all witnessed significant changes in the existing architectures of state power and social relations in the 1970s. But only in the Portuguese colonies of Africa did these involve actual decolonization projects of the kind that had characterized the "new nations" wave of the previous decades.

9   See Moyn, *The Last Utopia*, chapter 4.

10 The moralized rhetoric of outsider politics was not in itself something new. As W. H. Morris-Jones and Thomas Blom Hansen among others have pointed out, "saintly idioms" of political renunciation and transcendence, and the normative distinction between a "sublime" sphere of moral authority and the "profane" sphere of politics have structured public discourse in India since the early decades of the twentieth century, if not longer. In the aftermath of the Emergency, these rhetorical and discursive themes were given tangible institutional and material form. New kinds of extra-electoral actors and institutions, such as the media, the judiciary, civil society, and social movements gained influence in the arena of national politics, deploying moralized languages of political exit and transcendence to legitimize their political interventions. See W. H. Morris-Jones, *The Government and Politics of India* (London: Hutchinson, 1964); Thomas Blom Hansen, *The Saffron Wave* (Princeton: Princeton University Press, 1999).

11 Pierre Rosanvallon, *Counter Democracy* (Cambridge: Cambridge University Press, 2008): 8.

12 Gyan Prakash, *Emergency Chronicles* (Princeton: Princeton University Press, 2019).

13 In a further historical irony, Prakash establishes that many of the Emergency-enabling democratic norms and mechanisms were in fact continuous with the very state forms and practices of colonial domination that the postcolonial democratic state had staked its existence against.

14 For instance, Indira Gandhi remained an influential presence in political and public life and returned as prime minister in less than three years. Other figures like Naveen Chawla, Jagmohan, and Pranab Mukherjee who had played a prominent role in emergency government continued to enjoy social and political power and privilege after the Emergency ended, some up until today. The composition of lower-level bureaucracy did not change either, and investigations of the Emergency authorized by the Janata government often ran up against the obstructions of old regime bureaucrats who continued in office.

15 One of the first acts of the new Janata government in the early summer of 1977 was to set up an official commission of inquiry, the Shah Commission. The commission's initial scope was quickly narrowed down to an inquiry into the provable or evidenced excesses of the emergency. Only those acts that could be substantiated by official paper trails and a verifiable and accessible state record could be the subject of a lawful inquiry. This evidentiary and procedural imperative became paramount. In the end, the Shah Commission took up for investigation only four percent of the public complaints that it received (2000 out of 50,000) and just two hundred of these or less than half a percent of the total number of complaints were ultimately deemed excessive enough to receive a public hearing. This section is drawn from Sirupa Roy, "The Political Outsider," in *The People of India* eds. Ravinder Kaur and Nayanika Mathur (Gurugram: Penguin Viking, 2022): 66-87. Sirupa Roy, "Curative Democracy and the Political Outsider" (unpublished m.s., 2020).

16 See Robin Jeffrey, *India's Newspaper Revolution* (London: Hurst & Co, 2000), Adrian Athique, Vibodh Parthasarathi, and S.V. Srinivas, eds., *The Indian Media Economy*, vol. 1 and 2 (Delhi: Oxford University Press, 2018); Nalin Mehta, *Behind a Billion Screens* (Delhi: Harper Collins, 2015); Sevanti Ninan, *Headlines from the Heartland* (Delhi: Sage Publications, 2007); Pamela Philipose, *Media's Shifting Terrain* (Delhi: Orient Blackswan, 2019); Usha Rodrigues and Maya Ranganathan, *Indian News Media: From Observer to Participant* (Delhi: Sage Publications, 2014).

17 Multiple interviewees of the *Long Emergency* project, a digital archive of oral histories of Indian journalism and the Emergency, describe such life histories. See Sirupa Roy, "Long Emergency," Merian-Tagore International Centre for Advanced Studies, 'Metamorphoses of the Political' (ICAS:MP, 2018). See https://longemergency.demx .in/.

The generational shift in journalistic culture has been described by journalist Inderjit Badhwar as a shift from the era of "pontificators and thoughters" to that of "reporters and diggers." As Badhwar and also Gyan Prakash have noted, the Bombay-based tabloid *Blitz* was a notable exception in the pre-Emergency media field; *Blitz* published many investigative scoops and took on the government in bold and often angry terms, from the early post-independence years. See Inderjit Badhwar, "That Eighties Scoop Show: Indian Journalism Needs a Shot of the Past," *Outlook*, November 12, 2018, Prakash, *Emergency Chronicles*.

18 The genre of investigative journalism was actively encouraged by a wide range of print media organizations. Even niche magazines like *Debonair*, the men's magazine that was popularly known as the "Indian Playboy," commissioned and published investigative exposés of political leaders in the 1970s and 1980s, as former editor Vinod Mehta recounted in his memoir. See Vinod Mehta, *Lucknow Boy* (Delhi: Penguin Viking, 2011).

19 For instance, the immediate incident at the heart of the Kamala story of 1981 was the sale of a woman, Kamala, to Ashwini Sarin, an undercover journalist. The involvement of the political establishment was not readily evident; after all, the phenomenon of human trafficking at the core of the story could equally be linked to structural, economic and social forces that exceeded the ambit of any specific governmental authority. Some versions of the Kamala story did in fact offer such an analysis. For instance, for *The New York Times* the incident illustrated a larger Indian social problem that exceeded the role and responsibility of elected officials, bureaucracy, or police. In a similar vein, journalist Khushwant Singh observed that the story was about "endemic poverty" and in Vijay Tendulkar's play on the subject,

the common experience of patriarchy that united Kamala and the journalist's wife was the main focus. Undercutting the heroic narrative of the journalist who exposes the evils of the political classes, Tendulkar's dramaturgy of the Kamala story foregrounded the intersections and complicities between media and politicians, and their joint responsibility for the reproduction of gendered and classed inequalities; there were no clear-cut heroes or villains in Tendulkar's play. See Ashwini Sarin, "Buying Girls From a Circuit House," *Indian Express*, April 27, 1981, 1. Michael Kaufman, "Price of Woman in India: $306 and Much Sorrow," *New York Times*, August 11, 1981, A2, Vijay Tendulkar, "Kamala," in *Five Plays*, trans. Priya Tendulkar, Kumud Mehta, and Shanta Gokhale (Delhi: Oxford University Press, 1996).

20 See Srirupa Roy, *Beyond Belief* (Durham: Duke University Press, 2007), Chapter 4.

21 Nehruvian nation-building was invariably represented as a process of continual and open-ended becoming rather than being. See Partha Chatterjee, *The Nation and its Fragments* (Princeton: Princeton University Press, 1993), David Ludden, "India's Development Regime," in *Colonialism and Culture*, ed. Nicholas Dirks (Ann Arbor: University of Michigan Press, 1992), 247–87, Roy, *Beyond Belief.*

22 The constitution guaranteed a set of social and cultural group rights for religious minorities, and also attempted to redress the historical inequities of caste discrimination by introducing affirmative action measures of "reservations" that set aside a proportion of seats in educational institutions and government employment for individuals belonging to historically oppressed caste groups.

23 For a comprehensive overview of India's citizenship regimes and their transformations since independence, see Niraja Jayal, *Citizenship and Its Discontents* (Cambridge, MA: Harvard University Press, 2013).

24 Elsewhere I have discussed the genre of outrage journalism that arose after the Emergency, which focused on the problems and fears of urban middle-class citizens. Stories related to urban crime and lapses in urban security (e.g., the notorious Chopra children murder case of 1982), state failure to provide expected public services and entitlements (e.g., state pensioners who had not received their just dues), inadequacies in civic infrastructure, and everyday encounters with the indignities of petty corruption. See Srirupa Roy, "Angry Citizens," and also Arvind Rajagopal, "The Emergency as Prehistory of the New Indian Middle Class," *Modern Asian Studies* 45, no. 5 (2011): 1003–49 for a discussion of how the Emergency and its aftermath consolidated the urban middle class as the primary subject of political address.

25 "Crusader for justice" is a term that peppers many of the recollections about post-emergency journalism in the *Long Emergency* digital archive.

26 The choice of pronoun is deliberate: most of the big investigative stories of the post-emergency years involved male journalists.

27 Arun Shourie, "Why the Honorable Court Must Hear Us," *People's Union for Civil Liberties Bulletin*, July 30, 1981. http://arunshourie.bharatvani.org/articles/19810730 .htm.

The role of journalists in the Kamala story was not limited to reporting alone. Following the publication of the story, journalist Ashwini Sarin, who had purchased Kamala for 2300 rupees ($306) as part of his undercover investigation of trafficking, brought her to Delhi and placed the adult woman in an orphanage run by the Arya Samaj, a Hindu reformist social service organization. With the help of the People's Union of Civil Liberties (PUCL), an independent civil liberties organization, Sarin and his editor Arun Shourie then petitioned the Indian Supreme Court in the public interest to issue directions to the relevant state governments to take steps to end trafficking, and to find a suitable home for Kamala. The court ordered Kamala to stay in the Arya Samaj orphanage while the case was being heard. Six months later, in November 1981, Kamala escaped and no one ever found her again.

28 Concern networks drew on a relatively small group of individuals and organizations based in Delhi (and some from Bombay). Shourie, the *Indian Express*, the Supreme Court justice P. N. Bhagwati, and the PUCL featured repeatedly in many of the media and PIL interventions of the time.

29 This is one of the most common, and unexamined, phrases of Indian political and public culture. "Eminent citizens" are called upon not just by official agencies, but by civil society and social movement initiatives as well. The non-specification of "eminence" as a quality that "everyone recognizes" resembles the cognate term, "public spirit," and the two terms often work together in the claims-making practices of concern networks, public interest litigation, and other formations of non-electoral representative politics.

30 All of these occasioned much-cited public interest litigations. See (in order): *Hussainara Khatoon v. State of Bihar* 1979 SCR 3 532; *Olga Tellis v. Bombay Municipal Corporation*, 1985 3 SCC. 545; *Bandhua Mukti Morcha v. Union of India*, SCC 802; *Upendra Baxi v. State of Uttar Pradesh* 1983 2 SCC 308; *PUDR v. Union of India* 1983 SCR 1 456; *State of Himachal Pradesh v. Umed Ram Sharma* 1986 SCR 1 251.

31 The title of *New York Times* journalist Arthur Bonner's book on social movements in India. Arthur Bonner, *Averting the Apocalypse* (Durham: Duke University Press, 1990).

32 See among others Indu Agnihotri and Veena Mazumdar, "Changing Terms of Political Discourse: Women's Movement in India, 1970s-1990s," in *Writing the Women's Movement*, ed. Mala Khullar (New Delhi: Zubaan, 2005); Maitrayee Chaudhuri, *Feminism in India* (New Delhi: Kali for Women, 2004); Mary John, *Discrepant Dislocations* (New Delhi: Oxford University Press, 1999); Rajeswari Sunder Rajan, *The Scandal of the State* (Durham: Duke University Press, 2003); Malini Ghose, "Education and the Rural Woman Subject: Policy Discourses from the mid 1970s to the early 1990s" (unpublished m.s., 2020).

33 Dipta Bhog and Malini Ghose, "Mapping the Multiple Worlds of Women's Literacy: Experiences from Mahila Samakhya," in *Cartographies of Empowerment*, ed. Vimala Ramachandran and Kameshwari Jandhyala (New Delhi: Zubaan, 2012), 237–69, Malini Ghose, "Education and the Rural Women Subject," in *Logics of Empowerment*, ed. Aradhana Sharma (Minneapolis: University of Minnesota Press, 2008).

34 Yves Dezalay and Bryant G. Garth, *Asian Legal Revivals* (Chicago: University of Chicago Press, 2010), Rajeev Dhavan, "Law as Struggle: Public Interest Law in India," in *Journal of the Indian Law Institute* 36, no. 3 (1994): 302–38.

35 NANAP and the contemporaneous New World Information and Communication Order project (NWICO) were the two main "solidarities of decolonization" initiatives undertaken in the media and information/communication fields in the 1970s. See Carrie Buchanan, "Revisiting the UNESCO Debate on a New World Information and Communication Order," *Telematics and Informatics* 23, no. 2 (2015): 391–9; Paula Chakravartty and Katherine Sarikakis, *Media Policy and Globalization* (Edinburgh: Edinburgh University Press, 2006); Cees Hamelink, "Third World Call for New Order," *Journal of Communication* 29, no. 3 (1979): 144–8; Sean MacBride, *Shaping a New World Information Order* (Paris: UNESCO, 1979); Jésus Martin-Barbero, *Communication, Culture and Hegemony* (Thousand Oaks: Sage Publications, 1993).

36　*India Today's* first West Asia-themed issue was published during the Emergency. Even
　　at this high-point of state socialist rhetoric and economic protectionism, pro-business
　　and market forces, and the nascent beginnings of a consumer-citizenship that would
　　come to prominence in the 1980s and beyond, were in play. See "What people Say on
　　West Asian trade," *India Today*, April 15, 1976 and "End of the Boom," *India Today*,
　　April 15, 1980. The pages of *India Today* map the new locations that came to be
　　invested with international significance in the late 1970s and beyond and show us the
　　reconfigured contours of the Indian international.

37　On Freire's enthusiastic reception in India, and the diffusion and adaptation of
　　Freirean ideas, see Francis Cody, *The Light of Knowledge* (Ithaca: Cornell University
　　Press, 2013); Siddhartha, "From Conscientization to Interbeing: A Personal Journey,"
　　in *Rethinking Freire*, ed. C. A. Bowers and Frédérique Apffel-Marglin (Mahwah:
　　Lawrence Erlbaum, 2005), 83–100; Malini Ghose, "Refashioning Rural Women's
　　Subjectivities through Literacy Interventions in India in the mid 1980s" (unpublished
　　m.s., 2020).

38　See Rajni Kothari, *Memoirs* (Delhi: Rupa Publications, 2004), also the fiftieth
　　anniversary commemorative reflections on the history of CSDS that were published in
　　Seminar magazine (volume 639, 2012) and on the CSDS website (http://www.csds.in).

39　Kothari was close to the Congress government in the 1960s. As his colleague
　　Dhirubhai Sheth recalled, his first piece of original field research was commissioned
　　by the All India Congress Committee in the mid 1960s, to understand the reasons for
　　the Congress poor electoral performance in the Farukhabad and Rajkot parliamentary
　　constituencies in Kothari's home state of Gujarat. See Dhirubhai Sheth, "Interview,"
　　Seminar 639 (2012).

40　Along with *Seminar* magazine core intellectuals Romesh and Raj Thapar, CSDS
　　scholars played a leading role in developing a manifesto for the Janata Party ("An
　　Agenda for India"), where their ideas of a nonparty political formation committed to a
　　new grassroots process of democratization and development were explained to wider
　　political and public constituencies.

41　During the Janata regime, Kothari authored an important note on education policy,
　　and served as chair of the Indian Council for Social Science Research (ICSSR)
　　from 1978 to 1980, the apex state agency that funded and oversaw social science
　　research in India from 1978 to 1980 (Kothari had also been involved in the original
　　establishment of ICSSR in the early 1970s, a period when he was still close to the
　　Gandhi and the ruling Congress government). At the same time as these involvement
　　with state initiatives, CSDS and Kothari also began to play an active role in political
　　and social movements beyond academia. For instance, from the late 1970s, Kothari
　　was closely involved in the work of the civil liberties organization People's Union for
　　Civil Liberties (PUCL), and in other people's movements. The attempt to connect such
　　practical contexts of movement politics with academic and theoretical reflections on
　　the subject of democracy, development, and the non-political led to the establishment
　　of the *Lokayan* or people's dialogue initiative at CSDS in 1980 to foster engagements
　　and collaborations between intellectuals and activists, and to "bridge knowledge and
　　action." Lloyd and Susanne Rudolph, "Bridging Knowledge and Action," in *Seminar*
　　639 (2012).

42　American behavioralism's academic and pedagogical influence in India can be traced
　　to the mid-1960s when Robert Dahl and several other American social scientists
　　came to Delhi to conduct a six-week study program on political theory and behavior
　　sponsored by the Asia Foundation, an American institution. Following this encounter,

Kothari collaborated with scholars at the University of Michigan and the University of Pennsylvania to undertake election surveys in India (Kerala elections in 1965, national elections in 1967). Kothari then spent a year at Stanford University in 1968–9 on the invitation of political scientist Gabriel Almond, and wrote his widely acclaimed book on Indian politics as part of the Almond-edited series on modernization and comparative development that was sponsored by the Social Science Research Council. See Kothari, *Memoirs*.

43 The center was viewed as a "CIA den" in the polarized Cold War intellectual spaces of Delhi. In 1966, after the publication of several news articles claiming that the Asia Foundation was funded by the CIA created a stir in India, Kothari resolved to return the Asia Foundation funding and seek out government grants. According to Sheth, when a distraught Kothari went to see Indira Gandhi about the CIA revelations, she laughed it off and said that they had always known! See Dhirubhai Sheth, "Interview."

44 For example, Kothari pursued an "Inter-Asian" agenda, and encouraged the development of a China Group at CSDS.

45 This draws on the oral histories of the *Long Emergency* project, which has interviewed many of the journalists who were involved with *India Today* in the 1970s and 1980s. Interviewees include the magazine founder Arun Poorie, also journalists Dilip Bobb, Uma Vasudev, Inderjit Badhwar, Mohini Bhullar. See also Badhwar, "That Eighties Scoop Show," and the *India Today* archival collection, "India Today 40th Anniversary." https://www.indiatoday.in/india/photo/india-today-40th-anniversary-photographs-from-the-frontlines-376930-2015-12-10.

46 Shourie has changed his position yet again in recent years, and at the time of writing is a prominent public critic against the BJP-RSS regime that presently rules India. For a nuanced account of Shourie's political ambiguities, see Martha Nussbaum, *The Clash Within* (Cambridge, MA: Harvard University Press, 2008).

47 Burton, "The Sodalities of Bandung," 353.

48 Prashad, *Darker Nations*, xv.

Coda

Samuel Moyn

The recognition that most of modern history—most of all history for that matter—has been imperial history challenged the national frames that have served as default in the historical profession. But until recently, this same recognition left neoliberal globalization the narrative default. Like no other, this volume challenges that mistake.

The ascendancy of national histories had begun within a small number of European locales. That historiography both celebrated and masked that most of the states in question were in fact patchwork empires on their own lands, and held more and more massive territories overseas as time passed. By the time that formal colonialism collapsed, in stages after the Second World War, the coming of "the new states" of a decolonized world globalized the practice of national historiography, which had already emerged in the writings of nationalist intellectuals. As a result, what was screened out was far more than the fact that empire had been prevalent and the national frame contingent and recent. Lost, too, was the new global frame that the intellectuals and politicians of the decolonized new states themselves developed across a brief but fertile few decades. It is only now that global historians are recovering global but postcolonial aspirations to transcend empire and "nation-state" alike, plans for humanity that rose and fell on the ruins of formal empire.

The new global history has shone by providing an inescapable conviction of the endurance of the imperial form in the annals and across the world. Ironically, however, global history became essential—even fashionable—not in the era immediately after West European empires fell, but only when the Soviet one did, leaving United States hegemony unchallenged. Until recently, indeed, there was an unmistakable association between global history, and the "end of history" after 1989, and the neoliberal theories and practices that had gained traction before that date and went nearly unchallenged for a long time after. This meant that, as the new global history fulfilled its purposes in exploring the rule of empire, it also left a sense that the neoliberal globalization of our times was the only kind. At a moment of the crisis of this latest form of globalization, it is, therefore, of great value that this volume participates so successfully in writing in the alternative "world-making" that decolonizing states after the Second World War had attempted or at least envisioned. This book recalls that, once, another globalization was possible. Perhaps it still is.

Not that the postcolonial internationalists emerged without their own roots in the imperial age. Historians have shown that the reverse is true and not only because of the indispensable solidarity of initially ragtag movements and visionaries facing down far-flung and infinitely more powerful imperial might. For there were also disputes of principle that haunted the unity of strategic convenience that brought empire's opponents together. It was not obvious what should succeed what they hated and for a long time the nation-state remained one answer among others. One of the great historiographical breakthroughs of our time has been not merely to revive the plurality of anticolonialisms, and decenter the nation-state as preferred outcome, but also to show how long dissident forms remained active. Against their own steep odds, advocates of alternative decolonizations contested the clientelistic transfer of power at the end of empire that so often occurred. That handoff of imperial power converted alien rule into local predominance, frequently to maintain the essence of older forms of concessionary imperialism, and allowed the West to relinquish political control without obstructing its access to natural resources.

At the same time, it has been tempting to romanticize postcolonial world-making. As alternatives to empire were winnowed, the internationalism that surged to prominence—like the one originating across the Atlantic from the time of Woodrow Wilson or even before—presupposed nation-states as its building blocks. It was crucial to the emergence of "Third World" internationalism in the 1960s and 1970s that it was built on top of the victory of postcolonial nationalism and almost never portended a full-scale alternative to it. As much as our anti-romantic historiography today condemns any sense of unity in anticolonialism, it sometimes obscures that the postcolonial internationalism that won out almost never committed to any erosion of formal political control of new national elites.

It could hardly have been otherwise. Nationalism served as an extraordinary device of legitimation for the ascendancy of rulers in the postcolony. And among them, a certain amount of rhetoric to one side, they could never forget that "internationalism" could easily function as slogan for the return of meddlesome empire in a new guise. No wonder that it was postcolonial leaders around the world, not Europeans before, who attempted to bring a "Westphalian" myth of the complete impregnability of nation-states into being, whatever their commitment to another global vision. As an epitome of the first item on their agenda after the end of empire, consider the example of the United Nations "Declaration of the Inadmissibility of Intervention in the Domestic Affairs of States and the Protection of Their Independence and Sovereignty" of 1965. The title hardly forbade another globalization. But it did imply the version that could now succeed.

But the fact that postcolonial internationalism after the Second World War presupposed the nation-state, rather than planning for its obsolescence, hardly means that the globalizing credentials of postcolonial leaders were somehow false or ideological. What it does mean is that it was a tension-filled project that strove for global equity or fairness by taking advantage of the weak tools that postcolonial states could boast: not power or wealth but formal independence and a fiction of equal sovereignty that, for all its legitimating functions at home, might serve to justify a transformation of the global environment.

International norm-setting provides an excellent vantage point on these truths. First to be challenged—with Mexican antecedents before the Second World War—were the continuities with concessionary imperialism that postcolonial elites had been forced to allow at the brink of decolonization. Especially when it came to oil, nationalizations were justified in the name of the newfangled principle of "permanent sovereignty of natural resources." That principle asserted national control at the expense of outsiders, no matter the hierarchy in resources within the Global South that it intensified (not least that between oil-producing states and others). These seizures of power with one of the few tools that rulers in the Global South had available—the claim of sovereignty itself—were never easy. Ask Jacopo Arbenz or Mohammad Mossadeq, whom the newly hegemonic Americans did not allow to rule Guatemala or Iran for long after their nationalizations. But compared to building a globally fair world order, asserting ownership over natural resources was easy, enabled as it was by the triumph of the nation-state over alternative forms of liberation from empire.

Imagining new forms of globalism that would not threaten their newfound power and sovereignty, leaders of the Global South moved to supplement the Soviet Union's favored principle of world order—coexistence—with a new one—cooperation. Already in the Panchsheel principles negotiated between China and India in 1954, it was clear that postcolonial states would hew to coexistence as a nonnegotiable baseline. The year before the Bandung conference, these two great postcolonial states ratified mutual respect, nonaggression, and noninterference that made up "peaceful coexistence." Only one of the five principles, "equality and mutual benefit," suggested a project of world-making external to the postcolonial state. The job of securing the premises of sovereignty took pride of place instead, watchfulness at its borders the first and most important duty of its new bearers. And, as shown by the first (but by no means last) border war between China and India only eight years after the Panchsheel principles, in summer 1962, hopes for mutual benefit did not mean fidelity to the baseline principles went without saying.

Of course, at that early date it was not merely a matter of stabilizing extant borders: the completion of decolonization beckoned for all those who were forcibly kept under empire's thumb. Completing the globalization of the nation-state became the priority in the internationalism of those that already existed. The epoch-making Declaration on Colonialism of 1960 ratified this task. This auspicious event meant that the United Nations could become a forum of advocacy to denounce the crimes of late empire and South Africa's apartheid regime. Such internationalism was not always above self-interest. It could even authorize or at least justify the once imperial practice of territorial annexation, as when India cited the Declaration in annexing Goa from Portugal the year after it was propounded.

Other than the effort to liberate imperial subjects remaining around the world, ratifying new postcolonial sovereignty and strengthening the borders of the new states remained the essential foreign policy of the new states. For a long time, further world-making in the name of effective solidarity far remained far behind on any plausible accounting. Once achieved, sovereignty had to be jealously guarded. Indeed, commented R. P. Anand, the first great Indian international lawyer of the era, it fell to postcolonial states to create the world of state equality in the international order initially envisioned by eighteenth-century Swiss natural lawyer Emer de Vattel, which explained their "great stress on the otherwise dwindling concept of national sovereignty."[1] It was thus no accident that across these very decades it was ex-imperial states of Europe that took more significant steps toward federalization, on their road to the European community, than any postcolonial states did.

Even so, cooperation beyond coexistence beckoned. It might have to be compatible with the globalized state, after the prioritization of self-rule. Once again, however, the fact that postcolonial states had to make a virtue of weakness in the international system ended up planting the seeds of the destruction of their political project. What tools did postcolonial actors have at their disposal, for bringing economic fairness to a world where they had successfully multiplied the state form? Disturbingly, the great economic divergence that imperialism had wrought was exacerbated in the three decades after 1945 when northern economies boomed and ratified two centuries of prior gains over southern ones. Postcolonial leaders chose politics first, only to find economics haunting their choice. "Seek ye first the political kingdom," Ghana's Kwame Nkrumah had proclaimed in 1957, "and all things will be added to you." Only eight years later, in his classic indictment of *Neocolonialism*, it seemed things were not so simple.

Especially if they could disrupt the legacies of concessionary imperialism, what at least some postcolonial states boasted was raw materials for cultivation or extraction. At the time of Afro-Asian liberation, however, Argentine economist Raúl Presbisch had theorized the limits of a commodities-first strategy to undo the great divergence (because of the falling prices of commodities over time). Nor did the most obvious alternative, import-substituting industrialization, offer a lasting remedy. As Prebisch helped found the United Nations Conference for Trade and Development in 1966, however, a welfarist vision of commodity support seemed like the most plausible lever for closing the gap. If commodities prices fell relative to manufacturing on their own, supporting them through a collective welfare mechanism—in effect, global redistribution—might solve the problem.

Fulfilled in the New International Economic Order proposals of 1974, however, this plan failed to take account of what one might call the true great divergence of the late twentieth century, between the fortunate few of the Organization of Petroleum Exporting States (OPEC) and the great many states without oil (or, worse, without valuable commodities of any kind). The 1973 and 1978 price hikes in oil, advertised as a cause of postcolonial justice and initially sparking a great debate over how to remedy the widening gap between the Global North and South, were disastrous for many states and shattered postcolonial internationalism for good. After all, OPEC's gains meant far greater debt elsewhere in the Third World than the old imperial states of Europe or the United States of America ever incurred. Indeed, more than any other single factor it was not just OPEC's oil shocks but its decision to lend its money in showy generosity through the UN's Emergency Relief Fund—where Prebisch worked, in nearly his last act in public service—that sparked the global debt crisis of the next decade.

Of course, it is true that in the face of the New International Economic Order proposals US Secretary of State Henry Kissinger, and other participants in the early phases of the "North-South dialogue," understood that for the moment the Third World had the upper hand. Kissinger adopted an appeasement strategy, including in his appearance at the World Food Conference in 1974 to call for unprecedented aid for crisis management and to succor the worst off in global affairs. And West

Europeans like Willy Brandt could behave with more authentic generosity, even if the report that bears his name came too late, as brief Third World power eroded, to make a difference.

But that erosion occurred because the commodity support strategy, probably ill-advised in any event, ended up creating a class divide among southern states rather than moderating one between them and the Global North. The real story of the "world-making" of postcolonial internationalism thus, viewed with realism and retrospection, appears to be a terrible bet that ended up leaving many countries in more abasing hierarchy than they had been before. Calls for a pivot to postcolonial global solidarity through the weapon of commodity price fixing—the centerpiece of postcolonial world-making once it came—did far more to prepare the conditions for neoliberalism instead. Worse, even the functional sovereignty of many Third World states, which they enjoyed only briefly as they fell under the thumb of structural adjustment programs, was destroyed. World-making ended up eroding the effective power of the nationalist revolution that had preceded it.

For such reasons, the rise and fall of the Third World as a political project—to the study of which this volume contributes so many new perspectives—is hardly to be treated as a fund to draw upon now. If anything, it is a cautionary tale and object lesson for the future of global justice. No wonder, then, that contributors focus on alternatives to or sidelights on the dominant nationalist foundation of the distinctive Third World form of internationalism. No wonder, too, that the chapters capitalize on the fact that it took so long for the new global history to reach chronologically beyond empire to assess alternative globalizations before our neoliberal one. For, to return to my opening premise, the value of such inquiry has to be—beyond the gifts it gives in understanding the historical record—to help those who want to plot a next move in the present. For whatever else is true of the end of empire, it left dreams of global fairness that refuse to die.

Global history in recent scholarship has not been very presentist. Even though it arose in tandem with neoliberal globalization, it has tended to avoid becoming a prehistory of it. And it has been honorable for historians to recover bad and good alternatives in the annals to the specific overcoming of the nation-state that "the end of history" in the 1990s and since has involved. No doubt, global history has been good at defamiliarizing. It has presented story after story of how different global experience was before (in Thomas Friedman's slogan) the earth became flat in our time.

Yet, without recognizing how anticolonial internationalism—for all its heretical forms—was the true Westphalianism and how it helped create the conditions for the neoliberal breakthrough, it is impossible to connect prior globalizations to our own form of it. Nor is its relation to the overcoming of our neoliberal arrangements obvious. Revisiting anticolonial internationalism poses starkly how ironic and tragic its own self-undoing has turned out. Some of its aspirations remain pertinent in the extreme, and its demand for a genuine end to hierarchy a standing indictment of our unequal world. Perhaps nothing else is retrievable from decolonizing world-making than choices and commitments that led to its own collapse. If so, its dreams will have to find some other fulfillment.

Note

1   R. P. Anand, "Attitude of the Asian-African States Toward Certain Problems of International Law," *International and Comparative Law Quarterly* 15, no. 1 (1966): 69; see also R. P. Anand, "Sovereign Equality of States in International Law," *International Studies* 8, no. 3 (1966): 213–41 and 8, no. 4 (1967): 386–421.

Contributors

Gyan Prakash is the Dayton-Stockton Professor of History at Princeton University, USA. A member of the influential Subaltern Studies Collective until its dissolution in 2006, his recent books include *Mumbai Fables* (2010), which was adapted for the film *Bombay Velvet* (2015) and *Emergency Chronicles: Indira Gandhi and Democracy's Turning Point* (2019).

Jeremy Adelman is Henry Charles Lea Professor of History and Director of the Global History Lab at Princeton University, USA. His recent books include *Worldly Philosopher: The Odyssey of Albert O. Hirschman* (2013) and the forthcoming *Earth Hunger: Global Integration and the Need for Strangers*.

Cindy Ewing is an assistant professor of history at the University of Toronto. Her research focuses on the global history of the Cold War in postcolonial South and Southeast Asia.

Patrick Iber is an associate professor of history at the University of Wisconsin-Madison. His research focuses on twentieth-century Latin America and US foreign relations, and he is the author of *Neither Peace Nor Freedom: The Cultural Cold War in Latin America*.

Agustín Cosovschi is a historian of the global Cold War, with a primary focus on Southeast Europe. He is currently a postdoctoral research assistant at the Université Paris Nanterre and a postdoctoral fellow on the project "Photographing Revolution: Images of Cuban Solidarity in Transnational Contexts," funded by the Social Sciences and Humanities Research Council of Canada. He is also a research associate at the Centre d'Études Turques, Ottomanes, Balkaniques et Centrasiatiques in Paris.

Daniel Steinmetz-Jenkins is an assistant professor in the College of Social Studies at Wesleyan University. His book *Impossible Peace, Improbable War: Raymond Aron and World Order* is forthcoming from Columbia University Press. He has coedited (with Sarah Shortall) *Christianity and Human Rights Reconsidered* (2020) and coedited (with Stephen Sawyer) *Foucault, Neoliberalism and Beyond* (2019).

Marcelo Ridenti is a full professor of sociology at the State University of Campinas in Brazil and was a visiting professor at Columbia University (Ruth Cardoso Chair, 2014–15) and the University of Paris (Simon Bolivar Chair, 2017). His research focuses on cultural histories of the Cold War and the internationalization of Brazilian artists and intellectuals. He is the author of many books on culture and politics in Brazil.

Andreas Eckert is a professor of African history at Humboldt-Universität zu Berlin. His work is focused on global histories of labor and colonialism. He is the author of many books on modern African history and has edited several published volumes, including *Global Histories of Work* (2016) and *General Labour History of Africa* (2019).

Penny M. Von Eschen is the William R. Kenan, Jr., Professor in American studies and a professor of history at the University of Virginia. Her research focuses on decolonization, African American history, and the Cold War and its afterlives. Her publications include *Satchmo Blows up the World: Jazz Ambassadors Play the Cold War* (2004) and *Paradoxes of Nostalgia: Cold War Triumphalism and Global Disorder since 1989* (2022).

Atreyee Gupta is an assistant professor of Global Modern Art and South and Southeast Asian Art in the History of Art Department at the University of California, Berkeley. She specializes in Global Modernism, with an emphasis on the aesthetic and intellectual flows across Asia, Africa, the Middle East, and Latin America from the twentieth century onwards. She is the coeditor of *Postwar—A Global Art History, 1945-1965* (with Okwui Enwezor).

Naresh Fernandes is a journalist and the editor of Scroll.in, a digital daily based in India. He is the author of *Taj Mahal Foxtrot: The Story of Bombay's Jazz Age* (2012) and *City Adrift: A Short Biography in Bombay* (2013).

Jessica Bachman is a historian of modern South Asia, the Soviet Union, and the global Cold War. She is currently a doctoral candidate in the Department of History at the University of Washington.

Monica Popescu is the William Dawson Scholar of African literature and an associate professor of English at McGill University. She is the author of *At Penpoint: African Literatures, Postcolonial Studies and the Cold War* (2020) and *South African Literature beyond the Cold War* (2010).

Srirupa Roy is a professor and chair of State and Democracy, Center for Modern Indian Studies at the University of Göttingen, and codirector of the Merian-Tagore International Center of Advanced Studies (ICAS:MP). She is the author of *Beyond Belief: India and the Politics of Postcolonial Nationalism* (2007) and coeditor of *Violence and Democracy in India* (2006) and *Visualizing Secularism: Egypt, Lebanon, Turkey, India* (2012).

Samuel Moyn is the Chancellor Kent Professor of Law and Legal History at Yale University. His research focuses on legal and political thought, as well as the history of human rights. His publications include *Not Enough: Human Rights in an Unequal World* (2018).

Index

CPSIA information can be obtained
at www.ICGtesting.com
Printed in the USA
LVHW080212211122
733683LV00003B/35

9 781350 268159